INITIATION

STUDIES

IN THE HISTORY OF RELIGIONS

(SUPPLEMENTS TO *NVMEN*)

X

INITIATION

LEIDEN
E. J. BRILL
1965

INITIATION

CONTRIBUTIONS
TO THE THEME OF THE STUDY-CONFERENCE
OF THE INTERNATIONAL ASSOCIATION
FOR THE HISTORY OF RELIGIONS
HELD AT STRASBURG, SEPTEMBER 17th to 22nd 1964

EDITED BY

DR. C. J. BLEEKER

Professor of the History and Phenomenology of Religion at the University of
Amsterdam

LEIDEN
E. J. BRILL
1965

PRINTED IN THE NETHERLANDS

CONTENTS

PREFACE

This Supplementary Volume to Numen needs perhaps a word of introduction. As the sub-title indicates, the articles were originally papers given at the Study-Conference held in Strasburg from September 17th to 24th 1964. The theme of the Conference was the *Rites of Initiation*, but the scholars were invited to interpret this title broadly so as to include any theory or practice which introduces man to the hidden truths of religion. Several of the ensuing papers will be seen to make use of this broad interpretation of the term initiation.

The Study-Conference was therefore something of an experiment. We consider, however, that it was justified by success. As the meeting progressed, the meaning and implications of initiation became gradually clearer until it was generally agreed, though no official conclusions were formulated, that the following three important aspects should be distinguished:

i) The so-called 'rites de passage' which sometimes function as rites of initiation.

ii) Rites of initiation in the strict sense of the word, i.e. rites introducing people into closed religious societies.

iii) Initiation in the sense of introduction into the mysteries of religion.

It may be objected that such bold conclusions can scarcely be validly drawn from only twenty-eight lectures, which cannot of necessity cover all the important and relevant aspects of the field. Certainly this volume makes no pretence of giving a complete picture of the significance of initiation in religious past and present. No such complete treatment of the subject was planned when the scholars were invited to make their own choice of whatever aspect of the subject might interest them. The volume will nevertheless, we hope, make some contribution to a better understanding of the function of initiation in religion, and one which will serve to inspire further researches in this field.

THE EDITOR

L'INITIATION ET LE MONDE MODERNE

PAR

M. ELIADE

Chicago

Il est difficile de présenter dans ses grandes lignes le phénomène complexe qu'est l'initiation. Sans l'appui et l'illustration des documents, toute définition risque de paraître sommaire, toute généralisation semble arbitraire. C'est la raison pour laquelle nous avons conçu d'une manière différente notre communication. La première partie sera consacrée à une analyse rapide des diverses catégories d'initiation, en insistant surtout sur le rôle religieux et culturel des rites de puberté. Dans la deuxième partie, nous nous proposons de rappeler brièvement les progrès marqués par la recherche récente. Il serait, certes, utile de commencer cet examen sinon avec *Altersklassen und Männerbünde* (1902) de Heinrich SCHURTZ, *Primitive Secret Societies* (1908) de Hutton WEBSTER ou *Les rites de passage* de VAN GENNEP, livre qui fut publié en 1909, au moins avec *I Misteri*, de R. PETTAZZONI, publié en 1924. Mais il serait impossible de mener à bout une telle entreprise dans le temps limité dont nous disposons. Enfin, dans la dernière partie, nous allons mentionner les contributions de quelques historiens et critiques littéraires, qui se sont appliqués à déchiffrer et interpréter certaines œuvres à la lumière des symboles et des scénarios de type initiatique. Comme nous espérons le montrer, une telle tendance de la part des critiques littéraires n'est pas seulement réconfortante pour les historiens des religions; elle est également significative, car elle fait partie d'une orientation qui nous semble caractéristique pour la culture occidentale contemporaine.

I

Par initiation on comprend généralement un ensemble de rites et d'enseignements oraux, au moyen desquels on obtient une modification radicale du statut religieux et social du sujet à initier. Philosophiquement parlant, l'initiation équivaut à une mutation ontologique du régime existentiel. A la fin de ses épreuves, le néophyte jouit d'une toute autre existence qu'avant l'initiation: il est devenu un *autre*. On distingue trois grandes catégories — ou types — d'initiation.[1])

1) La première catégorie comprend les rituels collectifs par lesquels s'effectue le passage de l'adolescence à l'âge adulte, et qui sont obligatoires pour tous les membres de la communauté. La littérature ethnologique désigne ces cérémonies par les termes „rites de puberté", „initiation tribale" ou „initiation de classe d'âge". Les autres initiations se distinguent de celles du puberté en ce qu'elles ne sont pas obligatoires pour tous les membres de la communauté et que le plupart se pratiquent individuellement ou par groupes assez restreints.

2) La deuxième catégorie d'initiation comprend toutes les espèces de rites d'entrée dans une société secrète, dans un *Bund* ou dans une confrérie. Ces *Bünde* sont réservés à un seul sexe et sont très jaloux de leurs secrets respectifs. Bien que la majorité des confréries secrètes soit masculines, il existe également des *Weiberbünde*. Mais dans le monde méditerranéen et du Proche-Orient antique, les deux sexes avaient accès aux Mystères — et, quoique leur type soit un peu différent, on peut classer les Mystères gréco-orientaux dans la catégorie des confréries secrètes.

3) Enfin, le troisième type d'initiation caractérise la vocation mystique, c'est-à-dire, au niveau des religions primitives, la vocation du medicine-man ou du chaman. L'un des aspects spécifiques de ce troisième type d'initiation consiste dans l'importance considérable accordée à l'expérience religieuse personnelle. Précisons que les initiations des sociétés secrètes et les initiations de type chamanique sont en réalité assez proches les unes des autres. Ce qui contribue surtout à les distinguer, c'est l'élément extatique, très important dans les initiations chamaniques. Ajoutons aussi qu'entre toutes les catégories d'initiations il existe une sorte de solidarité structurelle qui fait que, vues d'une certaine perspective, toutes les initiations se ressemblent.

L'initiation de classe d'âge effectue la promotion de l'adolescent à l'état de membre responsable de la communauté. Le novice apprend non seulement les comportements, les techniques et les institutions des adultes, mais aussi les mythes et les traditions sacrées de la tribu, les noms des dieux et l'histoire de leurs œuvres; il apprend surtout les rapports mystiques entre la tribu et les Etres Surnaturels, tels

---

[1]) Cf. M. ELIADE, *Naissances mystiques. Essai sur quelques types d'initiation* (Paris, 1959:=*Birth and rebirth*, New York, 1958).

qu'ils ont été établis dans les temps mythiques. Dans de très nombreux cas, les rites de puberté impliquent également la révélation de la sexualité. Bref, par l'initiation on dépasse le mode naturel, celui de l'enfance, et on accède au mode culturel, c'est-à-dire qu'on est introduit aux valeurs spirituelles. A l'occasion de l'initiation la communauté toute entière est religieusement régénérée; car les rites initiatiques ne sont que la répétition des opérations effectuées, dans les temps mythiques, par les Etres Surnaturels.

Toute initiation de puberté comporte un certain nombre d'épreuves plus ou moins dramatiques: séparation d'avec la mère, isolement dans la brousse sous la surveillance d'un instructeur, interdiction de manger un grand nombre d'espèces végétales et animales, extraction d'une dent, circoncision (suivie en certains cas de subincision), scarification, etc. La révélation des objets sacrés (*bull-roarers*, images des Etres Surnaturels, etc.) constitue également une épreuve initiatique. Dans la majorité des cas, les initiations de puberté comportent une mort suivie d'une résurrection symbolique. Déjà chez certaines tribus d'Australie, l'extraction de l'incisive est interprétée comme la „mort" du néophyte, et le même symbolisme est encore plus évident dans les cas de circoncision. Les novices isolés dans la brousse sont assimilés aux spectres; ils ne peuvent pas se servir de leurs doigts, et doivent prendre la nourriture directement avec la bouche comme le font, croit-on, les âmes des morts. Parfois ils sont oints avec de la glaise, pour les rendre semblables aux spectres. Les huttes dans lesquelles ils sont enfermés ressemblent à un monstre ou à un animal aquatique: les néophytes sont censés être engloutis par le monstre et restent dans son ventre jusqu'au moment ou il seront "re-nés" ou "ressuscités". Car la mort initiatique est interprétée soit comme un *descensus ad inferos* soit comme un *regressus ad uterum*, et la "résurrection" est comprise parfois comme une „renaissance". Dans nombre de cas, les novices sont symboliquement enterrés, ou ils sont censés avoir oublié leur vie passée, leurs relations familiales, leur nom, leur langue, et doivent tout apprendre de nouveau. Parfois, les épreuves initiatiques deviennent de véritables tortures.

Aux niveaux archaïques de culture déjà (par exemple en Australie), l'initiation de puberté comporte une pluralité de degrés qui ne sont pas accessibles à tous les candidats. Ce qui veut dire que le sacré ne se laisse pas épuiser par les premières révélations. L'approfondissement de l'expérience et de la connaissance religieuses demande une vocation spéciale ou une force de volonté et d'intelligence hors du commun. Nous tenons ici l'explication de l'apparition des sociétés secrètes aussi bien que de l'organisation des confréries des medicine-men et des chamans. Les rites d'entrée dans une société secrète correspondent en tout point aux initiations tribales: réclusion, tortures et épreuves initiatiques, mort et résurrection, imposition d'un nom nouveau, révélation d'une doctrine secrète, enseignement d'une langue spéciale, etc. On remarque pourtant quelques innovations particulières aux sociétés secrètes: le rôle capital du secret, la cruauté des épreuves initiatiques, la prédominance du culte des ancêtres (personnifiés par les masques) et l'absence de l'Etre suprême dans les cérémonies. Là où il existe des *Weiberbünde*, l'initiation comporte des épreuves spécifiques suivies des révélations concernant la fécondité, la conception et la naissance.

La mort initiatique signifie à la fois la fin de l'homme „naturel", aculturel, et le passage à une nouvelle modalité d'existence: celle d'un être „né à l'exprit", c'est-à-dire qui ne vit pas uniquement dans une réalité „immédiate". La mort et la résurrection initiatiques font donc partie intégrante du processus mystique par lequel on devient *un autre*, façonné d'après le modèle révélé par les dieux ou les ancêtres mythiques. Ce qui revient à dire qu'on devient *homme véritable* dans la mesure où l'on ressemble à un Etre surhumain. L'intérêt de l'initiation pour l'intelligence de la mentalité archaïque réside surtout en ceci: elle nous montre que le *vrai homme* — l'homme spirituel — n'est pas *donné*, n'est pas le résultat d'un processus naturel. Il est „fait" par les vieux maîtres, selon les modèles révélés par les Etres divins et conservés dans les mythes. Ces vieux maîtres constituent les élites spirituelles des sociétés archaïques. Leur fonction est de révéler aux nouvelles générations le sens profond de l'existence et de les aider à assumer la responsabilité d'être un „homme véritable", et, par conséquent, de participer à la culture. Mais puisque, pour les sociétés archaïques et traditionnelles, la „culture" est la somme des valeurs reçues des Etres surnaturels, la fonction de l'initiation peut se ramener à ceci: elle révèle à chaque nouvelle génération un monde ouvert vers le trans-humain, un monde, dirions-nous, „transcendental".

Quant aux initiations chamaniques, elles consistent en une expérience d'ordre extatique (rêves, visions, transes) et en une instruction effectuée par les esprits ou les vieux maîtres chamans (communication des techniques chamaniques, noms et fonctions des esprits, mythologie et généalogie du clan, langage secret, etc.). Parfois, l'initiation est publique et comporte un rituel riche et mouvementé (par exemple chez les Bouriates). Mais l'absence d'un rituel de ce genre n'implique nullement l'absence de l'initiation: celle-ci peut très bien s'opérer en rêve ou dans l'expérience extatique du néophyte. En Sibérie et en Asie Centrale, le futur chaman tombe malade ou traverse une crise psychopathique pendant laquelle il est censé être torturé par les démons et les esprits qui jouent le rôle des maîtres d'initiation. Le scénario de ces maladies initiatiques comporte les moments suivants: 1) torture et morcellement du corps; 2) raclage des chairs jusqu'à réduction du corps au squelette; 3) remplacement des viscères et renouvellement du sang; 4) séjour aux Enfers, durant lequel le futur chaman est instruit par les âmes des chamans morts et par les démons; 5) ascension au Ciel; 6) „résurrection", c'est-à-dire accès à un nouveau mode d'être: celui d'un homme consacré, capable de communiquer personnellement avec les dieux, les démons et les esprits. Le même schéma est spécifique aux initiations des medicine-men australiens. [1]

Le peu qu'on sait des initiations à Eleusis ou dans les Mystères hellénistiques, laisse supposer que l'expérience centrale du myste consistait en une révélation en rapport avec la mort et la résurrection de la divinité fondatrice du Mystère. Grâce à cette révélation, le myste accédait à un autre mode d'être, qui lui assurait en même temps un sort optime après la mort.

II

Comme nous l'avons annoncé au début de notre communication, il serait instructif de rappeler, même très brièvement, les résultats obtenus durant les 30 ou 40 dernières années dans l'étude des diverses initiations. Il ne s'agit pas de faire un bilan ou de discuter les méthodes utilisées. Nous nous contenterons de mentionner quelques noms et de citer quelques titres, afin d'illustrer l'orientation actuelle de la recherche. Dès l'abord, une remarque s'impose: bien que les travaux sur les divers types d'initiation ne fassent pas défaut, les monographies présentant le complexe initiatique dans l'ensemble de ses manifestations sont assez rares. On peut citer le livre de O. E. BRIEM sur *Les Sociétés secrètes des Mystères* (trad. fr. 1941), *Geheimkulte* (1951) de W. E. PEUCKERT et *Naissances mystiques* (1959) de M. ELIADE.

---

[1] Voir notre livre *Le chamanisme et les techniques archaïques de l'extase* (Paris, 1951) pp. 45 sq. ,112 sq. et passim. (Une deuxième édition, corrigée et augmentée, est parue en traduction anglaise: *Shamanism. Archaic Techniques of Ecstasy*, New York, 1964; cf. pp. 33 sq., 110 sq., 508 sq.).

On peut faire la même remarque en ce qui concerne les initiations chez les „primitifs". Ad. E. Jensen a publié en 1933 un travail suggestif, *Beschneidung und Reifezeremonien bei Naturvölkern* et R. Thurnwald un important article intitulé *Primitive Initiation- und Wiedergeburtsriten.*[1]) Par contre, les monographies régionales abondent. Puisqu'on ne peut tout citer, rappelons, pour l'Australie et l'Océanie, *Aboriginal men of high degree* (1946) de A. P. Elkin et *Kunapipi* (1951) de R. M. Berndt, les études de F. Speiser,[2]) R. Piddington [3]) et D. F. Thomson [4]), les livres et les articles de J. Layard [5]), W. E. Mühlmann [6]), E. Schlesier, C. A. Schmitz [7]); pour les deux Amériques les travaux de M. Gusinde [8]), de Goeje [9]), J. Haeckel [10]), W. Müller [11]) et quelques autres; pour l'Afrique,

---

[1]) *Eranos-Jahrbuch* VII, 1940, 321-398. Cf. aussi E. M. Loeb, „Tribal Initiation and Secret Societies" (*Univ. of California Publications in American Archaeology and Ethnology*, XXV, 1929, pp. 249-288).

[2]) F. Speiser, „Über Initiationen in Australien und Neuguinea" (*Verhandlungen der Naturforschendenden Gesellschaft in Basel*, 1929, pp. 56-258); id., „Kulturgeschichtliche Betrachtungen über die Initiationen in der Südsee" (*Bulletin der Schweizerischen Gesellschaft für Anthropologie und Ethnologie*, XXII, 1945-46, pp. 28-61).

[3]) Ralph Piddington, „Karadjeri Initiation" (*Oceania*, III, 1932-33, pp. 46-87).

[4]) Donald F. Thomson, „The Hero-Cult, Initiation and Totemism on Cape York" (*The Journal of the Royal Anthropological Institute*, LXIII, 1933, pp. 453-537). Cf. aussi E. A. Worms, „Initiationsfeiern einiger Küsten -u. Binnenlandstämme in Nord-Westaustralien" (*Annali Lateranensi*, 1938, vol. II, pp. 147-174).

[5]) John W. Layard, *Stone Men of Malekula* (London, 1942); „The Making of Man in Malekula" (*Eranos-Jahrbuch*, XVI, 1948, pp. 209 sq.).

[6]) W. E. Mühlmann, *Arioi und Mamaia* (Wiesbaden, 1955).

[7]) Erhard Schlesier, *Die melanesische Geheimkulte* (Göttingen, 1956). Cf. aussi C. A. Schmitz, „Die Initiation bei den Pasum am Oberen Rumu, Nordost-Neuguinea" (*Zeitschrift f. Ethnologie*, 81, 1956, pp. 236-246); id., „Zum Problem des Balumkultes" (*Paideuma 6*, 1957, pp. 257-280); Dr. P. Hermann Bader, *Die Reifefeiern bei den Ngadha* (Mödling, sans date); C. Laufer, „Jugendinitiation und Sakraltänze der Baining" (*Anthropos*, 54, 1959, pp. 905-938); P. Alphons Schaefer, „Zur Initiation im Wagi-Tal" (*Anthropos*, 33, 1938, pp. 401-423); Hubert Kroll, „Der Iniet. Das Wesen eines melanesischen Geheimbundes" (*Zeit. f. Ethnologie*, 70, 1937, pp. 180-220).

[8]) M. Gusinde, *Die Yamana* (Mödling, 1937), pp. 940 sq.

[9]) C. H. de Goeje, „Philosophy, Initiation and Myths of the Indian Guiana and adjacent countries" (*Int. Archiv. f. Ethnographie*, XLIV, 1943). Cf. aussi A. Metraux, „Les rites d'initiation dans le vaudou haïtien", (*Tribus*, IV-V, 1953-55, pp. 177-198); id., *Le vaudou haïtien* (Paris, 1958, pp. 171 sq.

[10]) Josef Haeckel, „Jugendweihe und Männerfest auf Feuerland" (*Mitt. d. Oesterr. Gesell. f. Anthropologie, Ethnologie u. Prähistorie*, LXXIII- LXXVII, 1947, pp. 84-114); id., „Schutzgeistsuche u. Jugendweihe im westlichen Nord-amerika" (*Ethnos*, XII, 1947, pp. 106-122); id. „Initiationen u. Geheimbünde an der Nordwestküste Nordamerikas" (*Mitt. d. Anthropologische Gesellschaft in Wien*, LXXXIII, 1954, pp. 176-190).

[11]) Werner Müller, *Die blaue Hütte* (Wiesbaden, 1954); id., *Weltbild und Kult der Kwakiutl-Indianer* (1955).

les monographies d'E. Johanssen (*Mysterien eines Bantu-Volkes*, 1925), de Léo Bittremieux (*La Société secrète des Bakhimba*, 1934) et de A. M. Vergiat (*Les rites secrets des primitifs de l'Oubangui*, 1936); le travail sur les initiations des jeunes filles chez les Bemba, par Audrey I. Richards (*Chisungu*, 1956), et surtout les volumes de Dominique Zahan sur les initiations bambara[1]).

Grâce à la recherche récente, nous disposons maintenant d'informations précise et parfois abondantes sur quelques initiations primitives; qu'on se rappelle seulement les ouvrages de M. Gusinde sur les initiations des Fuégiens, de Zahan et d'Audrey Richards sur certaines initiations africaines, de Carl Laufer sur les rites des Baining, de Piddington, Elkin et Berndt sur les initiations australiennes. D'autre part, la compréhension des diverses formes d'initiation a été sensiblement améliorée à la suite d'analyses pénétrantes comme celles de Werner Müller, de Mühlmann, de Zahan, d'autres encore.

Quant aux initiations dans les religions des Mystères, les travaux publiés dans les dernières années se caractérisent plutôt par un certain scepticisme. A. D. Nock nous rappelait en 1952 combien nos informations concernant les Mystères hellénistiques étaient tardives et reflétaient parfois l'influence du christianisme[2]). En 1961, G. F. Mylonas déclarait dans son livre *Eleusis and the Eleusinian Mysteries* (Princeton) que nous ne savions presque rien sur les rites secrets, autrement dit sur la véritable initiation dans les Mystères d'Eleusis.

Par contre, la recherche a marqué des progrès importants dans un domaine assez négligé avant les années 30. Nous faisons allusion aux rites d'initiation de puberté et d'entrée dans les sociétés secrètes chez les différents peuples indo-européens. On n'a qu'à se rappeler les travaux de Lily Weiser (1927) et d'Otto Höfler (1934) sur les initiations germaniques, les monographies de G. Widengren et de Stig Wikander sur les mythologies et les rituels initiatiques indo-iraniens, les livres de G. Dumézil sur les scénarios initiatiques chez les Ger-

---

[1]) Dominique Zahan, *Sociétés d'initiation bambara* (Paris, 1960). Voir aussi Leopold Walk, ,,Initiationszeremonien u. Pubertätriten der Südafrikanischen Stämme'' (*Anthropos*, 23, 1928, pp. 861-966); M. Planquaert, *Les sociétés secrètes chez les Bayaka* (Louvain, 1930); E. Hildebrand, *Die Geheimbünde Westafrikas als Problem der Religionswissenschaft* (Leipzig, 1937); H. Rehwald, *Geheimbünde in Afrika* (München, 1941).

[2]) A. D. Nock, ,,Hellenistic Mysteries and Christian Sacraments'' (*Mnemosyne*, 1952, pp. 117-213). Cf. les bibliographies enregistrées dans *Naissances mystiques*, p. 231, n. 19, p. 233, n. 20, p. 241, n. 34.

mains, les Romains et les Celtes, — pour se rendre compte du progrès accompli [1]). Ajoutons qu'en 1936 le savant latiniste W. F. JACKSON KNIGHT publiait un petit livre, *Cumaean Gates* (Oxford), dans lequel il s'appliquait à dégager les éléments initiatiques du VIe livre de l'*Enéide*. Et récemment J. GAGÉ a étudié les traces des initiations féminines dans l'ancienne Rome [2]). Le beau travail de H. JEANMAIRE, *Couroï et Courètes* (1939), mérite une mention spéciale: le regretté helléniste avait réussi à reconstituer les scénarios initiatiques dans la saga de Thésée, dans la discipline spartiate de Lycurgue et dans les Thesmophories. L'entreprise de JEANMAIRE n'est pas restée isolée. A. BRELICH a mis en valeur la signification initiatique des mono-sandales dans la Grèce ancienne, c'est-à-dire de la curieuse habitude de chausser une seule sandale [3]). Et dans son livre *Gli Eroi Greci* (Rome, 1955), le même auteur a repris et prolongé les vues de JEAN-MAIRE sur les initiations féminines et sur la significations rituelle de la pénétration de Thésée dans le labyrinthe [4]). De son côté, Marie DELCOURT a pu identifier quelques traits initiatiques dans les mythes et légendes d'Héphaistos [5]).

Tout récemment le professeur R. MERKELBACH a publié un gros livre, *Roman und Mysterium in der Antike* (München-Berlin 1962), dans lequel il se propose de démontrer que les romans gréco-romains — qu'il s'agisse d'*Amor et Psyché*, des *Ephésiaques* ou des *Ethiopiques* — sont des ,,*Mysterientexte*", autrement dit, des transpositions narratives d'une initiation. Selon R. MERKELBACH, le rituel isiaque

---

[1]) Lily WEISER, *Altgermanische Junglingsweihen und Männerbünde* (Baden, 1922); Otto HÖFLER, *Kultische Geheimbünde der Germanen* (Frankfurt a. M. 1934); Geo WIDENGREN, *Hochgottglaube im alten Iran* (Uppsala, 1938), pp. 311 sq.; *id.* ,,Stand und Aufgaben der iranischen Religionsgeschichte", I (*Numen*, 1955, pp. 16-83), pp. 65 sq.; Stig WIKANDER, *Der arische Männerbund* (Lund, 1938); Georges DUMÉZIL, *Mythes et Dieux des Germains* (Paris, 1939), pp. 79 sq.; *id.*, *Horace et les Curiaces* (Paris, 1942). Voir maintenant Alwyn REES et Brinley REES, *Celtic Heritage* (New York, 1961), pp. 246 sq. *Cf.* aussi les indications bibliographiques dans *Naissances mystiques*, pp. 174 sq., nn. 2, 4, 7, 8-11. Marjan MOLÉ se demandait si, à l'époque ancienne, le passage du pont Cinvat ne constituait pas une épreuve initiatique; cf. ,,Daēnā, le pont Cinvat et l'initiation dans le Mazdéisme" (*R H R*, t. 157, 1960, pp. 155-185), p. 182.

[2]) J. GAGÉ, *Matronalia. Essai sur les dévotions et les organisations cultuelles de femmes dans l'ancienne Rome* (Bruxelles, 1963); cf. le compte-rendu de A. Brelich, *SMSR*, 34, 1963, p. 355 sq.

[3]) A. BRELICH, ,,Les monosandales" (*La Nouvelle Clio*, VII-IX, 1955-57, pp. 469-484).

[4]) Sur le symbolisme initiatique du labyrinthe, cf. Clara GALLINI, ,,Pontinjia Dapuritois" (*Acme*, XII, 1959, pp. 149 sq.).

[5]) Marie DELCOURT, *Héphaistos ou la légende du magicien* (Liège-Paris, 1957).

serait à la base du roman. Dans la longue analyse critique qu'il lui a consacré, R. TURCAN [1]) ne conteste pas les significations religieuses et même les allusions aux Mystères décelables dans certains romans alexandrins. Mais il se refuse à reconnaître dans ces textes littéraires, surchargés de clichés et de réminiscences, des indications concrètes concernant les Mystères. Nous ne discuterons pas ici le bien fondé de ces deux positions méthodologiques [2]). Mais il est significatif qu'un des maîtres de la philologie classique allemande ait cru pouvoir lire dans des textes littéraires de l'hellénisme le témoignage d'une expérience religieuse secrète, de structure initiatique.

III

Envisager la littérature, écrite ou orale, dans une perspective semblable nous semble une démarche caractéristique de notre époque, et, par conséquent, précieuse pour la connaissance de l'homme moderne. En effet, nous assistons depuis quelque temps à un effort concerté de la part des historiens, des critiques et des psychologues en vue de découvrir dans les œuvres littéraires des valeurs et des intentions qui débordent la sphère artistique proprement dite. Rappelons, par exemple, les romans du moyen âge qui mettent en vedette Arthur, le Roi Pécheur, Perceval et d'autres héros engagés dans la Quête du Graal. Les médiévistes ont démontré la continuité entre les thèmes et les figures de la mythologie celtique et les scénarios et les personnages des romans arthuriens. Or la plupart de ces scénarios sont initiatiques: il est toujours question d'une ,,Quête", longue et mouvementée, d'objets merveilleux qui impliquent, entre autres, la pénétration du héros dans l'autre monde. Ces romans énigmatiques ont donné lieu à des interprétations audacieuses. Ainsi, par exemple, une érudite prestigieuse comme Jessie L. WESTON n'a pas hésité à affirmer, en 1920, que la légende du Graal conservait des traces d'un ancien rituel d'initiation [3]).

Cette thèse n'a pas été acceptée par les spécialistes. Mais c'est le rayonnement culturel du livre de Jessie WESTON qui est à la fois

---

[1]) Robert TURCAN, ,,Le roman ,,initiatique'': A propos d'un livre récent" (*RHR*, 1963, pp. 149-199).

[2]) Voir aussi, dans les *Beiträge zur Klassischen Philologie*, Herausgegeben von Reinhold MERKELBACH (Verlag Anton Hain, Meisenheim am Glan), Ingrid LÖFFLER, *Die Melampodie. Versuch einer Rekonstruktion des Inhalts* (1962); Udo HETZNER, *Andromeda und Tarpeia* (1962); Gerhard BINDER, *Die Aussetzung des Königskindes* (1962).

[3]) Jessie L. WESTON, *From Ritual to Romance* (Cambridge, 1920).

important et symptomatique. Non seulement parce que T. S. ELIOT a pu écrire *The Waste Land* après l'avoir lu, mais surtout parce que le succès de ce livre a attiré l'attention du public sur la prolifération des symboles et des motifs initiatiques dans les romans arthuriens. On n'a qu'à lire l'excellent ouvrage de Jean MARX, *La légende arthurienne et le Graal* (Paris, 1952) ou la monographie d'Antoinette FIERZ-MONNIER, *Initiation und Wandlung. Zur Geschichte des altfranzösischen Romans in XII Jahrhundert* (Bern, 1951), pour se rendre compte que ces motifs et symboles initiatiques jouent un rôle essentiel de par leur propre présence et en dehors de toute solidarité génétique éventuelle avec des scénarios *réels*. Autrement dit, ils font partie d'un Univers *imaginaire* — et celui-ci est aussi important pour l'existence humaine que la vie diurne.

Des interprétations similaires ont été récemment formulées à propos d'autres littératures orales. En étudiant l'épopée néogrecque *Digenis Akritas*, J. LINDSAY n'hésite pas à écrire que: ,,Si nous analysons le vocables *Digenis* nous reconnaissons le terme initiatique ,deux fois né', terme utilisé pour exprimer la deuxième naissance d'un jeune homme qui a traversé avec succès ses épreuves. Et nous pouvons considérer notre héros comme le représentant d'un rituel initiatique: le jeune homme qui vainc les forces ténébreuses dans un moment de crise et qui, partant, symbolise son peuple dans sa mort et son renouvellement. Une telle interprétation s'accorde avec les nombreux éléments de rituels de fertilité qui accompagnent Digenis dans les ballades et les laïus, et qui se manifestent clairement dans les croyances populaires concernant son tombeau et sa massue" [1].

Dans son beau livre sur les l'épopée et le barde au Tibet R. A. STEIN dégage, d'une part, les rapports entre chamans et poètes populaires, et montre, d'autre part, que le barde reçoit ses chants d'un dieu et que pour recevoir cette révélation, il doit passer par une initiation [2]. Quant aux éléments initiatiques des poèmes ésotériques des *Fedeli d'Amore*, ils ont été mis en lumière par Luigi VALLI en 1928 et par R. RICOLFI en 1933 [3]. Récemment, H. CORBIN a profondément interprété un texte d'Avicene en tant que récit initiatique; il a montré en outre, dans plusieurs de ses ouvrages, les rapports entre philosophie, gnose et initiation [4].

---

[1] J. LINDSAY, *Byzantium into Europe* (1952), p. 370.

[2] R. A. STEIN, *Recherches sur l'épopée et le barde au Tibet* (Paris, 1959), spécialement pp. 325 sq., 332, etc.

[3] Cf. *Naissances mystiques*, pp. 259 sq.

[4] Henry CORBIN, *Avicenne et le récit visionnaire* (Téhéran-Paris, 1954). Cf. aussi

Evidemment, on n'a pas manqué d'approcher l'étude des contes populaires dans une perspective analogue. Dès 1923 P. Saintyves interprétait certains contes comme des ,,textes" accompagnant les rites initiatiques. En 1946, le folkloriste soviétique V. Ia. Propp est allé encore plus loin: il découvrait dans les contes populaires le souvenir des rites d',,initiation totémique" [1]). Nous avons montré ailleurs pourquoi une telle hypothèse ne s'impose pas [2]). Mais encore une fois, il est significatif que l'hypothèse ait été formulée. Ajoutons que le savant hollandais Jan DE VRIES a prouvé la persistance des thèmes initiatiques dans les saga héroïques et même dans certains jeux d'enfants [3]). Une psychologue suisse, Hedwig VON BEIT, dans un ouvrage considérable sur la symbolique des contes, s'est appliquée à interpréter les motifs initiatiques selon la psychologie de JUNG [4]).

Il était à prévoir que les psychologues s'intéresseraient à notre sujet. FREUD avait vivement encouragé les recherches d'Otto RANK sur le mythe de la naissance du héros. Depuis lors, la littérature psychanalithique sur les rites et les symboles des initiations n'a cessé d'augmenter. Citons une des dernières contributions, qui est aussi la plus originale: *Symbolic wounds* (Glencoe, 1954) de Bruno BETTELHEIM. Mais c'est surtout l'interprétation analythique de la littérature qui est instructive. En 1934 Maud BODKINS publiait son livre *Archetypal patterns in poetry*: en appliquant les idées de JUNG sur ,,l'archétype de la nouvelle naissance", l'auteur expliquait *The Ancient mariner* de COLERIDGE et *The Waste Land* de T. S. ELIOT comme la projection poétique d'un processus (inconscient) d'initiation.

Tout récemment, dans son ouvrage *Nerval: Expérience et création* (Paris, 1963), Jean RICHER a analysé avec perspicacité la structure initiatique d'*Aurélia*. D'ailleurs, Gérard DE NERVAL se rendait compte de la signification rituelle de son expérience: ,,Du moment que je me fus assuré de ce point que j'étais soumis aux épreuves de l'initiation

---

,,Le Récit d'Initiation et l'Hermétisme en Iran" (*Eranos-Jahrbuch*, XVII, 1949, pp. 149 sq.).

[1]) P. Saintyves, *Les contes de Perrault et les récites parallèles* (Paris, 1923); V. Ia. Propp, *Istoritcheskie korni volshenboi skaski* (Leningrad, 1946).

[2]) ,,Les savants et les contes de fées" (*La Nouvelle Revue Française*, Mai, 1956, pp. 884-891); cf. *Aspects du Mythe* (Paris, 1963), pp. 233-244.

[3]) Jan DE VRIES, ,,Betrachtungen zum Märchen, besonders in seine Verhältnis zu Heldensage und Mythos" (*FF Comm.* Nr. 150, Helsinki, 1954); id., *Heldenlied en heldensage* (Utrecht, 1959), spéc. pp. 194 sq.; id., ,,Untersuchung über das Hüpfspiel, Kinderspiel-Kulttanz" (*FF Comm.* Nr. 173, Helsinki, 1957).

[4]) Hedwig VON BEIT, *Symbolik des Märchens* (Berne, 1952); id., *Gegensatz und Erneuerung im Märchen* (Berne, 1956).

sacrée, une force invincible entra dans mon esprit. Je me jugeais un héros vivant sous le regard des dieux . . ." [1]) Selon Jean RICHER, le thème de la descente d'Orphée aux enfers domine toute l'œuvre de NERVAL. Or, le *descensus ad inferos* constitue l'épreuve initiatique par excellence. Certes, NERVAL avait lu quantité de livres occultistes. Mais il est difficile de croire qu'un poète de son envergure ait choisi le thème initiatique parce qu'il avait lu des livres sur ce sujet. *Aurélia* est en partie une œuvre autobiographique. Et il est significatif que NERVAL ait senti la nécessité de formuler et valoriser ses expériences réelles ou imaginaires dans un langage initiatique.

D'ailleurs, les critiques ont retrouvé des thèmes initiatiques chez des auteurs qui ignoraient la littérature occultiste. C'est le cas, par exemple, de Jules VERNE, dont certains livres — en premier lieu *Le Voyage au Centre de la Terre*, *L'Ile mysterieuse*, *Le Chateau des Carpathes* — ont été interprétés comme des romans initiatiques. Et on n'a qu'à lire l'étude de Léon CELLIER sur ,,Le Roman initiatique en France au temps du romantisme" [2]) pour se rendre compte de la contribution que la critique littéraire est susceptible d'apporter à notre recherche.

Mais ce sont surtout les critiques américains qui vont très loin dans cette direction. On pourrait même dire qu'un grand nombre de critiques interprètent les œuvres littéraires dans une perspective empruntée à celle des historiens des religions: mythe, rituel, initiation, héros, mort rituelle, régénération, nouvelle naissance, etc. font partie maintenant de la terminologie fondamentale d'une exégèse littéraire. Le nombre de livres et études analysant les scénarios initiatiques camouflés dans les poèmes, les nouvelles et les romans, est considérable. On a reconnu de tels scénarios non seulement dans *Moby Dick* [3]), mais dans *Walden* de THOREAU [5]), dans les romans de COOPER [4]), et ceux de Henry JAMES, dans *Huckleberry Finn* de Mark TWAIN, dans *The Bear* de FAULKNER [6]). Et dans un livre récent, *Radical Innocence*

---

[1]) Cité par Jean RICHER, *Nerval*, p. 512.

[2]) Léon CELLIER, ,,Le Roman initiatique en France au temps du romantisme" (*Cahiers Internationaux de Symbolisme*, Nr. 4, 1964, pp. 22-40).

[3]) Cf. Newton ARVIN, *Herman Melville* (New York, 1950).

[4]) Stanley HYMAN, ,,Henry Thoreau in our Time" (*Atlantic Monthly*, Nov. 1946, pp. 137-176); cf. also R. W. B. LEWIS, *The American Adam* (Chicago, 1955), pp. 22 sq.

[5]) Cf. R. W. B. LEWIS, *op. cit.* pp. 87 sq., 98 sq.

[6]) R. W. B. LEWIS, in *Kenyon Review*, Autumn 1951; *id.*, *The Picaresque Saint* (New York, 1961), pp. 204 sq.

(1963), l'auteur, Ihab HASSAN, consacre tout un chapitre à la „Dialectique de l'Initiation", en l'illustrant avec les écrit de Sherwood ANDERSON, SCOTT FITZGERALD, WOLFE et FAULKNER.

Il n'est pas question de juger ici la validité et les résultats de telles entreprises. Mais, pour le répéter, il est significatif que certaines œuvres littéraires, anciennes et modernes, aient été interprétées — par des historiens, des critiques ou des psychologues — comme ayant des rapports directs, bien qu'inconscients, avec l'initiation. Et ceci pour plusieurs raisons. D'abord, parce que dans ses formes les plus complexes, l'initiation suscite et contrôle la créativité spirituelle: dans nombre de cultures, la poésie, le spectacle, la sagesse sont le résultat direct d'un apprentissage initiatique. Et il est bon qu'on s'applique actuellement à étudier les rapports entre l'initiation et les expressions les plus „nobles", les plus créatrices d'une culture. On a mis en lumière le caractère „initiatique" de la maïeutique socratique [1]). On pourrait faire un rapprochement analogue entre initiation et phénoménologie: en effet, la phénoménologie se propose d'abolir l'expérience „profane", c'est-à-dire l'expérience de l'homme naturel. Or, ce que HUSSERL appelait l'„attitude naturelle" de l'homme correspond à l'état profane, pré-initiatique. A travers l'initiation de puberté, le novice a accès au sacré, c'est-à-dire au *réel*, tout comme par le truchement de la réduction phénoménologique l'esprit arrive à saisir le réel.

Mais des recherches semblables sont également significatives pour la connaissance de l'homme moderne. Le désir de déchiffrer des scénarios initiatiques dans la littérature et dans l'art (peinture, cinéma), dénote non seulement une revalorisation de l'initiation en tant que processus de régénération et transformation spirituelles, mais aussi une certaine nostalgie pour une expérience équivalente. On sait que les initiations dans le sens traditionnel du terme on disparu depuis longtemps en Europe; mais on sait aussi que les symboles et les scénarios initiatiques survivent au niveau de l'inconscient, surtout dans les rêves et dans les univers imaginaires. Il est significatif qu'on étudie aujourd'hui ces survivances avec un intérêt difficile à concevoir il y a 50 ou 60 ans. FREUD nous a appris que certaines tendances et décisions existentielles ne sont pas conscientes. Par conséquent, la forte attraction envers les œuvres littéraires et artistiques à structure initiatique est révélatrice. Le marxisme et la psychanalyse nous ont montré l'efficacité de la démystification lorsqu'on veut saisir le *vrai*

---

[1]) Cf. *Naissances mystiques*, pp. 239.

sens — ou le sens *premier* — d'un comportement, d'une action ou d'une création culturelle. Dans notre cas, il nous faut entreprendre une démystification à rebours; autrement dit, il nous faut ,,démystifier'' les univers et les langages apparemment profanes de la littérature, de la peinture, du cinéma, et montrer tout ce qu'ils comportent de ,,sacré'' — évidemment, d'un ,,sacré'' ignoré, camouflé ou dégradé. Certes, dans un monde désacralisé comme le nôtre, le ,,sacré'' est surtout présent et actif dans les univers imaginaires. Mais on commence à se rendre compte que les expériences imaginaires sont constitutives de l'être humain au même titre que ses expériences diurnes. Dans ce cas, la nostalgie pour les épreuves et les scénarios initiatiques, nostalgie déchiffrée dans tant d'œuvres littéraires et plastiques, révèle le désir de l'homme moderne d'un renouvellement définitif et total, d'une *renovatio* qui puisse transmuer l'existence.

C'est pour cette raison que les recherches récentes que nous venons de passer rapidement en revue ne représentent pas uniquement des contributions intéressant l'histoire des religions, l'ethnologie, l'orientalisme ou la critique littéraire; elles sont susceptibles d'être interprétées en tant qu'expressions constitutives du faciès culturel de l'époque moderne.

SOME INTRODUCTORY REMARKS
ON THE SIGNIFICANCE OF INITIATION

BY

C. J. BLEEKER
Amsterdam

Initiation has been chosen as the main subject of this Study-conference, because it plays an important part in practically all types of
religion. Rites of initiation are not to be found in all religions. However every religion introduces its adherents to eternal truth—into
a spiritual happiness of high quality. Therefore, it is no exaggeration
to contend that initiation is one of the key-notions of religion. Initiation is the gate, which leads to the knowledge of the nature and of
the will of the gods or of the deity.

It is the intention that the participants of this Study-conference
shall try to define the nature and the function of initiation in the
different religions, so that one is able to survey better the types of
initiation and thereby have a better understanding of the essence of
initiation. What the organizers had in mind is that this meeting should
function as a kind of joint scientific research. To this end a Study-
conference is a very appropriate means. A congress, attended by
several hundreds of persons, offers no opportunity and no leisure to
treat a subject of the history of religions exhaustively. No wonder
that there have been complaints about the scientific level of the congresses. Therefore, this Study-conference has been organized in
order to provide the participating scholars with an opportunity of
entering into a profound discussion in the restricted circle of persons
who are either experts or keenly interested in the subject at stake.
Obviously this meeting is an experiment. The organizers await the
results with interest. Please allow me to make a strong appeal to all
participants for their co-operation so that this Study-conference
becomes a real success.

It is evident, that this introductory talk does not intend to anticipate the results of the discussions of the forthcoming days. This is
not only impossible; it would also be senseless. However, it is extreme-

ly useful to reflect for a moment upon the function of the notion of initiation in the study of the history of religions. As a rule, students of the history of religions work empirically. They study texts and they try to interpret historic facts, without considering the import of the ideas which they employ for the interpretation of their material. It can be clarifying to ponder on the significance of these concepts. Thus the question arises: which are the implications of the idea of initiation?

Initiation presupposes a religious secret, which is only known to the initiated. Actually, true belief always is a secret. Therefore, Jesus gave in the Sermon on the Mount the well-known prescription concerning prayer: 'But thou, when thou prayest, enter into thy closet, and when thou hast shut thy door, pray to thy Father which is in secret; and thy Father which seeth in secret, shall reward thee openly.' True prayer takes place in the inner room. True belief belongs to the secret place of human life. It eludes the grasp of scientific research. The faithful are, in general, not inclined to discuss their religious belief with outsiders. One understands a religious truth only in so far as one is initiated into it by personal faith or by conversion. Here a clear limitation is placed on the study of the history of religions. This means, that the very essence of piety always escapes from scientific research and, moreover, that an outsider never fully manages to penetrate into the core of a religion which is not his own. Rud. OTTO had this experience when he once visited a Hindu-temple in the neighbourhood of Madras. Standing, at the entrance of the temple, he detected far away in the holy of holies a white object. It proved to be the temple-cow, ruminating in serene quiet and great dignity. Attracted by its mysterious appearance, Rud. OTTO intended to cross the sacred but forbidden threshold. At the same moment, a temple-bell was loudly rung, warning him not to profane the sanctuary by his unholy feet. His travelling companion who relates this story writes that, at that moment, a smile flitted across the face of the author of the famous study on the Holy, because he understood that nothwithstanding all his knowledge of the subject, he was not allowed to enter this Hindu holy place.

The preceding statement does not imply, that the student of the history of religions is incapable of understanding the characteristic features of whatever religion may be the object of his research. He certainly is able to penetrate deeply into the very essence of different religions. However, not everybody shares this opinion. And, I must admit, that here a serious and interesting problem arises. What are we to do, if the description which we give of a religion is contradicted by its adherents? There are in fact scholars who contend, that the best and most reliable information about a certain religion is to be obtained from its adherents, because they are supposed to know their religion better than uninitiated outsiders. In my opinion, this is only partly true. Sometimes, the initiated lack the survey of the whole system of their religion. They do not see the connection of certain lines of its structure. They are often badly informed about the history of their religion. Though the historians of religion are uninitiated people, they can by their unbiassed study make a most valuable contribution to the better understanding of the essence of the different religions.

And yet every expert knows that he very soon has reached the limit of his insight, a limit which he, to his despair, is unable to push back not even a centimeter. This holds particularly true for the study of the religions of antiquity. Here the difficulty is not only that the facts in this field of research often offer resistance to a satisfactory explanation, but also that the living informants of this type of religion are lacking. The adherents of these religions of the past—religions which have died—have taken the secret of their belief with them to their grave. They did not take the trouble to leave behind sufficient explanations by which scholars of the twentieth century could fully understand their course of religious thinking. Therefore, in the texts and in the symbols of these religions we are often confronted by riddles, so that we keenly feel: 'we are not initiated'. Moreover, one gets the feeling that the religious consciousness of the people of antiquity was orientated in another direction than ours. The late Dr. W. B. KRISTENSEN, who knew these religions better than anybody else, rightly has written: 'we can never reach a complete understanding of these religions. We shall never experience them as powers in our life, as the believers have experienced them. We shall never learn to fulfil their holy ceremonies. This proves best that we never can learn to understand their religions, as they themselves have conceived it. We only approximately can understand them; their experience can never fully become ours'. The difficulty is still more increased, when we are confronted by forms of religions, which pretend to possess an esoteric truth, one which is only disclosed by initiation. For the initiated have excellently kept their secret. We only know some fragments of the rites and of the formulae of initiation, which besides are capable of various explanations so that they only provide a vague idea of what happened in the closed meetings of these so called mystery societies.

The last fact gives rise to the remark that in regard to initiation a sharp distinction should be made between an inexpressible mystery and an esoteric truth. All believers are initiated in the ineffable mystery of their faith. Yet this is an open secret. One can get to understand it by faith. To him, who believes, the eyes are opened so that he discovers a new level of truth and of reality, which is unknown to the uninitiated. However, the secret also can be a religious truth, jealously guarded by a certain group of religious people. In this case, it is a privilege to belong to the initiated. It is true that theoretically everybody can be initiated, in practice it is the rule that people who want to be initiated must meet certain requirements. Now, attention should be paid to the fact that initiation into a hidden truth can have a twofold meaning. In the first place it can consist in the privilege of attending the actualization of a certain religious truth in the cult. This means that initiation introduces a person into the right to behold certain dramatic acts of mysterious character. This type of initiation occurs in several religions, e.g. in some religions of antiquity and in certain forms of Christianity. In these religions, everybody knows the truth which is dramatized in the cult. Nevertheless it is a mysterious truth. Therefore, its actualization is so holy and so secret, that only a limited number of people are allowed to attend to it. Moreover, it is strictly forbidden to depict or describe the cultic act in question. On the other hand, initiation can mean the disclosure of an esoteric truth, in the sense of a secret doctrine, which is taught or exemplified by dramatic action. In the latter case, the secret doctrine is mostly in the possession of a more or less closed society. Consequently, real rites of initiation of an elaborate character are here instituted and performed.

Thus initiation appears in various forms and can have a different significance in a different context. Though I am not making any attempt to exhaust the subject or to anticipate the results of this Study-conference, I may venture to enumerate the following types of initiation, because they are well-known.

1) the initiation into the tribal community, an initiation in which all young people, both the boys and usually also the girls, take part. Initiation means in this case, that the initiated are introduced to the knowledge of the myth and to the rules and the customs of the tribe.

2) the initiation into certain societies of men or women. This ceremony is generally celebrated by rites, which have either a symbolic or a realistic character, in which latter case they can consist of cruel ordeals.

3) the initiation into a closed society which possesses an esoteric truth, sometimes in the form of a secret doctrine.

4) the participation in a type of cult which dramatizes a religious truth of such a mysterious character that only privileged people are allowed to attend to it.

5) the initiation into an office, which requires certain personal qualities or extraordinary knowledge, such as the function of the shaman, the king or the prophet.

6) the initiation into religious truth, which happens when a man embraces a certain belief or is converted.

This enumeration of the types of initiation may serve to show that initiation is not exclusively bound to a certain age, i.e. to puberty, as some people think. Initiation can take place in different periods of a man's life. This is an important observation. It indicates that initiation accompanies man's spiritual growth and is, so to speak a milestone thereof. Now it is a wellknown fact that man's religious development in some cases runs smoothly but in other cases is interrupted by moments of crisis. In the latter case man must now and then take a leap in order to reach a new period of life. It is in these critical periods of transition that initiation becomes significant and exerts a beneficent influence. In my opinion, it is important to realize that these moments of transition do not only occur in the life of certain individuals, but also have a super-personal significance. For, human life as such moves on in a succession of periods. The transition to a new period always means the initiation into a new truth—into a new domain of reality. The main turning points of human life are wellknown, i.e. puberty, marriage and death. These events are so highly important, that a man, who evaluates them in a religious sense, cannot remain passive. Therefore, he performs certain rites in order to further the transition. They are the well-known 'rites de passage'. These ceremonies often function as rites of initiation. In that case the significance of initiation is that it marks the stages of the development of human life.

In conclusion, it can be stated, that initiation has both a religious and an anthropological meaning. Many instances of the religious significance of initiation could be given. Let me present one striking example, taken from the description of the initiation of Lucius into the mysteries of Isis given by APULEIUS in his famous book 'The Golden Ass'. I refer to the beginning of the veiled words in which Lucius describes his initiation, i.e. the sentence: 'I approached the borderline of death and I tread the threshold of Proserpine'. The meaning of these words is clarified by the explanation of the author that initiation must be understood 'as a voluntary death and as a salvation acquired by grace', that the initiated, by the grace of the goddess, 'in a certain sense was reborn and lead back on the path of new happiness' and that he celebrated the day of his initiation as his birthday. From these words it is clear that initiation meant to Lucius a religious re-birth. As to the anthropological value of initiation, I can refer to the wellknown studies of Professor ELIADE on this subject. He has time and again stressed the idea that initiation is an indispensable factor in the process by which men really become human beings. Only by initiation a man becomes a real man, a spiritual man, a man who knows the different dimensions of human life.

Initiation in this meeting is an object of study. It is worthwhile to note that this research in itself is an initiation, i.e. an introduction into unknown, hidden and fascinating regions of religious thinking and religious feeling. Each initiation is, in some respect an unmasking. A mysterious truth is deprived of its mask. The hidden world proves to be otherwise than one thought and imagined. One feels sometimes glad, sometimes disappointed. Every student of the history of religions shares in these experiences. Presumably this will also happen to us during this Study-conference. There is however one cause for consolation:—the essence of religion is more comprehensive than our acumen can ever grasp of. The real secret evades the most penetrating scientific research. Here we are reminded of the goddess in Ancient Egypt, whose statue was veiled and who took pride in the fact that nobody had ever lifted her veil.

TERMINOLOGIE
BAMBARA CONCERNANT L'INITIATION

PAR

D. ZAHAN
Strasbourg

Je n'ai pas l'intention d'analyser dans cet exposé les nombreux termes techniques que l'on rencontre dans les sociétés d'initiation bambara.

Mon dessein est de ne considérer que les deux vocables désignant l'acte par lequel une personne est admise dans ces communautés.

Les chercheurs qui se sont occupés de la religion bambara et moi-même d'ailleurs, avons nommé ces collèges: confréries religieuses ou sociétés d'initiation. L'action d'introduire un individu dans leur sein étant appelée l'initiation.

Mais ce mot possède dans notre langue un contenu très riche dont le sens général du point de vue religieux semble être, principalement, en rapport avec un nouveau mode de vie, une nouvelle „existence"; ou bien avec l'accès à une certaine connaissance; ou encore: avec ces deux idées, conjointement.

On est, alors, en droit de se demander si ce vocable convient parfaitement à son emploi par les chercheurs, ou s'il n'est qu'un de ces termes commodes, comme on en rencontre tant quand on procède à l'étude de cultures différentes. Comment les Bambara expriment-ils l'idée que nous nous faisons de l'admission de nouveaux adeptes dans leurs sociétés dites „secrètes"?

Il est évident que le problème ainsi posé, à propos de cette ethnie, n'est qu'un cas particulier. Nous pourrions en dire autant des „initiations" aux mystères d'Eleusis, des „initiations" australiennes ou indiennes. Nous nous servons à ce sujet d'une terminologie qui exprime le point de vue du tiers, de la personne étrangère au rite „initiatique" et qui n'exprime pas nécessairement la manière de considérer les choses de la part de l'„initié", ou de l'„initiateur".

Afin de mieux saisir la pensée des Bambara à cet égard, il convient de présenter d'abord une vue d'ensemble de leurs sociétés „initiatiques".

Ces dernières sont au nombre de six et embrassent la vie des individus de sexe mâle depuis l'enfance jusqu'à la maturité. Il s'agit, dans l'économie globale de ces sociétés, de donner à l'homme qui y est convié un certain statut religieux, moral et intellectuel qui affirme sa supériorité vis-à-vis des femmes et vis-à-vis des non initiés. Ces sociétés initiatiques proposent aux hommes de prendre conscience de leur destinée et, en fin de compte, de l'améliorer au point de transfigurer l'être humain en un être divin — condition de l'immortalité de l'homme.

La première de ces confréries, le *n'domo*, est ouverte uniquement aux enfants non circoncis qui en sont les régisseurs et les acteurs. Ce caractère enfantin du *n'domo* se veut exemplaire car toute son économie tend à présenter l'homme idéal: beau, équilibré, jouissant dans la même personne de l'égalité physiologique des sexes, mais entaché congénitalement du *wãẓo* qui est principalement ignorance et faiblesse morale. Le *n'domo* constitue la figuration de l'homme androgyne, tel qu'il est sorti des mains du créateur et tel qu'il apparaît avec chaque naissance dans le monde des vivants.

Le *n'domo*, en tant que première société d'initiation, possède également un caractère inchoatif, face aux cinq autres sociétés. Ses cinq classes préfigurent, en effet, les cinq autres sociétés d'initiation que l'homme devra aborder s'il désire parvenir à une connaissance intégrale de ce qu'il est et s'il convoite l'état d'immortalité.

A la sortie du *n'domo* les initiés à la confrérie sont circoncis puis introduits dans le *komo*, deuxième société d'initiation, où ils sont instruits sur la nature du savoir et de son rapport avec les humains.

Un pas de plus vers la conquête de la sagesse est franchi avec l'accès au *nama*, troisième confrérie initiatique. Celle-ci prodigue aux néophytes la démonstration des rapports sociaux entre hommes et femmes. La nature du mariage est son premier but, mais le *nama* ne néglige pas pour autant (loin de là) tout ce que les humains doivent savoir au sujet de l'eugénie de la personne humaine comme aussi ce qu'ils doivent faire pour prévenir les embuches des „sorciers". A vrai dire, le *nama* s'érige en précepteur habilité à prodiguer des lumières sur la nature des unions entre les sexes, en prônant la lutte contre les destructeurs des unions: les sorciers.

Avec le *kono*, quatrième société secrète, les néophytes se familiarisent avec l'enseignement concernant la nature de l'être humain, sa dualité départagée entre l'esprit et le corps, le jugement et la conscience morale de l'homme.

Le *tyiwara*, cinquième société d'initiation, jouit dans le contexte initiatique d'une situation toute spéciale. Elle est la seule société secrète qui ne se manifeste que de jour car la base de son enseignement est centrée sur l'agriculture et, partant, sur le soleil, générateur de l'humidité et de la chaleur indispensables à la germination des plantes de subsistance.

Le *korè*, sixième et dernière confrérie secrète, constitue le sommet de l'enseignement initiatique. Ce dernier a trait à la spiritualisation et à la divinisation de l'être humain. Son programme, le contenu et le caractère mystique de ses révélations marquent l'aboutissement du savoir humain, la frontière que l'homme ne peut dépasser car l'initié au *korè* acquiert la connaissance de l'être divin même.

Le programme global de ces six sociétés d'initiation pourrait, à première vue, paraître incohérent et dépourvu de fil conducteur. Or, il en existe un qui réside dans le rapport de la première confrérie (le *n'domo*) avec la sixième (le *korè*). Cette relation est celle-là même que l'on établit entre la connaissance de soi et la connaissance de dieu. C'est en se connaissant soi-même que l'on arrive à la connaissance de la divinité. En y intégrant les jalons intermédiaires entre ces deux extrêmes, le *continuum* qu'offrent les six sociétés d'initiation bambara est le suivant: la connaissance de soi (*n'domo*) engendre l'investigation au sujet de la connaissance elle-même (*komo*) et conduit l'homme en face du social (*nama*). De là naissent le jugement et la conscience morale (*kono*), puis la recherche de ce qui fait vivre l'être humain: le cosmos (*tyiwara*) et la divinité (le *korè*).

Mais ce *continuum* n'est pas senti par les Bambara comme un tout dont les parties se tiendraient entre elles sans contraste. Bien au contraire, sur différents plans les six sociétés d'initiation sont senties en termes d'opposition complémentaire.

L'opposition fondamentale est celle qui existe entre le *n'domo* et le *korè*, c'est-à-dire (en termes imagés bambara) entre l'homme à l'état larvaire et le même homme à l'état pleinement développé et transfiguré.

D'autres oppositions sont décelables entre le *komo* et le *kono*, entre le *komo* et le *korè*, entre le *nama* et le *tyiwara*. Je n'en parlerai pas ici afin de ne pas m'éloigner de mon sujet.

La terminologie très stricte employée pour désigner l'initiation est fondée, elle aussi, sur le contraste et l'opposition entre ces sociétés.

Deux termes sont en usage à ce point de vue. L'appellation *biri* ou *bri* est réservée uniquement à l'action par laquelle de nouveaux adeptes sont introduits dans les cinq premières sociétés d'initiation. Le vocable *fa* est de rigueur pour l'initiation au *korè*. Se tromper dans l'application exacte et appropriée de ces termes quand il s'agit de différentes initiations est signe, aux yeux des Bambara, que l'interlocuteur n'est qu'un piètre profane ne comprenant rien à l'économie des sociétés secrètes.

Le mot *biri* exprime l'action de „mettre sur" (pour couvrir). Il traduit aussi l'action de se baisser, se prosterner, se courber. *Biri* évoque donc à la fois: l'action de revêtir quelqu'un ou quelque chose d'un objet afin de le cacher, de le protéger ou de l'orner et l'action de s'incliner vers la terre. Sur le plan moral *biri* exprime la soumission à un enseignement et l'acceptation. Les *n'domo birĩ dẽw* ou les *nama birĩ dẽw* p. ex. sont ceux qui se sont soumis à l'enseignement et à la discipline du *n'domo* ou du *nama*, ceux qui sont revêtus comme d'une couverture ou comme d'un habit de la doctrine exprimée par ces sociétés d'initiation. Le *biri de*, l'initié (comme nous l'appelons) à ces sociétés, est donc celui qui se sent recouvert, caché, protégé et même orné par la confrérie à laquelle il s'est soumis.

Considérant les choses du point de vue de l'initié, le terme *biri* fait appel à la volonté et à la liberté de choix de l'adepte. Si ce dernier est un „soumis", c'est parce qu'il l'a voulu ainsi. D'où l'importance et le rôle joué dans ces cinq sociétés d'initiation par le serment d'en garder le secret. Celui-ci n'est de mise et ne se justifie pleinement, en effet, que si celui qui le prête ne subit pas de contrainte à l'égard du secret qu'il doit respecter. Volontairement soumis, le silence que l'initié s'impose à lui-même constitue le meilleur atout de l'efficacité de sa cachette. Parler de ce qu'il entend autour de lui, au sein de la confrérie, équivaudrait pour lui au déchirement de sa „couverture", au dévoilement, état justement contraire à son statut d'„initié". Ceci explique aussi le rôle justicier de ces sociétés à l'égard des parjures dont la première et profonde punition est celle qu'ils s'infligent à eux-mêmes. Sur le plan psychique ceci se traduit par un choc psychologique voisin, sinon identique, de la folie. L'homme qui agit à l'encontre de ses intérêts peut-il être considéré en possession de sa raison?

Mais cette analyse conduit à se demander quelle est la nature de l'enseignement dispensé aux „soumis". Ce dernier apparaît en premier lieu comme une chose qui les enveloppe. Cette caractéristique est importante car elle montre bien qu'à ce stade de la vie initiatique l'adepte n'est pas censé assimiler ce qu'il entend. La connaissance à lui dispensée n'est pas considérée comme une chose qui le pénètre; elle est une donnée objective qui s'impose par son objectivité si le disciple remplit pleinement son rôle d',,élève", s'il en prend conscience et s'il mesure à sa juste valeur la mission protectrice de son ,,voile". Tout ceci est admirablement démontré, dans l'institution du *komo* en particulier où le débat porte justement sur la nature de la connaissance, ce ,,fumier du milieu du fleuve que seuls les grands oiseaux peuvent atteindre" (chant du *komo*).

L'enseignement est, en second lieu, une œuvre humaine; il est forgé par les hommes; il est à l'échelle et à la mesure humaines. C'est là, d'ailleurs, la raison de la soumission qui, à cet égard, caractérise l'attitude des adeptes. On se soumet à ce qui vient de la part des hommes et on l'accepte; on subit, comme nous le verrons tout à l'heure, et on supporte ce qui vient de la part de la divinité.

En somme, point n'est question dans les cinq premières sociétés d'initiation, d'intelligence et de compréhension de l'enseignement proposé aux adeptes. Celui-ci recouvre ces derniers comme un habit dont la présence seule est garante de son efficacité. S'y soumettre et en admettre la protection signifie opérer librement un choix de moyens pour requérir la force de vaincre son ignorance.

Le deuxième terme employé pour désigner l',,initiation" est *fa*, tuer. Il est réservé uniquement à la sixième société d'initiation: le *korè*.

Lors de l'entrée dans cette confrérie, un des moments fondamentaux du rite consiste en une mise à mort symbolique des néophytes. Par ailleurs, pendant toute la durée des cérémonies du *korè*, la nouvelle de la mort de ces derniers est répandue et entretenue d'une façon ouverte. Tout est mis en œuvre pour donner l'illusion de la mort des postulants. Eux-mêmes s'abstiennent de se servir de leurs membres pour se nourrir et il leur incombe d'éviter tout contact de leur ombre avec un être humain. La signification profonde du *korè* se rapporte essentiellement à la mort, mais une mort qui doit aboutir à la résurrection, afin que l'homme puisse se rire de la mort.

Comme devant la nécessité inflexible de son anéantissement l'être humain doit subir la mort du *korè*. La raison fondamentale de ce fait réside premièrement dans le caractère divin de l'institution. Les sages de la confrérie sont persuadés que l'enseignement dispensé aux néophytes et aux adeptes est d'inspiration divine, que les révélations des maîtres ne sont pas l'œuvre des hommes mais viennent de Dieu lui-même. La raison de l'absence de choix de la part de l'homme vis-à-vis de son entrée au *korè* gît, en second lieu, dans le postulat religieux, et sans doute philosophique, que l'on ne peut être en mesure de vaincre la mort qu'en se faisant mettre à mort dans certaines conditions spéciales définies par l'économie de l'institution.

Ainsi se dessine, selon la terminologie utilisée dans les sociétés initiatiques bambara pour désigner l'initiation, le dualisme et l'opposition qui marquent ces confréries. Les unes (les cinq premières) possèdent les caractéristiques des entreprises humaines. Aussi, l'attitude des néophytes à leur égard, au moment des rites sacrés d'initiation, est-elle connotée par un acte volontaire signifiant l'acceptation des épreuves. L'autre, le *korè*, se détache de cet ensemble à cause de son origine supposée divine. D'où sa nature contraignante à l'égard de laquelle le postulant n'a pas de choix: il doit subir le *korè* à l'instar de la mort physique devant laquelle il demeure impuissant.

Mais cette terminologie est révélatrice, à n'en pas douter, de la nature même de ce que nous appelons ,,initiation" qui consiste moins dans un ,,passage" que dans un *continuum* qui, au lieu de se référer à l'accès à une connaissance, connote la force morale de l'adepte à la prendre et à la garder comme ,,cachette".

Ce dernier trait de la notion bambara d'initiation est fondamental dans l'esprit de ces Soudanais. Voilà pourquoi toutes leurs sociétés d'initiation insistent, tant dans les rites que dans l'enseignement oral, sur le rôle de la maîtrise de soi — par la maîtrise de la parole — pour le perfectionnement de l'homme.

*

* *

L'analyse ici esquissée pose, comme on a pu s'en rendre compte, d'autres problèmes intéressant l'histoire des religions: la nature du serment qui lie l'adepte à la société qui l'accueille, la punition des parjures, la notion de nouvel habit qui peut ne pas être nécessairement en rapport avec le changement de personnalité.

Je ne fait qu'effleurer ici ces questions: elles dévoilent, cependant, toute la complexité du concept d'initiation quand on s'efforce de l'approfondir dans une société actuelle.

DIE SPRACHE VON ZUYUA ALS INITIATIONSMITTEL

VON

GÜNTER LANCZKOWSKI

Heidelberg

Eine der heiligen Schriften der yukatekischen Maya, das Buch des Chilam Balam von Chumayel, tradiert umfangreiche Texte, die die Formulare für jene Prüfungen enthalten, denen die Anwärter für Statthalterschaften und höhere Verwaltungsposten durch den Halach Uinic unterzogen wurden, den „wahren Mann", den obersten und offensichtlich mit theokratischen Qualitäten versehenen Herrscher der Maya des Neuen Reiches [1]. Durch diese Prüfungen, die jeweils zu Anfang einer *katun*-Periode, also am Beginn eines Zyklus von etwa zwanzig Jahren [2], veranstaltet wurden, stellte der Halach Uinic die Legitimität der Kandidaten fest [3], er verschaffte sich, wie der Text des Chilam Balam von Chumayel ausdrücklich angibt, Klarheit darüber, ob die Bewerber „von Herrschenden abstammten, ob sie zum Stammbaum der Häuptlinge gehörten" [4]. Dieses Examen, das die adlige Herkunft der Kandidaten ermitteln und diesbezügliche Täuschungsversuche verhindern sollte, hatte esoterische Kenntnisse zum Inhalt und setzte mithin die Einweihung in ein Geheimwissen voraus, das in den herrschenden Familien vom Vater auf den Sohn übertragen wurde [5]. Es handelte sich also um eine bereits vollzogene Initiation, deren Geheimwissen überprüft wurde und daher in den Fragen und deren jeweils beigefügten Lösungen des Prüfungstextes voll zutage tritt. Dabei werden sowohl das gesamte Examen als

---

[1] Ralph L. ROYS, *The Book of Chilam Balam of Chumayel* (*Carnegie Institution of Washington*, Publication No. 438), Washington 1933, S. 88-98.

[2] Es handelte sich um einen Zyklus von 7200 Tagen.

[3] Vgl. Ferdinand ANDERS, *Das Pantheon der Maya*, Graz 1963, S. 47, S. 51; ROYS, *a.a.O.*, S. 192; Sylvanus Griswold MORLEY-George W. BRAINERD, *The Ancient Maya*, 3. Aufl., Stanford, California 1958, S. 88; Hans-Dietrich DISSELHOFF, „Das Alte und das Neue Reich der Maya", in: *Saeculum* 2, 1951, S. 544; Victor W. VON HAGEN, *Die Kultur der Maya*, Hamburg u. Wien 1960, S. 165.

[4] ROYS, *a.a.O.*, S. 89.

[5] MORLEY-BRAINERD, *a.a.O.*, S. 88.

auch — in stereotyper Wiederholung — jeder einzelne Prüfungsabschnitt mit *Zuyua than*, „Sprache von Zuyua", bezeichnet.

Die Etymologie dieses Terminus *zuyua* ist noch nicht eindeutig
geklärt. Wollte man sie im Bereich der Maya-Idiome suchen, so böte
sich hierfür am ehesten das Quiché-Wort *zivan* an, das „Schlucht"
bedeutet und an einer Stelle des Popol Vuh, des heiligen Buches der
guatemaltekischen Maya, dem Begriff *zuyua* nachfolgend in einer
Weise koordiniert wird, die gerade nach den Gesetzen indianischer
Stilistik eine Erläuterung des vorangehenden durch den ihm folgenden
Begriff beabsichtigen kann [1]). Jedoch ist es auch möglich, *zuyua* als
ein Fremdwort innerhalb der Maya-Sprache aufzufassen, wobei
mehrfach an eine Herkunft aus dem Zapotekischen gedacht worden
ist, in dem *zoo-paa* sich als Etymon anbietet, das den „Westen"
bezeichnet [2]).

Diese unterschiedlichen sprachlichen Ableitungsmöglichkeiten, die
einerseits zur Kennzeichnung eines Landschaftscharakters, andererseits zur Bestimmung einer Himmelsrichtung führen, bereiten jedoch
auffälligerweise in sachlicher Hinsicht keine Schwierigkeiten. Denn
sie verweisen übereinstimmend auf die Vorstellung einer im Westen
von Yucatan zu lokalisierenden Landschaft und auf deren Sprache.
Dass hiermit primär der Bereich der Tolteken gemeint war, bezeugen
zweifelsfrei zahlreiche Textstellen, die zugleich Tollan oder Tula,
die Metropole des Toltekenreiches, als Ursprungsort der herrschenden
Geschlechter zur Zeit des Neuen Reiches der Maya angeben. Von
den Tutulxiu, den Herrschern von Mani, berichtet das ebenfalls
unter dem Priestertitel *Chilam Balam* überlieferte Buch des Chilam
Balam von Mani [3]): „Aus dem Westen kamen sie, aus dem Lande
Zuiva [4]), aus Tula." Die gleiche Vorstellung einer Wanderung von
Zuyua in das Gebiet der Maya tradiert der Chilam Balam von Tizi-

---

[1]) Leonhard SCHULTZE JENA, *Popol Vuh. Das heilige Buch der Quiché-Indianer
von Guatemala* (*Quellenwerke zur alten Geschichte Amerikas*, Bd. II), Stuttgart u.
Berlin 1944, S. 108; vgl. Eduard SELER, *Gesammelte Abhandlungen zur Amerikani-
schen Sprach- und Altertumskunde*, Bd. III, Berlin 1908, Neudruck Graz 1960, S. 574;
Ders., *Ges. Abh.* Bd. IV, Berlin 1923, Neudruck Graz 1961, S. 109.

[2]) SELER, *Ges. Abh.* Bd. II, Berlin 1904, Neudruck Graz 1960, S. 7; Walter
LEHMANN, *Zentral-Amerika*, Teil I: *Die Sprachen Zentral-Amerikas*, Bd. II, Berlin
1920, S. 987; Ders., „Ein Tolteken-Klagegesang", in: *Festschrift Eduard Seler*,
Stuttgart 1922, S. 302. — Maud WORCESTER MAKEMSON, *The Book of the Jaguar
Priest, a Translation of the Book of Chilam Balam of Tizimin*, New York 1951, S. 50
Anm. 135, S. 101, leitet *zuyua* von *suy-vah*, „ewiges Leben", ab.

[3]) SELER, *Ges. Abh.* III, S. 48; Daniel G. BRINTON, *The Maya Chronicles*, Philadelphia 1882, S. 95, S. 108 ff.

[4]) Die Schreibungen von *zuyua* differieren in den verschiedenen Handschriften.

min [1]). Und in den Cakchiquel-Annalen findet sich die Aussage [2]): „Aus Tullan . . . kommen wir. Das ist das Tullan, wo wir von unseren Müttern, unseren Vätern geboren und erzeugt wurden."

Nun haben im mexikanischen Raum die Begriffe „Tolteken" und „Tollan" nach dem Untergang des geschichtlichen Toltekenreiches, an dessen Historizität heute nicht mehr zu zweifeln ist [3]), in aztekischer Zeit zunehmend einen Bedeutungswandel und eine Wertsteigerung erfahren. Wie die menschliche Persönlichkeit Quetzalcoatls, des grössten Toltekenherrschers, vergöttlicht wurde [4]), so haben die Azteken nicht allein willig die kulturelle Überlegenheit des toltekischen Erbes anerkannt [5]), sondern darüber hinaus Tollan in einer Weise idealisiert und glorifiziert, die — nach Aussage vor allem der „Historia Tolteca Chichimeca" [6]) — zur Identifikation mit dem mythischen Ursprungsort der Tolteken, Azteken und anderen Nahuastämme führte, nämlich zur Gleichsetzung mit *Chicomoztoc* [7]). *Chicomoztoc* heisst „Ort der sieben Höhlen"; und Chimalpahin, der in der ersten Hälfte des 17. Jahrhunderts wirkende indianische Historiker, erklärte die mit der mythischen Ursprungshöhle der Nahuastämme verbundene Siebenzahl, indem er schreib [8]): „Deswegen heisst (der Ort) Chicomoztoc, weil an sieben Stellen hohl ist der Felsen, die Höhle".

Es ist nun sehr bezeichnend, dass von den herrschenden Geschlechtern der Maya mit dem Begriff Zuyua nicht allein die primäre Vorstellung von Tollan verbunden wurde, sondern ebenso diejenige von Chicomoztoc, womit zugleich das Bild der „Schlucht" Bedeutung

---

[1]) Maud WORCESTER MAKEMSON, *a.a.O.*, S. 38, S. 100 f.

[2]) SELER, *Ges. Abh.* III, S. 574.

[3]) Vgl. Paul KIRCHHOFF, „Das Toltekenreich und sein Untergang", in: *Saeculum* 12, 1961, S. 248-265.

[4]) Vgl. G. LANCZKOWSKI, „Quetzalcoatl - Mythos und Geschichte", in: *Numen* 9, 1962, S. 17-36.

[5]) Vgl. G. LANCZKOWSKI, „Die Begegnung des Christentums mit der aztekischen Religion", in: *Numen* 5, 1958, S. 60.

[6]) Konrad Theodor PREUSS, „Der Ursprungsort Chicomoztoc nach der mexikanischen Bilderhandschrift Historia Tolteca Chichimeca", in: *Baessler-Archiv* 19, 1936, S. 97-101; SELER, *Ges. Abh.* IV, S. 108.

[7]) Vgl. SELER, *Ges. Abh.* II, S. 1019 ff.; Walter KRICKEBERG, *Altmexikanische Kulturen*, Berlin 1956, S. 58 f.; W. Jos. DE GRUYTER, „De Mythe van den gevederden Slangengod", in: *Primitief Denken en Beelden* 5, o.J., S. 172.

[8]) Walter LEHMANN u. Gerdt KUTSCHER, *Das Memorial Breve acerca de la fundacion de la ciudad de Colhuacan von Domingo de San Anton Muñon Chimalpahin Quauhtlehuanitzin (Quellenwerke zur alten Geschichte Amerikas*, Bd. VII), Stuttgart 1958, S. 18; Günter ZIMMERMANN, *Das Geschichtswerk des Domingo de Muñon Chimalpahin Quauhtlehuanitzin*, Hamburg 1960, S. 34 f.

gewann. Diese Übernahme mexikanischer Anschauungen findet ihren knappsten Ausdruck in einer Stelle des Popol Vuh, wo jener Ort, aus dem die Urväter der Quiché ihre Götterbilder holten, bezeichnet wird als *tulan zuiva, vucub pec, vucub zivan*, „Tulan-Zuiva, sieben Höhlen, sieben Schluchten" [1]); — worin deutlich die direkte Übersetzung von *Chicomoztoc* enthalten ist. Der Begriff Zuyua kann mithin im Gebrauch der Maya als eine Art sakraler Richtungsname verstanden werden, der in spezifischer Weise mit toltekischen Traditionen verbunden war.

Dass gerade die adligen Schichten der Maya sich dieses Begriffes zur Kennzeichnung ihres Geheimwissens bedienten, ist als eine Pflege toltekischer Traditionen zu verstehen, denen sie sich besonders verbunden fühlten und die im Bereich der Maya jener Einfluss begründet hatte, der mit den Berichten über die Reise Quetzalcoatls und seiner Getreuen nach Yucatan verbunden ist [2]). Aber auch vereinzelt greifbare mexikanische Vorstellungen deuten auf Überlieferungen, die die Ursprungshöhle nicht generell als Ausgangspunkt der Nahuastämme fassten, sondern bereits in erster Linie mit den Geschlechtern der Herrschenden verbanden; denn in einem altaztekischen Gesang heisst es [3]): „Aus Chicomoztoc stammen und kommen alle eure Gebieter hierher." — Jedenfalls verweist die Vorstellung jener Sprache von Zuyua, in der im Chilam Balam von Chumayel die Weisheit von adligen Initiierten tradiert wird, eindeutig auf die Pflege toltekischen Erbes.

Es ist deshalb mit grosser Wahrscheinlichkeit anzunehmen, dass der Terminus „Sprache von Zuyua" ursprünglich auch in idiomatischer Hinsicht relevant war, dass mithin die Prüfungen, denen die Anwärter auf die Häuptlingswürde durch den Halach Uinic unterzogen wurden, in toltekischer Sprache vor sich gingen. Es spricht für diese Vermutung noch in besonderer Weise, dass der Text nicht allein jeden Prüfungsabschnitt stereotyp als „Sprache von Zuyua" kennzeichnet, sondern an einer Stelle ausdrücklich konstatiert [4]): „Alles wird in der Sprache von Zuyua gefragt."

Aber überliefert ist uns eine toltekische Version der Texte leider

---

[1]) SCHULTZE JENA, *a.a.O.*, S. 108 f.; Wolfgang CORDAN, *Das Buch des Rates, Popol Vuh*, Düsseldorf-Köln 1962, S. 111, S. 206; ANDERS, *a.a.O.*, S. 73; SELER, *Ges. Abh.* III, S. 574.

[2]) LANCZKOWSKI, *Quetzalcoatl, a.a.O.*, S. 22 ff.

[3]) Leonhard SCHULTZE JENA, *Alt-Aztekische Gesänge (Quellenwerke zur alten Geschichte Amerikas*, Bd. VI), Stuttgart 1957, S. 36 f.

[4]) ROYS, *a.a.O.*, S. 96.

nicht; ihre Fragen und Antworten sind vielmehr im Chilam Balam von Chumayel im Mayathan, also im yukatekischen Zweig der Maya-sprachen, niedergelegt, wodurch der Begriff „Sprache von Zuyua" für uns heute eine ausschliesslich inhaltliche Relevanz gewinnt. Das bedeutet zweifellos eine Erschwerung des Textverständnisses gerade im Hinblick auf die Frage, ob auch für Intention und Inhalte der Prüfungen toltekischer Einfluss wahrscheinlich ist.

Die Intention der im Chilam Balam von Chumayel überlieferten Befragungen geht eindeutig aus den Konsequenzen hervor, die der Halach Uinic am Ende des Examens zieht. Diejenigen, die die Prü-fungen bestehen konnten, anerkennt er als wahre Adlige, nimmt sie mit bewegten Worten in den Häuptlingsstand auf und verleiht ihnen Matte und Thronsitz, die auch hier, wie durchweg im mexikanischen Bereich, als Zeichen der herrscherlichen Autorität gelten [1]. Die Nichtwissenden aber werden als Betrüger angesehen, die sich zu Unrecht ihre adlige Stellung angemasst haben. Die Strafe, die sie trifft, ist hart. Sie werden gänzlich verworfen, die Zungenspitzen werden ihnen abgeschnitten, die Augen ausgerissen, und durch Erhängen finden sie den Tod [2]. Es ist deutlich, dass somit der ererbte soziale Rang einer zusätzlichen Bewährung unterzogen wird, die, nach diesem Text, im Bereich der Maya ein esoterisches Wissen betrifft.

Es ist zumindest bemerkenswert, dass sich der exklusive Besitz alter Traditionen innerhalb der herrschenden Schichten in durchaus vergleichbarer Weise bei den ebenfalls durch toltekische Kultur ge-prägten Pipil [3] findet [4]. Jedoch ist an sich die Erscheinung eines Sonderwissens der Herrschenden, wie es in Mesoamerika nach dem Verlust der staatlichen Eigenständigkeit teilweise von der privile-gierten Gruppe auf den Geheimbund überging [5], nicht allein auf diesen kulturellen Raum beschränkt. Deshalb ist es für die Frage toltekischen Einflusses wesentlicher, ob wir ein Prototyp jener für die Maya im Chilam Balam von Chumayel ganz singulär überlieferten Prüfungen im mexikanischen Bereich nachweisen können.

Die uns aus Mexiko in so reichem Masse tradierten Relationen

---

[1] ROYS, *a.a.O.*, S. 95.

[2] ROYS, *a.a.O.*, S. 92.

[3] Leonhard SCHULTZE JENA, *Indiana II. Mythen in der Muttersprache der Pipil von Izalco in El Salvador*, Jena 1935, S. 1.

[4] Franz TERMER, „Die Bedeutung der Pipiles für die Kulturgestaltung in Guatemala", in: *Baessler-Archiv* 19, 1936, S. 111 f.

[5] Daniel G. BRINTON, *Nagualism*, Philadelphia 1894, S. 30 f. u. ö.

in aztekischer Sprache müssen wir, wenn wir nach spezifisch toltekischen Sachverhalten fragen, jeweils der kritischen Frage unterziehen, inwieweit diese von aztekischen Vorstellungen überlagert
sind. Bringen wir aber die von dem betont kriegerischen Geist der
Azteken bestimmten Qualitäten in Abzug, so finden wir in der Tat
in einem von Sahugún überlieferten Text eine Antizipation des
formalen Schemas der Maya-Prüfungen [1]). Denn auch in Mexiko vollzog sich keine automatische Übernahme des ererbten Ranges. Die
jungen Adligen mussten sich vielmehr — aztekischem Brauche
entsprechend — zunächst in einer kriegerischen Aktion bewähren.
Es ist aber bezeichnend, dass sich daran eine Befragung anschloss,
die auch hier der oberste Herrscher, der König Mexikos, vornahm.
Er befragte die jungen Adligen über ihren Kampf, und er liess ihre
Antworten überprüfen. Erst wenn er sich von der Richtigkeit dieser
Antworten überzeugt hatte, verlieh er ihnen die Insignien des Adels.
Dagegen wurde der falsch Antwortende auch hier mit dem Tode
bestraft. Wenn auch der Inhalt dieser Befragungen im aztekischen
Geiste überliefert ist, so findet sich doch in formaler und intentioneller
Hinsicht Übereinstimmung mit denen der Maya.

Ob derartige Bezüge zu mexikanischen Überlieferungen auch
hinsichtlich des sachlichen Gehaltes der Maya-Prüfungen feststellbar
sind, ist m.W. bislang noch nirgendwo untersucht worden. Der
bedeutende Maya-Forscher MORLEY hat die Texte zur Sprache von
Zuyua als eine Serie gänzlich unsinniger Rätsel bezeichnet [2]), und
zweifellos stellen sich der Erschliessung dieser schwierigsten Urkun-
den zur mesoamerikanischen Religionsgeschichte beachtliche Hinder-
nisse entgegen. Diese resultieren zum geringeren Teil aus der Text-
geschichte jener unter dem Titel des „Jaguar-Wahrsagepriesters",
des *Chilam Balam* [3]), mit unterscheidender Angabe des jeweiligen
Entstehungsortes überlieferten Bücher. Denn wenn auch diese
— wahrscheinlich auf verlorene Bilderhandschriften zurückgehenden
Texte in der frühen Kolonialzeit niedergeschrieben wurden [4]), so
lässt sich doch das in sie eingedrungene spanisch-christliche Gut
ebenso wie die Erwähnung europäisch importierter Tiere und Pflanzen

---

[1]) Eduard SELER, *Einige Kapitel aus dem Geschichtswerk des Fray Bernardino de
Sahagun*, Stuttgart 1927, S. 330 ff.

[2]) MORLEY-BRAINERD, *a.a.O.*, S. 88.

[3]) *chi* „Mund", *chilam* „Mundstück, Sprachrohr, Übersetzer", *balam* „Jaguar".

[4]) ANDERS, *a.a.O.*, S. 3, S. 7 f.; W. KRICKEBERG, „Die Religionen der Kultur-
völker Mesoamerikas", in: KRICKEBERG-TRIMBORN-MÜLLER-ZERRIES, *Die
Religionen des alten Amerika*, Stuttgart 1961, S. 61.

leicht ausscheiden oder — im religiösen Bereich — auch auf synkre-
tistische Bezüge zu indianischen Dingen zurückführen.

Eine weitaus grössere Schwierigkeit besteht in dem Symbol-
charakter einer esoterischen Sprache, in der die Prüfungen sich
vollzogen [1]. Diese symbolische Redeweise tritt hier besonders stark
in Erscheinung, sie ist jedoch generell charakteristisch für religiöse
Aussagen im indianischen Bereich. Darauf hat LAFITEAU [2] zuerst
hingewiesen, BRINTON [3] hat diese Symbolik seiner Konzeption des
Begriffes „Nagualismus" eingeordnet, und für den aztekischen Bereich
hat HÖLTKER [4] das damit im Zusammenhang stehende metapho-
rische Sprechen analysiert.

Eine weitere Komplikation besteht darin, dass in den Prüfungs-
texten keineswegs durchweg ein Zeichen durch das von ihm Bezeich-
nete aufgelöst, sondern häufig seinerseits nur durch ein neues Symbol
ersetzt wird, das, um sinnvoll genannt zu werden, vom Prüfling
gewusst werden muss, von uns aber zu erschliessen ist.

Beispielsweise fordert in der fünften Frage [5] der Halach Uinic
vom Prüfling, dass er ihm das „Herz" des obersten Gottes bringe.
In den Mayasprachen wird durchweg, im Aztekischen erst im Laufe
der Sprachentwicklung anstelle eines ursprünglichen Gebrauchs von
„Leber" [6], das „Herz" als Sitz der Empfindung und als Wesens-
essenz der angesprochenen Persönlichkeit verwendet. — Der Prüfling
beantwortet diese Aufforderung mit der Darbringung einer „Perle
aus kostbarem Stein". Es ist deutlich, dass damit die Lösung der
Frage durch ein Symbol gegeben wird. Und zwar ist im mexikanischen
Bereich die Perle Opfergabe für den Regengott Tlaloc [7]. Sie symbolisiert die ihrerseits in magischer Analogie zum Regen stehenden
Tränen geopferter Kinder, und sie kann das Kinderopfer ersetzen;
cozcatl, die „Perle", ist neben *quetzalli*, der „Schmuckfeder", auch in

---

[1] ANDERS, *a.a.O.*, S. 51.

[2] J. FRANÇOIS LAFITEAU, *Moeurs des sauvages américains*, Paris 1724, S. 123; vgl.
auch R. Fr. MERKEL, „Anfänge der Erforschung amerikanischer Religionen",
in: *Studi e Materiali di Storia delle Religioni* 12, 1936, S. 77; vgl. ferner Theodor-
Wilhelm DANZEL, *Mexiko* II, Hagen i.W.u. Darmstadt 1923, S. 27 f.; DE GRUYTER,
a.a.O., S. 148.

[3] BRINTON, *Nagalism, passim*.

[4] P. GEORG HÖLTKER, *S.V.D.*, „Einige Metaphern im Aztekischen des P.
Sahagun", in: *Anthropos* 27, 1932, S. 249-259.

[5] ROYS, *a.a.O.*, S. 91.

[6] W. LEHMANN, *Zentral-Amerika*, Teil I: *Die Sprachen Zentral-Amerikas*,
Bd. I, Berlin 1920, S. 283.

[7] SELER, *Ges. Abh.* II, S. 884 u. ö.

der aztekischen Sprache die häufigste Metapher für „Kind" [1]). — Die
Darbringung der Perle durch den Prüfling beantwortet also die Frage
des Halach Uinic dahingehend, dass sie das Wesen des obersten
Gottes bestimmt als vegetative, lebensspendende Macht.

Allerdings ist eine solche Interpretation im Hinblick auf die
Mehrdeutigkeit der Symbole [2]) nur dann haltbar, wenn sie der Ge-
samtintention des Textes entspricht. Die vordringliche Aufgabe
gerade eines erstmaligen Erklärungsversuchs sollte es daher sein, zu
prüfen, inwieweit einige methodische Gesichtspunkte zur Ordnung
des zweifellos stark korrumpierten Textes und zu seiner Deutung
beitragen können.

Wichtig scheint zunächst zu sein, dass der Halach Uinic nicht
einfach Fragen stellt, sondern dass er in verschlüsselter Form das
Holen und Überreichen der gemeinten Dinge und damit den Beweis
einer Einsicht in die von ihm angesprochene Symbolik fordert. Diese
in einer Aktion sich vollziehende Bewährung der Kandidaten scheint
dafür zu sprechen, dass die Prüfungen in den Vollzug eines Rituals
eingeordnet waren.

Als Kriterium für dessen sinnvolle Ordnung und damit für die
Voraussetzung zur Erschliessung seiner Intentionen kann zünächst
die Beobachtung eines bereits formal in Erscheinung tretenden
Unterschiedes zwischen zwei Prüfungsgruppen geltend gemacht
werden. In der einen nennt der Halach Uinic eine sakrale Realität,
deren symbolisches Abbild der Prüfling zu besorgen hat. In der
zweiten Gruppe bezeichnet der Halach Uinic umgekehrt ein Symbol,
dessen Repräsentation ihm der Prüfling überbringen muss. — Ferner
dürfte es für Aufgliederung und Verständnis des Textes wichtig sein,
auf die unterscheidende Erwähnung symbolischer Farben und, wo
solche genannt werden, auch auf diejenige symbolischer Zahlen zu
achten.

Überprüft man den Text unter diesen Gesichtspunkten, so hebt
sich deutlich eine Gruppe von Fragen ab, in denen der Halach Uinic
primär ein Symbol nennt, dem er häufig das Attribut der grünen
Farbe beifügt. Die Antworten der Kandidaten bestehen hierbei im
Überreichen der häufigsten pflanzlichen und tierischen Lebensmittel
— wie des Maises, der Bohne, des Honigs, des Kakaos, der Hühner

---

[1]) Eduard SELER, „Die achtzehn Jahresfeste der Mexikaner" (Erste Hälfte), in:
Veröffentlichungen aus dem Kgl. Museum für Völkerkunde, Bd. VI, Berlin 1899, S. 123.
[2]) Zum Symbolbegriff vgl. zusammenfassend G. LANCZKOWSKI, „Artikel
„Symbole" und „Symbolismus" " (mit Lit.) in: *RGG*[3], Bd. VI, 1962, Sp. 541 ff.,
Sp. 548 ff.

und Truthähne [1]) — sowie der Darbringung der wichtigsten kultischen Mittel, nämlich des Kopalharzes für Räucherungen [2]), des für priesterlichen Gebrauch unerlässlichen Tabaks [3]) und des berauschenden Zeremonialtrankes des *balche* der Maya, der bedeutungsmässig dem *octli* der Mexikaner entspricht und seit der spanischen Zeit mit *pulque* bezeichnet wird [4]). Es dürfte keinem Zweifel unterliegen, dass damit, unterstrichen durch die vegetative Symbolik der grünen Farbe [5]), ein Ritus vollzogen wurde, der der Erneuerung und Verjüngung der Lebensmittel dienen sollte.

Es ist auffällig, dass sich unter den dargebrachten Tieren die hier — wie vereinzelt auch sonst [6]) — durch einen Stein symbolisierte Wachtel befindet [7]), obwohl dieser Vogel in den Maya-Handschriften nicht mit Sicherheit nachzuweisen ist [8]) und jedenfalls im Kultus keine Bedeutung besass, während im mexikanischen Bereich Wachtelopfer häufig waren und dort als Substitut für sakrale Menschenopfer innerhalb jener deutlich verfolgbaren Richtung mexikanischer Religiosität feststellbar sind, die im Gegensatz zum offiziellen aztekischen Kult stand, in den rituellen Praktiken der aztekischen Grosskaufleute zur Zeit Motecuçomas II. ihren Ausdruck fand [9]) und im historischen Rückblick auf den Tolteken Quetzalcoatl und seine Vogelopfer zurückgeführt werden kann[10]). Dabei war die Bedeutung der Wachtel vegetativer Art [11]).

Dies ist jedoch inhaltlich nicht der alleinige Bezug des Maya-

---

[1]) Zum Truthahn als Festgericht vgl. SELER, *Ges. Abh.*, Bd. I, Berlin 1902, Neudruck Graz 1960, S. 285.

[2]) Vgl. u.a. Alfred M. TOZZER, *Landa's Relación de las Cosas de Yucatan (Papers of the Peabody Museum of American Archaeology and Ethnology*, Harvard University, Bd. XVIII), Cambridge, Mass. 1941, S. 75 Anm. 338.

[3]) Zum Tabaktäschen *(yequachtli)* als Hauptausrüstungsstück der mexikanischen Priester vgl. SELER, *Ges. Abh.* III, S. 371; zur mythologischen Bedeutung des Tabakrauchens im Maya-Bereich vgl. SELER, *Ges. Abh.* I, S. 464.

[4]) Georg FRIEDERICI, *Amerikanistisches Wörterbuch und Hilfswörterbuch für den Amerikanisten*, 2. Aufl., Hamburg 1960, S. 529 f. Zu Tabak und *balche* vgl. auch BRINTON, *Nagualism*, S. 9; SELER, *Ges. Abh.* II, S. 779 f., S. 820; *Ders., Ges. Abh.* III, S. 569.

[5]) Jacques SOUSTELLE, *La pensée cosmologique des anciens Mexicains*, Paris 1940, S. 71.

[6]) ROYS, *a.a.O.*, S. 128, S. 130.

[7]) ROYS, *a.a.O.*, S. 94.

[8]) SELER, *Ges. Abh.* IV, S. 627 ff.

[9]) G. LANCZKOWSKI, „Die religiöse Stellung der aztekischen Grosskaufleute", in: *Saeculum* 13, 1962, S. 346-362.

[10]) Walter LEHMANN, *Die Geschichte der Königreiche von Colhuacan und Mexico (Quellenwerke zur alten Geschichte Amerikas*, Bd. I), Stuttgart u. Berlin 1938, S. 76.

[11]) SELER, *Ges. Abh.* IV, S. 627 ff.

Textes zu mexikanischen Dingen. Es lässt sich vielmehr in der Tat nachweisen, dass sowohl das Festformular als auch seine Intentionen in genauer Entsprechung zu einem mexikanischen Zeremoniell stehen. In den Texten, die uns Sahagún zum *tonalamatl*, dem augurischen Kalender der Mexikaner, überliefert hat, finden sich für den Tag des Gottes Xiuhtecutli Zeremonien, die mit einem Wachtelopfer beginnen, die Darbringung von Speisen vorschreiben und Kopal, Tabak und Pulque als kultische Mittel nennen [1]). Beweiskräftig für die Übereinstimmung mit dem Bericht der Maya ist aber vor allem die gleiche Intention: auch im mexikanischen Bereich begleitet dieses Zeremoniell die Amtseinführung hoher adliger Herren, der *tlatoque* [2]).

Dass hierin eine Ideenassoziation zwischen der Sicherung der menschlichen Ordnung durch das Herrschertum und der Erhaltung des vegetativen Jahreskreislaufs zum Ausdruck kommt, können wir nicht nur postulieren, sondern auch als mexikanischem Denken entsprechend nachweisen; denn gerade das Formular für das *Uei Tecuilhuitl*, das grosse Fest der vornehmen Herren [3]), verzeichnet einen Ritus, als dessen Zweck ausdrücklich die Fortsetzung des Kreislaufs der Jahre angegeben wird [4]).

Fragen wir nach spezifisch toltekischen Bezügen sowohl des yukatekischen Prüfungstextes als auch seiner Entsprechung im mexikanischen Formular für die Amtseinführung der *tlatoque*, so finden wir diese für beide Texte charakteristische Verbindung der Sicherung des natürlichen Kreislaufs mit derjenigen der menschlichen Ordnung personifiziert in der Gestalt Quetzalcoatls, dessen grünes Federschlangengewand die Funktion des Lebensspenders symbolisiert [5]), und der gleichzeitig als Begründer der irdischen Herrschaft verehrt wurde; für letzteres sind im mexikanischen Bereich die Texte zum

---

[1]) Leonhard SCHULTZE JENA, *Wahrsagerei, Himmelskunde und Kalender der Azteken* (*Quellenwerke zur alten Geschichte Amerikas*, Bd. IV), Stuttgart 1950, S. 182 ff.

[2]) SCHULTZE JENA, *a.a.O.*, S. 184 f.; zur sozialen Stellung der *tlatoque* vgl. Friedrich KATZ, *Die sozialökonomischen Verhältnisse bei den Azteken im 15. und 16. Jahrhundert*, Berlin 1956, S. 115 f.

[3]) Der Bezug des Festes auf die Herrschenden kommt im Codex Telleriano Remensis und im Codex Vaticanus A besonders deutlich dadurch zum Ausdruck, dass das *Uei Tecuilhuitl* durch einen Vornehmen (*tecutli*) in Festtracht dargestellt wird, der das Zeichen für „Fest" (*ilhuitl*) in der linken Hand hält; vgl. SELER, *Die achtzehn Jahresfeste der Mexikaner, a.a.O.*, S. 60 f.

[4]) SAHAGÚN (SELER), *a.a.O.*, S. 150.

[5]) LANCZKOWSKI, *Quetzalcoatl, a.a.O.*, S. 18 f.

Krönungszeremoniell der aztekischen Könige beweiskräftig [1]), für die Anschauung der Maya aber vor allem ein Text des Popol Vuh, nach dem die Quiché von ihm die Abzeichen der Herrscherwürde empfingen [2]).

Eine scheinbare Schwierigkeit dieser Interpretation besteht noch darin, dass der mexikanische Einsetzungstext als Herrn der Feier nicht Quetzalcoatl, sondern den Feuergott Xiuhtecutli nennt. Jedoch hat bereits Eduard Seler dessen Wesensgleichheit und Verschmelzung mit Quetzalcoatl herausgestellt [3]), und historisch wurde diese relevant, als die Gesandten Motecuçomas II. dem bei Vera Cruz gelandeten Cortés angeblich ein Gewand Quetzalcoatls überreichten, in Wahrheit aber, wie die Beschreibung zeigt, ein solches des Xiuhtecutli gaben [4]).

Die Bezugnahme auf Quetzalcoatl charakterisiert nun auch eine zweite Gruppe der yukatekischen Prüfungsabschnitte, in denen der Halach Uinic primär eine sakrale Realität kosmischer Art nennt, in denen mit einer nur für den mexikanischen Bereich nachweisbaren Vorstellung die Zahl 13 auf die Gliederung der Himmelsspären verweist [5]) und weiss als Symbolfarbe der obersten Region des Himmels [6]) häufig erwähnt wird. Sakrale Realitäten und symbolische Abbilder dieser Textgruppe stellen makrokosmisch—mikrokosmische Korrelationen her, und sie fügen damit den Intentionen zur Sicherung des Jahreskreislaufs und des Herrschertums diejenigen zur Erhaltung des ganzen Kosmos hinzu.

Der inneren Struktur des Textes entsprechend, haben wir auch hier die Bezüge auf Quetzalcoatl in verschlüsselter Form zu erwarten. Einige Beispiele aus der oft vielfach verschlungenen Symbolik dieser Textgruppe scheinen charakteristisch zu sein.

Zunächst ist das Weiss nicht allein Symbolfarbe der obersten Region des Himmels, sondern auch des Gottes Quetzalcoatl [7]).

Sodann ist aufschlussreich die Forderung nach einem „erhabenen Kreuz", die der Halach Uinic in seiner ersten Frage im Rahmen

---

[1]) Seler, *Ges. Abh.* IV, S. 104; Lanczkowski, *Die Begegnung des Christentums mit der aztekischen Religion*, a.a.O., S. 76.

[2]) Schultze Jena, *Popol Vuh*, S. 144 f.

[3]) Seler, *Ges. Abh.* II, S. 415 f., III, S. 343 f.

[4]) Sahagún (Seler), a.a.O., S. 461; vgl. W. Lehmann, „Altmexikanische Mosaiken und die Geschenke König Motecuzomas an Cortés", in: *Globus* 90, 1906, S. 320.

[5]) Krickeberg, *Altmexikanische Kulturen*, S. 188.

[6]) Seler, *Ges. Abh.* III, S. 297.

[7]) Soustelle, a.a.O., S. 69, S. 75.

kosmischer Grössen erhebt [1]). Die Aufnahme eines ausschliesslich
christlichen Zeichens in den Text ist vor allem deshalb höchst unwahrscheinlich, weil sich gerade mit dem Kreuz bis heute ein Fort-
leben indianischer Vorstellungen verbindet [2]). Ursprünglich aber
war dieses Zeichen als kosmisches Symbol der vier Weltrichtungen
mit Quetzalcoatl verbunden, dessen Hut und Schild mit der crux
decussata, dem chi-förmigen Andreaskreuz, verziert waren [3]).

Allein mittels einer Bezugnahme auf Quetzalcoatl lässt sich schliesslich eine sonst ganz rätselhafte Stelle des Prüfungstextes verstehen,
in der der Mond als „das gemeine Ding der Nacht" bezeichnet wird [4]).
Bei den Maya ist das Wesen der Ixchel, der Herrin des Mondes, —
wie das so vieler Maya-Numina — ambivalent, enthält aber keineswegs eine restlos negative Wertung, wie sie von der Metaphorik dieses
Textes angesprochen wird [5]). Dagegen ist im mexikanischen Bereich
die Mondgöttin Tlazolteotl, die ursprünglich huaxtekische Ixcuinan,
die Göttin des Unrats und der Sünde [6]). Ausserdem galten in Mexiko
die Kaninchen als Mondwesen und zugleich als Numina des Pulque-
Rauschtrankes [7]). Diese beiden mit dem Monde verbundenen nega-
tiven Vorstellungen der Sünde und des Rauschtrankes treffen sich
in der Vita Quetzalcoatls, dessen Gegnern es gelang, ihn zum sündigen
Genuss des Pulque zu verführen und damit zum Versäumnis seiner
Bussübungen und dem hieraus resultierenden Entschluss des Ver-
lassens seiner Stadt [8]).

Der Pater Francisco Hernandez, der Gewährsmann von Las Casas
für yukatekische Dinge, hat berichtet, dass nur die Fürsten des Landes
Bescheid wüssten über Kukulcan [9]), jenen Gott, der mit dem toltekischen Quetzalcoatl identisch ist und wie dieser den Namen
„grüne Federschlange" trägt [10]). Als allgemeine Aussage ist diese

---

[1]) Roys, a.a.O., S. 89.

[2]) Charlotte ZIMMERMAN, „The Cult of the Holy Cross: an Analysis of Cosmolo-
gy and Catholicism in Quintana Roo", in: *History of Religions* 3, 1963, S. 50-71;
Wolfgang CORDAN, *Mayakreuz und rote Erde*, Zürich u. Stuttgart 1960, S. 34 f.;
F. V. SCHOLES - R. L. ROYS, *The Maya Chontal Indians of Acalan-Tixchel* (*Carnegie
Instit. Publ.*560), Washington 1948, S. 341 ff.; BRINTON, *Nagualism*, S. 48; ANDERS,
a.a.O., S. 55.

[3]) KRICKEBERG, *Altmexikanische Kulturen*, S. 201.

[4]) Roys, a.a.O., S. 94.

[5]) ANDERS, a.a.O., S. 310 ff.

[6]) KRICKEBERG, a.a.O., S. 206 f.

[7]) SELER, *Ges. Abh.* III, S. 315, IV, S. 518.

[8]) LEHMANN, *Die Geschichte der Königreiche*, S. 85 ff.

[9]) SELER, *Ges. Abh.* I, S. 389, S. 670.

[10]) MORLEY-BRAINERD, a.a.O., S. 81.

Behauptung höchst unwahrscheinlich. Sie hat aber spezielle Gültig-
keit für jenes toltekische Geheimwissen, dessen Kenntnis die Prüfungen in der Sprache von Zuyua voraussetzten. Indem aber diese
Prüfungen in den Vollzug eines bedeutungsreichen Rituals eingeordnet waren, vermittelten sie den Herrschenden anlässlich ihrer Beauf-
tragung zur Sicherung der irdischen Ordnung zusätzlich eine zweite
und abschliessende Initiation, die die esoterische Kenntnis der Sprache
von Zuyua voraussetzte und die die kultische Sicherung des Jahreskreislaufs und die Geheimnisse des Kosmos betraf.

THE SIGNIFICANCE OF
TIME IN SOME ANCIENT INITIATORY RITUALS

BY

S. G. F. BRANDON

Manchester

This paper is based upon my conviction that religion is the expression of man's fundamental instinct to seek security from the menace of Time. To be conscious is to be aware of Time, in its threefold aspect of past, present and future, and of our personal involvement in its process. In the struggle for existence this Time-consciousness has given mankind its mastery over all other species, and also indeed over most of its environmental contingencies. The ability to draw upon the memory of past experience to deal with future situations is truly the 'first cause' of all civilisation, whether in the remote past or today. Thus the Palaeolithic hunter who sat in his cave, fashioning a stone axe to use in some future hunt, was employing in his primitive way the same basic ability as that which lies behind the complex scientific and technological planning required to send a rocket to the moon.

This Time-consciousness has, however, another side. Not only does it enable man to plan for the future, it makes him aware of the inevitability of his own personal end—he knows that at some time in the future he must die. Man's Time-consciousness, therefore, involves consciousness of his own mortality. Accordingly, man knows himself to be subject to Time's inexorable law of decay and death. Faced with this grim threat to his very existence, man has instinctively sought for immunity or security from Time. His conceptions of such immunity or security, also of the cause of his subjection to Time, and of the means whereby he can escape from its power, have found expression in his religions. Indeed, I would go as far as to assert that the *raison d'être* of religion is the seeking for salvation from Time and its dread consequences.

The ways in which this deliverance or security from Time has been sought have been many and various. In a forthcoming book, entitled

History, Time and Deity, I have discussed them at length.[1]) In this paper I want to show how the menace of Time is to be discerned as a factor of fundamental import in certain initiatory rituals.

I shall begin with the mortuary ritual of ancient Egypt. This may seem at first sight a rather strange choice, and the question may fairly be asked: how can a mortuary ritual be an initiatory ritual? The paradox disappears on analysis. A mortuary ritual may serve to initiate or introduce those, on whose behalf it is performed, into a new form of life. This was certainly so with the mortuary ritual of ancient Egypt, as we shall see.

All study of ancient Egyptian religion has to start with the evidence of the *Pyramid Texts*. This great corpus of spells and prayers, hymns and incantations, was compiled by the priests of Heliopolis during the third millennium B.C. to secure the safe passage of the dead pharaohs from this life to the next. These *Texts* undoubtedly formed part of the funerary liturgy, and it would seem that the various sections were inscribed in the chambers and passages of the pyramids where the corresponding ritual was performed.[2])

The material used in these *Texts* is very amorphus, and often the ideas expressed in them are mutually contradictory; however, there runs throughout a common *motif*, namely, to unite the dead king to some thing unchanging and eternal, i.e. to put him beyond the menace of Time. Thus, for example, arrangements are made for the deceased to join the sun-god, Re, in his solar boat. The idea involved here is obvious. The Egyptians believed that the sun-god unceasingly made a voyage across the sky each day, and then through the underworld each night. It was an eternally repeated journey, untouched by the change and decay wrought by Time. If, therefore, one could secure a place with the sun-god, one would be for ever safe with him on his eternal journey.[3]) The belief here in the possibility of union with the

---

[1]) Published by the Manchester University Press, 1965. See also the author's book *Man and his Destiny in the Great Religions*, Manchester University Press, 1962.

[2]) Cf. H. BONNET, *Reallexikon der ägyptischen Religionsgeschichte* (Berlin, 1952), pp. 620b-623a; I. E. S. EDWARDS, *The Pyramids of Egypt* (Harmondsworth, 1947), pp. 151-4; S. A. B. MERCER, *The Pyramid Texts* (New York, 1952), I, pp. 1-7; SPIEGEL, J., „Die Auferstehungsritual der Unaspyramide", in *Annales du Service des Antiquités de l'Egypte*, LIII (1956).

[3]) E.g. *Pyr.* 366c, 367b. An alternative idea was that the dead king should join the company of the circumpolar stars (the 'Imperishable Ones'), cf. *Pyr.* 656c. Cf. H. FRANKFORT, *Ancient Egyptian Religion* (New York, 1948), pp. 100, 103, 106-8; C. E. SANDER-HANSEN, *Der Begriff des Todes bei den Aegyptern* (Copenhagen, 1942), pp. 18-20.

sun-god is expressed in terms of a complete absorption in a Middle Kingdom document (*The Story of Sinuhe*). There it is said of the dead pharaoh Amenemmes I: "He flew to heaven and was united with the sun's disk (*itn*); the flesh of the god (i.e. the king) was merged in him who made him". [1]

The ritual action that would enable the deceased king to ascend into the heavens and join the sun-god, thus initiating him to a new life, is necessarily obscure. It seems mainly to have taken the form of magical incantations to transform him into a bird, thus to wing his way to heaven, or for the setting up of a ladder to reach the sky. [2] We are, however, much better informed about the complex of ritual centred on Osiris, which came to form the classic pattern of Egyptian mortuary ritual, from the Pyramid Texts onwards.

The legend of Osiris is too well known to need outlining here. What is important to remember about it is that it provides the *rationale* of a ritual drama designed to initiate the dead into a new and eternal life. The process of initiation was developed along three distinctive lines, each of which was designed to achieve a specific end in the post-mortem life. This Egyptian funerary ritual reached its completest form in the so-called *Book of the Dead*, during the New Kingdom period. We shall, therefore, draw upon material from this source as well as from the earlier evidence of the *Pyramid* and *Coffin Texts*. [3]

From the Egyptian point of view three things were essential for initiation into an eternal state of beatitude: (i) the body had to be secured from the decay and corruption occasioned by death (ii) the dead person had to be raised to life again, or, rather, to a new life (iii) he had to be declared morally worthy of enjoying eternal beatitude.

To render the body eternally secure from corruption, it was embalmed. But this was not regarded merely as a practical measure to prevent chemical decomposition. The whole process was conceived as ritually accomplishing on behalf of the deceased what had once been done, so it was believed, by the deities Isis, Nephthys and Anubis

---

[1] K. SETHE, *Aegyptische Lesestüke* (Leipzig, 1928), 3(5); A. H. GARDINER, *Notes on the Story of Sinuhe* (Paris, 1916), pp. 121-2, 168.

[2] E.g. *Pyr.* 365-6. According to EDWARDS, *op. cit.*, pp. 236-7, the pyramid itself was the 'Place of Ascension'. On the dead king's ascent to heaven see generally H. KEES, *Totenglauben und Jenseitsvorstellungen der alten Aegypter* (Berlin, 1956), pp. 68-72.

[3] Cf. BRANDON, "The Ritual Technique of Salvation in the ancient Near East", in *The Saviour God: Essays presented to E. O. James*, ed. S. G. F. BRANDON (Manchester University Press, 1963).

to save the dead body of Osiris from physical disintegration. The concluding ceremony of this part of the funerary ritual constitutes a very striking instance of a 'rite de passage'. After the body had been embalmed, and before it was actually placed in its 'eternal house', i.e. the tomb, the so-called ceremony of 'Opening the Mouth' was performed. The idea behind the rite was an essentially practical one. The magical efficacy of the embalmment ritual, as well as its chemical effect, was calculated to preserve the body for eternity; but, for the new life in the tomb, it was necessary that the body should be able to see, hear, breathe, and take nourishment. The rite of the 'Opening of the Mouth' was designed to restore these faculties to it, thus initiating it to its new mode of being.[1])

To raise the deceased person himself from death, and endow him with a new and eternal life, two ritual acts, both based upon the principle of magical assimilation, were employed. In one of these the dead man was ritually assimilated to, or identified with, Osiris in his resurrection from death. Thus, in the following passage from the *Pyramid Texts*, the sun-god, Atum of Heliopolis, is invoked to raise the dead pharaoh Unas, whose situation is paralleled with that of Osiris: "Recite: O Atum, it is thy son—this one here, Osiris, whom thou hast caused to live (and) to remain in life. He liveth (and) this Unas (also) liveth; he (i.e. Osiris) dieth not, (and) this Unas (also) dieth not".[2]) In another passage the parallelism becomes an actual identification of the dead king with Osiris: "Thy (i.e. Osiris') body is the body of this Unas. Thy flesh is the flesh of this Unas. Thy bones are the bones of this Unas. (If) thou walkest, this Unas walks; (if) this Unas walks, thou walkest".[3]) In another words, we see operative here the belief that by assimilation to, or identification with, a divine being, who had passed through death to a new eternal life, a like immortality could be obtained.

The other ritual act, to secure rebirth or renewal of life, took the form of a lustral bathing of the corpse. Several motifs were involved here. The historical precedent was provided by the legend of Osiris —his body had been so washed by Isis and Nephthys; the mythological precedent came from the idea that the sun-god Re rejuvenated himself each day be bathing in the mystic waters of Earu; the

---

[1]) Cf. BRANDON, *Man and his Destiny*, pp. 35-47, in *The Saviour God*, pp. 19-23. where full documentation is given.

[2]) *Pyr.* 167a-d.

[3]) *Pyr.* 193a-c.

principle on which the efficacy of the rites was based was doubtlessly that of contagious magic, in this instance in connection with the life-giving virtue ascribed to water.[1]

The third requirement, according to Egyptian thought, for initiation into eternal beatitude was that the character of one's life on earth should be tested and vindicated. Accordingly, a post-mortem judgment was conceived, which is vividly depicted in the illustrated copies of the Book of the Dead. This judgment had two parts: the solemn declaration by the deceased of his innocence in regard to a long catalogue of sins; and the ordeal of the weighing of his heart (i.e. his conscience) against the symbol of 'maat' or truth. If he passed this ordeal successfully, he was declared 'maa kheru', i.e. 'true of voice'—in other words, vindicated. This vindication enabled him, as the corresponding vignette of the Papyrus of Ani so graphically shows, to be introduced into the presence of Osiris, thus to enjoy the beatitude of his everlasting kingdom.[2]

We see, then, in the Osirian mortuary ritual a complex of faith and practice that was designed both to secure the deceased from the physical consequences of death and introduce him to a new life of eternal beatitude. In the Book of the Dead this immunity from death takes a most significant form from our point of view. The deceased, by virtue of his initiation into a new and eternal form of being, does not only escape from the menace of Time, but he is conceived as becoming Time himself. Thus he is represented as declaring: "I am Yesterday, Today and Tomorrow"—in other words, he comprehends in his own being the three constituent parts of Time as experienced by man.[3]

The concern to escape from the destructive power of Time, which thus finds expression in the Egyptian mortuary cultus, involving as it

---

[1] *Pyr.* 841a-843b. Cf. Mercer, *op. cit.*, IV, pp. 54-6; Bonnet, *Reallexikon*, pp. 635a-636a; Brandon in *The Saviour God*, pp. 21, 22-3, 24, 27.

[2] See *The Book of the Dead: Facsimile of the Papyrus of Ani*, 3, 4, (British Museum, 2nd edition, 1894). Cf. Brandon, *Man and his Destiny*, pp. 50-7 (with documentation); J. Yoyotte, "Le jugement des morts dans l'Égypte ancienne", in *Sources orientales*, IV (Paris, 1961); Brandon, "The Judgment of the Dead", in *History Today*, XIV (1964), pp. 564-70.

[3] Cf. E. A. W. Budge, *The Book of the Dead* (London, 1910), Text, I, p. 177: *ink sf dw3 bk3* (cap. lxiv. 2, *Papyrus of Nebensi*). S. Morenz, *Aegyptische Religion* (Stuttgart, 1960), pp. 74-84, has shown how essentially fate was connected with time in Egyptian thought; cf. J. Zandee, *Death as an Enemy* (Leiden, 1960), p. 70 (A. 5. .); C. J. Bleeker, "Die Idee des Schicksals in altägyptischen Religion", in *Numen*, II (1955), pp. 40-6. Cf. Brandon, *History, Time and Deity*, chap. II.

did initiation into a new life, can be discerned in some other ancient religions. We may just mention two here, before passing on to consider the Christian rite of baptism in this connection. Evidence has been presented recently by certain specialists in Iranian studies for identifying the lion-headed monster, whose statues have been found in Mithraic sanctuaries, with Zurvān *dareghō-chvadhāta*, i.e. 'Time of the Long Dominion', who in turn was also equated with Ahriman, the principle of evil and darkness in Zoroastrian dualism.[1]) What part this personification of the destructive power of Time had in the initiation rites of Mithraism is unknown; but there is reason for thinking that in some way therein the sovereignty of Zurvan-Ahriman over mankind in this world was recognised.[2])

The other instance, to be mentioned briefly, in which the idea of deliverance from Time undoubtedly inspired an initiatory ritual, occurs in Orphism. The evidence comes from some lines engraved on a gold leaf found in what seems to have been an Orphic grave near Timpone Grande, in Southern Italy. The lines concerned form part of a kind of affidavit addressed by the deceased to Persephone, the queen of the underworld:

> Out of the Pure I come, Pure Queen of Them Below
>
> . . . . .
>
> I have flown out of the sorrowful weary Wheel;
> I have passed with eager feet to the Circle desired.[3])

The 'sorrowful weary Wheel' (κύκλου ... βαρυπενθέος ἀργαλέιοι), mentioned here, is, without doubt, the endless cycle of metempsychosis, to which the Orphics believed every unenlightened soul was condemned. This process, like the Indian concept of saṃsāra, was equated with the cyclic process of Time in which all existence in the phenomenal world was involved. Although Time seems to be conceived differently here from the manner in which it was viewed in

---

[1]) Cf. R. C. ZAEHNER, *Zurvān: A Zoroastrian Dilemma* (Oxford, 1955), pp. viii-ix, in *Bulletin of the School of Oriental and African Studies*, XVII (1955), pp. 237-43; J. DUCHESNE-GUILLEMIN, "Ahriman et le Dieu Suprême dans les Mystères de Mithra", in *Numen*, II (1955), pp. 190-5; "Aiōn et le Léontocéphale, Mithras et Ahriman", in *La Nouvelle Clio*, X (1960), No. 3, p. 6, *Symbolik des Parsismus* (Stuttgart, 1961), pp. 86-9.

[2]) Cf. BRANDON, *Man and his Destiny*, pp. 290-8; *History, Time and Deity*, chapter III.

[3]) Translated by G. Murray in J. HARRISON, *Prolegomena to the Study of Greek Religion* (3rd edition, New York, 1955), pp. 667-9. Cf. W. K. C. GUTHRIE, *Orpheus and Greek Religion* (2nd edition, London, 1952), p. 173.

Egyptian or Iranian thought, namely, as a cyclical, and not a linear, process, its menace is the same, and is as keenly felt. In some way, therefore, initiation into the Orphic mysteries was believed to lead to ultimate deliverance from Time as manifest in the 'sorrowful weary Wheel' of the unceasing transmigration of the soul.[1])

We come now to consider the involvement with Time in the Christian initiatory rite of baptism. In effect, this involvement is of a twofold character, and it implicates two very different conceptions of Time. This may be seen, on analysis, in the earliest and classic statement concerning the significance of baptism given by St. Paul in the 6th chapter of his Epistle to the Romans. It is necessary to cite the passage concerned *in extenso*: "... are ye ignorant that all we who were baptised into Christ Jesus were baptised into his death?... We were buried therefore with him through baptism into death: that like as Christ was raised from the dead through the glory of the Father, so we also might walk in newness of life. For if we are become united (σύμφυτοι) with him by the likeness (τῷ ὁμοιώματι) of his death, we shall also be by the likeness of his resurrection; knowing this, that our old man was crucified with him (συν εσταυρώθη), that the body of sin might be done away, that we should no longer be in bondage to sin; for he that hath died is justified from sin. But if we died with Christ, we believe that we shall also live with him συζήσομεν αὐτῷ); knowing that Christ being raised from the dead dieth no more; death no more hath dominion over him" (vi. 3-9).[2])

Of the two very different concepts of Time involved here, let us first briefly notice that which is of a more primitive nature. In other published studies I have defined this concept as 'the Ritual or Magical Perpetuation of the Past'.[3]) We have already met the earliest historical example of it in the Osirian ritual, where it took the form of the ritual re-presentation of various events in the legendary history of Osiris. For example, the ceremony of 'Opening the Mouth' reproduced, with the dead man as the subject, what it was believed had once been done to Osiris, to re-endow him with his lost faculties. The principle

---

[1]) Cf. BRANDON, *History, Time and Deity*, chapter IV.

[2]) In his *Das religionsgeschichtliche Problem von Römer* 6, 1-11 (Zürich/Stuttgart, 1962), G. WAGNER provides a valuable discussion of the passage, but his concern to prove Paul's independence of the Mysterie-cults causes him to overlook the significance of the phenomenological factor, i.e. the common use of the 'ritual perpetuation of the past' motif.

[3]) *Time and Mankind* (London, 1951), pp. 17-18; "The Ritual Perpetuation of the Past", in *Numen*, VII (1959); *Man and his Destiny*, pp. 25, 37-8, 39, 215(3), 235.

involved was that of the magical efficacy of ritual simulation, i.e. by miming a past action, with a clear statement of intention, the virtue or power of that action could be reproduced and utilised. Thus, as the magical acts of the 'Opening of the Mouth' had enabled the resurrected body of Osiris to see, and breathe, and take food, so a repetition of them, on behalf of a dead person who was ritually identified with Osiris, would enable his embalmed body also to see, breathe, and receive food.[1])

In the Christian rite of baptism, the neophyte was accordingly ritually assimilated to Christ in his death by immersion in water— indeed the primitive custom of baptismal nudity and descent into the water signified death and the going down into the grave, which Christ had once experienced. Emergence from the 'waters of death', the re-clothing, and the reception of a new name and mystic food in the early baptismal ritual, in turn re-presented the resurrection of Christ, so that the neophyte might also participate in this new risen life. In other words, it was believed that the ritual of baptism perpetuated the virtue or efficacy of a past event, namely, the resurrection of Christ, so that the baptised person should also be raised to a new and glorious life.[2])

The other aspect of the conception of Time involved in the rite of baptism is the more fundamentally significant one of deliverance from Time's menace of personal extinction. The Christian, by dying with Christ, rises with him to a new and immortal life. Paul describes this new life elsewhere as living 'in Christ', so that one is created anew. In other words, the neophyte became incorporated with the divine Saviour, whose very nature placed him beyond Time—it is indeed worth noting here that, in the Epistle to the Hebrews, Jesus Christ is proclaimed as being "the same yesterday, and today, and for ever" (xiii 8: χθὲς καὶ σήμερον ὁ αὐτός, καὶ τοὺς αἰῶνας). Thus, the initiation of baptism united the neophyte with one who both comprehended the whole Time-process and transcended it. And so, in a very true sense, the Christian could claim, as did the Osirian devotee, "I am Yesterday, Today and Tomorrow".[3])

[1]) Cf. BRANDON in *The Saviour God*, pp. 22-3.

[2]) Cf. M. WERNER, *Die Entstehung des christlichen Dogmas* (Berne, 1941²), pp. 420-31; L. DUCHESNE, *Christian Worship*, (E. T., London, 1927), pp. 308-16; H. RAEHNER, "The Christian Mystery and the Pagan", in *The Mysteries: Papers from the Eranos Yearbooks* (London, 1955), pp. 387-401; E. DINKLER in *Religion in Geschichte und Gegenwart* (3. Aufl., 1962), VI, 631a.

[3]) Cf. BRANDON, *History, Time and Deity*, chapter II.

Christian baptism has, of course, always been an initiatory rite administered to the living—although it may be recalled that baptism for the dead was practised in the Early Church.[1]) In this sense, therefore, it appears to differ from the Osirian rites; but the difference here is only apparent. For Christian baptism really anticipated the physical death of the neophyte, and was designed to introduce him, while in this world, to a new state of life which presupposed a dying to his former state of existence. Thus the essential purpose of both the Osirian mortuary ritual and Christian baptism was to place the initiate into a state of eternal beatitude beyond the destructive touch of Time. And the Pauline idea of an eternal incorruptible spiritual body, that would replace the physical one, significantly parallels the ancient Egyptian embalmment ritual, to render the body impervious to decay.[2])

We may, accordingly, summarise our brief survey. The impetus behind both the Osirian mortuary ritual and Christian baptism is found, on the final analysis, to be the desire for security from Time's threat of personal extinction. Each was, in effect, a 'rite de passage' to a state of eternal blessedness, beyond the power of Time and its Doppelgänger, Death.

---

[1]) I *Cor.* XV. 29. Cf. DINKLER in *Religion in Geschichte und Gegenwart*, VI, 958.

[2]) I *Cor.* xv. 53: Δεῖ γὰρ τὸ φθαρτὸν τοῦτο ἐνδύσασθαι ἀφθαρσίαν καὶ τὸ θνητὸν τοῦτο ἐνδύσασθαι ἀθανασίαν.

INITIATION IN ANCIENT EGYPT

BY

C. J. BLEEKER
Amsterdam

The history of religions teaches that all over the world certain rites were celebrated at the critical moments of human life. They arose from the perception that life proceeds in periods, which are separated by a kind of threshold. At a certain moment a critical situation arises in which man cannot remain idle. By special ceremonies, he tries to further his passage from one period into the next and to effect his initiation into a new state of life. The most salient of these critical moments are puberty, marriage and death. Several of these so called 'rites de passage' function as rites of initiation. A description of these well-known rites would be beyond the framework of this paper. It should only be noted that the rites of puberty in most cases include the initiation into the secret knowledge of the tribe, which either men or women possess. In other cases the rites of initiation mean the introduction into a secret society. Closed societies of this sort play an important part in a later and higher phase of religious life, notably in the Hellenistic era. The mystery-religions of that age claimed to possess an esoteric wisdom, into which only those individuals could be initiated who satisfied certain requirements.

This short description of the meaning and of the function of the rites of initiation may serve as a guiding principle to answer the question whether ceremonies of this sort existed in Ancient Egypt. In this respect the texts give an unambiguous answer. Nowhere are rites of puberty mentioned. It is true, that circumcision occurred, but it is not clear whether it was generally applied or whether it had the significance of a rite of initiation. Apparently the ancient Egyptians did not assign religious significance to puberty. Neither had marriage any sacral significance, in the sense that its celebration was considered as an initiation. However, death was in a somewhat different case. The ancient Egyptians were extremely fascinated by the mystery of life and death.[1] On the one hand they looked upon life and death

---

[1] W. B. Kristensen, *Het leven uit de dood*, 1949[2].

as implacable enemies; on the other hand, they were convinced that these two powers could be reconciled, at least in a divine life, in so far as the deity proves its creative power by rising from death. Sincerely they hoped, that mortal beings by death could take part in eternal life. Thus it will be a matter of further research to discover how far death was deemed to be an initiation. In order to gain a clear idea of the function of initiation in Ancient Egypt, it is further very useful to state, that the texts never mention the existence of secret societies. This point should be stressed, because there are authors who promulgate the opposite opinion. Aided more by imagination than by expert knowledge, they boldly contend, that the ancient Egyptians possessed a profound esoteric wisdom, which, by the initiates of secret societies of priests and scholars, was transmitted from one generation to the following. It can not be doubted that the ancient Egyptian religion testified to a deep insight into the nature of divine life, as it revealed itself to the inhabitants of the valley of the Nile, but the texts nowhere allude to the existence of a kind of esoteric wisdom, only disclosed to the initiated. Considering these facts, it needs to be understood clearly that rites of initiation, in the strict sense of the word, may not be expected to have existed in Ancient Egypt. Yet initiation played a not unimportant part in ancient Egyptian religion. It is worthwhile to make an inquiry into its meaning, though the relevant facts are scanty and hard to interpret.

The best way of tackling the problem of the significance of initiation in Ancient Egypt is by making an inquiry into the nature and the function of mystery. This notion plays a certain part in the structure of the temples, in the Egyptian cult and in several cultic and funeral texts. Even in such matters mystery proves to have been an important component of the religious consciousness of the ancient Egyptians. And when mystery somewhere occurs, then the initiation into that hidden truth or spiritual reality can not be totally absent.

In regard to the structure of the temples and to the nature of the cult, attention should be payed to the following peculiarities:

1) Apparently certain parts of the temples were inaccessible to ordinary people. This fact was known to the Greek authors. PLU-TARCH alludes to it, when he illustrates his thesis, that myth has a metaphoric meaning. He then refers to the structure of the Egyptian temple which as he says partly consists of open and airy corridors and colonnades, partly contains hidden, dark, subterranean rooms,

which have a likeness to caves and graves.[1]) As regards these sub-terranean rooms it is a well-known fact, that the temple in Dendera contains crypts, of which the function is not yet satisfactorily explain-ed. It may be, that they have served as repositories, i.e. of images. However, it is curious, that the walls are decorated with religious texts and pictures. One does not expect this in a store room. It could point to a cultic function of these crypts. The texts even record, that the crypts are entered, but that their entrance and their place are hidden. Actually the entrance is narrow and difficult. There is also a short description of the festivals which were held in the crypts.[2]) All the facts suggest that the crypts contained a mystery to which only a few people had access. At any rate they belonged to those parts of the temple which were inaccessible to common people.

One can even move a step further. The very structure of the temple prevented ordinary people from partaking in the cult and stressed thereby the mysterious character of the rites performed in its interior. This fact is apparent from the Ptolemaic temples, which have re-mained nearly undamaged. The walls of their enclosure are so high that nobody could see or hear what was going on in the temple when the gates were closed. Moreover so little light managed to penetrate into the central parts of the temple that an atmosphere of mystery and awe were created. It is clear, that the Egyptian temple was not meant to let the masses of the people participate in the religious services. In regard to the temple of Dendera MARIETTE writes: 'Le temple égyptien n'a rien à faire, soit avec le temple grec, soit avec l'église chrétienne. Les fidèles ne s'y assemblent pas pour la prière. Les prêtres n'y sont pas les intermédiaires entre les fidèles et la divinité ... Tout s'y fait au nom du roi et en faveur du roi. En Egypte, les rois ne sont pas seulement les représentants de la nation; ils s'élèvent plus haut et se proclament les fils du soleil et les représentants des dieux. A ce titre, ils sont vraiment dignes de voir la divinité face à face: dans la silence et dans la retraite des temples ils conversent avec elle; ils sollicitent pour eux-mêmes et pour l'Egypte la faveur des dieux et c'est à eux que les dieux répondent.'[3]) These beautiful words anticipate one of the conclusions of this paper, i.e. the thesis that the king is to be considered as initiated on account of his descent and of his dignity. Primarily these words cast a clarifying light on the function of the

---

[1]) PLUTARCH, *De Iside et Osiride*, cap. 20.
[2]) A. MARIETTE, *Denderah, Description générale*, 1875, pg. 323, 326.
[3]) MARIETTE, *op. cit.*, pg. 301.

Egyptian temple. This sanctuary served for the celebration of a cultic mystery.

It is no wonder that regulations were made to guard the temple, and specially the holy of holies against profanation. There is a text, published by H. JUNKER, which contains the decree of the gods concerning the abaton.[1]) The decree consists of rules, issued by Re himself, and written down by Thoth, concerning the abaton, i.e. the 'pure place', where Osiris has been buried. The prescriptions contain several prohibitions: it was forbidden to make music, that means to beat the drum, and to sing with the harp or the flute; it was not allowed to shoot birds and to catch fishes within the holy territory; people should not break the silence during the holy time that Isis was dwelling there, by speaking loudly. These regulations testify to a deep respect for the mysterious character of the temple. The sense of awe is clearly reflected in the prohibition to enter the abaton. It literally runs like this: 'nobody is ever allowed to enter it', i.e. the abaton. This prescription in fact refers to an absolutely inaccessible secret.

2) From the preceding argument follow that the celebration of a part of the cult was concealed from the eyes of the laity. The ordinary people could at any time pray to the gods outside the gates of the temenos and bring them their modest offerings. The daily ritual, which contained three services, mainly took place in the innermost of the temple in the presence of a limited number of priests. It was a mystery-service, though everybody knew what happened there. The same can be said of the celebration of the festivals, which culminated in a procession. Sometimes the procession left the temple, for various reasons. In that case the general public could to a certain degree be witness of the ceremonies. As a rule even the festivals chiefly had the character of mysteries.[2])

3) This does not presume however, that there existed a secret doctrine in Ancient Egypt, which was only known to the initiated. H. O. LANGE rightly declares: ‚Von einer solchen Geheimlehre enthalten die Denkmäler keine Spur'. [3]) H. BONNET reaches in his 'Reallexikon der ägyptischen Religionsgeschichte' the same con-

---

[1]) H. JUNKER, *Das Götterdekret über das Abaton* (*Denkschriften der Kais. Ak. d. Wiss. in Wien, phil.-hist. Klasse*, Band LVI, 1913).

[2]) H. W. FAIRMAN, "Worship and Festivals in an Egyptian Temple" (*Bulletin of the John Rylands Library*, Volume 37, 1954/5, pg. 165 sq.)

[3]) H. O. LANGE, *Die Aegypter* (*Lehrbuch der Religionsgeschichte* 1925 I pg. 444).

clusion when treating the notion 'Mysterien'.[1]) As a matter of fact the idea of a secret doctrine fully misjudges the character of the ancient Egyptian religion. It is prompted by the modern conception that the essence of a religion is to be found in certain dogmatic tenets, in a myth or a doctrine. When studying the Egyptian texts attentively and critically one comes to the conclusion that myth therein is a vague and hardly definable entity. The texts are predominantly of a cultic nature. This can best be exemplified by the way in which the famous myth of Osiris is handed down. The Egyptian texts nowhere present a connected tale. They only contain allusions to the myth, which sometimes are hard to harmonize, because they contradict each other. Apparently there was no authoritative myth, and certainly no secret doctrine. The living religious and mythical consciousness expressed itself in the cult. What one could know about the gods, was commonly known.

Yet some cultic ceremonies were celebrated, which were so holy and which so strongly had the character of a mystery that no one was allowed to describe or to depict them. There are Greek authors who mention the fact. IAMBLICHUS speaks about 'the inexpressible and hidden affairs which take place in Abydos'.[2]) HERODOTUS alludes to them. He refers a few times to the god 'whose name it is not allowed to mention in this connection' i.e. Osiris. He records that in Saïs, during the night, a dramatic performance of the sufferings of Osiris took place, which 'the Egyptians call mysteries'. His words suggest that he was informed about these holy rites, but he adds: 'hereupon I keep silent'. [3]) The Egyptian documents confirm this information. I myself was forced to draw the conclusion that a certain rite has not been depicted on account of its mysterious character, when I studied the great festival of the god Min, which is represented in the temple at Medinet Habu.[4]) The texts record that the Min-festival consisted of the celebration of three highly important rites, i.e. firstly a ritual harvest, secondly the renewal of the dignity of the king and thirdly the elevation of Min on his staircase or platform. The two first ceremonies are represented with all desirable clarity. However, the representation of the third rite, which has paramount importance, because, in my opinion, it dramatizes and actualizes the birth of Min,

[1]) *Op. cit.* pg. 494 sq.
[2]) A. MORET, *Mystères égyptiens*, 1922, pg. 19.
[3]) HERODOTUS II: 86, 132, 170, 171.
[4]) C. J. BLEEKER, *Die Geburt eines Gottes*, 1956.

is fully lacking. This can not be accidental and that the less, because one clearly sees, how the parts of this so called staircase are carried in the procession by some servants. Apparently the elevation of Min on his staircase was a secret rite. It must have been performed in the presence of a chosen company.

In the preceding part of this paper, general considerations have been used to prove that the notions of mystery and of secret actions played a certain part in the ancient Egyptian religion—a statement, which leads to the conclusion that there must have been certain persons who were initiated into the mystery, though no trace of official rites of initiation has ever been found. However the argument needs not merely rest on general considerations, drawn from the structure of the temple and from the nature of the cult. It can also have recourse to the results of researches into the significance and the function of the Egyptian word by which mystery is indicated, i.e. *št3*.

št3 is used both in a secular and in a sacral meaning .[1]) In daily life *št3* means: concealed, hidden, difficult, unprecedented, curious. It is evident, that in this connection attention should be focussed on the sacral significance. Here the Egyptologist meets a curious difficulty. In my opinion insight into the purely religious meaning of *št3* is not acquired merely by philological researches, that means by studying the texts. One has also to take into account two general points of view, one with regard to the literary character of the texts and the other in the nuances in the Egyptian language. Thus two questions arise: 1) what type of literature had been created in Ancient Egypt? 2) how far does our insight reach into the peculiarities of the Egyptian religious language? This paper does not allow me to pursue very far these two questions. I must be brief. In respect to the first point, it is evident that the religious significance of *št3* is dependent on the judgment about the literary character of the cultic and funeral texts, in which it is used. To be more precise, the controversial question among Egyptologists is whether the Egyptian literature has known the drama. The French Egyptologist E. Drioton has tried to prove that, in Ancient Egypt, the theatre existed, both in a secular and in a religious form.[2]) In his opinion certain religious texts have a dramatic tendency, that means: they refer to the theatrical representation of mythical ideas. The same conception is expressed by the title which

---

[1]) W.B. 4: 55 sq.
[2]) f.i. in *Pages d'Egyptologie*.

K. Sethe gave to his study on the famous Schabaka-text and on the Ramesseumpapyrus, which contains the rite of the ascension to the throne. It reads: 'Dramatische Texte zu altaegyptischen Mysterienspiele'. On the other hand G. Jéquier denies that dramatic performances existed in Ancient Egypt, as is shown from this quotation: 'En Égypte rien dans les textes ni dans les tableaux de la vie civile ne nous permet de supposer l'existence de représentations dramatiques ... Dans tous les actes du culte d'Osiris ... il n'y a pas de drame, c'est à dire de représentations scèniques mimées ... il n'y a que des rites'.[1]) H. Frankfort comes to a similar conclusion: the typical Egyptian literary genres are the novel, the proverbs and lyrics. Epos and drama are lacking.[2]) If the last opinion were true, it would mean that *št3* can not have any reference to some kind of cultic performance. The question is too complicated to be settled in a few words. However, in my opinion, there are indications that certain cultic texts have a dramatic intention.

The second point is of no less importance. It is the question: what do we know about the Egyptian religious terminology? The answer must be: preciously little. Curiously enough many Egyptologists do not seem to realize, that well-known words must have had a sacral shade of meaning and that it is worthwhile to make inquiries into this field, which is practically untrodden. The result is that several Egyptologists neglect or deny the existence of certain religious notions or elements of religious truth, because they do not take the religious sense of certain words into account. Needless to say, it is decisive for the conception of the essence and the function of *št3*, whether the existence of a sacral terminology is accepted or not.

In view of the fact, that no agreement has been reached concerning these two points, it is self-evident, that the conclusions in regard to the significance of *št3* can only have provisional value. They are the following:

1) obviously there existed in Ancient Egypt certain cultic mysteries which were only known to the initiated. For, the texts record, that people took pride in the fact that they had beheld certain secret rites. Thus one person declares: 'I am therein initiated', (i.e. certain cultic ceremonies) ... but I do not tell it to anybody'.[3]) Therefore the

---

[1]) "Drames, mystères, rituels dans l'ancienne Egypte" (*Mélanges offerts à M. Max Niedermann*, 1944).
[2]) H. Frankfort, *Ancient Egyptian Religion*, 1948.
[3]) Ä.Z. 57, 1922, 27, 35.

admonition is given: 'Do not reveal what you have seen in the mysteries of the temples'.[1] It has already been indicated what the contents of such cultic secrets were likely to have been. At the great festival of Min, it seems to have been the elevation of the god on his staircase. In regard to the cult of Osiris the texts, which describe the celebration of the festivals in the month of Choiak, lift a corner of the veil, covering *št3*. The texts date from the Ptolemaic period, but they refer to a ceremonial which must be ancient. Unfortunately the texts are far from lucid. So much is clear, viz., that the death and the resurrection of Osiris were actualized by shaping his broken and his reconstructed body in certain moulds. These forms were shaped out of earth and other ingredients and possessed so to speak sacramental power. In this connection the texts mention 'the mystery chest' and then speak about 'knowing the mystery of the shaped dough, in the mould of Sokaris, in the form of an object, which is absolutely unknown'.[2] These veiled words hint at a cultic secret. Presently it will appear, that the funeral texts contain similar allusions.

2) the netherworld contains secrets which under certain circumstances can be disclosed to gods and to men. Sometimes they are inaccessible even to gods. In respect to the last point, attention should be paid to the fourth and the fifth hour of the journey of the sungod through the netherworld. These hours are the domain of Sokaris. The texts inform us, that this territory is absolutely closed to the sun-god, though the pictures represent Sokaris and his domain. Obviously there is a mystery in these two hours of the night. Moreover the inscription on the gate of the domain of Sokaris reads: 'the mysterious gate, which the sun-god does not enter, though he hears his voice' i.e. of Sokaris. In regard to Sokaris it is said: 'the body of Sokaris, the mysterious image, which is neither seen nor perceived'.[3] In another text, describing the voyage of the sun-god through the netherworld, it is told that the god penetrates into several secrets.[4] As to mortal man, these texts presuppose that he can get to know the mysteries. This knowledge provides him with all kinds of spiritual and material goods in the hereafter.[5] This corresponds to the Egyptian conception that man by death is initiated into a deeper wis-

---

[1]) Chassinat, EDFU III 360, 361, 5.
[2]) V. LORET, "Les fêtes d'Osiris au mois de Choiak" (*Rec. de Trav.* III, IV, V).
[3]) M. E. LEFÉBURE, *Le Tombeau de Séti* I, 1886, I, 23, 24.
[4]) H. FRANKFORT, *The Cenotaph of Seti I at Abydos*, 1933, Volume I, pg. 39.
[5]) G. JÉQUIER, *Le livre de ce qu'il y a dans l'Hades*, 1894, passim.

dom. This remark leads to further research into the funeral texts.

3) the notion *št3* is mostly used in the funeral texts, for instance in the Book of the Dead and in Papyrus Leiden T 32, which has been studied by B. H. STRICKER very excellently. In these texts, the dead man emphatically declares, that he has entered the secrets of the netherworld, that he has seen the mysteries of *R3-št3w*, i.e. the sphere of Sokaris, that he has beheld the faces of the gods, that he has heard some mythical words, viz., the conversation between the ass and the cat, presumably Seth and Re, that he has seen labour, which even the mystagogue does not know, that he knows the names of the parts of the gate of the realm of Osiris, that he has performed the ceremonies which should be done there and that he has been a witness to quite a series of secret rites.[1]) Curiously enough one point is not quite clear. There is uncertainty in regard to the question whether these rites are all performed in the netherworld or whether the enumeration includes the remembrance of the celebration of secret rites in which the dead took part on earth. In the cases when the names of wellknown sanctuaries are mentioned, the last explanation seems plausible. That means, that the funeral texts might contain pieces of evidence which are useful for the knowledge of the cultic mysteries.

Finally two questions arise, namely 1) what were in general the contents of *št3* ? and 2) who were initiated into these mysteries? The first question can be quickly answered. It has become clear that the knowledge of *št3* does not consist in the introduction into a secret doctrine, but means the participation in the celebration of a secret rite, which actualized a mythical idea. The answer to the second question should be: in the first place the pharaoh must be considered as initiated, and that on account of his descent and of his function: in his capacity of king he was at the same time high priest, who mediated between heaven and earth and therefore was deemed to possess superhuman wisdom.[2]) Thus he is addressed in the following words: '*Hw* (the creative word) is in thy mouth. *Sj3* (the true insight) is in thy heart, the place of thy tongue is a temple of Ma-a-t. (the cosmic order)'.[3]) Secondly the priests, who took his place in the cult, took part in the cultic mysteries. Finally there must have existed a group of persons who enjoyed the privilege of assisting in the secret rites.

---

[1]) *Book of the Dead* 1, 15 B III, 125; B. H. STRICKER, *De Egyptische mysteriën*: *Pap. Leiden* T 32 (O.M.R.O. 31, 34, 37).
[2]) C. J. BLEEKER, *La fonction pontificale du Roi-Dieu* (The Sacred Bridge 1963).
[3]) C. J. BLEEKER, *De betekenis van de Egyptische godin* Ma-a-t 1929, pg. 33.

This number of initiated must have been enlarged in the course of time, if we rightly interpret the relevant cultic and funeral texts.[1])

----

[1]) In the discussion following the delivery of this paper Dr. J. ZANDEE from Utrecht made the remark, that the verb *bs*: to introduce, several times means: to initiate into a mystery, into hidden knowledge. He gave interesting quotations from the Coffin Texts and from the Book of the Dead, which confirm the thesis of this study. It appears that *bs* is used for the introduction of the king and of the priest into their office—also into the special knowledge, connected therewith—and for the initiation into the mysteries of the cult and of the netherworld, especially of Osiris. The '*Wörterbuch der Aegyptische Sprache*' I: 473 and its 'Belegstellen' give instances of this significance of the verb *bs* and moreover mention a noun *bs* which means: mystery.

VORAUSSETZUNGEN DER EINWEIHUNG
IN ELEUSIS

VON

K. KERÉNYI
Ascona

Von gewissen Voraussetzungen der Einweihung in Eleusis wollte ich reden, einen kleinen Beitrag zu diesem Colloquium über Initiationsriten vorlegen, und zugleich einen Nachtrag zu meinem Buch „ Die Mysterien von Eleusis" von einem Standpunkt aus, den ich seit dessen Erscheinen (Zürich 1962) hinzugewonnen habe und den ich jetzt im Zusammenhang mit anderen, allgemeineren Gesichtspunkten zu bedenken geben möchte. Zu diesen gehören zwei Thesen, die, wie ich sehe, zum gemeinsamen Gut des Gesprächs über Initiationen und mit ihnen verbundenet Geheimkulte geworden sind. Sie stehen in meinen Arbeiten der Vierzigerjahre oder waren aus ihnen als Folgerung abzuleiten.

Die erste ist die Anwendung eines berühmten Verses von GOETHE, aus dem „Epirrhema" zum Gedicht „Die Metamorphose der Pflanzen", auf solcher Art „naturhafte" — so nannte ich sie — Geheimkulte. Sie waren — „mit GOETHES Worten

— „ein heilig öffentlich Geheimnis."—

„Das Geheimgehaltene im griechischen Kult war" — so führte ich es aus[1] — „sicherlich allen, die im Umkreis des betreffenden Kultortes wohnten, bekannt, es war aber ein Nicht-Auszusprechendes. Ja es besass diesen Charakter — den Charakter des Arreton — unabhängig von der Willkür der Kultteilnehmer. Denn es war zutiefst — in jener Tiefe, in der es Gegenstand des Kultes sein konnte — eben unaussprechlich: ein echtes Geheimnis. Erst nachher machen ausdrückliche Verbote das Arreton zu Aporreton."

Die Begründung in dieser Ausführung wurde von Anderen vielleicht nicht — oder nicht ausdrücklich — angenommen, doch angenommen die Konsequenz, die aus meinem „Urmensch und Mysterium" folgt. Dessen Ergebnis war „die nicht nur griechische Anschau-

---

[1]) *Die Geburt der Helena*, Zürich 1945, 49.

ung" — ich habe eine ganz genaue ethnologische Parallele angeführt [1])
— „dass zum Menschwerden aus dem Urmenschen eine zweite
Formung, Schöpfung oder Geburt notwendig ist. Bei den Griechen
war diese zweite Formung die Heiligung durch das Brot und durch
das Geschenk der Mysterien, auf dem nach dieser Anschauung, nicht
weniger als auf dem Ackerbau selbst, die Zivilisation beruht. Der
Mensch kommt aus der Erde, doch zum Menschen wird er erst
durch die zweite Phase seiner Erschaffung". Das griechische Wort
ἀτελής, das ich angeführt habe, bedeutet sowohl den Unfertigen
als auch den Uneingeweihten. Es kann also gefolgert werden, dass
Initiationen im Grunde genommen Initiationen zum Menschsein
sind. Doch müssten auch die Gebiete genau aufgewiesen und in die
Landkarte der Erde eingetragen werden, wo sie es tatsächlich waren,
um die Reichweite der Feststellung zu überblicken.

Gehört auch Eleusis zu den Gebieten, auf denen dieser allgemeine
Sinn der Einweihung — Initiation zum Menschsein — zutraf? Ich
möchte eine noch allgemeinere Formulierung vorschlagen, die für
alle naturhaften Initiationen, ja auch für viele nicht naturhaften, wie
Einweihungen in Berufe, Klassen (nicht Altersklassen) und Stände,
zutrifft. Jede Initiation, die mehr als leere Formalität oder ein Scherz ist,
setzt einen Lebensinhalt (x) voraus, der allen übrigen, den Einzuweihenden schon bekannten Lebensinhalten (n) gegenüber um etwas —
um ein y — mehr oder höher ist: $n+y=x$, in eine Formel gebracht.
Einen Lebensinhalt — auch den neueren und höheren oder volleren,
etwa den Lebensinhalt eines reiferen Alters — *hat* man. Die darin
sind, denen genügt ein Wink, um sich über das Gemeinsame, das
sie haben, zu verständigen. Die noch nicht darin sind, denen
wird kein Wort dasselbe mitteilen können. Daher konzentriert sich
die initiatorische Mitteilung auf y. Man versucht mit allen Mitteln
den *Unterschied* — nicht bloss den Übergang (den *passage*) — bemerk-
bar, fühlbar, wissbar zu machen.

Darin liegt unsere grosse Schwierigkeit in bezug auf die Mysterien
von Eleusis: es wirken sich da zwei Unbekannte aus. Bei allen
naturhaften und den meisten nicht-naturhaften Initiationen vermögen
wir uns etwas unter x vorzustellen. Dadurch wird auch das, was
jeweils von den Initiationsriten ermittelbar ist, begreiflich. Nicht so
in Eleusis. Auch da kann manches von den Zeremonien ermittelt
werden. Wir werden aber nicht klug, um welchen Unterschied es

---

[1]) Niobe, Zürich 1949, 86.

geht. Die Vielschichtigkeit und Kompliziertheit der Riten ermutigt uns nicht, als x einen Lebensinhalt anzunehmen, der mit einem völlig naturhaften verwandt wäre, in den die Reifezeremonien initiieren. Die Verbindung der Agrikultur mit einem besseren, menschenwürdigeren Leben ist als eleusinische Anschauung bekannt. Die Reihenfolge, ob der Ackerbau der primäre Inhalt der Mysterien war und das menschenwürdige Leben dessen Deutung, oder ob das durch die Initiation erreichte Menschsein erst nachträglich als Leben in der Agrikultur gedeutet wurde, ist von vornherein nicht zu entscheiden.

Ich möchte mich auf gewisse Voraussetzungen der Einweihung in Eleusis beschränken und hebe nur das hervor, worin der Unterschied zwischen dem Eingeweihtsein und Nichteingeweihtsein als höchste Stufe der Initiation zum Ausdruck kam und auch für Nichteingeweihte genau bezeichnet werden konnte. Es steht im homerischen Demeterhymnus mit einem Perfectum (480) ausgesprochen: ὄπωπεν. Man hatte gesehen, und was man gesehen hatte, hat man behalten. Das besagt das Perfectum. Die Initiation wurde durch Sehen vollbracht — Sehen in einem intensiven Sinne, da es, der Perfektform entsprechend, als Abschluss der vorausgehenden Phasen der Initiation einen bleibenden Inhalt hatte: das Eingeweihtsein. Ausser jenen Phasen gab es auch Vorbereitungen, die nicht zur Initiation gehörten, aber als deren Voraussetzungen ebenso klar bezeichnet werden, wie die Wichtigkeit des Sehens.

Eine ganz allgemeine Voraussetzung war, die nur für uns als solche bezeichnet werden muss, in der historischen Zeit der Mysterien die griechische Mythologie. Im homerischen Demeterhymnus geht die griechische Göttin der Agrikultur mit ihrem Beispiel durch alle Vorbereitungen den Einzuweihenden voran. Diese Beobachtung ist längst gemacht worden und darf als allgemein anerkannt gelten. Die Göttin des Ackerbaus musste erst eingeweiht werden — sicher nicht in die Geheimnisse der Agrikultur und deren Segen, deren Inbegriff sie war —, damit sie die Mysterien den Eleusiniern zeigen konnte. Das spricht nicht für eine ursprüngliche, im Wesen dieser Einweihung liegende Verbindung des Eingeweihtseins in Eleusis mit dem Ackerbau, eher für eine nachträgliche Vereinigung. Aus dem Beispiel der Göttin wird ersichtlich, dass eine der Voraussetzungen der Einweihung das Fasten war. Als Voraussetzung wird es klar bezeichnet durch das Bekenntnis — das σύνθημα — das die Einzuweihenden ablegen mussten, ehe ihre Initiation vollbracht werden konnte. Die Länge und die Strenge des Fastens — neun Tage ohne Nahrung

— ergibt sich aus den Angaben des homerischen Hymnus über den Zustand der Demeter, ehe sie die Mysterien zeigte:

47 ἐννῆμαρ μὲν ἔπειτα κατὰ χθόνα πότνια Δηὼ στρωφᾶτ' αἰθομένας
δαΐδας μετὰ χεζσὶν ἔχουσα, οὐδέ ποτ' ἀμβροσίης καὶ νέκταρος
ἡδυπότοιο πάσσατ', ἀκηχεμένη, οὐδὲ χρόα βάλλετο λουτζοῖς...
200 ἀλλ' ἀγέλαστος ἄπαστος ἐδητύος ἠδὲ ποτῆτος ἧστο...

Das σύνθημα (Clem. Al. Protr. 2. 21) bezeichnet nach dem Fasten als zweite Voraussetzung das Trinken, nach Arnobius (Adv. nat. 5. 26) das „Austrinken", des Kykeon: Ἐνήστευσα, ἔπιον τὸν κυκεῶνα, *ieiunavi atque ebibi cyceonem*. Im homerischen Hymnus befolgt Demeter dieses Nacheinander und gibt die Anweisung zur Bereitung des Getränkes. Die Mischung bestand aus Gerste, Wasser und zarten Blättern [1] des *Mentha pulegium*. Nachher wird es besonders betont, dass dies der κυκεών war, der Kykeon κατ' ἐξοχήν, denn es gab auch andere Mischgetränke, die gleichfalls κυκεών hiessen. Die eleusinische Mischung war kein Geheimnis, die Anweisung der Göttin ist aber als rituelle Anweisung aufzufassen:

208 ... ἄνωγε δ'ἄρ' ἄλφι καὶ ὕδωρ δοῦναι μίξασαν πιέμεν γλήχωνι
τερείνηι. ἡ δὲ κυκεῶ τεύξασα θεᾶι πόρεν ὡς ἐκέλευε...

Die Göttin trinkt das Getränk aus einem, für die eleusinischen Mysterien charakteristischen rituellen Gefäss aus, das im Hymnus, in der nach 211 ausgefallenen Zeile, wahrscheinlich auch erwähnt war, wie in der orphischen Version (fr. 52, 5 Kern) [2]. Wir kennen die Form des Gefässes von zahlreichen Abbildungen [3] und Nachbildungen, ja, von mehr oder weniger fragmentierten Stücken, die in Eleusis ausgegraben wurden. Die Frage, ob in solchen Gefässen nicht ein gärendes — oder schon gegorenes — Getränk in der Prozession von Athen nach Eleusis mitgetragen wurde, ist vom griechischen Archäologen Andreas SKIAS aufgeworfen [4], doch von Anderen schnell abgetan worden, mit der Begründung, dass im homerischen Hymnus zwischen der Anweisung der Göttin und dem Darbringen des fertigen Getränkes keine Zeit zur Gärung war. Man dachte an die

---

[1] So interpretiert, richtig, das homerische Beiwort A. DELATTE: *Le Cyceon*, Paris, 1955, 33. Die grünen Blätter sind wirksamer als die getrockneten.

[2] *Symbolae Osloenses* 36, 1960, 15.

[3] DAREMBERG-SAGLIO: *Dict. des ant.* III 1, 823 f.; in meinen *Mysterien von Eleusis* Abb. 1a; 20 und 24 mit Anm. 173. Das gemeinte Gefäss, das bei der Prozession von Frauen auf dem Kopf getragen wurde, ist weder Kernos, noch Thymiaterion, es gibt aber Exemplare, die die Funktionen kombinieren.

[4] *Ephem. Arch.* 1901, 19 ff.

Macht der Göttin nicht, die die Gärung hervorrufen konnte, wie Dionysos ein Weinwunder. In den eleusinischen und athenischen Häusern wurde das Getränk der fastenden Einzuweihenden wohl mehrere Tage, bevor sie es trinken durften, vorbereitet. Man brauchte wahrscheinlich geröstete Gerste dazu — *tosta polenta* nach OVID (Met. 5. 450) — die Röstung war aber nicht notwendig. Getreide dient als Grundstoff alkoholischer Getränke auch in ungeröstetem Zustand. Hinzukam das *Mentha pulegium*.

Die Beachtung der Tatsache, dass die Einzuweihenden, bevor sie in Eleusis „gesehen haben", nach langem strengen Fasten ein — wenn auch nur leicht — alkoholisches Getränk zu sich nahmen, ergibt einen zusätzlichen Standpunkt, von dem aus das im Telesterion, dem Ort Vollendung der Initiation Gesehene beurteilt werden müsste, selbst wenn wir nichts von dessen Inhalt wüssten. Inbezug auf die Wirkung des *Mentha pulegium*, das bei uns nur als Carminativum, Beruhigungsmittel in der Form des Pfefferminztees bekannt ist, habe ich mich an einen Fachmann der Phytochemie gewandt, der durch seine Forschungen auf dem Gebiete der in der Religionsgeschichte auftretenden Drogen, wie Psilocybin, Mescalin und ihrer Verwandten, bekannt ist, an Dr. Albert HOFMANN in Basel. Von ihm erfuhr ich, dass das Polei-Öl (Oleum Pulegii), das in Südeuropa für Aromatisierungszwecke aus dem *Mentha pulegium* gewonnen wird, in hohen Dosen Delirien, Bewusstlosigkeit und Krämpfe erzeugt. Zwischen dem Minimum und dem Maximum — Pfefferminztee und hochdosiertes Polei-Öl — gibt es natürlich auch mittlere Stufen.

Besonders wertvoll war mir daher das, was Dr. HOFMANN mir vom Kykeon schrieb, nachdem ich ihm das gesamte philologische und archäologische Material vorgelegt hatte. Er schickte voraus, dass der Inhalt der Visionen bei chemisch, d.h. durch Drogen, induzierten visionären Zuständen „weitgehend oder vielleicht ganz durch die Erwartungen, durch die geistige Vorbereitung und seelische Ausgangslage und durch das Milieu" bestimmt werden, und setzte in seinem Brief fort: „Nach den Belegen, die Sie beibringen, wäre es denkbar, dass das Fasten allein in diesem Fall die 'doors of perception' um mit Huxley zu reden, geöffnet hat. Der Inhalt des Geschauten, die Bilder, wurden dann durch die Erwartungen, das Ritual und durch die Symbole bestimmt. Als 'Initialzündung' könnte in einem solchen Zustand schon eine geringe Dose Alkohol genügen, wie Sie es als eine Möglichkeit der Erklärung zur Diskussion stellen. Dem *Mentha pulegium* käme dann tatsächlich nur noch die Rolle eines Carminativum zu, eine Qualität, die unbestritten ist. Andererseits könnten die ätherischen Öle, die im Polei-Öl enthalten sind, zusätzlich zum Alkoholgehalt des kykeon, auf durch Fasten sensibilisierte Personen sehr wohl eine halluzinogene Wirkung ausgeübt haben''.

Die Wichtigkeit von Faktoren, für die der Naturforscher Zuständig ist, wurde von einem hervorragenden Spezialisten bestätigt, *neben* derjenigen der historischen und geistigen, der mythologischen und religiösen Voraussetzungen der Einweihung in Eleusis. Die Wirkung eines langen Fastens und des Kykeontrinkens bei Initiationsriten, bei denen Aristoteles das παθεῖν und διατεθῆναι betonte [1]), verdient, dass sie in Betracht gezogen, und das *Mentha pulegium*, dass es zum Gegenstand besonderer Forschung gemacht wird. Die Vorbereitung durch Fasten und ein solches Getränk ist aber schon jetzt verständlich, wenn sie zum Gelingen der Einweihung, durch eben diese Kombination, beitragen konnte. Der Inhalt der Vision, deren Zustandekommen sie förderte, ist aus ihr nicht abzuleiten. Da spielte die bei dem Mysterienfest vergegenwärtigte *Mythologie* die richtunggebende Rolle — womit noch nicht alle möglichen Faktoren genannt wurden [2]).

Der Inhalt der Vision steht weniger klar im „Herakles'' des Euripides (613), wo die Worte des Helden, er habe das gesehen, was die Eingeweihten in Eleusis, nicht eindeutig auf seine Hadeserlebnisse zu beziehen sind, klar in einem Mailänder Papyrus [3]), wo Herakles bereit ist, die Einweihung in Eleusis zurückzuweisen, da er Persephone doch schon in der Unterwelt gesehen hatte. Die Begegnung mit dem Tode, in der Gestalt der Unterweltskönigin, war etwas, um das Menschsein völlig erfahren zu lassen und zugleich mit einer Hoffnung zu bereichern, weil eine solche Erfahrung überhaupt möglich war. Dieser Lebensinhalt, in dessen Besitz sich die Eingeweihten in Eleusis nach ihrer Vision anders befanden als die Nichteingeweihten, ist vielleicht nicht ganz unvorstellbar: er berührt sich mit der gemeinsamen Voraussetzung naturhafter Initiationen, wo sie immer das Menschwerden meinten. Der voragrikulturale menschliche Kern der Mysterien von Eleusis ist — um es mit einer kleinen Aenderung am Goethevers zu sagen — ihr heilig offenbar Geheimnis.

---

[1]) Fr. 15 Rose; *meine Mysterien von Eleusis*, Zurich 1962, S. 105 f.

[2]) Weiteres in meinem *Grund zur Eleusinischen Vision, Spectrum Psychologiae,* Festschrift für C. A. Meier, Zürich 1965, S. 13 ff.

[3]) I 1937 S. 177 Nr. 20, 31, in seiner Bedeutung erkannt von W. F. OTTO, *Eranos Jahrbuch* 1939, 105; vgl. *Paideuma* 7, 1959, 69 ff.; *meine Mysterien von Eleusis* 90-100.

„LE SECRET CENTRAL DE L'INITIATION AUX MYSTERES D'ELEUSIS"

PAR

MAURICE MEHAUDEN
Bruxelles

1. Thèse

Les Mystères d'Eleusis constituaient la plus prestigieuse, et sont actuellement la moins mal connue, de toutes les sotériologies païennes. C'était une promesse de Bonheur posthume, de caractère rétributif par suite du mode de recrutement des mystes, promesse octroyée aux seuls Initiés sous forme d'un mot de passe pour l'Au-delà et le Paradis de Déméter. Cette sotériologie était étroitement liée à un culte de la Maternité, à savoir la maternité de la Divinité chthonienne et agraire Déméter, dont les initiés, hommes et femmes, devenaient au cours de leur initiation, et grâce à une seconde naissance mystique, les enfants, après avoir participé à des manipulations et à des cérémonies symbolico-mystico-génésiques, en rapport elles-mêmes avec le ἱερός γαμος de Zeus et de Déméter. C'était comme fils ou fille de Déméter que les initiés, désormais des δευτερόπτομοι, étaient accueillis après leur mort par leur Mère Déméter dans son Paradis chthonien. Tel quel ce *résultat* de l'initiation n'était nullement secret, (cf. „Les Grenouilles" * et de nombreux autres textes), ce qui resta un secret sévèrement gardé, c'étaient les rites de l'initiation et surtout son *rite central*. (cf. 3 C).

2. Deux remarques préliminaires

A. Il faut avoir *vu* les ruines d'Eleusis (entre les usines!) pour ne pas faire certaines fautes, comme de négliger de développement des énormes souterrains, les dénivellations aptes à expliquer certains détails étranges, l'aspect saisissant de la grotte d'Hadès, qui dispensait d'employer machinerie ou mise en scène dans la nuit de Boedromion.

---

* Aristophane, Βατραχοι , cf. vers 107-420-421 à 886.

Il ne faut pas non plus se laisser trop influencer par des mensurations d'architecte comme NOACK, car ce qui subsiste des murs et du gros œuvre ne donne pas une idée réelle des possibilités passées.

Espoir: des fouilles à Agra, où avaient lieu les petites Eleusinies de printemps, d'où possibilité de trouvailles pour nouveaux recoupements avec élimination correspondante de certaines hypothèses — Egalement des fouilles renouvelées sous la chapelle ortodoxe devant le bois sacré de l'acropole d'Eleusis, où se trouvait le *Temple* de Déméter (le Télestérion ou monument civil des initiations était construit au-dessus d'un μεγαρον où temple mycénien, peut-être d'origine en partie crétoise.).

B. Il ne faut pas sous-évaluer la portée psychologique et la valeur révélatrice de la pudique indignation et du dégoût furieux des Chrétiens ex-initiés d'Eleusis, pour lesquels le tabou sexuel chrétien revêtait toute son acuité et toute son intransigéance. Il est compréhensible que ces Chrétiens ex-initiés d'Eleusis aient rejeté avec horreur la mentalité mystico-symbolico-génésique des antiques cultes chthoniens et maternels, celle qui imprégnait le *secret central* de l'initiation éleusinienne, après avoir marqué les premiers cultes anthropomorphiques préhelléniques. Mais le témoignage de leur indignation n'en est que plus solide en faveur de l'hypothèse contemporaine de ce secret central (cf. 3 C).

Ne pas perdre de vue que parmi les Chrétiens déchaînés à mots couverts contre les indécences et les hontes d'Eleusis (Grégoire de Nazianze, Clément d'Alexandrie, Amasius, Hippolyte, etc....) beaucoup avaient étudié à Athènes, avaient pu être tentés par le prestige des Mystères d'Eleusis avant leur conversion personnelle au Christianisme, et que les rapports d'amitié entre l'empereur Julien l'Apostat et St. Grégoire de Nazianze dataient de leur enfance en CAPPADOCE et de leurs études à Athènes et appuient l'hypothèse de leur initiation éleusinienne.

Ne pas minimiser les nécessités de la polémique entre païens et Chrétiens et les ménagements obligés des adversaires opposant le Paradis ouranien, sévère et abstrait du Christianisme au Paradis chthonien, riant et parfumé, de Déméter, ni la gêne ou le ridicule que risquaient les Chrétiens ex-initiés d'Eleusis s'ils avaient avoué trop clairement ce qu'ils avaient dû voir, et faire, lors de leur initiation, ou s'ils avaient acculé leurs adversaires païens à leur en dire trop clairement le but et la signification.

3. Le secret central de l'initiation éleusinienne

A. Il s'agit de l'initiation aux *Grandes Eleusinies* d'automne (mois de Boedromion) et plus spécialement, du *premier grade* de cette initiation (bien que l'existence des cinq grades supérieurs ait pu, en présence du secret obligatoire, amener des confusions de rites partiels et de textes précis).

B. Les ouvrages généraux renseignés à la bibliographie du présent article présentent d'une façon excellente, sous des formes et à des points de vue divers, le spectacle d'ensemble des Grandes Eleusinies, jusqu'à — et parfois y compris — une conception de leur *secret central*.

C. De même qu'à un moment donné de son initiation le myste avait dit: ἐνήστευσα (j'ai jeûné, comme Déméter cherchant sa fille Corè) — ἔπιον τον κυκεῶνα (j'ai bu le cycéon) — ἐκ τύμπανου ἔφαγον (j'ai mangé du tympanon) — ἐκ κύμβαλου ἐπίον (j'ai bu au cymbalon), de même il dira plus tard, et en tout cas avant de recevoir le mot de passe pour l'Au-delà (le fameux „prends à droite"): ἔλαβον ἐκ κίστης — ἐργασάμενος — ἀπεθεμήν εἰς καλαθον, και ἐκ καλαθου εἰς κιστην.

C'est à dire:

J'ai pris hors de la Ciste — ayant manipulé j'ai mis dans la corbeille, et hors de la corbeille ... (j'ai remis) ... dans la Ciste. Mais qu'est-ce-qui a été pris, manipulé, et *replacé* dans la Ciste, (évidemment à l'intention et à l'usage du myste suivant)? Dans l'ambiance mystique de la préfiguration symbolico-génésique de la naissance à une seconde vie, une seule hypothèse est désormais retenue par l'immense majorité des spécialistes: Hors de la Ciste — souvent ornée d'un φαλλος et sur laquelle trône souvent Déméter — le myste doit prendre non seulement l'image — en métal ou en pâte de froment — d'un φαλλος. mais aussi celui d'un κτεις, celui de la grande Déesse Déméter. Il doit appliquer ce κτεις sur la statue d'or de la Déesse, simuler avec le φαλλος un rapprochement sexuel, mettre le φαλλος dans la corbeille en gardant le κτεις, poser le κτεις contre sa propre hanche et le faire descendre le long de sa propre cuisse pour simuler un accouchement ou en éveiller l'idée (et l'idée de sa seconde naissance comme enfant accouché par Déméter) et replacer le κτεις auprès du φαλλος dans la ciste, à l'usage du myste suivant (celui-ci peut d'ailleurs être du sexe féminin!)

D. Simple remarque d'ordre pratique: lorsqu'il y avait parfois jusqu'à trois mille mystes à initier, un rapide calcul permet de vérifier que les manipulations de la litt. C ne pouvaient être positivement effectuées par chacun d'eux, il aurait fallu de nombreux jours et de nombreuses nuits, et tout devait être terminé à l'aurore. Un mystagogue représentant de nombreux mystes, ou un myste „principal" choisi par le mystagogue et représentant de nombreux co-initiés, devait s'en charger à leur place.

E. Pour donner plus de poids à la seconde naissance liée aux manipulations de la litt. C, et *avant* de recevoir le mot de passe pour l'Au-delà (la branche droite de l'Y mystique), les mystes devaient assister dans la pénombre au ἱερος γαμος de Zeus et de Déméter, représenté par l'Hiérophante et la Grande-Prêtresse de Déméter. L'Hiérophante disait à la Grande-Prêtresse: ὕε-κύε — „pleus" — „conçois" (preuve nouvelle du caractère chthonien et agraire de Déméter) et aussitôt après: Brimô a enfanté Brimos, l'Auguste a enfanté le Sacré (c'est-à-dire le deutéroptomos).

F. Après le mot de passe, les mystes désormais les initiés, montaient à l'étage supérieur du Télestérion, où un lanterneau orienté vers l'est (ὀπαιον) leur fera voir le soleil levant du vingt-deux de Boedromion, dont les rayons viennent dorer d'abord un épi d'or (peut-être symbole phallique) tenu à bout de bras au-dessus de sa tête par l'Hiérophante, et inondé peu à peu toute la pièce, dernier spectacle d'éblouissement des initiés dans la technique d'alternance de ténèbres et de lumière éblouissante qui était à la base de l'initiation éleusinienne, qui n'était ni moralisatrice ni propédeutique mais devait frapper violemment comme un stigmate indélébile.

G. L'hypothèse symbolico-mystico-génésique décrite litt. C a trouvé un poids supplémentaire dans un élément plastique important, bas relief et peinture de vase, signalé par SAMTER (*Mysterienweihe*), MAGNIEN (*Les Mystères d'Eleusis*) et le *Bulletin communal de Rome* no. VII: Déméter assise sur la ciste s'entretient avec Corè debout, toutes deux ont une torche à la main, autour du corps de Déméter s'enroule le serpent chthonien dont la tête est caressée par Dionysos Bacchos. A côté, un myste voilé est assis, au-dessus de la tête duquel une hiérophantide secoue le van mystique (λίκνος). A côté le Hiérophante (avec bandelettes de tête et longue robe consacrée) tient à la main gauche un κυμβαλον contenant trois φαλλοι et il verse de la main droite de l'eau lustrale sur la tête d'un porcelet (symbolique des instincts inférieurs), maintenu la tête en bas par les pattes de derrière, par un myste en costume classique.

H. *Histoire des recherches modernes relatives aux Mystères d'Eleusis*

1°) Vers le milieu du XVIème siècle, les précurseurs immédiats et les maîtres de Jan VAN MEURS (1579-1639), qui publie en 1619 un important *Variorum Divinorum Liber unus*, plein de fragments importants pour les Mystères d'Eleusis.

2°) l'évêque anglican WARBURTON, qui vers 1740 lance la première hypothèse sur l'origine égyptienne des Mystères d'Eleusis dans ses *Essais sur les Hiéroglyphes*.

3°) LOBECK, qui, en 1829, donne une belle étude d'ensemble des Mystères d'Eleusis, mais essaie d'écarter le fait des manipulations génésiques en proposant: ἐγγευσάμενος au lieu de ἐργασάμενος („après avoir goûté" au lieu de „après avoir manipulé").

4°) les modernes: Goblet d'ALVIELLA (cf. la Migration des Symboles) — NOACK SAMTER — MÉAUTIS — MAGNIEN — FOUCART — LEGGE — DEUBNER — etc. . . . (cf. bibliographie). FOUCART essaie sans succès de reprendre la théorie égyptienne de WARBURTON.

5°) les contemporains: DESPLACES — FUSTIGIÈRE — DELATTE — OTTO KERN — PETTAZZONI — GUTHRIE — REITZENSTEIN — WOLTER — HEIGL — ZIELINSKI — etc. . . . (cf. Bibliographie).

Résumé général de quatre siècles de recherches, d'hypothèses, et de recoupements: *le secret central de l'initiation d'Eleusis est mystico-symbolico-génésique*, comme il a été dévelloppé au 3 C.

BIBLIOGRAPHIE

I. Auteurs grecs, romains, et latins (chrétiens) étudiés par les auteurs des ouvrages cités plus loin (en II et III):

Apollodore d'Athènes, Apulée, Aristide-Aelius, Aristote, Aristophane, Cicéron, Diogène Laërce, Diodore de Sicile, Denys d'Halicarnasse, Eschyle, Euripide, Hérodote, Hésiode, Isocrate, Jamblique, Kallimaque d'Alexandrie, Lucien, Ménandre, Pausanias, Philistrate l'Athénien, Pindare, Platon, Porphyre, Simonide de Céos, Sophocle, Strabon, Thucydide, Xénophon — et l'Hymne (pseudo-) homérique à Déméter — en outre Clément d'Alexandrie, St Grégoire de Nazianze, Lactance, St Hippolyte, Tertullien, Astérius d'Amasia, et l'auteur des Philosophouména.

II. Auteurs modernes en Français (originals ou traductions):

Goblet d'ALVIELLA, *Une initiation aux Mystères d'Eleusis*, 1898.
Paul FOUCART, *Les Mystères d'Eleusis*, 1914.
Victor MAGNIEN, *Les Mystères d'Eleusis*, 1929.
George MÉAUTIS, *Les mystères d'Eleusis*, 1934.
Maurice BRILLANT et René AIGRAIN (dans *Histoire des Religions*, 1916): „Les Mystères d'Eleusis — Orphisme et Pythagorisme".

Richard KREGLINGER, *l'Evolution religieuse de l'Humanité.*
LOISY, *Les Mystères païens et le mystère chrétien*, 1930.
Jeanne CROISSANT, *Aristote et les Mystères* (*thèse publiée par l'Université de Liège*, 1926).
Thadée ZIELINSKI, *La Religion de la Grèce antique*, 1926.
PRZYLUSKI, *La Grande Déesse*, 1950.
P. GRIMAL, *Dictionnaire mythologique.*
FESTUGIÈRE (A. J.), *Religion personnelle*, 1954.
R. PETTAZZONI, *la Religion dans la Grèce antique*, 1953.
GUTHRIE (W. K. C.), *Les Grecs et leurs Dieux*, 1951.
M. P. NILSON *La Religion populaire dans la Grèce antique*, 1954.
Armand DELATTE, *Le Cycéon*, 1957.
P. DES PLACES, ,,Mystères d'Eleusis" dans *Histoire des Religions* de BLOND et GAY, 1955.
DARENBERG et SAGLIO, *Dictionnaire des Antiquités grecques et romaines* (édition Hachette).
Louis GREUNING, *l'Initiation de Cicéron aux Mystères d'Eleusis*, 1950.

III. Auteurs modernes en d'autres langues:

a) *allemand*

Chr. A. LOBECK, *Aglaophamos ou Théologie mystique des Grecs* (*surtout en latin*), 1829.
RUBENSOHN, *Die Mysterienheiligentümer in Eleusis*, 1892.
R. REITZENSTEIN, *Die Hellenistischen Mysterienreligionen*, 1927.
E. SAMTER, *Die Religion der Griechen*, 1914.
HEIGL, *Antike Mysterienreligionen und Urchristentum*, 1932.
E. NOACK et Ludwig ZIEHEN dans GNOMON 1929. (pp. 228, 229, 238, 152).
THASSILO DE SCHEFFER, *Hellenische Mysterien*, 1943.
DEUBNER, *Zum Weihehaus der Eleusinischen Mysterien*, 1946.
KERN, Otto, *Die Eleusinischen Mysterien*, 1927.
Ulrich von WILAMOWITZ-MOELLENDORF, *Der Glaube der Hellenen*, 1949.
PRÜMM, *Die Religion der Griechen*, 1930.

b) *italien*

Nicola TURCHI, *Religioni misteriche*, 1948.

c) *néerlandais*:

Albert ZWART, *Heidense en Kristelijke Mysterien*, 1946.

d) *anglais*

F. LEGGE, *Forerunners and Rivals of Christianity*, 1915.
H. R. WILLOUGHBY, *Pagan Regeneration and Mystery Initiations*, 1929.
G. E. MYLONAS, *Eleusis and the Eleusisian Mysteries*, 1960.
George THEMISTOCLES MALTESO, *Eleusis and Mysteries*, 1961.

INITIATION IN LATER HINDUISM ACCORDING TO TANTRIC TEXTS

BY

D. J. HOENS
Utrecht

1. *Introduction*

Mircea ELIADE in the third impression of the German encyclopedia *Die Religion in Geschichte und Gegenwart* describes initiation as follows: "Initiation ist die Bezeichnung für eine Folge von Riten und Unterweisungen mit deren Hilfe eine radikale Änderung des religiösen und sozialen Status des Einzuweihenden herbeigeführt wird." [1]

This definition indicates the formal, phenomenological framework of this lecture.

Now, as is well known, initiation in this sense occurs already in the texts dealing with the Vedic-Brahmanic period of the history of Indian religion.

Several forms of initiation can be traced here.

a. Firstly the so-called *upanayana* ("leading to himself": i.e. "the guru leads the pupil to himself".[2]) In ancient India every young man belonging to the three higher classes of society had to be instructed in certain rites, texts, and their interpretations. Without this instruction the man could not act as a full member of his class. Now the upanayana rite gave him admission to this instruction.[3]

b. Another form of initiation was the *dīkṣā*, the "consecration". The term is perhaps a derivation of the desiderative of the root *dakṣ*, which means "to be able, to be fit".[4]

By means of the *dīkṣā-rite* the institutor of a sacrifice (the *yajamāna*) and his wife become fit for participation in the performance of a soma-sacrifice.[5]

---

[1] See *o.c.* Tübingen 1959, vol. III, col. 751.
[2] See M. MONIER WILLIAMS, *A Sanskrit-english dictionary*, Oxford 1899, p. 201.
[3] Cf. M. ELIADE, *Naissances mystiques*[6], 1959, pp. 113-115.
[4] See MONIER WILLIAMS in *o.c.* p. 480.
[5] Cf. P. V. KANE, *History of Dharmaśāstra*, Porna 1941, II[II] pp. 1133 ff.

c. Sometimes the dīkṣā is followed by an *abhiṣeka*, an aspersion-rite. So the king was *aspersed* during the consecration ceremony.[1]

d. In ancient *Buddhism* adherents who wished to become monks had to pass through *two* initiation ceremonies: first the *pravrajya*, "going away (sc. from the family)", this can be considered a parallel of the upanayana and secondly, the *upasampadā*: "the arrival (sc. of the aspirant in the community of monks)".[2]

These forms of initiation being generally known it would not be superfluous to make further investigations into them in detail but I shall not deal with them here.

In this lecture I hope to give you some information on the dīkṣā in *later* Hinduism, according to Tantric texts.

This title includes two restrictions. Firstly, that we deal with one *form* of initiation only, and secondly that we confine ourselves to the *Tantric* current in the tradition of later Hinduism.

These tantric schools, however, represent a very important part of the whole later Hindu tradition. In this context it may be remembered that the fact that the well-known schools of Kashmir Śaivism, the Śaiva Siddhānta, the Vīraśaiva on one hand and the Śrī Vaiṣṇava school,[3] the school of *Rāmānuja* on the other hand, all belong to this Tantric current of tradition. Another point which can be mentioned is the great number of Tantric scriptures which are the vehicles of this tradition.[4] Many of these have already been edited. Unfortunately we know very little about the time and the circles in which these scriptures originated.

The material for this lecture has been drawn from those texts which I had access to and could study. I mention:

1. the *Tantrasāra of Abhinavagupta*[5]—a work which may be dated in the twelfth century—

2. the *Rauravāgama*.[6]—It is a pity that this text which is one of the

---

[1] Cf. J. C. HEESTERMAN, *The Ancient Indian royal consecration*, 's-Gravenhage 1957, pp. 114 ff.

[2] Cf. J. TAKASUKU in *Hasting's Encyclopedia of Religion and Ethics*, Edinburgh 1925, vol. 7, pp. 319-320.

[3] As to these schools see *The cultural heritage of India*[2], vol. IV, Religions ed. by H. BHATTACHARYYA, Calcutta 1956, pp. 79 ff.; 74 ff.; 98 ff and 163 ff. and J. GONDA, *Die Religionen Indiens II*, Stuttgart 1963, pp. 224 ff.; 229 ff.; 243 ff. and 131 ff.

[4] Cf. *The cultural heritage*, pp. 220 ff.

[5] Edited in *Kashmir Series of Texts and Studies* no. XVII, Bombay 1918.

[6] Edited by M. BHATT as *Publications de l'Institut Français d'Indologie* no. 18, Pondichéry 1961.

main original sources of the Śaivasiddhānta, in its already published parts gives no description of the ritual of the dīkṣā.

3. The *Iśānaśivagurudevapaddhati*, a Śaiva Tantric manual edited in the Trivandrum Sanskrit Series [1] especially part III on the *kriyāpāda*—

4. the *Kulārṇava Tantra* edited by Sir J. WOODROFFE in his Tantric texts.[2]

Moreover I must mention:

T. A. GOPINATHA RAO, *Elements of Hindu Iconography, II, I*,[3]
V. A. DEVASENAPATHI, *The Saiva Siddhānta*;[4]
S. C. NANDIMATH, *A Handbook of Vīra Śaivism*, [5]
K. RANGACHARI, *The Sri Vaisnava Brahmans*;[6]
R. V. JOSHI, *Le Rituel de la devotion Krṣṇaite*;[7]
E. THURSTON, *Castes and Tribes of Southern India*,[8] Vol. IV s.v. Lingāyats; Vol. VI s.v. Pandaram;
H. V. NANJUDAYYA & C.K. ANATAKRISHNA IYER, *The Mysore Tribes and Castes*,[9] *Vol. IV*. s.v. Saivas;
and some more works of Sir J. WOODROFFE.[10]

Considering the small quantity of texts and taking into consideration the variations in the data of these texts, nobody could be more convinced of the rather provisional character of several of my statements than the present lecturer.

2. *Dīkṣā*

a. First some remarks about the person who wishes to be initiated. He commonly is called *śiṣya*—pupil. Not everybody can be initiated; he has to come up to certain requirements. The pupil has to see a

---

[1] Vol. LXXVII Trivandrum 1922 especially Patalas 16, 17, 18 pp. 137 ff.

[2] *Kulārṇava Tantra* ed. by T. VIDYĀRATNA in *Tantrik Texts* vol. V, London 1917 especially 14: 17, 19, 20, 23, 24 p. 210.

[3] Madras 1916 especially pp. 6-15.

[4] Madras 1960 especially pp. 233 ff.

[5] Dharwar 1942 especially pp. 66 ff.

[6] Madras 1931 especially pp. 34 ff. and 101 ff.

[7] *Publications de l'Institut Français d'Indologie* no. 17, Pondichçry 1959, especially chapt. II pp. 8-28.

[8] Madras 1909 vol. IV pp. 263 ff.; vol. VI pp. 45 ff.

[9] Mysore 1931, vol. IV pp. 91 ff.

[10] *Principles of Tantra*[2], Madras 1952; *Introduction to Tantra Śāstra*[3], Madras 1956 and Sv. PRATYAGĀTMĀNANDA SARASWATĪ and Sir J. WOODROFFE, *Sādhana for self-realization*, Madras 1963.

guru who is qualified to initiate him. The pupil must be carefully watched to see whether he is of good intention (*sat*) and whether he is devoted (*bhakta*) to the guru. The latter has to test him as to his insight (*jñāna*) and his ritual performance (*kriyā*), each for half a year. The guru treats him respectfully when the latter is doing menial work, and contemptuously when he has to do higher work. The pupil must honour the guru under all circumstances and finally must show signs of religious emotion.[1]

b. The function of the guru in the dīkṣā is an essential one as might have already been concluded from my foregoing remarks. There can be no dīkṣā without a guru. He watches the pupil during the period of preparation for the dīkṣā; he performs the initiation rites, he further instructs the initiated pupil in the holy utterances (*mantra*) which he has to mutter daily, in his future conduct, in the form of yoga to which he has to devote himself, and in theological and mystical knowledge. He also decides when the pupil will be able to undergo another dīkṣā.[2] The guru, according to the Kulārṇava Tantra is "*Śiva* without having three eyes, *Viṣṇu* without having four arms, and also *Brahmā* without four heads". "O, Pārvatī, there is no difference at all between the god Sadāśiva and the venerable guru. He who makes a difference between them commits a sin".[3] At the same time, however, he is a human being, whose ability has to be examined.[4] "Both the guru and the pupil who, being spiritually blind, instructs or is instructed without mutual examination will become Piśācas (demons)".[5]

3. *Several Forms of Dīkṣā*

Let us now consider the dīkṣā ceremonies. The texts distinguish between several forms of it. Thus there is a *spṛṣadīkṣā*: "consecration by touching". This means that the guru, by concentration produces Śiva, as a guru, on his arm; then he mutters a certain mantra and touches the body of the pupil on several spots.[6] The meaning of this rite is clear. In touching the pupil's body by the arm which is Śiva,

---

[1] As to these data see *Kulārṇava Tantra* pp. 209, 210.
[2] On guru see A. AVALON, *Principles of Tantra*², Madras 1952, pp. 798, 815, 816.
[3] See *Kulārṇava Tantra* 13:57, 61 p. 198.
[4] See *o.c.* 14:25, 26 p. 211.
[5] See *o.c.* 14:11 p. 209.
[6] Cf. *o.c.* 14:53 p. 214 and *Īśānaśivagurudevapaddhati* III, 16: 15 p. 138.

the former would participate in the communion with Śiva, indeed, even would become Śiva.

Another form of dīkṣā is the vāgdīkṣā: "the consecration by the voice." "The guru, having identified the found with the essence by concentration *samādhāya*, pronounces several interconnected mantras which are powerful by the highest principle".[1]) This means by concentration, having identified the visible reality with the essential reality, pronounces several interconnected mantras which draw their power from the name of the highest principle, the Absolute. These mantras consist of three syllables of the mūlamantra (main mantra of the school) combined with some very sacred sounds such as hṛiṃ, krīṃ, huṃ. All together they represent the divine reality and power. By muttering these mantras in the ear of the pupil the guru causes the divine reality and power to penetrate and transform the pupil.

A third form of dīkṣā is called the *nayanadīkṣā* or *dṛkdīkṣā*: "the consecration by seeing". The guru having closed his eyes, and with a calm mind concentrates the highest Principle (the Absolute) in his eye, and then looks at the pupil in the right way.[2]) Whereas the 'evil eye' harms beings by its destructive power, here the divine eye gives its brilliance and its essence to the pupil. In a similar way there are other forms of dīkṣā, such as: the *manasādīkṣā*, that is "the consecration by the mind". The guru has the way to liberation in his mind and then concentrates on the pupil and so purifies him and liberates him from all evil;[3]) the *yoga dīkṣā*: "the consecration by yoga". The guru instructs the pupil in one of the existing forms of yoga by means of which the latter comes to Śiva;[4]) and finally, the *kriyādīkṣā*: "the consecration by ritual acts" such as oblations and sacrifices.[5]) I shall return to this later on.

The texts make yet another distinction between dīkṣās, namely between the *samaya*- and the *nirvāṇadīkṣā*. In the practice of Indian religion this distinction has been of much greater importance than the list of dīkṣās we have mentioned before. The books of Gopinatha Rao, Rangachari, Devasenapathi [6]) and others prove to us that these dīkṣās are still in existance. The first dīkṣā, the *samaya*—so called be-

---

[1]) See, *o.c.* 14: 54 p. 214 and *Īśāna* III, 16: 16 p. 138.
[2]) See *o.c.* 14: 55 p. 214 and *Īśāna* III, 16: 17 p. 138.
[3]) Cf. *o.c.* 14: 57, 58 p. 215 and *Īśāna* III, 16: 19, p. 138.
[4]) Cf. DEVASENAPATHI *o.c.*, pp. 239 ff.
[5]) Cf. *Īśāna* III, 16: 13, 14 p. 138.
[6]) In *o.c.*; l.c.

cause it unites the pupil with the deity [1])—is the normal rite by which the initiated becomes a member of a religious group. The other type, the *nirvāṇadīkṣā* is prescribed for anyone who is going to become a temple priest or a guru. It is, however, not only modern authors who especially mention these dīkṣās. Abhinavagupta in his *Tantrasāra* already gives an elaborate description of these two dīkṣās only.[2]) So does the *Īśānaśivagurudevapaddhati*.[3]) I cannot deal with the whole complicated ritual now. I can only try to give you a general idea, with some details, which, according to me, are important for the purpose of this lecture.

samayadīkṣā

As in the Vedic dīkṣā a hut with four door openings to the four points of compass is erected.[4]) In the centre of it a jar is placed into which the main god is called. It is clear that the hut represents the universe, of which the deity is the centre.

The person to be initiated, first has to look at the *aṅkurārpaṇam*, the so-called "seed-sowing rite". In this rite, first, mud with several kinds of grain seeds is placed in jars and afterwards some young plants of several kinds of grain.[5]) So it is a rite which symbolizes and represents the arising of new life.

The ritual of the dīkṣā is not always the same. The sequence of the acts is not always identical, sometimes the rites themselves vary.[6])

There are many preliminaries, such as worshipping and consecrating the great jar into which the main god is called, and the appeasing of the mantras which are used.[7]) After that, the pupil whose eyes are blindfolded, is led several times round the hut by the guru and finally led inside. He sits down on a special seat with his face turned to the North East. The bandage over his eyes is removed and he now may look at the great jar, which represents the main deity.[8]) The guru lays his right hand, which is the hand of Śiva himself, on the head of

---

[1]) Cf. *Tantrasāra* p. 149 and *Īśāna* III, 16: 19 p. 138.

[2]) See *o.c.* Ahnikas 13 and 14, pp. 133-161.

[3]) See *Patalas* 16, 17, 18 pp. 137-186.

[4]) Cf. *Tantrasāra* pp. 133, 143; *Īśāna* III, 16: 23 ff.; RANGACHARI *o.c.* p. 101 and GOPINĀTHA RAO *o.c.*, p. 11.

[5]) Cf. RAURĀVĀGAMA pp. 65-67 and RANGACHARI *o.c.*, pp. 101 ff.

[6]) Cf. *Tantrasāra* pp. 138 ff and GOPINATHA RAO *o.c.*; l.c.

[7]) Cf. *Tantrasāra* pp. 144, 145, GOPINĀTHA RAO *o.c.*; l.c. and RANGACHARI *o.c.*; l.c.

[8]) Cf. *Tantrasāra* p. 146 and *Īśāna* III, 16: 57 p. 145.

the pupil and mutters into his ear the mantra which he has henceforth to recite daily. This mantra is very difficult to understand and is elaborately explained by the guru. By means of this rite the *śakti* (energy) of the deity is thought to have descended upon the pupil.[1]) The latter kneels down and throws the flowers which he holds in his hand, away, in the direction of the great jar, round which a *yantra*, a cosmic diagram has been drawn on the earth. The part of the diagram on which the flowers descend, determines which god henceforth is to be worshipped by the pupil as his *iṣṭadevatā*, (his chosen deity), his tutelary deity whose name he will now bear.[2])

In the next rite, the guru, with his right hand touches the head, the place of the heart, and of the navel of the pupil in order to remove the *pāśas*, the "bonds" by which he is bound, and throws them into the fire. With the left hand he touches the same places, but in reverse, muttering a certain mantra, the *Śuddhatattvāpyayanam*, i.e. "which makes the pure principles thrive".[3]) These are the principles of which the universe as the macrocosmos and of which the human being as the microcosmos consist. In this way the pupil has become an *aṃśa* (part) of Rudra, a particular form of Śiva.[4])

I should like to stress two points of this ritual.

Firstly: There are several rites such as the leading of the pupil into the hut, the communication of the mantra and the purification of the pupil which all have the same meaning, namely: the introduction of the pupil into the world of the gods in general and that of a certain god in particular. This means a new creation, a new birth of the pupil (symbolized by being blindfolded, receiving a new name and pure principles).

Secondly: the pupil is introduced into a new cult. This also implies a new pattern of socio-religious conduct. So the initiated one should honour the guru and not perform vulgar acts in his presence. An initiated Śaiva should not mix with Vaiṣṇavas and other people who have inferior views. And so on.[5])

The second form of dīkṣā which we come across in the texts is the *nirvāṇadīkṣā*. It is of a higher grade than the *samaya* and can only be taken by those pupils who always have fulfilled their religious duties

---

[1]) Cf. *Tantrasāra o.c.*; l.c.
[2]) Cf. *Īśāna* p. 146.
[3]) Cf. *Tantrasāra* p. 147 and *Īśāna* pp. 147, 148.
[4]) Cf. *Tantrasāra* p. 149 and *Īśāna* p. 148.
[5]) Cf. *Tantrasāra* pp. 150-154.

very strictly.[1]) Again, it is the guru who determines if the pupil is ripe for the nirvāṇadīkṣā.

I want to stress three important points from the ritual of this dīkṣā. Firstly, the purification of the six *adhvas* (paths) takes place. This is to say that by means of oblations the six different components of the pupil are purified. These components are *mantras*, *padas* (syllables), *varṇas* (letters), *tattvas* (principles), *bhuvanas* (worlds) and finally, *kalās*. The latter are five in number each consisting of certain mantras, padas, varṇas, tattvas, and bhuvanas, and each being a manifestation of a special śakti and connected with its own deity: so, for instance, the fifth state, which is the highest one, has Sadāśiva himself for its deity.[2]) In this way the pupil, by means of sacrifices is integrated with the universe and its divine centre.

A second rite to which I should like to draw your attention shows the liberation of the pāśas in a realistic way. Threads are fastened to the pupil's body from the hairtuft to his toes. Then the mind of the pupil is called into these threads. The guru meditates upon the several lives of the pupil. Then the threads are cut into pieces and cast into the fire.[3]) Or a string is twined round the pupil's body as many times as there are tattvas. Afterwards the string is cut into pieces according to the number of tattvas and cast into the fire.[4]) Finally the guru pronounces the tattvas in *sṛṣṭikrama*—cosmogonical sequence —and touches the body of the pupil at several places. The latter now is definitely liberated from all pāśas and is a new creature.[5])

The nirvāṇadīkṣā further knows a special form of yoga by means of which the pupil is able to reach *Śivapada*, the abode of Śiva.[6]) The man who has been initiated to the nirvāṇa has special rights and special duties. As the underlying ideas of both dīkṣās are the same, namely an introduction into the divine world and a new birth it might be asked, what is the difference between them? According to the Śaivasiddhānta tradition in the *samayadīkṣā* the pupil is liberated from certain *pāśas* only, whereas in the nirvāṇa all pāśas are definitely destroyed and the pupil gets the six qualities of Śiva himself.[7])

Further, after the first dīkṣā, man is only entitled to perform the

---

[1]) Cf. *Īśāna* III, 16: 19 p. 138.
[2]) Cf. *Tantrasāra* p. 158 and *Īśāna* pp. 149 ff.
[3]) Cf. GOPINĀTHA RAO *o.c.*, pp. 13 f. and *Īśāna* III, 16: 20 p. 138.
[4]) Cf. RANGACHARI *o.c.*, pp. 103 ff.
[5]) Cf. RANGACHARI *o.c.*; l.c.
[6]) Cf. *Īśāna* III, 16: 20 p. 138.
[7]) Cf. GOPINĀTHA RAO *o.c.* pp. 13, 14.

daily pūjā, whereas after the *nirvāṇa* he is qualified to perform all public rites or to become a guru.[1]) These functions of a priest and a guru he can only perform after having received an aspersion (*abhiṣeka*). The aspirant is aspersed by means of a liquid—water or wine—out of a jar into which Śiva has been called.[2]) The meaning is quite clear. Of course the accompanying mantras are different according to the purpose. Sometimes these abhiṣekas are also called dīkṣā.[3]) When we survey the *samaya-* and *nirvāṇadīkṣā* it is clear that they are a mixture of the different kinds of dīkṣā which have been discussed first, namely, *spṛśa-*, *vāg-*, *yoga-*, and *kriyādīkṣā*.

There is a third list of four dīkṣās in the texts: *kriyā-*; *varṇa-* (letter); *kalā-* and *vedha-*dīkṣā.[4]) The kriyā such as *samaya-* and *nirvāṇadīkṣā* are for those who have only minor religious "insight". The *varṇadīkṣā* is for those who have higher qualifications. It runs as follows: the guru lays down the letters of the alphabet in the shape of the pupil; then he gathers them again in the reverse order, "in this way uniting the spirit of the pupil with the highest Self." Further the guru lays down the letters again in the shape of the pupil. Thus his divine nature (*devatābhāva*) arises, full of bliss.[5]) Pupils who have still greater spiritual insight may be initiated by means of the *kalādīkṣā*. The five kalās which have been mentioned before and according to which the human mind and body is divided, will be meditated upon in yoga by the guru from numbers one to five.[6]) Number 1 corresponds with the legs up to the knees and 5 corresponds with the forehead to the skull. Thus the pupil is taken up into the divine centre of the universe, the supreme deity.

The shortest way to liberation and bliss is the *vedhadīkṣā*: "consecration by piercing" which is the same as the *manasādīkṣā* which has already been mentioned.[7])

Thus the dīkṣā is an important phenomenon in later Hinduism. No wonder that the *Rauravāgama* says: "As darkness, having reached dawn, disappears quickly, so man having reached dīkṣā is liberated from good and evil (*dharmairadharmaiḥ*)".[8])

---

[1]) Cf. GOPINATHA RAO *o.c.*, p. 15 and *Tantrasāra* pp. 173 ff.

[2]) Cf. GOPINATHA RAO *o.c.*; l.c. and *Mahānirvāṇa Tantra* in *Tantrik Texts*, vol. XIII Calcutta/London 1929 X: 140-143; 160-181 pp. 307, 311-313.

[3]) Cf. DEVASENAPATHI *o.c.*, p. 240 and C. G. DIEHL, *Instrument and purpose, Studies in rites and rituals in S. India*, Lund 1956 pp. 51, 52 note 5.

[4]) Cf. *Kulārṇava* 14: 39 ff. pp. 212 ff.   [5]) Cf. *o.c.* 14: 42-45 p. 213.

[6]) Cf. *o.c.* 14: 46-50 p. 214.   [7]) Cf. *o.c.*, 14: 57-63 p. 215.

[8]) Appendix I, Dīkṣāvargaḥ 3.

"As water which is poured out into water, and as milk which is added to milk, so the mantraknower by means of the dīkṣā turns to union (with the deity)" And the *Kulārṇāva* Tantra states briefly: "Without dīkṣā no liberation (*mokṣa*).[1])

Nevertheless we should not forget that the dīkṣā is not always directly connected with liberation. The *samayadīkṣā* with appropriate mantras may also serve other purposes, as for instance, to obtain wealth, to gain superiority over enemies, and so on.[2]) So they can have the same function as the *kāmyeṣṭis* in the Vedic-Brahmanic period of Indian religion.[3])

When we now briefly summarise, we may say: the dīkṣā according to Tantric texts is a ceremony which *can* consist of rites or words or yoga or religious insight, but in practice most probably actually consists of a mixture of these elements. The dīkṣā requires a mutual examination of the master and the pupil. The underlying conceptions of the dīkṣā are: purification, a new creation and a new birth, and reaching the sphere of a deity. By the dīkṣā the pupil becomes qualified to perform the daily rites or to become a priest or a guru of a certain religious group, and has to act according to certain standards.

The term religious does, however, not imply that the dīkṣā only serves the purpose of final liberation (*mokṣa*); it may also serve the desire for well being in daily life.

---

[1]) 14: 3 p. 208.

[2]) Cf. DIEHL *o.c.*; l.c. and JOSHI *o.c.* p. 27.

[3]) Cf. W. CALAND, *Altindische Zauberei, Darstellung der altindischen Wunschopfer*, Amsterdam 1908.

DĪKṢĀ

BY

A. BASU

University of Durham, England

The Sanskrit word *Dīkṣā* which is translated by 'initiation' in English means many things. Consecration, e.g. as a king, dedication to a noble cause, serious preparation for any undertaking, e.g. for battle, complete restriction or resignation to a particular thing, exclusive preoccupation with something, a rite e.g. that of marriage entry into a certain stage of life and its attendant duties and responsibilities e.g. *brahmacarya* which is the stage of moral training and intellectual and practical education, devotion to a person or God, initiation into spiritual life—all these meanings are covered by *dīkṣā*. There is an underlying significance common to all these meanings of this comprehensive term, namely, the entry into a new stage of life with its appropriate duties and responsibilities the successful discharge of which require special training and also the rites marking this entry. We shall in this paper deal with diksha as initiation into spiritual life, as commonly understood in Hinduism.

It is well-known that Hinduism makes a distinction between *dharma* and *mokṣa*. Life according to dharma, moral law, is or may be a preparation for the pursuit of *mokṣa*, spiritual liberation. A seeker of liberation must be initiated into spiritual life, that is, the kind of life that will lead him to Freedom. That life includes certain disciplines. What specific disciplines a particular seeker will be taught depends on the particular tradition of *yoga* which he chooses and to which he is called. Just as the idea of moksha is not the same in the different schools of Hinduism, so also the teachings and the disciplines given to all seekers are not identical. But just as there is a common idea among the different conceptions of liberation, so also there are certain features in the various disciplines which are identical. And initiation is indispensable whatever tradition of spiritual discipline a seeker is guided to follow. That which gives pure Knowledge, exhausts *karma* and desire for *karma*, confers Divinity and cuts the thread of sin is famed as diksha.

Why is initiation indispensable? Man is separated from the Ground of his being, is ignorant of the real nature of his true Self and thus of his relationship with the Reality. All his imperfection and suffering is due to this ignorance. Liberation the goal of spiritual life, is release from *Māyā*, the Cosmic Ignorance, due to which there is loss of awareness of the real nature of the true Self of man. Knowledge therefore is essentially necessary for liberation. But even to begin the practice of the disciplines which will enable him to rend the veil of Ignorance, man must have an initial contact with something beyond Maya, indeed he must have the touch of the Reality. Diksha is the means of establishing this necessary contact between the seeker and the Ground of his being which is in its nature free. Diksha is thus the infusion of Spirit into man. It is the transmission of spiritual force or substance into the aspirant.

The monistic spiritual philosophies in Hinduism are of the view that the main purpose of diksha is to rouse or unveil the Spirit which is inherent in man. In whatever manner initiation may be interpreted, whether it is the transmission of spiritual substance-force into a seeker or it is the unveiling of the Relity in him, our main point remains unaffected. For even in the monistic systems it is admitted that the Supreme Self shows itself to him whom it chooses.[1]) In the dualistic systems, that is, in those philosophies which do not accept the identity of the individual Self with the Supreme Self, the former is still *ātman* and of the same nature as the latter. In others words, both *Jīva* and *Īśvara* are *cit*, pure Consciousness, essentially free, uncreated, distinct from mind, life-force and body. But liberation in these systems which include union with God, can not be attained unless knowledge of the true spiritual Self is obtained. And for that initiation is necessary. The point is that man in the world is a mixture of *cit* and *acit*, Consciousness and unconscious principles viz. mind, life-force and matter. He therefore needs something from outside of his formed nature, with which he mistakenly identifies himself, to open the way to the realisation of the Self in him and its relation with the Reality, however that relation may be conceived—union with Ishwara in the dualistic systems or identity with Brahman in the monistic ones. The answer to this need may be called Grace, though not always in the same sense as in Christianity.

A word must be said about the monistic systems which unlike the

---

[1]) Katha Upanishad, I. 2. 23 and Shankara's commentary on it.

Adwaita philosophy of Shankara proclaim both the identity of the
Supreme Self and the individual Self *and* the reality of the latter. In
these systems—the Trika philosophy or Kashmir Shaivism and the
Integral Adwaita of Sri Aurobindo are examples—the Supreme Self
through its dynamic Consciousness-Force manifests istelf as many
individual selves. Here also, indeed more than in other systems, the
Power of *anugraha* or Grace is ultimately the most important thing for
liberation. It should be mentioned that in the Trika philosophy
liberation is a much more comprehensive goal than in the pure
adawaita of Shankara or in the dualistic systems like those of Rama-
nuja and Madhva. Sri Aurobindo's ideal is not only the freedom from
our ignorant nature, not only union with God and identity with the
Absolute but also the realisation of all the aspects of the Divine and
added to all that, the liberation of nature also. In other words, it is
not enough to attain liberation from the tharldom of mind, life-force
and body and to realise the Reality in all its aspects—transcendent,
universal and individual, static and dynamic, Being and Becoming,
Impersonal and Personal as that which becomes through self-limi-
tation mind, life-force and body, the One and Many—but there must
also be the descent of the creative Knowledge—Will of the Divine
into ordinary nature and its supramental transformation through
that. This is the end of the Integral Yoga. Not only can this not be
attained except through the Grace of the Divine but also the yoga can
not be started without it. It is God's Power in us which functions
as aspiration and will to spiritual life which is the first step of the yoga
of Aurobindo.

The seeker is initiated into spiritual life by the Guru. The Guru
teaches dharma and delivers from Ignorance. Truly speaking the
Reality in its aspect of the intermediary between the spiritual soul in
bondage and its own Freedom is the Guru. It is secretly lodged in the
heart-cave of man and when the time comes, it opens the eyes of the
seeker blinded by Ignorance with Knowledge. Man however needs
something more concrete and an Incarnation of God takes on the
role of the Guru. Krishna, Buddha, Christ are World-Teachers and
to humanity groping in darkness they are like the effulgent Sun
dispelling the veil of Ignorance and suffering and sin. The Prophets
and the Rishis also fulfil the function of the Guru as they act as chan-
nels of the Divine as Teacher. But man finds it necessary to have a
living person to give him guidance, to teach him, to act as an example
and influence and inspire him through silence or words to spiritual

effort. Hinduism believes that certain human beings can be gurus and have the capacity of initiating others into spiritual life. It must be remembered however that the doctrine is that it is God who is still the true guru and the human guru is only a representative of the Divine in his aspect of the Saviour and Liberator and Teacher. Just as the different atmans are manifestations of the Atman, so also gurus are expressions of the One Guru. When the Hindu says 'my Guru is the World Guru, my *nātha*, master, is the Lord of the world', what he really means is that God is his Guru and Master.

It is primarily because of this that the disciple should revere his guru. Faith, humility and obedience to the guru are virtues which the disciple must have. These help develop the right attitude in him and changes his temperament and purifies his *buddhi*, intelligence, in a way that it becomes receptive and reflects the Light of Atman-Consciousness shining upon it. They also enable those who are *bhakta*, devotees, to develop loving adoration for the Divine Beloved and the capacity to receive the love of the Supreme Lover. To please the guru is essential because it is his Grace and powerful blessings which assure success for the seeker-disciple. There are stories in the Upanishads of how disciples had spiritual illumination not so much through yoga but by pleasing their respective gurus who just said: 'Let all the wisdom of the Veda be revealed in you' and the disciples became knowers of Truth. In the guru occurs the miraculous fusion of the Divine and the human. That is why while the disciple looks upon his guru as Divine in so far as he is guru, the spiritual preceptor makes it clear to the disciple that it is the manifestation of the Saviour and Teacher aspect of the Divine in him that makes him a guru. The following words of Sri Aurobindo regarding the guru of the Integral Yoga could be applied to all genuine teachers: '. . . he does not arrogate to himself Guruhood in a humanly vain and self-exalting spirit. His work, if he has one, is a trust from above, he himself a channel, a vessel or a representative. He is a man helping his brothers, a child leading children, a Light kindling other lights, an awakened Soul awakening souls, at highest a Power or Presence of the Divine calling to him other powers of the Divine'.[1])

There are many means of giving initiation, many are the rites of diksha. The transmission of the spirit-force and spirit-substance can be done by the guru just by looking at the candidate for initiation or

---

[1]) The Synthesis of Yoga, The Sri Anrobindo Library Inc. New York, 1950, p. 18.

by touching him, in dreams in which case however it is said that the initiation should be repeated during waking hours, and by *mantra*. A mantra is a word or a collection of words charged with spiritual power. It can purify the mind and heart of the seeker, it helps concentration. It is authoritatively said that spiritual perfection is certain as a result of *japa* or repetition of a mantra. The Names of God are also mantra. 'The *mantra*', says Sri Aurobindo, 'is a direct and most hightened, an intensest and most divinely burdened rhythmic word which embodies an intuitive and revelatory inspiration and ensouls the reality of things and with its truth and with the divine soul-forms of it, the Godheads which are born from the living truth. Or, let us say, it is a supreme rhythmic language which seizes hold upon all that is finite and brings into each the light and voice of its own infinite'.

We have referred to Kashmir Shaivism above. It should be mentioned that according to this system, initiation by a human guru is not indispensable. On the other hand it is Shiva's Power of Grace that starts a spiritual pilgrim on the journey to his goal which in this case is the recognition of the limited self as Shiva and through this recognition, the realisation of identity with everything as the glory of one's own absolute Self's manifestation.

Diksha thus is the transmission of the Spirit into man enabling him to realise his true self as spirit. All initiation is from Heaven.

(1) In the approach to the Reality through various *sādhanās*, spiritual paths, the Gods and Goddesses may and do play a prominent part. These deities are God in various aspects, they are not independent beings but Powers and Personalities of the Supreme Deity. The initiated disciple will have an *iṣta devatā*, a chosen deity, who is nothing but God in the Form that the seeker finds most appealing and helpful to him. The chosen deity presides over the spiritual efforts of the aspirant and prepares him for the realisation for which he is trying to live a life of discipline or *sādhanā*. The consummation of this line of development in spiritual life is the vision and later the realisation of the unity of the chosen Deity and God and the Guru.

(2) Much of the process and rites of initiation are symbolic of the opening of the seeker to different aspects of psycho-spiritual states and activities and to contact with supernatural beings connected with progress in spiritual life. To take an example from Tantric Buddhism in which the term *abhiṣeka* is used instead of *dikṣā* but which is deeply influenced by Tantric Hinduism. First, let us point out the importance of abhisheka in Tantric Buddhism. The *Kriyā-saṁgraha-pañjikā* says: 'The yogi who though not abhishikta or initiated follows the state of yogihood, that is, practises yoga, darts a blow to the sky and drinks the water of a mirage'. *Pabajjā, parivrajyā*, going out is the first abhisheka, the second being arrival, *upasampadā*, which is entry into the circle of fully accredited members of the Samgha or Order of Buddhist monks. But then there are four kinds of more advanced initiation. They are by outward purification by water, into the secret cult,

into perfect Wisdom and finally, into the 'Thunderbolt' Truth and Reality. And these are connected with different *Tathāgatas*. In one classification, a first initiation is called *Kalasa-abhiṣeka*, 'pitcher initiation' and includes six different kinds, namely, with water, crown, thunder, bell, name and preceptor and these are connected with different Tathagatas. Water signifies ideal knowledge, crown equalising knowledge, thunder discriminative knowledge, bell performance of duties, name knowledge of pure *dharmadhātu*, Law-Substance and the initiation by the preceptor Thunder knowledge. The Tathagatas connected with these are respectively *Akṣobhya, Ratnasaṃbhava, Amitābha, Amoghasiddhi, Vairocana*.

Initiation into the secret cult is the start of instruction in deep yogic processes. The seeker has to develop the *bodhicitta*, the intuitive mind, its downward tendency is to be checked and it is to be sent upward into the *uṣṇiṣa-kamala*, the Lotus in the Crown of the Head, because there is the seat of the highest Wisdom. After the secret initiation, the disciple is taught the void nature of the empirical self and of all dharma, objects in the world. Initiation into the perfect Wisdom and then into the Vajra, thunder-like adamantine, Truth follow.

In the mystical sadhana as given in the Veda one finds something similar. *Agni*, the first deity invoked in the Rigveda is the Divine Will and is the Flame of aspiration in the soul of mystic pilgrim to the Home of Truth. Without aspiration sadhana can not begin. Then follows the purification of the vital force of which *Vāyu* is the god. The vital force is the seat of all movements of desire and ambition in man as also of magnanimity, love and other expansions of consciousness of a similar kind. This leads to the operation in the seeker of *Mitra* and *Varuna*, the gods of harmony and vastness. Mitra breaks down all pettiness in man and Varuna endows him with the knowledge of the illimitable infinity of God. *Indra*, the god of the pure mind, then becomes the most important deity guiding the sacrificer, the aspirant of immortality. The pure mind, freed from pettiness and the disturbing movements of the vital force is ready to open to *Sūrya*, the Sun, who is the deity of the full supramental Knowledge. It may be said that each god in his turn initiates the seeker into the next phase of the sadhana. Agni is the *purohita*, one standing in the front as will and aspiration and he is the deity who also brings all the other deities to the seeker. The sacrifice is an ascent, an inner journey to the heights of Truth the realisation of which confers immortality. *Caraiveti*, fare forward, says the Veda.

In the Upanishads several *Vidyā-s* are described. The *Prāṇa, Śāṇḍilya*, and *Madhu* vidyas for example are famous. They all represent, sometime clearly, sometime symbolically, instructions regarding the different aspects of the integral Reality. Nowhere are the actual disciplines described in so many words, for these had to be learnt personally from the Guru. But enough hints can be found not only about the philosophical standpoints of the various teachers—and they are not speculative in the modern sense of the word philosophical but statements of spiritual experiences and realisations of different aspects of Brahman and Atman—and of the disciplines they recommended to their respective disciples. The vidyas were secrets to the uninitiated but progressively revealed their treasures to the initiated. The Guru was the revealer of Truth. Sanatkumara for example showed the shore beyond darkness to Narada who inspite of knowing thirty-six sciences found he was lacking in something and went to Sanatkumara for the Knowledge that would enable him to tide over to the other side of 'Sorrow'. Sanatkumara taught Narada the nature of the One Self the seer of which sees neither death nor disease nor sorrow. And the Guru not only taught but showed the other side, that of Truth, of darkness to his accepted and initiated disciple.

INFORMAL INITIATION
AMONG HINDUS AND MOSLEMS

BY

HENRY H. PRESLER
Jabalpur, m.p., India

The histories of the religions of Mid-India and extensive field work among the adherents have pointed to the need for expanding the conceptual system to handle initiatory rites. To classify our data we require, in the opinion of the writer, the concept of formal initiation and the concept of informal initiation. By formal initiation I mean a *rite de passage* regularized within one's inherited religious community; one is expected to undergo the rite, usually at a prescribed period in the life cycle of the individual, and the pattern of the rite is fixed by tradition and religious orthodoxy. As an example of formal initiation, the sacred thread ceremony of the Brahmins may be mentioned. The thread ceremony is a feature of the religious community into which the candidate has been born; the youth is expected to present himself and would be excommunicated should he refuse; the ritual is unalterably fixed in sacred Sanskrit scripture. Such is formal initiation.

By informal initiation I mean induction into a religious community not one's own; one is not expected to have the initiatory experience and he himself may not have intended it, may be surprised that it became his lot; the occurrence is not an orthodox ritual but a conventionalized procedure, known better by the masses than by the religious functionaries who generally frown upon it. The Mid-India illustrations for informal initiation will be given below. Meanwhile, I have sought some other illustration shared by my readers and me. After some thought I have selected one which is not satisfactory, but which will do for a beginning, namely, the association of Saul with the ecstatic prophets. You may recall that on one occasion Saul fell in with the possessed members of another religious community, and after observing their behavior for some time, he began to act like them, giving evidence of being himself possessed; but his entrance into the cult activity was not expected of him, and the account does not suggest any intention on his part to engage with the prophetic community to which he did not belong. There was no ritual for which he prepared, no ceremonial pattern sanctified by tradition; rather he began to dance and sway in the customary way of the ecstatics. The experience of the prophetic religion seems to have been real, and the sociological consequences were paradoxical. On the one hand, Saul appears to have been accepted by the ecstatics as one of them during the day; on the other hand, he did not continue to be classified as a member of their community. Thus, Saul was religiously "in" but socially "out". Whether this description of what happened to Saul is exegetically correct, the Old Testament scholars can decide, but does not matter in this paper; the unsatisfactory illustration supplied by Saul is useful here as an aid to conceptualizing what I mean by informal initiation. It is, so to speak, only a convenient channel through which to communicate the new concept of informal initiation proposed in this paper. Let me proceed with Mid-India illustrations that seem to demand the concept being proposed.

The context for informal initiation in Mid-India has a history based on oral literature down to about 1650 A.D. This cultural island became the refuge for the aboriginals fleeing before the invading Aryans, and from later invaders entering from the west and south. The tribal refugees piled in upon the aboriginals already there, resulting in the distribution of three main tribes, the Gonds with over two million living persons, the Bhils with somewhat less, and the Kols with somewhat less. The total tribal population of Mid-India exceeds the population of some of the smaller nations of Europe. The religions of these tribes have no connection with the Sanskrit tradition of Hinduism, and may be designated by such terms as *mana, totemism, animism*, etc. The crucial point here is that the tribal religions provided a matrix over which Hinduism and Islam began to flow about 1653 a.d., resulting in an amalgamation conducive to informaliation. The history of the last three centuries saw the development of a tribal capital into the unsophistical city of Jabalpur with 300.000 inhabitants, distributed between Hinduism, Islam, Sikhism, Jainism, Parsiism, and Christianity. The context is therefore a cultural island containing peoples who regard themselves as strangers in an urban center surrounded by a tribal hinterland. The religious mentality is somewhat unstable. Beliefs and practices are fluid. On their part, the tribals have created a lively interest in magic and in spirit possession. The Hindus have supplied one of the institutions about to be described, and the Moslems have provided some organization to the complex. In the space allowed for this article, interesting strands of the history cannot be presented.

Against this background the sort of informal initiation defined above occurs, initiation outside one's own religious community, initiation unplanned and unexpected but nevertheless real, initiation governed not by established ritual but by customary procedure, initiation that ends with the person being religiously "in" but socially "out". The case study materials may be classified under three types: the *akhara*, the practice of *tona vidya*, and the practice of *hal*.

The *akhara* is a male youth organization for the cultivation of gymnastics, music and religion. *Tona vidya* may be loosely translated as the secret knowledge of magic. *Hal* is translated here as ecstatic seizure. The *akhara* is an institution something like the German *Turnverein* but with the addition of music and religion; it is the Hindu alternative to the Y.M.C.A. except being a small club with music added. *Tona vidya* is like an informal secret society with its own functionary and obscure clientele. *Hal* is a type of religious experience arising out of local institutions associated in the Cult of the Dead.

At this point a motion picture film was projected to aid in the conceptualization, showing an *akhara* and *hal*. *Tona vidya* is secret and therefore difficult to film.

I. *The Akhara*

The *akhara* represents a Hindu institutional pattern with a history reaching back into the distant past. Orders of Hindu holy men go by the same name, and are comprised of adults practicing celibacy, obeying monastic rules, and divided on sectarian lines. The Gond tribe through its local kings adopted the institution and patronized it, so that *akharas* in Jabalpur are notable for their frequency, our city having some two hundred of them, and for the peculiarity that the adherents cross over religious boundaries and manifest overt behaviour while shouting religious slogans. Moreover, our *akharas* have become youth groups, whereas two hundred years ago they were adult groups. The males come together around an older man reputed for athletic prowess, and who agrees to teach them. Usually somebody donates a one to three room house, or the members erect the mud walls and combine to purchase what we call rafters and tiles. In the main room is a wrestling pit with gravel prepared religiously, and also weights for body building, and fencing weapons. At one end of the room containing the wrestling pit is a three dimensional symbol for the Hindus, generally the god of strength, the monkey god named Hanuman. But some *akharas* have the patron god of the Gond rajas, named Bhairon. In a Moslem *akhara* the symbol is usually a green pennant upon which appear Arabic letters from the Koran. In another room there are, in the fully developed institutions, a room for the practice of daily religious rituals superintended by a priest, and another room for the cultivation of music with instruments.

The memberships of these *akharas* distinguish them. Some have exclusively Hindu members, even restricted to a certain caste or status bracket of castes. Other have exclusively Mohammedan members, and still others have both Moslems and Hindus. In the exclusively Hindu *akhara*, the wrestlers or fencers or gymnasts turn towards the statue, bow their heads, place the palms together, murmur appropriate words, and then try their strength. In the exclusively Moslem *akhara*, the members make practically the same gestures towards the pennant. It is the mixed *akhara* that provides us with pertinent illustration of informal initiation. Mixed clubs, that is, having both Hindu and Moslem members, fall into three types illuminating the subject before us: 1) those having Hindu symbols at one end of the gymnastics room, and Moslem symbols at the other end of the same room; 2) those having only Moslem symbols at one end; 3) those having only Hindu symbols at one end.

In the mixed *akharas* having both Hindu and Moslem symbols, the Hindu boys turn towards one end of the room, and the Moslem boys towards the other end; each prays to his own divinity for strength to win. But what happens in those clubs having only one kind of religious symbol? This is the situation in which informal initiation occurs. We observe the unusual case of Hindu boys in a Moslem *akhara* rendering obeisance to the Moslem symbols, and, of Moslem boys in a Hindu *akhara* turning towards the Hindu symbols. Thus, the three characteristics of informal initiation are met: the boy comes to the club only to wrestle, but he finds himself unexpectedly seeking divine help from the divinity of an outside community; he is not required to do it, may not intend to submit, usually has no thought for or against; yet he finds himself following conventionalized procedure impelled by human need. And, lo, he wins. The Hindu god is believed to have helped the Moslem, or Allah is thought to have helped the Hindu. In his exhileration he feels himself to be "in", but not "of". He freely and gladly confesses the power of the god of the outside community, but does not classify himself with it socially, nor does his society think it has lost him.

The reality and the effectiveness of this informal initiation was tested in 1956 and 1960 during the communal riots between Hindus and Moslems in which death and arson fragmentized the city for from two weeks to a month. In those geographical areas in which informal initiation had taken place, many *akharas* presented an impregnable unity. Hindu boys and young men defended their Moslem brothers whose god they knew, and Moslems protected their Hindu brothers whose god they knew, from roving bands of cutthroats and looters. Nevertheless, the Hindus would not acknowledge themselves to be Moslems nor vice versa. Rather, a theological bond had sprung up between them through informal initiation, and they defended the mob a brother who was within the "in-group" religiously speaking, but in the "out-group" sociologically speaking.

Emphasizing the fluidity of this situation, some Christian converts have been observed to enter the process of informal initiation.

II. *Tona Vidya*

Tona vidya is actually black magic, evil intentioned, destructive. Our respondents speak also of *jhar phoonk* or white magic, well intentioned, remedial, curative, helpful, and are prepared to talk more freely about it. I have not become acquainted with any word in Mid-India which covers both black and white, so the English word, magic, may be used to cover both. (*Jadu* does not seem to me to be suitable because it also refers to sleight-of-hand-tricks).

The most feared magicians in and around Jabalpur are the Gond tribals, who periodically enter the city to sell jungle produce. They are believed to be so powerful that one should never argue with them about a price, and should even buy an unwanted article if asked by them. The Gonds have taught some Hindus their magic art. In addition we have the Moslem magicians called *fakirs*, wandering into town for a week or so and then withdrawing before public wrath against black magic forms and identifies them as the perpetrators of local suffering.

For several years I tended to accept the local evasion as to magic; people would tell me to go to the jungle to visit the Gonds, or to wait outside on the highways for the *fakirs*. But as rapport with the people increased, cases of magic, of stationary magicians with clienteles, began to be reported. Also, I came to know where outside magicians periodically set up their temporary stands. After plotting these on a map of the valley, and of the city, I noticed magic falling into a particular type of area which the sociologist calls, interstitial. An interstitial area is a natural area of the city characterized by high indices of poverty, disease, crime, and social disorganization. Yet, magic occurs not in every interstitial area of Jabalpur, but in one kind of such area, namely, one in which a Moslem and a Hindu settlement share a common border between them. That border may be a dirty stream inhabited by rats and plague-bearing fleas, or an old burial ground, or a political ward boundry, or a miserable *gulli* with gunny sacks hanging over Moslem house doors on one side, and low caste Hindu hovels on the other side. *Tona vidya* and *jhar phoonk* (black and white magic) occur in an interstitial area divided between a phalanx of Moslem houses on one side of a border, and another phalanx of Hindu houses on the other. In this situation informal initiation also occurs.

When the Mohammedan *fakirs* come to town and squat on their side of the border, the Hindus cross over surreptitiously to them, driven by motives of revenge or relief. When the Gonds come to town the Moslems cross to the Hindu side, even more stealthily because local maulvis are enemies of magic. Either party goes to the secret practitioner of the other, seeking supernatural power to destroy a rival or to heal a beloved. Upon arriving he may not intend to go through the customary procedures of the gentile magician; but in time he is doing it. The magician requires him to bring from the bazar the necessary ingredients for the motions of the ritual, later to sit so, to say thus and so, to prostrate himself now and then, and so on. The myth, the spell, the actions are procedural, not scriptural, but they are equally real to the client who would have been astonished the day previously to have it predicted of him. Later, when the magic appears to "work"—when the rival falls sick or the son is healed— the client will testify that the magic of the other religion has mighty power in it, and on the quiet, he will recommend it to his co-religionists. He will say that he knows this from "the inside", so to speak, meaning that he is magically "in" but socially "out". Informel initiation made this possible.

III. *Ecstacy or Hal*

The Urdu word, *hal*, (here translated ecstasy) indicates a religious experience in which the devotee feels a religious thrill, and interprets the thrill as a direct visitation of the divinity. Orthodox Sunni Islam makes a place for *hal* in a milder form than about to be described, and looks askance at the Jabalpur variety. The latter expresses itself in abnormal behaviour, such as losing consciousness, weeping, cataleptic fixation, frothing at the mouth, shouting and roaring, leaping into the air in proxyms of twisting. *Hal* occurs at the graves of Moslem saints, and particularly at the relic of one of the greatest of the Baghdad saints, Pir-i-Jilani Gaus, on his death anniversary. The relic is located in the wall of a *dargah* or shrine, on the top of a rocky hill within our city. At graves on Thursday nights (weather permitting), and at this shrine, the spirit of the departed Moslem saint is believed to return, and to enter into the person of the religious functionary, rendering him *behosh* or unaware and beside himself. After a period of extraordinary physical exertion, the possessed functionary quiets sufficiently to become a medium to whom the believers (of any religion) address questions. The answers from the tongue of the medium are believed to come from the spirit of the saint. Finally, the functionary collapses and lies inert for some time, and at last struggles to his feet rather exhausted but in his normal state. The annual gathering at the relic draws as many as seventy separate functionaries (*mujavirs*) from their stations at the graves of other lesser saints, and becomes a festival for ecstatic participation.

One would expect that these functionaries would be Moslems only, but roughly one third of them are Hindus. The saints are Moslems, but their representatives on earth whom they favor with their visitations include Hindus. This provides the third illustration of informal initiation. The explanations given by the masses inform us as to the customary procedures. The illiterate and even literate Moslems (not maulvis) interpret the informal initation of Hindus about as follows: "Our saints", they say, "are very powerful and in favor with Allah; it is good that the Hindus recognize them and beseech them; not all of us Mohammedans have the qualities and worthiness necessary for the reception of the spirits of these saints, nor do all Hindus; spiritual virtues are peculiar to individuals, and our saints recognize virtue wherever found, possessing worthy Hindus; if the saint chooses a Hindu to be his vehicle for manifestation, we accept his selection".

The Hindus interpret their possession in a way that seems to point toward the concept of informal initiation. They talk like this: "You see, we came here after hearing about this powerful *pir* (saint). We (or I) expected to ask one of those Moslem *mujavirs* to intercede with the saint for his recommendation to the Mohammedan's Allah. But what happened? I myself do not know. I cannot recall what happened. People told me afterwards that the *pir* came upon me while I was approaching the sacred table to claim a rose petal as a charm. They say I got *hal*, fell down from the platform twenty feet on to the stone slabs, and yet no bruise marks my body; that I leaped and cavorted as those *mujavirs* are now doing, for twenty-seven minutes, and then became unconscious. I only know that I woke up lying under a sheet to shade my face, and was utterly exhausted, and that the *pir* brought back my stray cow to me, which had occasioned my seeking help. That was 17 years ago, and ever since I have served the *pir* as a Hindu".

Now the writer would suggest that the psychology of collective behavior throws some light on what happened, but not all the illumination required. We have to account for the routinization of the experience and the subsequent conformity to customary procedures. That is, why do the Hindus proceed in the customary manner of the Moslem masses? We need the sociological concept of informal initiation to assist us. The initiate, after resuming consciousness, has himself defined to himself by the laymen who observed his behaviour during the period of unconsciousness. They tell him, in effect, that he was chosen by the saint as a favored vehicle, causing him to behave thus and so, and that in the future he may be expected to conduct himself according to the legendary account of the saint of Baghdad. In his amazed and humbled state of mind, he accepts what they are telling him without question, and thus his informal initiation is completed. His future procedures are regularized according to custom. Henceforth, he is an adherent of that fragment of Islam devoted to saint worship, never having intended it so, but conforming to the routinization supplied by mass disobedience to the wishes of the maulvis.

Some Observations

Informal initiation occurs into a religion not one's own, unintentionally and unexpectedly; there is no conversion, no shift of religious affiliation, no apostasy. Informal initiation occurs outside the official church, and contrary to the preferences of its stated functionaries. The populations affected are characterized by poverty, illiteracy, low social status, and desperate need, and live in urban areas. The driving power behind informal initiation is the driving power of a felt need.

The question arises as to whether informal initiation occurs in other parts of the world under similar conditions and among similar populations in urban areas. In other words, the usefulness of the concept—informal initiation—may be tested by historians and field workers for other cultures and localities.

INITIATION IN THE SHUGENDO:
THE PASSAGE THROUGH THE TEN STATES
OF EXISTENCE

BY

CARMEN BLACKER
Cambridge

The Shugendō is one of the sects in Japanese religion closely concerned with the worship of mountains. It is one of those minglings of Buddhist doctrine with the indigenous folk religion of Japan which until the Meiji government in the early 1870s set about its drastic policy of 'purifying' Shintō from Buddhist elements was the religion of the great majority of Japanese. In the Shugendō we find ancient beliefs in the holiness of mountains enriched by the complex symbolism and doctrine of Tantric Buddhism, which spread to Japan in the form of the Shingon and Tendai sects in the course of the 9th century.

Little of the doctrine of the sect was committed to writing until late in the medieval period, for the reason that the Shugendō has traditionally stressed the esoteric quality of its teachings. Its instruction was revealed only orally and in secret to those disciples who had undergone the requisite training. But the image of the Shugendō adept which appears in the literature of the 12th-13th century is of an ascetic who retired voluntarily to mountain fastnesses in order to accumulate power. The *yamabushi*, or man who 'lies in the mountains', is a figure endowed with powers of a magical kind which could be used benevolently to relieve the sufferings of ordinary folk in the world below. After climbing numerous sacred peaks, standing under waterfalls and fasting, the *yamabushi* was thought to be able to subdue demons and expel the evil beings which caused sickness and madness. With clairvoyant eyes he could see into the causes of disease. With clairaudient ears he could understand the language of animals and the sounds of nature. With a special concentration he could subdue the essence of fire. He was thus akin to a magician or a thaumaturge, rather than to a saint or a bodhisattva.

But the early works from the 13th century onward which expound Shugendō doctrine give a rather different picture. From these we gather that the *yamabushi* goes into the mountains not merely for power, however beneficent, but for spiritual enlightenment of a much more loftily Buddhist kind. The works of SOKUDEN, for example, the celebrated *sendatsu* or high ranking *yamabushi*, from Hikosan in Kyūshū who flourished during the first half of the 16th century, expound a doctrine deeply imbued with the Tantric teachings of the Shingon sect.

The goal of the *yamabushi*, he tells us, is to discover in himself the Buddha nature which lies hidden in all mankind. We are all, in our original essential natures, Buddhas, one with the cosmic Buddha Vairochana whose body is manifested in the whole universe. We have merely been deluded by the phenomenal world into losing sight of our true nature, so that we do not realise that we are Buddhas. Our task is therefore to bring about this realization in ourselves.

To do this we must go into the mountains, and there undergo a series of ascetic disciplines of such transforming power that by the time we reach the summit of the mountain we are brought to the realisation of our identity with the cosmic Buddha [1]). The initiation of the *yamabushi*, the process whereby his nature is transformed into something beyond the ordinary human state, thus takes the form of an ascent of a mountain. It is a physical climb invested with the powerful symbolism of a spiritual journey.

Why should mountains play so important a part in this particular process of transformation? Because from early times certain mountains in Japan have been looked on as the Other World.

In most mythical traditions there are stories of a mysterious Other World. It may be an island in the mist or beyond the horizon, to be reached by boat through perilous seas. Or it may lie under the sea or under the earth, an unexpected fair land at the bottom of a well or down a long staircase. Or it may be found inside a hollow hill, through a deep cavern, or on certain nights of the year when the hill is raised up on pillars.

The Other World may either be inhabited by the dead, or by gods or fairies, but always it is 'other', removed from the ordinary human

---

[1]) SOKUDEN's two main works are the *Shugen Shuyō Hikesshū* and the *Sambu Sōjō Hossoku Mikki*, both of which are included in *Nihon Daizōkyo Shugendō Shōso* Vol. 2. The above argument may be found in the first work, p. 380. See also the references to SOKUDEN in the extremely useful article by MIYAKE HITOSHI "Shugen-dō no Shisō", in *Tetsugaku*, No. 43. January 1963.

world, mysterious and strange. Time there is not human time. It
moves either much more quickly or much more slowly. Nor is the
food there for ordinary mortals. Once a man eats of it he can never
again return happily to his own world.

In the earliest records in Japan the Other World seems to have
been imagined as a land lying beyond the sea where the dead dwelt and
whence mysterious divine visitors came at certain seasons. At some
later date, however, a shift seems to have occurred. The Other World,
the dwelling place of the dead and of the mysterious visitors, moved
from the sea to the tops of certain mountains. Not mythical mountains,
where no one has actually been save the heroes of legend, but geographical places accessible to anyone who cares to climb them.[1]

Usually these Other World mountains are of a rather distinctive
shape. They do not lie deep and inaccessible in layers of hills, but rise
up isolated and symmetrical, easily visible from the world below.
Mt Fuji, until modern tourism destroyed most of it numinous
quality, was the perfect example of such a holy mountain. But it
was only one among many such hills scattered over the whole country
and associated with some aspect of the Other World. Gassan and
Osorezan, to name only two in the north, were the abodes of the dead.
Mt Tateyama was believed to be the entrance to Hell, where travellers,
might hear voices calling from beneath the earth, or meet the sem-
blances of dead people allowed a few hours' respite above ground
from their torments below. In the Kumano mountains pilgrims could
find the paradise of Kannon, or the Pure Land of Amida. [2]

Such mountains are thus sacred ground, inhabited by beings more
powerful than ordinary men. It follows therefore that if a man wishes
to transcend the ordinary human state and participate in the powers
of the sacred world, the mountains are the best place for him to
pursue his religious discipline.

---

[1] Studies of *tokoyo*, the Japanese Other World, may be found in MATSUMOTO
NOBUHIRO, *Nihon no Shinwa*, Chapter 3, and in ORIGUCHI SHINOBU, *Kokubungaku no
Hassei*, Part 3, *Origuchi Shinobu Zenshū*, Vol. 1, p. 3-62. An interesting discussion
in English is in Dr. C. OUWEHAND's *Namazu-e and their Themes*, p. 85-105.

[2] Stories of the hell on Mt. Tateyama may be found in the 11th century
collection *Konjaku Monogatari*, *Nihon Bungaku Taikei* Vol. 8, p. 912, 914; Vol. 9,
p. 161. WAKAMORI TARŌ's *Yamabushi* (1964) discusses the paradise in the Kumano
mountains, p. 55-7. A most useful appendix to this book gives a list of all the
sacred mountains in Japan. See also the first chapter of Marco PALLIS's *The Way
and the Mountain* for an interesting discussion of the association in various traditions of the mountain with the spiritual Way. Also of the mountain as the *axis
mundi*, the pillar through the centre of the world joining the earth to the sky.

Thus from ancient times in Japan various transforming disciplines (*shugyō*) have been carried out in mountains. One could circum-ambulate the mountain, pausing at various holy spots on the way to recite sutras and mantras. Or one could climb to the summit, following a similar sacred route. Or one could retire there in seclusion, under-going such austerities as fasting, standing under a waterfall and reciting sacred texts. The last practice, known as *komori*, seems to have been the most ancient, and in the early medieval period such recluses were much sought after as exorcists. Their austerities were thought to have given them unrivalled power to subdue the angry ghosts and resentful emanations of living people which at the time were held responsible for nearly a'l sickness and calamity.[1]

The discipline of the Shugendō, once it emerges as a distinct doctrine and practice, is a blending of these ancient folk practices with Buddhist symbolism. The yamabushi's *shugyō* took the form of a ceremonial climb at certain seasons up one of the sacred peaks, with Buddhist rites and symbols enacted on the way which would serve to identify the journey with a spiritual pilgrimage.

The mountain for the *yamabushi* is not only the Other World of folk religion. It is also a mandala, the symbol which in Buddhist practice serves supremely to make space sacred, to cordon it off and make it qualitatively different from the profane world outside. Thus when the mountain itself becomes a mandala, those who set foot on it become themselves figures on the mandala, in a sacred dimension out of ordinary space and time. When the Shugendō disciple climbed Mt Kimpu, he was thought to be treading through the nine divisions of the Diamond-world (*kongōkai*) mandala. When he climbed the Kumano mountains, he likewise passed over the eight petals of the Womb-world (*taizōkai*) mandala. While Mt Ōmine, lying between the two, combined in its extra holiness the mandalas of both worlds. The summit of Mt Ōmine was "the secret place where the Two Mandalas and the Ten Worlds meet".[2] On Mt Ōmine "the thickly wooded slopes are the nine divisions of the Diamond World. The

---

[1] A full account of the origin and development of these early ascetics can be found in HORI ICHIRŌ's "On the Concept of the Hijiri", *Numen* April and September 1958.

[2] *Shugen Shuyō Hikesshū*, p. 388. See also the *Gempei Seisuiki*, book 40, for an early reference to the association of these mountains with mandalas. *Nihon Bungaku Taikei* Vol. 16, p. 591. A very detailed and valuable study of the development of these two mandalas in Shingon doctrine is TOGANOO SHŌUN's *Mandara no Kenkyū*, 1927.

deep and gloomy caverns are the eight petals of the Womb World. Here the streams, trees and plants are all of themselves the body of Vairochana. The sound of the storm wind in the valley is the voice of the cosmic Buddha".[1])

The powerful symbolism which in the course of the climb impresses on the disciple that he is indeed in a sacred dimension, climbing towards a spiritual as well as a physical goal, is the *jikkai-shugyō* or discipline of the Ten Worlds. Here the disciple must pass symbolically through the Ten States of Existence—the Six Realms (*rokudō*) of transmigration into which those still subject to the laws of karma are reborn, followed by four states of enlightened consciousness leading to final Buddhahood. The Six Realms, to be found depicted on the wheel of life, are Hell (*jigokudō*), the Hungry Ghosts or pretas (*gakidō*), the Beasts (*chikushōdō*), the Titans or Asuras (*shuradō*), men (*jindō*) and lastly Heaven, the realm of the gods (*tendō*). Above these lie the four holy states of the sravaka (*shōmon*), the pratyeka-buddha (*engaku*), the bodhisattva (*bosatsu*) and finally completely enlightened Buddhahood.

In the *jikkai-shugyō* each of these worlds or states must be negotiated by means of an ordeal or a rite, which is held to be a concentration and hence an expiation of the experience usually undergone in that state. Instead of passing a lifetime in hell, for example, the disciple may suffer a concentrated symbolic ordeal representing hell. In a similarly symbolic ordeal he may pass through the Hungry Ghosts, the Beasts and all the subsequent seven states until he finally emerges at the summit of the mountain in the full realisation of his own Buddhahood.

We gather that in medieval times the *jikkai-shugyō* was an important if not a dominant feature of the *yamabushi*'s initiatory climb. One of the earliest accounts of the practice is to be found in a story in the *Kokonchomonjū*, a collection of tales compiled about the year 1215. It describes how the poet Saigyō Hōshi, who was also a Buddhist priest, had long wished to join the *yamabushi* in their ritual climb up Mt Ōmine, but had always hesitated to ask, thinking that his shaved head and Buddhist attire would look embarassingly conspicuous among the *yamabushi*. But eventually his desire came to the ears of a famous *sendatsu* by the name of Shunambō Sōzu Gyōsō, who assured him that there was no objection to his joining the party provided that

---

[1]) *Shugen Shuyō Hikesshū*, p. 396.

he made the climb in a truly Buddhist spirit. Saigyō was delighted, but asked to be excused from observing all the rules of discipline during the climb on the score that he was not a *yamabushi*. "To be sure", Shunambo replied, "we do not insist on everyone conforming to our rules". Saigyō therefore set out with the party in high spirits, but was soon dismayed to find that Shunambō, far from treating him more leniently than the others, insisted with ferocious severity that he performed all the required disciplines to the letter. Saigyō was soon weeping with pain and exhaustion, and inveighing loudly against such barbarous doctrines.

Shunambō called him over and sternly explained the meaning of their practices. "When the *sendatsu* orders you", he said, "to perform arduous tasks such as cutting wood and drawing water, confessing your sins and being beaten with a stick, this means that you are redeeming the pains of Hell. When he allows you so little to eat that you are nearly dying of starvation, you shall thereby redeem the miseries of the Hungry Ghosts. When you carry heavy burdens over steep mountains and valleys, you are thereby expiating the pains of the Beasts. So after exerting ourselves all day and night to the very limits of our strength, when dawn comes we read the Sembō to wipe away our sins. At that moment we feel exactly as though we have passed through all the sufferings of the Three Evil Ways and emerged into a perfect and spotless paradise. You are sadly misled if you imagine that we undergo such trials merely for the sake of power and fame".

Thus admonished, Saigyō was needless to say enlightened as to the meaning of the Shugendō discipline, and conducted himself for the rest of the climb with exemplary fortitude.[1]

This story mentions only those disciplines associated with the three lowest and most painful of the Ten States. For a complete description of all ten stages we must look in the various books of Shugendō doctrine and rules. These works were usually compiled from the slips of paper called *kirigami* on which the various points of doctrine were noted down to help the disciple remember the oral instruction imparted to him in secret. One of the earliest of these

---

[1] *Kokonchomonjū*, book 2, *Nihon Bungaku Taikei* Vol. 10, p. 382-4. For discussions of the *jikkai-shugyō* see also MURAKAMI TOSHIO, *Shugendō no Hattatsu* (1943), p. 304-318; WAKAMORI TARŌ, *Shugendōshi Kenkyu* (1943), p. 138-146; and *Yamabushi* (1964) p. 82-87; TOGAWA ANSHŌ, "Shugendō to Minzoku", *Nihon Minzoku Kaihō*, No. 31, 1963, p. 5-6.

works, the *Shugen Hiōshō*, compiled in 1215 from a collection of thirty-three leaflets, contains the following prescription for the *jikkai-shugyō*.

„First, the rite of Hell is that of weighing one's Karma *(gōhyō)*.
Second, the rite of the Hungry Ghosts is fasting *(kokudachi)*.
Third, the rite of the Beasts is abstaining from water *(mizudachi)*.
Fourth, the rite of the Titans is wrestling *(sumō)*.
Fifth, the rite of the human world is repentence *(sange)*.
Sixth, the rite of Heaven is the Dance of Long Life *(ennen)*.

There follow the first two of the four holy states, where the rites are concerned with the symbolic attire of the yamabushi, while the last stage of final Buddhahood is celebrated by the *seikanjō*, the abhisekha ceremony of the Shingon sect.[1]

Thus by the early part of the 13th century the *jikkai-shugyō* seems to have become an accepted part of the ceremonial climb. Rather surprisingly, for we should expect some variation with time and place, the description given in the *Shugen Hiōshō* for the first six stages at any rate seems to have been followed fairly consistently right up to the 18th century. The same scheme is repeated in the works of Sokuden in the early 16th century, and also in the *Shūren Hiyōgi* of 1720 and the *Shugen Sanjūsan Tsūki* of 1734.[2] The issue in these later works is complicated by the inclusion of a second, overlapping set of ten disciplines, known as *jisshu-shugyō*, some of which are not specifically associated with any of the Ten Worlds. It seems clear too that the rites corresponding to the four holy states soon ceased to be practised. Possibly such realms were too lofty and remote to be meaningful to most *yamabushi*, for they find no place in any of the later schemes of *jisshu-shugyō*. Instead, we find rites associated with *aka* and *kogi*, water and firewood—objects familiar and essential to the ascetic living in the mountains, and at the same time deeply symbolic in their aspect of the water for the *abhisekha* baptismal ceremony and the wood for the *goma* fire ritual. They are not, however, given a place in any of the Ten Worlds.

The *Shugen Hiōshō* gave only a bare and enigmatic list of the ten

---

[1] *Shugen Hiōshō, Nihon Daizōkyō Shugendō Shōso* Vol. 1, p. 395. A useful note on the contents and provenance of this work by HATTORI NYOJITSU is in *Bussho Kaisetsu Jiten*.

[2] *Shūren Hiyōgi, Shugendō Shōso* I, p. 605. *Shugen Sanjūsan Tsūki, Shugendō Shōso* II, p. 409. The relevant passages in SOKUDEN's works are in II, p. 367 and 455.

Fig. 1. Yamabushi reciting the Heart Sutra at the Shōgoin temple in Kyoto at the start of their annual ascent of Mt Ōmine.

Fig. 2. The start of the *akimine* ascent of Mt Haguro.

Fig. 3. Arrival at the temple on Mt Haguro for the week of initiation.

Fig. 4. A daytime pilgrimage during the initiation week on Mt Haguro.

(Photographs by the author)

rites, with no explanation of their nature or proper mode of performance. Such details were still presumably imparted only orally and in
secret. But by the time of Sokuden in the early 16th century a fuller
written description must have been allowed, for we find in his *Sambu
Sōjō Hossoku Mikki* some indication of the nature of these ordeals.

The ordeal of Hell, 'weighing one's karma', should always, he
insists, be enacted closely with the rite of the human world, *sange*
or repentence.[1]) Here we find exemplified one of the most distinctive
features of Shugendō discipline.

Sange signifies not only a confession of sins, but also the complete
purging of the neophyte from his ordinary mode of consciousness
which must precede the realisation of his Buddha nature. It is the
exposure of his worldly thoughts and passions in such a light that
he immediately perceives their futility. Thereupon they slough off
like an unwanted skin. Shugendō practice holds that this process of
repentence and realisation can be facilitated by a sudden shock. The
neophyte is deliberately put in positions of danger or terror, where he
is exhorted with threats towards *sange*. The *Kokonchomonjū* story seems
to indicate that the *sendatsu* beat the neophyte with a stick as he made
him recite the *sange* text. Sokuden's insistence on coupling the rite
of *sange* with that of Hell has the same significance. For with *Gōhyō*,
or weighing one's karma, he says, the neophyte's hands are tied with
cord and he is seated on a kind of balance, projecting over a precipice,
with a large stone to act as counterweight. In this terrifying position
he must confess all his sins to the assembled company. If he refuses
or conceals anything he will be hurled over the precipice. If he confesses all, his karma is lightened, the counterweight sinks and he is
out of danger. [2])

This practice of shocking or startling the disciple out of his ordinary
profane human nature into the realisation of his own Buddhahood is
still to some extent carried out by the Shugendō in their annual
summer climb of Mt Ōmine. This mountain is one of the few left in
Japan still closed to women, so that I was not allowed to accompany
the *yamabushi* on their journey further than the lower slopes. But even
in that short distance vestigial remnants of these practices were still

---

[1]) *Sambu Sōjō Hossoku Mikki*, p. 481. An almost identical description is given
in the apparently anonymous and undated work *Buchū Jisshu Shugyō Sahō*, in
Shugendō Shōso II, p. 263.

[2]) *Ibid*, p. 481. The Portugese Jesuit Father Frois in a letter of 1583 describes
this ordeal as it was related to him by one of his converts, who had undergone
it seven times. See EBISAWA Arimichi *Kirishitanshi no Kenkyū*, p. 109-113.

observed. When we reached, at about four o'clock in the morning, the ancient shrine of Kimpu Jinja, the neophytes were bidden to follow the shrine priest to a small building a few yards away called the *kakuredō*, or hall of hiding. Here we found ourselves squashed inside round a central pillar and instructed to put a hand on the shoulder of the person in front. The doors were then banged shut, and we were plunged into total darkness. The priest thereupon instructed us to move round the pillar, repeating what he said. We shuffled round, clutching on to the person in front, while the priest boomed, "The *kakuredō* at Yoshino has always been the abode of emptiness", and other phrases, several times repeated, calculated to lead us to recall our Buddha nature. Suddenly there was a deafening clanging on a bell, which made everyone jump, and the doors were flung open to let in the early morning sunlight. The *sendatsu* in charge of the party afterwards told me that this was an old technique known as *kyōgaku-kaishi*, enlightenment through shock.

The same technique is repeated at a point near the summit, beyond the limit permitted to women, known as the Nishinonozoki. The neophyte is hung head downwards over a precipice, his legs firmly held by several companions, and made to repeat, in this critical posture, various collects designed to bring about *sange*. He is also sternly questioned by the *sendatsu* on his recent misdemeanours and forced, on pain of being thrown over the cliff, to make full repentence.[1]

The rites associated with the Hungry Ghosts and the Beasts, if less dramatic than that of Hell, were nonetheless not for the faint-hearted. Appropriately enough the world of the pretas was celebrated by fasting. *Kokudachi*, which all the books of doctrine alike prescribe for this realm, means literally abstinence from the Five Cereals. In practice howeve r it often meant a fast more or less complete for seven days.

Less understandably, the world of the Beasts was celebrated by *mizudachi*, abstinence from water — a prohibition on washing and rinsing the mouth for an unstated period.[2]

With the rites of the Titan world and of Heaven, we come to ancient practices, originating probably in folk religion, clothed in Buddhist symbolism. *Sumō*, wrestling, although justified by Sokuden as symbolising the "anger, strife, pride and lust for victory" which characterised the Titan world, was nevertheless far older than Bud-

---

[1]) See for instance MIYAKE, *op. cit.*, p. 211.

[2]) *Sambu Sōjō*, p. 482, 485. *Shūren Hiyōgi*, p. 611-2. *Sanjūsan Tsūki*, p. 428-9.

dhism in Japan. A ritual bout of *sumō* on the occasion of the descent of a deity at a festival, was, like other contests of horse racing or a tug-of war, a method of divining the deity's will on any humanly insoluble problem.

The *ennen-no-mai* or dance of Long Life, again prescribed by all the works of doctrine as the correct celebration of the Heaven world, was likewise an ancient magical dance, performed as a spell for warding off calamity and prolonging life. It was doubtless designed as a relief and a diversion for the *yamabushi* after the ordeals of the lower worlds. At the end of the Nō play *Ataka*, Benkei when the danger is passed dances the *ennen* dance for the assembled company.[1]

The crowning moment of the progress through the Ten Worlds, the moment corresponding to the 'perfect and spotless paradise' of the *Kokonchomonjū* story, should naturally be the last of the ten rites, the *kanjō* or 'pouring on the head' ceremony. Here, as the name implies, some sort of baptismal rite, wherein the two elements of water and consciousness are conjoined, was performed over the neophyte. Sokuden then closes his description of the Ten Realms by repeating that the purpose of the discipline is to impress on the disciple that profane and sacred are one; that the Six Profane States and the Four Holy ones are one, and that his own mind and body are part of the cosmic body of the Buddha.[2]

Such writings would lead us to believe that the Shugendō was predominantly Buddhist in intention, that the disciple underwent his initiation in the mountains in the hope of achieving the truly Buddhist goal of emancipation from worldly passions. In practice however, this seems rarely to have been the case. In the mingling of Buddhist elements with folk religion which constituted Shugendō practice, the more ancient elements seem to have proved the stronger. The mountain initiation, with its stress on the painful ordeals of the lower worlds, produced not an enlightened saint, but the magician who figured so prominently in the pre-Buddhist cult. The founder prototype of the *yamabushi* was after all not a Buddhist exemplar, but En-no-Gyōja, a magician, and certainly the image of the *yamabushi* appearing in medieval literature has little about him of wisdom, compassion or saintliness. He is a demonic figure, uncanny and

---

[1] A discussion of the origin of the *ennen* dance is in WAKAMORI, *Shugendōshi Kenkyu*, p. 142. SOKUDEN's instructions for its performance are in *Sambu Sōjō*, p. 479.

[2] *Sambu Sōjō*, p. 486. See also MURAKAMI, *op. cit.*, p. 314.

strange, akin to a goblin rather than to a bodhisattva.[1]) We can only conclude that despite the Buddhist homilies in the works of doctrine, the passage through the Ten States produced power rather than holiness.

What of this practice in modern times? Has the same pattern of initiation still survived?

The most noticeable trend, dating back probably to the 17th century is a mitigation in the severity of the discipline. The painful elements have tended to give way to formalised ritual, the beatings with a stick to mere sounds on wooden clappers. The length of the fasts have been reduced, the efforts towards *sange* slackened. As a result the quality in the order of *seishin-tōitsu*, or the intense concentration of mind which is for the Japanese th beginning of power or skill or wisdom, began to weaken, and with it the demonic quality seems to go out of the *yamabushi*, leaving him a faintly debased figure. KAEMPFER at the end of the 17th century described those he encountered on his journeys with the Dutch embassy from Nagasaki to Edo as little more than noisy and importunate charlatans, making on their conch shells "such a horrid frightful noise as would make one mad or deaf".[2]) MOTOORI NORINAGA, the Shintō scholar, watched the procession of *yamabushi* as it passed through Kyoto in the year 1757 at the beginning of the annual ascent of Mt Ōmine. The route was lined with dense crowds of spectators and the procession was nearly six miles long, but what most impressed Motoori was not the ascetic or demonic mien of the *yamabushi*, who on the contrary seemed loutish and uncouth, but the elegant attire of the Imperial Prince who was accompanying the party. He was wearing "very pale blue satin with a figured pattern of *shinobu* flowers", and rode in an unusually splendid palanquin lacquered all over with gold.[3]) Hardly a suitable costume in which to climb even an ordinary mountain, let alone one which leads through the Ten States of Existence.

Proscribed by the government in the early 1870s in the effort to 'purify' Shintō from Buddhist elements, the Shugendō survived surreptitiously until 1945. Then, with the religious freedom proclaimed by General MCARTHUR, it revived prolifically in a number of sects and branches.

---

[3]) Many stories identify the *yamabushi* with the *tengu*, a winged, beaked goblin who figured as a subtle of Buddhism. See for instance *Shasekishū* (1312) book 8, Iwanami Shoten edition Vol. 2, p. 75. *Kokonchomonjū*, p. 728.

[1]) KAEMPFER, *History of Japan* Vol. 2. Glasgow edition of 1906, p. 342.

[2]) MOTOORI NORINAGA, *Zaikyō Nikki. Koji Ruien* Vol. 33, p. 1105.

The ancient strictness, however, has not been revived. There has been a still further breaking up of the *kata* or prescribed forms. The Shōgoin branch of the order, for example, still performs the annual climb of Mt Ōmine, but in an attenuated form. The *jikkai shugyō* is no longer observed in formal ritual. Instead, the disciple is instructed that in the ordinary courseof his climb he will automatically undergo the salient characteristics of each of the Ten Worlds. Hell, for example, is no longer signified by a special rite, but the disciple as he climbs the mountain will suffer from heat and cold much as though he were passing through the Eight Hot and the Eight Cold Hells. Likewise he will feel hungry and thirsty, as though he were travelling through the realm of HungryGhosts. Even the ritual bout of *sumō* has gone, and in its place is a bland exhortation to turn the spirit of strife of the Titan world into one of *striving* and effort.[1]) The rites, with their transforming power, have disappeared.

But in the northern branch of the Shugendō based on the three mountains of Dewa Sanzan, the disciplines of some at least of the Ten Worlds are still preserved in their initiatory form. They are enacted in the course of the *akimine* or 'autumn ascent' of Mt Haguro, one of the sect's four main seasonal rites. The *akimine* involves a formal climb in procession up the mountain, a sojourn of a week in a remote temple near the top, and finally a triumphal descent.[2]) During the week symbolism of an unmistakeably initiatory kind is enacted on two separate levels. At the same time as the *yamabushi*, in his capacity of a Buddhist disciple, struggles upwards through the Ten Worlds, he is also undergoing a symbolic transformation of an obviously older order of folk religion.

Here the mountain is the mother's womb. The disciple starts his climb as a newly conceived embryo, and at the end of the week emerges from the mountain as a newly born child.[3])

On the first day the procession of *yamabushi*, brilliant with many

---

[1]) *Nyūbu no Shiori*, the booklet issued to all those about to embark on the climb, 1963, p. 3-5.

[2]) A description of the *akimine* may be found in KISHIMOTO HIDEO, "Dewa Sanzan wo chūshin to seru shūkyōteki shugyō ni tsuite", in *Teikoku Gakushiin Kiji*, Vol. 1, No. 2, July 1942. The most detailed account of the ritual of this branch of the Shugendō is undoubtedly SHIMAZU DENDŌ's *Haguroha Shugendō Teiyō*, but see also the distinguished writings of TOGAWA ANSHŌ, *Haguroha Yamabushi to Minkan Shinkō* (1950), and „Shugendō to Minzoku", in *Nihon Minzokugaku Kaihō*, Nos. 31 and 32, 1963 and 1964.

[3]) Compare the Taoist imagery of the growing embryo in the training of the adept. See K. L. REICHELT, *Meditation and Piety in the Far East*, (1953), p. 112-210.

colours and a panoply of ceremonial axes, conch shell trumpets and large red umbrellas, arrived at a shrine near the gateway to the mountain. Here the *Daisendatsu*, the leader of the party, knelt on the steps wearing a white hat of peculiar shape and holding in his hands a very long pole. For several seconds he crouched on the steps shaking the pole from side to side in a curious fashion, then flung it with all his might in the direction of the mountain. This act, I was told, represented our initial conception. As we trudged up the mountain-side through the cedar forest, we were all embryos in the womb of the mother mountain. The curious white hat worn by the Daisen-datsu, which played a prominent part in subsequent rituals during the week, represented the placenta.

The image of the mountain as a womb is carried over into the Buddhist symbolism in so far as Mt Haguro represents the mandala of the Womb-world (*taizōkai*). But on the whole this ancient symbol-ism of rebirth seemed to run unconnected with the passage through the Ten Worlds.

The week was further divided into three *shuku* or lodgings, symbolic shifts of dwelling to another plane of existence. A hundred years ago before the Meiji Restoration when the whole period of seclusion lasted not a week but seventy-five days, the passage from one to another was marked by a physical change of lodging to another temple. Now, however, the shift is symbolic only.

To the first lodging, lasting three days, belonged the ordeals of the three lower worlds, Hell, Hungry Ghosts and Beasts. The ordeal of Hell practised here is undoubtedly peculiar to the Haguro sect, for no mention of anything similar can be found in any other branch of the Shugendō.

It is known as the *namban-ibushi*, or 'southern smoking', and was enacted in the small hours of the morning after each of the two services or *gongyō* which together occupied most of the night. As the chanting died away the outer shutters of the hall were flung open, and three *yamabushi* entered with braziers full of hot charcoal, which they set down in the front, middle and back of the hall. The shutters were firmly closed and a command came from the *dōshi*, one of the five officiating *sendatsu*, "*Kamidoko e yakumi, shimodoko e yakumi*"—herbs to the front, herbs to the back. At once the *yamabushi* threw on to the charcoal trays of red pepper flakes, rice bran and a smelly plant called *dokudami*. A thick cloud of smoke rose up from the braziers, which the *yamabushi* fanned vigorously with large red fans. Every few seconds the *dōshi* would call, "More herbs to the front, more herbs to the back", and more pepper flakes would be thrown on to the braziers until the thick white smoke spread over the whole room. It had a peculiarly stinging and suffocating quality, and soon everyone was coughing and choking, and the *dōshi* could only with difficulty splutter out, "More herbs to the front." Thicker and thicker rose the smoke, until the figures the other side of the room were almost blotted out, and those near me loomed as though through a fog. At last, after what I subsequently learned was only about five minutes, the *dōshi* called "*Toko-yurugi*", and the shutters were flung open. Some of the party continued to sit bravely in their places, but most people rushed choking to the open windows and gasped for air. It was some time before I could stop coughing, and the peculiar smell of the smoke lingered over the whole temple for hours afterwards.

Why this particular symbol for Hell, I asked the *dōshi*. Why pepper smoke? Burning pepper smoke, he answered, was an old method of driving out evil or impure spirits from the body. In remote parts of the country they used often to burn pepper smoke in the faces of people suspected of being possessed by foxes, in the belief that it was a sure way of driving out the fox. In the old days when the whole period of seclusion lasted for seventy-five days, the ordeal was incomparably more severe. They used to perform the *namban-ibushi* some forty times, instead of the present five, and it was no unusual thing for people to be carried out unconscious. Like much else about the *akimine* ritual, the prescribed forms for the ordeal of Hell had lately been much modified.

From Hell we proceeded to the Hungry Ghosts, where the ordeal was the traditional one of fasting. When we arrived at the temple on the first afternoon, we were told that there would be nothing to eat for twenty-four hours. For the three days of the first 'lodging' we were reduced to one meal a day, though we were allowed to accept *segaki*, or 'offerings to the Hungry Ghosts'. On the third day these assumed substantial proportions when some villagers from the foot of the mountain appeared with beans and water melons in return for sutras recited for the repose of their ancestors.

The austerity of the Beast World was also the traditional one of *mizudachi*, abstention from washing. No one was supposed to wash face or body, clean the teeth, rinse the mouth or shave for the whole week, though some members of the party were seen to make use of the nearby stream to wash their faces in the early morning. The Titan

World was also celebrated by the traditional bouts of *sumō*, with one of the *yamabushi* acting as umpire.

No special rite was enacted to mark the human world. Heaven was supposed to be celebrated by the traditional *ennen* dance, but for some years back no one had known how to perform it. Instead, in the small hours of the morning of the fifth day, we were given, with saucers of rice wine, a performance of the *utai* chanting of the Furukawa school.

No rites were performed for the four holy states lying above the Heavens, and hence none to mark the final stage of Buddhahood. The only indication that we were indeed supposed to be Buddhas was a curious ritual on the steps of the Haguro shrine on the last day. Here a steep flight of ten steps leads up to the great hall, each of which is said to represent a stage on the way to final Buddhahood. On our way up the mountain on the first day we passed the shrine without climbing the steps. But on the last day we were bidden to tramp up to the very top. Here the *dōshi*, in the formal medieval language in which during the week he had made all his announcements and commands, proclaimed that the tenth step represented not only our transformation into Buddhas, but also our birth into the world from the mother's womb. Hence we must all give the *ubugoe*, the first cry of the new born child. Everyone at once gave a loud yell, and clattered down the steps.

Thus the older stream of symbolism of conception and birth was brought to its climax.

But in the case of the Buddhist passage through the Ten Worlds, the climactic moment of the initiation seems in a curious manner to have been lost. The higher the stage through which we were supposed to be passing, the less dramatic became the rites, until the last four, culminating in final Buddhahood, were lapsed and imperceptible.

It was as though the initiation, having laid great stress on the early ordeals, had stopped just short of the climax of final transformation. It had stopped, indeed, at the stage of the magician or shaman who in the traditional Japanese folk religion had sought to accumulate his magical powers from austerities in mountains. The basic folk tradition, like a strong background colour which persistently shows through any pattern imposed on it, proved too obstinate to be moved by later Buddhist accretions. The state of Buddhahood proved in practice to be too remote to be comprehended and striven for by those who became *yamabushi*. Certainly none of the party who climbed Mt

Haguro in the summer of 1963 had any thought in their minds of becoming Buddhas. Strength of one kind or another, and that vague concept *seishin-shūyō*, mental and moral training, was what they sought by their efforts in fasting, sleeplessness, strenuous pilgrimages by day and strenuous recitation of sutras by night.

Though the Buddhist intention in devising the passage through the Ten Worlds seems to have fallen short of fulfilment, yet it remains an outstanding example of a physical journey identified by powerful symbolism with a spiritual pilgrimage. Like the Christian disciple walking the stations of the Cross or following on his knees the labyrinthine pattern on cathedral floors.[1]) the *yamabushi* undoubtedly by this pilgrimage achieved some emancipation from the confines of ordinary human habits of mind.

---

[1]) See Dr. E. SCHNAPPER, *The Inward Odyssey* (1964) for a full discussion of the labyrinth as a religious symbol.

L'INITIATION MAZDÉENNE

PAR

J. DUCHESNE-GUILLEMIN
Liège

L'initiation mazdéenne est dépourvue de la riche symbolique du baptêmechrétien, sur laquelle le professeur Brandon, dès le premier jour du colloque, et d'autres orateurs ensuite ont attiré notre attention; elle ignore aussi les variations si diverses que connaît l'hindouisme dans les rituels de la *dīkṣā*.

A première vue, l'initiation parsie n'est pas un rite de renaissance; elle n'a rien d'ésotérique; il semble lui manquer les caractères les plus frappants de ce qu'on appelle, à la suite de Van Gennep, rite de passage et enfin, presque totalement, ce qu'on pourrait appeler la dimension cosmique.

Elle diffère évidemment, à cet égard, du mithraïsme. Dans celui-ci, on distinguait sept degrés, placés chacun sous la protection d'une planète et dont chacun entretenait une relation particulière avec Mithra. Au lieu de ces sept degrés, l'initiation parsie n'en connaît que trois, dont le premier est seul commun à tous les fidèles, tandis que les deux autres concernent les deux catégories de prêtres, *herbad* et *mobad*.

Le fidèle de Mithra avait certainement conscience d'être initié à un mystère, à un secret — quels que fussent les moyens employés: baptême de l'eau, baptême du sang. Dans le mazdéisme, seule la légende garde témoignage de révélations obtenues par des moyens particuliers: Arda Viraf, pour connaître le monde de l'au-delà, prend un narcotique, et son âme s'en va dans le séjour d'après la mort, dont elle nous rapporte une description qui est comme le premier état de la Divina Commedia.

Vištasp aussi, le protecteur et patron de Zarathuštra, but, selon la légende, un mélange stupéfiant pour connaître l'histoire du monde, passé et futur, substance de l'apocalypse qui porte son nom.

L'initiation du premier degré, qui concerne tout jeune mazdéen à sept ans dans l'Inde, à dix ans en Perse, s'appelle dans l'Inde *naojōt*, mot dont nous étudierons ci-dessous l'étymologie, et en Perse *jašn i sadre pušti* ‚fête du revêtement de la chemise'.

La cérémonie consiste essentiellement à investir l'enfant d'une chemise, *sadre*, et d'un cordon, *kusti*. On peut y distinguer des préliminaires, la cérémonie proprement dite et un rite supplémentaire.

Préliminaires.

1) Le premier acte est une ablution (*nahn*), ce qui met en évidence le caractère de purification et rappelle la lustration juive, d'où est sorti le baptême chrétien.

2) Caractère d'épreuve: il est aujourd'hui effacé, mais, jusqu'à récemment, l'enfant devait jeûner depuis le matin jusqu'à l'achèvement de la cérémonie.

3) Caractère cosmique: on assied l'enfant face à l'est.

4) Caractère d'une conversion: l'enfant peut réciter le Patēt; en tous les cas, les assistants le font pour lui.

Cérémonie proprement dite.

1) Avant de revetir la chemise, l'enfant invoque la religion personnifiée, *Dēn*, et récite une formule de profession de fois envers la loi mazdéenne, don de Mazda. En revêtant la chemise, il récite la prière *Ahunvar*.

2) Le prêtre se tient debout derrière l'enfant assis, tous deux face au soleil. Avant de passer le cordon, l'enfant récite le commencement du Yašt à Mazda, un bref sommaire de la doctrine mazdéenne et une confession.

3) Il récite enfin le Fravarāne ou grande profession de foi avestique, adhésion aux bonnes pensées, paroles, actions.

Rite supplémentaire.

On administre à l'enfant le *kunkun*, dont il sera parlé ci-dessous, et une bénédiction finale, qui s'accompagne de présents: noix de coco, fleurs, feuilles de bétel, noix, etc.

Analyse. A part ce rite supplémentaire, qui est de fécondité, l'initiation parsie consiste essentiellement en une admission à la Religion, *Dēn*, car elle fait pour toujours de l'enfant un *beh-dēn* ‚appartenant à la bonne religion'. La *Dēn* est un ensemble de croyances et de pratiques: ceci se traduit, comme nous allons le voir, dans le symbolisme du *kusti*.

En étudiant ce symbolisme, il ne faut pas se laisser égarer par diverses interprétations adventices du *kusti*. Deux d'entre elles jouent sur l'étymologie (visiblement fausse) de ce mot: *kusti*, dit-on, est ce qui montre la bonne direction (persan *kušt*); ou bien c'est un bateau,

persan *kaštī*, qui nous conduit au havre bienheureux. Ces deux interprétations sont récentes, puisqu'elles présupposent le persan moderne.
Deux autres interprétations ont plus d'autorité, puisqu'elles figurent
dans le traité pehlevi *Cīm i Kustīk*: selon l'une, le *kustī* est le signe de
l'obéissance, puisqu'un serviteur, pour exécuter un ordre, se ceint les
reins; c'est, selon l'autre, le symbole de la division du corps entre une
part noble au dessus et une part ignoble, au-dessous. Ces deux interprétations ne sont pas à dédaigner, mais elles doivent se comprendre
en fonction d'une troisième, laquelle se trouve dans plusieurs livres
pehlevis et a déjà pour elle, en outre, l'autorité de l'Avesta.

Selon l'Avesta, la ceinture *est* la religion mazdéenne, formule très
forte en sa simplicité: on ne dit pas que la ceinture représente la religion, on les met tout simplement en apposition l'une à l'autre. Vue
à la lumière de cette équation, l'une des deux interprétations pré-
cédemment citées apparaît comme un effort pour comprendre l'origine
de cette identité: si la ceinture est la religion, c'est parce qu'elle est le
signe de l'obéissance.[1])

L'autre interprétation reflète une spéculation morale qui subor-
donnait le ventre et le bas-ventre au cœur et à la tête. Je serais enclin
à ne voir dans ces deux interprétations que des prolongements de
l'équivalence fondamentale

$$kustī(k) = d\bar{e}n.$$

L'importance de celle-ci est confirmée par diverses correspondances
de détail, qui en donnent en quelque sorte, comme dirait Malraux,
la monnaie. Les 72 brins qui composent le *kustī* symbolisent les 72
hās ou chapitres du Yasna; les six tresses, de 12 brins chacune, représentent les 6 devoirs religieux d'un zoroastrien (célébration des fêtes
saisonnières, des cérémonies funéraires, prières 3 fois le jour en l'honneur du soleil, 3 fois la nuit en l'honneur de la lune, etc.). En outre,
la *Dēn* est conçue de façon en quelque sorte spatiale. En effet, la
ceinture, à laquelle elle est identifiée, a un équivalent cosmique: la
Voie Lactée — qui semble ceinturer le ciel comme le *kustī* ceinture
l'initié. De plus, le creux du brin symbolise l'espace entre ce monde-ci
et l'autre, et le fait de plier en deux le cordon symbolise la connexion
entre le monde actuel et le monde futur. MODI, à qui nous empruntons
ces détails, ajoute, *Religious Ceremonies and Customs of the Parsees*,
Bombay ²1937, p. 179, que le tressage final des 72 brins symbolise la
fraternité ou union universelle. On peut dire que pénétrer dans la

---

[1]) GEO WIDENGREN a étudié, en une conférence faite à l'Université de Liège
mais demeurée inédite, le symbolisme de la ceinture comme signe de vasselage.

Dēn, c'est accéder à un univers. Rappelons que l'initié, par l'orientation vers le soleil, est placé en connexion avec cet astre.

Précisons encore : en recevant la *Dēn*, l'initié reçoit ce qu'il appelle expressément un don de Mazda. Ce don sacré est un secret, puisque l'Avesta prescrit de ne transmettre la parole sacrée que de père en fils.

Ce caractère ésotérique n'est pas accentué dans le cérémonial, mais c'est peut-être seulement parce qu'il est suffisamment sous-entendu ? Peut-être la ceinture est-elle l'image appropriée d'un monde fermé ?

Par la ceinture, en tout cas, l'initié a accès aux doctrines, aux cérémonies, au droit de contempler le feu sacré — privilège refusé aux étrangers. Cependant, il ne ressort pas manifestement de la cérémonie que l'initié entre dans un groupe.

La cérémonie d'initiation n'est-elle pas encore autre chose ? Etudions-en le nom. Elle s'appelle, chez les Parsis, comme nous l'avons vu, *naojōt*. Selon l'étymologie la plus plausible, le *naojōt* est une renaissance. Cette étymologie, déjà indiquée par WEST, SBE XXIV, 262, est confirmée — comme l'a montré JUNKER, *Der wissbegierige Sohn*, 1959, 27 sq. — par le texte pehlevi du *Šāyast nē Šāyast*, chap. 13, où on lit qu'un jeune homme de 15 ans qui veut devenir prêtre, confesse ses fautes an grand-prêtre, récite les gâthâs et accomplit la cérémonie de *navēt-χātīh*, littéralement ,nouvelle naissance'.

Or, la prononciation s'est altérée de *nauχāt* en *naozōt*, jusqu'à effacer le souvenir même du sens du mot. Modi interprète celui-ci comme *navō χaotā*, nouveau prêtre', ce qui n'a guère de sens puisque l'initiation concerne n'importe quel fidèle et non pas seulement ceux qui veulent accéder à la prêtrise. Il est donc évident que l'idée de renaissance n'a pas retenu l'attention des Parsis.

Cette carence résulte peut-être d'une épuration — si du moins on admet avec WIDENGREN, *Iranisch-semitische Kulturbegegnung*, 62 sq., qu'autrefois les grottes servaient à symboliser la renaissance de l'initié, lequel, plongé d'abord dans la nuit de la grotte, sortait ensuite de celle-ci comme d'un sein maternel. Mais cette interprétation reflète peut-être seulement nos propres rêveries freudiennes.

Les Iraniens, mithraïstes ou mazdéens, n'ont peut-être jamais vu si loin. Ou peut-être ont-ils tenu à effacer une allusion trop grossièrement physiologique et par là indécente. La parsisme est une religion chaste, pudique.

On trouverait confirmation de ceci dans le fait que lorsqu'un usage étranger, de caractère évidemment sexuel, s'est imposé aux Parsis — je veux parler de l'usage du *kunkun*, qui consiste à marquer le front de l'enfant d'un trait rouge si c'est un garçon, d'un point si c'est une fille — les Parsis tendent à voiler par l'allégorie le caractère sexuel de cet usage: „The red pigment on the forehead of a girl is always round and that on the forehead of a boy always long and vertical, explique Modi, *Ceremonies*, 22. The reason is this: the long vertical mark of the male symbolizes a ray of the sun, and the round mark of the female symbolizes the moon. A handsome man is compared by oriental writers with the sun, but the beauty of a woman is always compared with that of the moon. The sun is always represented in ancient pictures as a round disc with shooting rays. Again, the sun, through its rays, is a fructifying agent, but the moon is represented as a conceiving agent. She absorbs the rays of the sun. Just as the sun is a fructifying agent and the moon a conceiving agent, so is man in his relation to woman. Hence it is that the mark on a man's forehead is long and vertical like the rays of the sun and that on a woman's forehead round like the moon.''

Quoi qu'il en soit, il ne reste dans le rite parsi, pour symboliser la renaissance, que l'ablution, la chemise et les vêtements neufs. D'autre part, le caractère d'épreuve physique et morale, nous l'avons vu, manque aujourd'hui totalement à l'initiation parsie — du moins à celle du premier degré. Il n'y reste que l'épreuve d'intelligence ou de mémoire que constitue la récitation de formules de profession de foi.

Le caractère d'épreuve est plus développé dans les initiations du deuxième et du troisième degré, celles qui élèvent le candidat au rang de *herbad* et de *mobad*.

Ces initiations, en effet, durent tout un mois et comportent une retraite, un jeûne sévère, ainsi qu'un abstinence sexuelle qui s'étend même jusqu'à l'interdiction de *pollutio nocturna*.

D'autre part, le candidat prouve sa capacité en récitant presque tous les textes liturgiques: le Yasna, le baj, l'afringan, etc. Le troisième degré, qui fait les prêtres du degré supérieur, diffère seulement par l'addition du Videvdat. Ce troisième degré qualifié le candidat à accomplir le yasna et les baj.

Il est curieux, et d'abord inexplicable, que le seul texte qui l'habilite à cela soit le Videvdat. Mais ceci s'expliquera plus loin. Il faut d'abord parler du *barešnūm*.

Le trait le plus important des cérémonies des deux degrés supérieurs, c'est le *barešnūm*, qui se présente évidemment comme une purification, puisque le candidat y est frotté d'eau, de sable et d'urine de bœuf, au dessus de trous faits dans le sol et par où est censée disparaître l'impureté. Mais je me demande si ce rite n'avait pas autrefois une autre valeur. En effet, tandis que le candidat est lavé à l'urine, à l'eau et au sable, le prêtre récite, et le candidat répète après lui, une formule d'hommage à l'entité *Armaiti*. MODI ne voit dans celle-ci que ,la pureté de pensée', comme il dit. Il me semble que cette interprétation néglige l'essentiel: *Spentā Armaiti* était (aussi) la patronne de la Terre. Il est donc naturel qu'on l'invoque au moment où les impuretés sont, par les trous rituels, évacuées dans la terre. L'invocation veut-elle propitier la Terre au moment où on lui fait cette injure? Je ne sais. Il y a peut-être ici plutôt trace d'une véritable offrande à la Terre, ou plus exactement d'un sacrifice, c'est-à-dire d'un sacrement d'union à la Terre, lequel ferait pendant aux sacrifices offerts devant le feu aux divinités du ciel. Rappelons-nous la présence du feu au naojot.

C'est là une hypothèse, mais elle aurait le mérite d'expliquer un terme qui ne l'a pas encore été jusqu'à présent. Je veux parler du mot *maγa* qui, dans la langue de l'Avesta récent, désigne le trou rituel. On a longtemps hésité, malgré l'identité de forme (la différence phonétique tenant à la différence de dialecte), à rapprocher ce mot du gâthique *maga*, qui veut dire ,l'union, le don rituel, le sacrement'. Il me semble que si l'on admet que le *barešnūm* était primitivement un sacrifice chtonien, on trouvera naturel que le trou, *maγa*, qui en était l'instrument porte le nom même, *maga*, qui désignait plus généralement un sacrement.

Le *barešnūm* serait ainsi une union aux puissances divines de la Terre? En tout cas, voici un fait: le candidat doit dormir à même le sol.

Et voici encore un trait qui manquait jusqu'ici à notre description et dont l'absence était de nature à nous gêner (si nous pensions à ce qu'est, dans l'hindouisme, la *dikṣā*: accès à des vérités, incorporation à une société, union à un dieu). Le candidat mazdéen à la prêtrise est gratifié d'une massue: *gurz*. Par là, il est assimilé à un dieu, car la massue n'était pas seulement l'attribut d'anciens héros tueurs de démon, tel *Frētōn*, mais il l'était aussi de Mithra. (Signalons en passant que l'importance décisive du Videvdat pour habiliter le prêtre à célébrer le yasna trouve ici son explication: le Videvdat, code anti-démoniaque, est l'arme qui lui permettra, comme la massue, d'abattre les démons).

Mithra a encore ici la place — c'est-à-dire la première — qu'il partageait jadis, semble-t-il, avec un autre ahura, avec celui qui, par l'action de Zarathustra, a tendu, sans jamais y parvenir complètement — à règner seul dans le ciel: Ahura Mazda, le Seigneur Sage.

D'autre part, le temple dans lequel l'initié est admis comme prêtre s'appelle *dar i mihr* ,porte ou maison de Mithra'. Il me semble assez remarquable que, quand on examine les rites et non pas seulement les formules, on s'aperçoive que ce n'est pas Ahura Mazda qui est en jeu, mais Mithra, le Soleil, et Spenta Armaiti, la Terre.

En résumé, l'initiation mazdéenne se présente, au terme de cette analyse, avec les caratères suivants:

1) c'est une épreuve, bien que le caractère d'épreuve physique soit, au premier degré, entièrement aboli;

2) c'est une renaissance; sans doute, le caractère sexuel ou biologique fait défaut, mais le symbolisme de renaissance est cependant exprimé par l'ablution et les vêtements neufs;

3) c'est une purification: ablutions et *barešnūm*;

4) (ceci est le trait central): c'est une adhésion ou incorporation à un univers spirituel, par suite d'une conversion-confession; cet univers spirituel, la *Dēn*, est conçu comme un ensemble de vétités et de devoirs, et aussi comme une réalité cosmique;

5) cet univers est un monde fermé, interdit aux profanes; mais ceci n'est pas souligné;

6) enfin l'initiation mazdéenne comporte union à des dieux qui sont plus anciens que Mazda, à savoir: le Soleil et la Terre; et, en ce qui concerne l'initiation des prêtres, l'assimilation à l'un de ces dieux, Mithra.

L'initiation parsie n'est peut-être, après tout, pas si pauvre qu'on l'aurait cru.

POUR UNE ETUDE DE
L'INITIATION DANS L'ANCIEN ISRAEL

PAR

ANDRÉ CAQUOT
Paris

Une enquête sur l'initiation dans l'acception la plus large de ce terme nous invite à examiner les données de chaque civilisation sur deux types de complexes rituels qui peuvent avoir des traits morphologiques communs, mais dont le rôle social est différent. La distinction est clairement établie par M. Eliade [1] — il s'agit: 1.) des rites de puberté (les *Reifezeremonien* d'A. Jensen), "grâce auxquels les jeunes gens accèdent au sacré, à la connaissance et à la sexualité, deviennent véritablement des êtres humains"; 2.) des „initiations spécialisées, que certains individus entreprennent afin de transcender leur condition humaine et de devenir les protégés des êtres surnaturels ou même leurs semblables", initiation qui agrège un individu dans une société vouée à une activité particulière ou à une spéculation particulière. A ces deux domaines d'étude, il faudrait peut être en joindre un troisième, celui des „thèmes initiatiques" détachés en apparence de toute connexion sociale et rituelle.

Le secteur géographique et historique qui est le nôtre se prête assez mal à ce genre d'études; nos documents les plus utiles, ceux de la littérature israélite et juive ancienne ne sont pas des plus explicites sur l'initiation, et l'interprétation est rendue difficile par l'écart constant entre les faits rituels qui nous sont communiqués et qui remontent peut-être au fond des âges, et l'interprétation des faits, la "justification subjective", ce que les ethnographes appellent le „native point of view", de ces mêmes faits. Pour le rite qui doit longuement retenir notre attention, la circoncision, il est incontestable que la justification „classique" — la circoncision signe de l'alliance — est tardive: on a surimposé une interprétation religieuse, qui peut s'éclairer par les conditions dans lesquelles vivait la communauté juive

---

[1] *Naissances mystiques*, Paris, 1959, p. 263.

post-exilique, à une vieille coutume dont les origines mêmes sont indiscernables, et non seulement les origines, mais encore la fonction que pouvait avoir la pratique dans la société israélite antique. L'étude des rituels israélites se heurte à la même difficulté que celles des mythes, ou des thèmes mythiques de l'A.T., difficulté parfaitement mise en lumière par C. Lévi-Strauss [1]). „L.'A.T. qui met certainement en œuvre des matériaux mythiques les reprend en vue d'une autre fin que celle qui fut originellement la leur. Des rédacteurs les ont sans nul doute, déformés en les interprétant ... Il faudrait commencer par un travail préliminaire, visant à retrouver le résidu mythologique et archaïque sous-jacent à la littérature biblique ...'' Plus loin, Lévi-Strauss dénonce le cercle vicieux que comporterait l'analyse structurale, mais nous pourrions dire aussi bien l'étude fonctionnelle, des mythes (et des rites) bibliques: „Leur sens ne nous est accessible que par référence au contexte ethnographique, c.à.d. à ce que nous pouvons connaître du genre de vie, des techniques et de l'organisation sociale, or dans le cas de l'ancien judaïsme, le contexte ethnographique fait presque entièrement défaut, sinon celui précisément qu'on peut extraire des textes bibliques.'' Tout ce que nous pouvons saisir à propos d'un rituel, „initiatique'' ou autre, c'est une justification subjective ou une série de justifications subjectives, plus ou moins situables ou explicables à un certain moment de l'évolution religieuse d'Israël, avec un degré déjà assez grand d'hypothèse. C'est tout ce à quoi peut prétendre, me semble-t-il, l'histoire des religions. La recherche du dernier mot, de la „justification objective'' nous ne pouvons que la confier à l'anthropologie, mais là la part de l'hypothèse n'est-elle pas encore plus considérable? Autrement dit, il s'agirait pour nous d'abord de décrire le rituel dans sa matérialité, de déterminer sa constance, ensuite et surtout de relever le sens qui est donné à la pratique aux différents niveaux chronologiques et sociaux, dans la mesure où nous pouvons les discerner. Parler de niveaux sociaux est sans doute mal approprié à notre sujet, car notre littérature n'est guère „populaire'', c'est l'œuvre de spécialistes religieux, et s'il y a bien dans l'A.T. les matériaux folkloriques chers à Frazer, ils ont en général pris place dans une synthèse „tendancieuse'' qui les fait servir à ses fins, et ce sont parfois elles les plus évidentes. Les justifications présentées sont celles de penseurs qui réfléchissent sur ce qu'on fait et essaient de lui donner un sens. C'est de ces justifications

---

[1]) Voir *Esprit*, Novembre 1963, p. 631.

que nous pourrions, au mieux faire l'histoire. L'histoire du rituel lui même ne doit pas être trop ambitieuse: peut-on poser en termes d'histoire le problème de *l'origine* de la circoncision par ex? J'en doute. Une hypothèse diffusionniste comme celle d'A. LODS[1]) qui ne fait que reprendre l'argumentation d'HÉRODOTE II, 104, à savoir que la circoncision est d'origine égyptienne (et d'abord africaine: passée d'Afrique en Égypte et de là chez les tribus sémitiques de la région syro-arabe) est-elle vérifiable?

Après avoir posé ces quelques principes, et avant de voir de plus près les questions relatives à la circoncision, je crois utile d'esquisser tout de suite quelques lignes de recherche sur le problème de l'initiation dans la civilisation et la religion d'Israël. Il y aurait trois champs de recherche:

a) celui des thèmes iniatiques (déplacés par rapport à tout contexte rituel ou social, éléments d'un „pattern" désintégré): il en est un assez important qui reparaît dans la littérature apocalyptique: celui du révélateur des secrets sur la fin des temps, qui reçoit, si l'on veut, une initiation individuelle dans le ciel où il est mystérieusement monté: le prototype serait *Hénoch*, mais la littérature apocalyptique attribue une aventure semblable à Abraham, Isaac, Lévi (dans le *Testament des XII Patriarches*), Moïse, Élie, Isaïe, Baruch, Esdras. A propos des ch. 3-4 et 8 du *Testament de Lévi*, G. WIDENGREN[2]) a étudié tous les éléments d'un rituel effectif que nous y trouvons transposés (rituel d'intronisation qui est une forme priviligiée d'initiation). Le nom d'Hénoch à lui seul invite à mettre cette figure au centre d'une étude des thèmes initiatiques dans la littérature israélite: son nom se rattache à la racine *ḥnk* que signifie en hébreu „inaugurer" ou „consacrer", et en arabe *ḥanaka*=„frotter le palais des nouveaux nés avec du jus de datte" est un dénominatif de *ḥanak* ,hébreu *ḥek* „palais". Il est probable que c'est pour le qualifier d'initié que le récit *P* de Genèse 5: 22 donne le nom d'Hénoch au septième patriarche antédiluvien qui, comme on l'a remarqué depuis longtemps, paraît correspondre au septième roi antédiluvien En-men-dur-an-na/ En-me-dur-an-ki de la liste royale mésopotamienne, le roi légendaire de Sippar, connu ailleurs comme favori du dieu Shamash et fondateur de la corporation des devins, donc détenteur et révélateur des secrets célestes. Il faut noter que le récit *J* de Genèse 4: 17, prononçant le nom d'Hénoch à propos de l'inauguration de la première ville, joue

[1]) *Israël des origines au milieu du VIIIe siècle*, Paris, 1930, p. 227.
[2]) *Sakrales Königtum im A.T. und im Judentum*, Stuttgart, 1955, p. 49-53.

aussi sur son nom.[1]) Dans la même ligne, on pourrait chercher des
thèmes d'initiation individuelle au sens d'accès à un mode supérieur
de connaissance, dans des récits d'expérience prophétique, tel celui
d'Isaïe 6. Mais là on aborde peut-être le deuxième champ de recherche.

b) Celui des initiations spécialisées, grâce auxquelles l'individu
pénètre dans une communauté restreinte consacrée à des exercices
particuliers. On peut deviner d'après quelques traces, que de telles
initiations existaient à haute époque. Il en est une assez bien connue
à basse époque: le rituel d'agrégation dans la communauté sectaire de
Qumran, caractérisé par une catéchèse et un noviciat [2]). Cette initiation essénienne pose le problème historique des rapports avec des
initiations occidentales, comme celle des Pythagoriciens. Elle représente en tout cas une innovation du bas-judaïsme par rapport à la
religion traditionnelle. A haute époque, les indices de communautés
initiatiques restreintes sont beaucoup plus fuyants. Pourtant, on peut
supposer qu'il existait une initiation prophétique, bien que nous n'en
ayons que des indices exterieurs. D'une part l'existence de guildes
prophétiques (*bənē nəbî'îm*) groupées autour d'un maître ou „père",
institution qui apparaît pour la première fois dans les temps qui ont
précédé immédiatement les débuts de la royauté et qui paraît à son
apogée au moment de la grande crise sociale du IXe siècle dans le
royaume du Nord (cycles d'Élie et d'Élisée dans les livres des Rois).
D'autre part, I Rois 20: 38 et s. nous apprend tout à fait incidemment
que les prophètes se reconnaissent à une marque sur le front. Allusion
qu'éclaire Ézéchiel 9: 4: les justes qui doivent être préservés lors de
la visite de YHWH sont marqués par l'ange d'une croix au front
(*taw*): cette marque est donc interprétée comme signe d'une consécration particulière de celui qui la porte. Un pareil usage a dû se
maintenir assez longtemps, puisque Zacharie 13: 6 fait allusion à
une marque que le prophète porte „entre ses mains", c'est-à-dire sur
la poitrine. D'après le récit de I Rois 20: 35 et s. il est permis de
penser que le prophète qui pour dissimuler son état a mis un voile
(*'aper*) au dessus de ses yeux est rasé. C'est pourquoi selon II Rois
2: 23 Élisée — qui n'est pas particulièrement âgé — est traité de

---

[1]) Sur le personnage d'Hénoch et l'influence sur ses légendes d'une notion
babylonienne de l'initiation, voir H. LUDIN-JANSEN, *Die Henochgestalt. Eine vergleichende religionsgeschichtliche Untersuchung*, Oslo, 1939, et P. GRELOT, „La légende
d'Hénoch dans les apocryphes et dans la Bible: origine et signification", dans
Recherches de science religieuse, 46, 1958, p. 5-26 et 181-210.
[2]) Voir M. DELCOR, „Le vocabulaire juridique, cultuel et mystique de l'„initiation" dans la Secte de Qumran", dans *Qumran-Probleme*, Berlin, 1963, p. 109-131.

„tondu" (*qereaḥ*) par les gamins irrespectueux. Le prophète était rasé comme l'homme en deuil, et peut-être la marque prophétique doit-elle être rapprochée des incisions, autre manifestation extérieure du deuil [1]). Il y avait sans doute là un moyen de distinguer le prophète du prêtre, puisque le „Code de sainteté", un des éléments les plus anciens du cycle *P*, interdit au prêtre le rasage et les incisions (Lévitique 21: 5). Quel est le sens de ces marques extérieures, qu'on peut tenir pour des marques initiatiques? Une hypothèse psychanalytique verrait dans le rasage le symbole d'une répression de l'agressivité. Une hypothèse structuraliste, comme celle de E. LEACH [2]), qui conteste la valeur symbolique absolue conférée par la psychanalyse à de tels comportements, pour ne leur reconnaître qu'une signification „de position", permettrait d'opposer par ce biais à l'homme quelconque qui porte une chevelure coupée et soignée le „prophète" tondu, et également le nazir hirsute, à propos duquel nos textes établissent nettement la connexion entre chevelure entière et défaite et l'agressivité (on connaît l'histoire de Samson, voir Juges 16: 17). Il se peut que l'institution israélite du naziréat ait son origine dans la guerre sainte: Samson représente le type du combattant charismatique et invincible. Elle a en tout cas perdu sons sens, la loi „sacerdotale" sur le *nazir* de Nombres 6 le définit comme consacré à YHWH sans qu'on sache quel est le but de cette consécration, et ce que l'histoire présente comme un charisme est devenu un vœu individuel et volontaire (à ce titre, il est encore question de nazir dans le livre des Actes 21: 21-24). Si je pense à une fonction originellement guerrière du *nazir*, c'est qu'il s'oppose aussi à la civilisation cananéenne en s'interdisant l'usage du vin. Y avait-il à l'époque de la conquète des confréries de *nəzirim*? Nous n'en savons rien. Mais il est frappant qu'Amos 2: 11-12 mette en parallèle *nəbi'im* et *nəzirim* (ceux-ci recrutés parmi les *baḥurim*) comme des personnes suscitées par Dieu pour le salut commun et empêchées d'exercer leur fonction par la perversité du peuple.

c) Le troisième domaine d'étude serait celui des „rites de puberté". Le judaïsme actuel connaît un seuil d'âge comportant une cérémonie de maturité, à treize ans on devient *bar miṣwåh*. La cérémonie qui

---

[1]) Le Deutéronome (14: 1) interdit de se raser et de s'inciser „pour un mort". La pratique est cependant attestée par les prohètes, d'Amos à Ézéchiel sans encourir leur censure.

[2]) „The Magical Hair", dans *Journal of the Royal Anthropological Institute*, 88, 1958, p. 147-164.

marque ce seuil d'âge est tardive, bien que la Mishna (*Abot* 5: 24) signale qu'à treize ans l'homme est „sujet au commandement." Le seul rite de passage anciennement connu est celui de la circoncision qui est dans le judaïsme un rite de la toute première enfance. Mais était-ce le cas dans un passé plus reculé? On l'a contesté, et les historiens admettent d'ordinaire que la circoncision était à l'origine une pratique pré-nuptiale, une cérémonie de maturité qu'on aurait „adoucie" — dit WELLHAUSEN [1]) — en la reportant au huitième jour après la naissance. Telle est l'opinion courante [2]), appuyée sur de nombreux parallèles ethnologiques et sur l'exégèse de Genèse 34 et Exode 4: 24-26. Seuls quelques historiens plus „fondamentalistes" considèrent que la circoncision du nouveau-né est une donnée des plus anciennes [3]).

Avant de reprendre ce problème, examinons le vocabulaire et quelques modalités de la circoncision israélite.

Le verbe *mâl* „circoncire" n'est pas employé en un autre sens; l'usage métaphorique qui en est fait dépend toujours étroitement de l'acception usuelle: c'est „circoncire le prépuce du cœur" (voir Jérémie 4: 4 Deutéronome 10: 16). L'étymologie en est inconnue: on ne peut donc constater l'équivoque présentée une fois par l'égyptien entre „circoncire" et „châtrer", qui pourrait être instructive. Les autres termes techniques se rattachent à la racine *ġrl*. Ce sont *ʿârel* „incirconcis" et *ʿorlâh* „prépuce", les emplois métaphoriques en sont plus nombreux, mais dérivés eux aussi de la circoncision rituelle: „cœur incirconcis" (Lévitique 26: 41) incirconcis de cœur" (Ézéchiel 44: 9), „incirconcis de lèvres" (=bègues, Exode 6: 12, 30, textes *P*), „oreille incirconcise" (Jérémie 6: 10). Ces images révèlent que la circoncision passe pour une perfection de l'individu, que le „prépuce" est un obstacle au bon fonctionnement de l'organe; on saisit là une „justification subjective" de la pratique. Selon Lévitique 19: 23 (également un texte *P*) les fruits d'un arbre nouvellement planté constituent son prépuce pendant trois ans, c'est-à-dire qu'ils sont impropres à la consommation. La circoncision est synonyme de pureté rituelle dans la logique de la législation „sacerdotale" qui place le commandement de circoncire les enfants le huitième jour parmi les lois sur le pur et l'impur. Notons enfin un emploi métony-

---

[1]) *Prolegomena to the History of Ancient Israel* (réimp. New York, 1957) p. 340.

[2]) Voir en dernier lieu H. RINGGREN, *Israelitische Religion*, Stuttgart, 1963, p. 183 et s.

[3]) Ainsi M. BUBER, *Moïse*, Paris, 1957, p. 64 et s.

mique de ʿorlåh à I Samuel 18: 25-27 et II Samuel 3: 14: Saül demande
à David en guise de *mohar* pour sa fille Mikal cent prépuces de Philistins. Il est clair que c'est une ,,pars pro toto'' et que la pratique à
laquelle il est fait allusion est l'émasculation de l'ennemi dont G.
WIDENGREN a recueilli des attestations sur tous les points de l'aire
sémitique, de l'Assyrie à l'Éthiopie [1]). Les Philistins étant désignés
dans les textes historiques comme les incirconcis par excellence, le
prépuce représente ici les parties sexuelles. Etymologiquement
ʿårel ʿorlåh ont un équivalent exact en arabe *ġurla* ,,prépuce'' ,'*aġral*
,,incirconcis'', on ne peut remonter au delà du sémitique. C'est donc
encore un terme au champ sémantique très restreint et qui n'autorise-
rait aucune spéculation, si l'étymologie pouvait jamais prouver
quelque chose . En ce qui concerne la technique, rien ne permet de
penser que la circoncision ait jamais été autre chose que la περιτομή.
On a cru pouvoir remarquer que la partie du prépuce enlevée n'avait
pas toujours été aussi grande, parce que selon *I Maccabées* 1: 15 les
juifs hellénisants qui fréquentaient les gymnases se faisaient ,,refaire
des prépuces'' et reniaient ainsi l'alliance; l'ablation totale du prépuce
serait l'effet d'une exigence des piétistes d'alors [2]). Le texte des
Maccabées n'est pas des plus clairs, mais Saint Épiphane a donné
quelques détails sur l'opération qui invalident cette opinion [3]). Selon
Josué 5: 2, la circoncision était pratiquée avec des couteaux de pierre,
signe incontestable d'archaïsme [4]).

A la seule exception de Josué 5, nos textes présentent la circoncision
comme une cérémonie privée, qui n'est soumise à aucune détermina-
tion de lieu ou de temps. Les autres modalités (qui opère? âge de
l'opéré?) et la raison d'être de la pratique ne peuvent être examinées
qu'à propos des textes qu'on va passer en revue et dont les données
ne sont pas toujours concordantes.

Nous partirons des textes les plus récents, ceux qui remontent à
l'époque d'après l'Exil. La loi de Lévitique 12: 3 ordonne incidemment
la circoncision du nouveau-né le huitième jour, dans un règlement sur
la purification de l'accouchée. Le sujet qui circoncit n'est pas indiqué,
car la phrase est au passif (*yimmōl baśar ʿorlåtō*), ce qui laisse penser
que l'opération est faite par un *mōhel*. On ignore à quelle époque s'est

---

[1]) Dans *Studia orientalia J. Pedersen dicata*, Copenhague, 1953, p. 377-384.
[2]) Voir R. BRIFFAULT, *The Mothers*, édition abrégée, New York, 1963, p. 399.
[3]) MIGNE, *Patrologia graeca*, 43, col. 264; voir F. M. ABEL, *Les livres des Maccabées*, Paris, 1949, p. 8.
[4]) Exode 4: 25 parle de ,,caillou''.

établie la coutume de circoncire à huit jours, mais il est admis sans doute depuis une haute antiquité que l'âge de huit jours est un seuil dans la vie de l'enfant. C'est ainsi que dans le texte ougaritique *II Aqhat* II, 2, 26-40, les *kṯrt* demeurent sept jours auprès de la mère d'Aqhat qui vient d'accoucher [1]). Les textes *P* contiennent deux autres allusions à la circoncision. L'une est législative: Exode 12: 44-48 ordonne de circoncire l'esclave et le client qui participent à la cérémonie domestique de la Pâque. L'autre est historique et tient lieu dans le cycle *P* de mythe d'origine de la pratique: Genèse 17 fait de la circoncision opérée à huit jours sur les enfants et les esclaves nés à la maison le signe de l'alliance. Après avoir reçu cet ordre, Abraham se fait circoncire et circoncit lui-même tous les mâles de sa maison. Il a alors quatre vingt dix neuf ans, et son fils Ismaël treize ans. Isaac né plus tard est circoncis a huit jours (Genèse 21: 4). La circoncision a alors le sens d'un rite d'agrégation dans la société juive et se comprend à un âge où les juifs vivent au milieu de peuples incirconcis [2]). La communauté juive trouvait dans cette pratique un moyen de se distinguer des païens au milieu desquels elle vivait, et c'est pourquoi les rabbins ont défendu si fermement la circoncision, l'imposant même aux prosélytes. Margaret MEAD [3]) souligne cette signification „de position" que la circoncision peut encore présenter de nos jours: pour les Grecs vivant en symbiose avec des Turcs et des Juifs, le prépuce est une marque de nationalité, et ils résistent à la circoncision ordonnée par un médecin. Une marque de cette sorte n'a donc pas besoin d'être extérieurement visible pour jouer son rôle de signe distinctif [4]).

Attachait-on alors d'autres „justifications subjectives" à la circoncision [5])? A. WENDEL [6]) suggère qu'on lui prêtait encore le pouvoir d'accroître la fecondité, en raison des promesses contenues dans le contexte (Genèse 17: 5-6); il semble au contraire que la fixation de

---

[1]) Voir A. VAN SELMS, *Marriage and Family Life in Ugaritic Literature*, Londres, 1954, p. 85 et s.

[2]) La circoncision paraît inconnue des Babyloniens. Chez les Sémites occidentaux, elle semble avoir passé de mode: d'après Jérémie 9: 25 les Ammonites étaient circoncis, or selon Judith 14: 10, l'Ammonite Ahior se fait circoncire. Il est vrai qu'on ne peut guère tirer parti de ce texte qui prend les Ammonites comme type de païens.

[3]) *Cultural Patterns and Technical Change*, U.N.E.S.C.O., 1955, p. 222.

[4]) Contre A. BERTHOLET, *Histoire de la civilisation d'Israël*, Paris, 1929, p. 128.

[5]) P. RADIN, *Primitive Religion*, New York, 1957, p. 91, cite une série de justifications subjectives avancées par les Australiens à propos de la circoncision.

[6]) *Das Opfer in der israelitischen Religion*, Leipzig, 1927, p. 17.

l'âge à huit jours ait fait perdre de vue un lien immédiat entre le rite et la capacité procréatrice. En revanche, comme la circoncision est le signe de l'alliance, et comme les rites archaïques d'alliance comportent une effusion de sang, il est possible qu'elle ait été alors interprétée comme une sorte de pacte de sang entre l'homme et la divinité. C'est aussi un rituel de purification de l'enfant comme l'indique le contexte de Lévitique 12: 3 et l'emploi métaphorique de ,,prépuce'' signalé plus haut. Isaïe 52: 1 met en parallèle ,,incirconcis'' et ,,impur''.

Avant les textes *P*, trois passages d'Ézéchiel (28: 10, 31: 18, 32: 19-32) renferment une allusion assez mystérieuse à la ,,mort des incirconcis'' décrite comme un sort particulièrement redoutable et assimilée à la mort violente (,,percé par l'épée''). On retiendra la solution proposée par A. LODS [1]) et O. EISSFELDT [2]): Les incirconcis, dont le sort est comparé à celui des assassinés, sont comme les ἄωροι, les βιοθάνατοι ou les ἄταφοι des Grecs. Mourir avec son prépuce, c'est mourir prématurément, avant d'être un homme fait. Sans nous dire à quel âge on devient un homme fait, cette allusion révèle une interprétation de la circoncision comme achèvement de l'homme. Interprétation souvent reprise par les phénoménologues: les mutilations initiatiques, qu'aucune considération utilitaire ne peut justifier [3]) sont destinées à parfaire la nature, à marquer la transcendance de la condition humaine par rapport à la nature [4]). Ce sens a pu être prété par les juifs à la circoncision, même détachée de tout le contexte d'initiation sexuelle qui est le sien dans les ethnies les plus diverses, dans la mesure où elle marquait, non une maturité physique, ni même une maturité sociale, mais ce qu'on pourrait appeler une maturité idéale reconnue à tout nouveau-né mâle.

Telles sont les données des textes postérieurs à la captivité de Babylone, c'est à dire au moment où Israël s'est replié sur lui-même pour préserver son existence. La vieille pratique acquiert alors une fonction sociale de distinction que les textes antérieurs ne lui recon-

---

[1]) ,,La mort des incirconcis'', dans *Comptes rendus de l'Académie des Inscriptions*, 1943, p. 271-283.

[2]) ,,Schwerterschlagene bei Hezechiel'', dans *Studies in the O.T. Prophecy*, Edimbourg, 1950, p. 72-81.

[3]) Au sujet de la circoncision, on a renoncé aux justifications hygiénistes qu'une certaine propagande mettait en avant au siècle dernier dans les pays anglo-saxons.

[4]) Voir G. VAN DER LEEUW, *La religion dans son essence et ses manifestations*, Paris, 1948, p. 190 et s. (§ 22, 5); J. CAZENEUVE, *Les rites et la condition humaine*, Paris, 1958, p. 349. Selon le Midrash Tanhuma (*Wayyiqra*, 18*a*), c'est à propos de la circoncision que Rabbi Aqiba déclare que les œuvres de l'homme sont plus belles que celles de Dieu.

naissent pas au même titre. La réflexion religieuse s'y est alors attachée pour lui prêter un sens ou des sens. Il fallait essayer de dégager ces „justifications subjectives", sans les prendre nécessairement pour argent comptant. Il importe de saisir les motivations conscientes des actes religieux, mais aussi de ne pas croire qu'elles livrent le dernier mot.

En remontant le cours du temps, nous rencontrons des textes d'une nature beaucoup plus mystérieuse.

Josué 5 est une notice incluse dans l'histoire sainte deutéronomiste. Elle contient du matériel traditionnel, réinterprété sans aucun doute, mais trop peu pour ne pas laisser transparaître une représentation de la circoncision différente de celle qui a prévalu. YHWH ordonne à Josué de faire des couteaux de pierre et de circoncire tous les Israélites nés pendant la traversée du désert, ce qu'on n'a pu faire pendant le voyage. La scène se passe à Gilgal, au lieu dit „la colline des prépuces". Le récit est suivi de celui de la célébration de la Pâque à Gilgal. Le toponyme Gilgal est expliqué par la parole de YHWH à Josué (v. 9) „aujourd'hui j'ai roulé (*gallōtī*) l'opprobre de l'Égypte (*ḥerpat miṣrayim*) loin de vous". On peut attribuer au traditionniste deutéronomiste la présentation de la circoncision comme une qualification cultuelle pour la Pâque, et le jeu de mot du v. 9 sur *gal* „rouler" et *gilgal*. L'expression *ḥerpat miṣrayim* est équivoque: ce peut être l'opprobre qui entache les Égyptiens aux yeux des Israélites, ou l'opprobre infligée aux Israélites par les Égyptiens. Dans le premier cas, on pourrait considérer que cet opprobre n'est autre que le prépuce, ce qui signifierait que les Égyptiens étaient tenus pour incirconcis. Dans le second cas, l'expression signifierait que les Égyptiens faisaient honte aux Israélites de leur prépuce, et Josué, en les circoncisant, aurait supprimé ce motif de raillerie. Mais il est peu probable que „rouler l'opprobre loin de . . ." soit une allusion directe à la circoncision. La locution signifie simplement „dégager de l'opprobre" [1] et rappelle la délivrance d'Israël de l'esclavage égyptien. C'est pourquoi le v. 9 tout entier peut être mis au compte du Deutéronomiste qui développe son thème de la „délivrance de l'Égypte". Pour lui, la circoncision est un signe d'affranchissement et une marque distinguant l'Israélite de ses oppresseurs étrangers. Derrière la re-élaboration deutéronomiste on devine cependant une tradition du vieux sanctuaire amphictyonique de Gilgal [2], qui expliquait le toponyme „la colline des prépuces" et

---

[1] Comparer Psaume 119: 22.
[2] Voir H. J. Kraus, „Gilgal", dans *Vetus Testamentum*, 1, 1951, p. 181-199.

gardait peut-être le souvenir d'une circoncision collective à l'occasion d'une solennité en ce lieu saint. Le passage rappelle bien des données ethnographiques sur les circoncisions par classes d'âge. S'agit-il d'une pratique propre à la Gilgal antique, plutôt que d'une coutume de tous les ancêtres d'Israël? Il me semble en tout cas que l'institution, telle qu'elle apparaît au niveau de la tradition de base, n'a rien à faire avec l'Égypte, ce n'est ni une imitation des Égyptiens, ni une réaction contre leur usage.

Le récit „élohiste" de Genèse 36 paraît nous placer sur un terrain plus solide. Sichem le Hiwwite a violé Dina fille de Jacob et veut l'épouser (v. 3-4). Les fils de Jacob ne consentent au mariage de leur sœur que si Sichem, son père et tous les siens se font circoncire, comme le sont les Israélites „Nous ne pouvons ... donner notre sœur à un homme qui aurait son prépuce, car ce serait une honte pour nous" (v. 14).

Sichem accepte, mais les fils de Jacob ont accueilli par ruse les propositions de Sichem, ils ne songent qu'à venger l'honneur de leur sœur et massacrent Sichem et sa maisonnée. L'analyse de ce chapitre est des plus délicates, et l'accord n'est pas fait à son sujet [1]). A première vue, Sichem l'incirconcis a commis un acte monstrueux en violant une Israélite et en voulant l'épouser. Cela permet de penser que la circoncision est présentée ici comme une condition requise pour la nuptialité, et tel était peut-être le sens du récit à un certain niveau de la tradition. Mais dans son état actuel Genèse 34 est explicable autrement. Reportant à l'époque patriarcale un épisode qui se situerait mieux à l'âge de la „Conquête", le récit traite de quelque chose de plus important qu'une affaire de famille. Il rappelle à quelle condition un groupe ethnique étranger pouvait entrer dans la communauté israélite, le *connubium* n'est qu'un aspect du synoecisme, c'est pour former avec les Israélites „un seul peuple" (v. 16) que se font circoncire les gens de Sichem, et non le seul héros de l'histoire. Sichem est ici l'éponyme de la cité bien plus qu'un individu, et les rapports sociaux sous entendus dans Genèse 34 sont des rapports de groupes tribaux, non de groupes familiaux. Genèse 34 rappelle, ou suggère, que des incirconcis habitaient la Palestine pré-israélite [2]). La circon-

---

[1]) Voir la discussion dans E. NIELSEN, *Shechem. A Traditio-Historical Investigation*, Copenhague, 1955, p. 241-259.

[2]) Il est question à Genèse 34 de „Hiwwites", c'est à dire de non-Sémites, à l'époque de la „Conquête", les cités-états de Canaan paraissent avoir été dominées par une aristocratie non-sémitique, vraisemblablement incirconcise.

cision serait ainsi revêtue de son sens „de position" qu'on a dégagé
des textes postérieurs.

Exode 4: 24-26 est le plus énigmatique de tous nos documents.
Il apparaît comme un „bloc erratique", mal rattaché au contexte. Il
est précédé d'un paragraphe où YHWH ordonne à Moïse de partir
avec sa femme et ses fils pour aller en Égypte, annoncer au Pharaon
les malheurs qui l'attendent. Moïse devra dire au Pharaon, au nom de
YHWH: „je tuerai ton fils" (v. 23). C'est sans doute à cause de ces
mots qu'on a fait suivre les versets 24-26 parlant d'une menace pesant
sur un autre enfant.

V. 24 Et ce fut en route, à la halte de la nuit que YHWH *le* ren-
contra et chercha à *le* faire mourir.

V. 25 Et Sipporah (— femme de Moise —) prit un caillou et coupa
le prépuce de son fils (à elle), et elle toucha *ses* pieds (c'est à dire *ses*
parties sexuelles, à lui). Et elle dit: „Tu es pour moi un mari de sang
(*ḫătan dămīm*).

V. 26 Et il se retira de lui. Alors elle dit „mari de sang" à propos(?)
des circoncisions.

Les pronoms posent la principale difficulté. Qui est rencontré par
YHWH? De qui Sipporah touche-t-elle les „pieds"? A qui dit-elle
„tu es pour moi un mari de sang"? Et que signifie cette dernière
expression, que les Septante ont renoncé a comprendre?

Pour toute une série d'exégètes, ce fragment rappelle la circoncision
pré-nuptiale de Moise. „Tu es pour moi un mari de sang" fait allusion
aux noces de Sipporah. WELLHAUSEN [1]) en rapproche l'usage de
certaines tribus arabes où la fiancée regarde si le jeune homme frémit
pendant l'opération. J. HENNINGER [2]) signale que chez certains
Bédouins des chants de noce accompagnent la circoncision. L'opération pratiquée par Sipporah sur Moise serait une manière d'écarter
un démon revendiquant le *ius primae noctis*, on le trompe en lui mettant
du sang sur le sexe et en lui disant „mari de sang". La pratique
s'inscrirait dans une catégorie de charmes pré-nuptiaux largement
attestée. Cette histoire aurait été édulcorée, et Moïse remplacé par
son fils. De fait, il n'est pas question de Moïse dans la péricope, et la
reconstitution proposée, si séduisante soit-elle en raison des parallèles qu'elle peut invoquer, pèche surtout par la nécessité de postuler
cette substitution ou un transfert symbolique de l'opération du père

---

[1]) *Reste arabischen Heidentums*[2], Berlin, 1897, p. 175, note 5.
[2]) „Eine eigenartige Beschneidungsform in Südwestarabien", dans *Anthropos*,
33, 1938, p. 952-958 et 35-36, 1940-41, p. 370-376.

sur le fils [1]), qui revient de toute manière à prescrire la circoncision infantile.

Selon les Rabbins, Moïse a négligé de faire circoncire son fils, il est attaqué par un ange qui veut le punir de cette négligence, Sipporah se hâte de couper le prépuce de l'enfant et le jette aux pieds de Moïse [2]) en lui disant: ,,tu as été pour moi un mari de sang", c'est à dire" un mari meurtrier". Il s'agit d'une histoire effrayante destinée à inculquer la règle de la circoncision infantile [3]).

D'autres interprètes essayent d'expliquer le texte comme se rapportant bien au fils de Moïse et laissant Moïse lui-même hors de cause. H. KOSMALA [4]) voit dans la circoncision de l'enfant un sacrifice partiel de préservation. La mère touche le pied de son fils avec le prépuce qu'elle vient de trancher et les mots qu'elle lui addresse signifieraient: ,,tu es pour moi un circoncis marqué de sang". H. KOSMALA traduit ḥătan d'après le verbe arabe ḫatana ,,circoncire". Alors, la divinité qui attaquait l'enfant le laisse tranquille. J. MORGENSTERN [5]) tient aussi la circoncision, telle qu'elle apparaît à Exode 4, pour un rite de rédemption de l'enfant et d'agrégation sociale dont il s'efforce de préciser la fonction dans la société israélite archaïque. La circoncision établissait la relation de parenté entre l'enfant et la famille de sa mère. C'est pourquoi le nom du ,,beau père", arabe ḫatn, hébreu ḥōten est dérivé de la racine de ḫatana ,,circoncir". C'est à l'origine celui qui circoncit l'enfant de sa fille. En raison de l'urgence, Sipporah a procédé à la circoncision à la place de son père, ou de son frère aîné, et prononcé la parole rituelle: ,,tu es mon ḥătan dămīm, mon parent par le sang", le sens de ,,mari" pris par le mot ḥătăn est tenu pour secondaire. On ne peut discuter ici toute l'hypothèse sur les institutions familiales israélites que suppose cette interprétation [6]). Elle me paraît viciée par un contre-sens sur ḥătan dămīm. En inter-

---

[1]) Ainsi H. JUNKER, ,,Der Blutbräutigam", dans Bonner Biblische Beiträge, 1, 1950, p. 120-128.

[2]) On discute pour savoir si les ,,pieds" sont ceux de l'ange, de Moïse ou de son fils (Talmud de Babylone, Nedarim 32 a).

[3]) H. HUBERT et M. MAUSS (Mélanges d'histoire des religions, Paris, 1909, p. 125 et s.) adoptent cette exégèse en présentant la péricope comme un récit de sacrifice partiel de rachat opéré sur un substitut (le fils de Moïse).

[4]) The ,,Bloody Husband", dans Vetus Testamentum, 12, 1962, p. 14-28.

[5]) The ,,Bloody Husband" once again", dans Hebrew Union College Annual, 34, 1963, p. 35-70.

[6]) Sur la question des ,,survivances du matriarcat" en Israël, voir en dernier lieu W. PLAUTZ, ,,Zur Frage des Mutterrechts im A.T.", dans Zeitschrift für die A.T. Wissenschaft, 74, 1962, p. 9-30.

prétant „mari qui a failli verser le sang", les Rabbins étaient plus près de la vérité, car dans toutes les expressions ou *dâmîm* détermine un substantif il signifie „sanguinaire" [1]). Cette objection vaut aussi contre l'hypothèse de KOSMALA. Il reste à préciser ce qu'est un „mari de sang". L'interprétation la plus simple consiste à y voir un époux ou un fiancé capable de verser le sang, c'est à dire de déflorer une vierge. Malgré les obscurités dont le texte est entouré, peut-être à dessein, il laisse entrevoir que la circoncision était bien à haute époque un rite prénuptial.

Mais cette mutilation, qui est censée rendre l'homme apte au mariage est effectuée sur un enfant. La teneur d'Exode 4: 24-26 nous l'impose, et mieux vaut s'abstenir de reconstituer un texte „antérieur", entreprise que guettent tous les risques d'arbitraire. L'âge de l'enfant est tenu caché, on voit seulement qu'il est encore sous la dépendance de sa mère. Nous devinons de la sorte l'existence à haute époque d'une circoncision familiale exercée par la mère, et encore au IIème siècle avant notre ère, la mère était tenue pour responsable de la circoncision de ses fils (voir *I Maccabées* 1: 60, *II Maccabées* 6: 10) [2]). Le sens attaché à cette pratique était celui d'une préparation à la nuptialité, et les mots prononcés par Sipporah, qu'on pourrait gloser: „j'ai fait de toi un mari capable de déflorer une vierge", accompagnaient probablement l'opération comme formule rituelle, ainsi que l'a vu MORGENSTERN. C'est sans doute une particularité d'Israël, au moins parmi les Sémites, d'avoir placé la circoncision à un âge assez éloigné de la puberté physique, sans qu'on puisse savoir quand s'est instauré l'usage de circoncire à huit jours, et d'avoir ainsi reconnu aux jeunes enfants une maturité idéale. Cette particularité explique la fidélité à l'usage devenu un signe distinctif de l'appartenance à la communauté. Les valeurs attachées à la circoncision, et qui du point de vue social peuvent être considérées comme secondaires, se laissent mal discerner. Peut-être l'a-t-on présentée comme un sacrifice partiel de rachat, avant d'en faire le „signe de l'alliance".

L'usage qu'atteste Exode 4: 24-26 et qui a prévalu n'était sans

---

[1]) '*îš dâmîm*=„un homme sanguinaire"; '*îr dâmîm*=„une ville sanguinaire". Ajoutons que „sang" n'est pas employé en hébreu, comme il l'est en grec, au sens de „parenté".

[2]) Pendant la persécution d'Antiochus Épiphane, on déférait en justice les femmes „qui avaient circoncis leurs enfants". Même si on admet que c'est là une pratique de détresse, en l'absence de *môhel* régulier, ou si l'on traduit „qui avaient faire circoncire", il est incontestable que la responsabilité pouvait être reconnue à la mère ou lui incombait.

doute pas le seul qu'ait connu l'Israël antique. Je ne vois pas le moyen
d'harmoniser cette circoncision infantile pratiquée par la mère avec
ce que la vieille tradition de Gilgal décelable à Josué 5 paraît représenter. Mais ne faudrait-il pas éviter de concevoir l'histoire la plus
ancienne d'Israël d'une manière trop unilinéaire? N'y a-t-il pas eu
convergence dans l'amphictyonie de groupes d'origines diverses, aux
institutions différentes [1])?

---

[1]) J'ai évité d'aborder ici la question des valeurs „métaphoriques" à la recherche
desquelles la psychanalyse nous convie. F. Sierksma („Quelques remarques sur
la circoncision en Israel, dans *O.T. Studiën*, 9, 1951, p. 136-169) a esquissé une
brillante histoire de la circoncision d'un point de vue à la fois psychanalytique
et évolutionniste, mais elle doit demander à nos textes peut-être plus qu'ils ne
peuvent donner. On trouvera de nombreuses indications dans les *Symbolic Wounds*
de B. Bettelheim, New York, 1962, dont on connaît les critiques à l'égard de
Freud.

QUMRAN UND DIE ZWÖLF

VON

DAVID FLUSSER

Jerusalem

Die essenische „Einung" von Qumran war eine streng in sich geschlossene Gemeinde mit einer esoterischen Geheimlehre, einem Noviziat, Initiationen sowie einer vollkommenen hierarchischen Organisation. Das Christentum war stets offener als jene jüdische Sekte, doch fehlte es auch bei ihm nicht an Ansätzen zu einer Arkandisciplin und die Taufe ist nicht weit von einer Initiation entfernt. Der essenische Ursprung der Taufe ist nahezu allgemein anerkannt und auch die Möglichkeit eines gleichen Ursprungs des Messsakraments ist weitgehend zugestanden. Doch ist damit die Natur der Gemeinschaft Jesu selbst noch nicht bestimmt und es bleibt insbesondere die Frage offen, ob er etwas gleich der Gründung einer Kirche angestrebt hat. In dieser Allgemeinheit entzieht sich die Frage auch heute noch einer Lösung. Doch mögen wir wenigstens etwas über die vorchristlichen Wurzeln der Ideologie der wichtigen urchristlichen Institution der zwölf Apostel in Erfahrung bringen, wenn wir unsere Aufmerksamkeit einem essenischen Text zuwenden, der vor einigen Jahren veröffentlicht worden ist.

Der leider nur fragmentarisch erhaltene Text [1] ist ein „pescher", d.h. eine typologische Erklärung zu der Jesaiah-Stelle 54: 11-12 über das neue Jerusalem. „Wohlan, ich lege deine Steine in Hartmörtel ein, ich gründe dich in Saphire, aus Rubin mache ich deine Zinnen, deine Tore von Karfunkelstein, all deine Umfassung von Edelgestein". Die Deutung der Worte „ich gründe dich in Saphire"

---

[1] Die Ausgabe des Textes: J. M. ALLEGRO, „More Isaiah Commentaries from Qumran's Fourth Cave", *JBL*, 77, 1958, pp. 215-221; der Text wurde neu interpretiert durch Y. YADIN, „The Newly Published Pesharim of Isaiah", *Israel Exploration Journal* 9, 1959, pp. 39-42. Der Text wurde übersetzt durch Johann MAIER, *Die Texte vom Toten Meer*, Bd. I, München 1960, p. 189. Ich benutze hier diese Übersetzung mit einigen kleinen Änderungen und in der nächsten Zeit wird mein hebräischer Artikel erscheinen, der sich mit der ganzen Problematik des Fragments befassen wird.

ist nach der Rolle „dass sie die Gemeinschaft der Einung gegründet haben . . . die Priester . . . die Gemeinde Seiner Erwählten wie einen Saphir unter den Steinen". Die aus Rubin gemachten Zinnen des neuen Jerusalems werden „auf die zwölf" gedeutet. Das Ende der Zeile ist leiden abgebrochen. Von der nächsten Zeile sind die Anfangsworte „leuchten im Gericht [1]) der Urim und Tummim" erhalten. In den folgenden Zeilen wird die Umfassung von Edelgestein typologisch „auf die Stammeshäupter Israels" gedeutet.

Die Worte des Propheten über das endzeitliche Jerusalem verstand also die Sekte als eine symbolische Beschreibung ihres eigenen Wesens. Seltsam ist nur, dass in unserem Text die Zahl zwölf dreimal angedeutet ist, einmal wörtlich, das zweite Mal in der Erwähnung des Gerichtes der Urim und Tummim: die Brustplatte des Hohepriesters war nämlich aus zwölf Steinen zusammengesetzt, „auf den Namen der Söhne Israels, zwölf auf ihren Namen" — und am Ende unseres Textes sind obendrein die Stammeshäupter Israels erwähnt. Dies ist umso auffallender, als die Zahl Zwölf in dem Texte des Propheten Jesaiah selbst nicht vorkommt. Die Deutung des pescher ist anscheinend von dem Propheten Ezechiel beeinflusst, der in seiner Schilderung des Jerusalems der Endzeit sagt (48: 31), dass „die Tore der Stadt nach dem Namen der Stämme Israels" sein werden; von den „Toren von Karfunkelsteinen" spricht ja auch Jesaiah, und da nach der Auffassung der Sekte die zwei Propheten, Ezechiel und Jesaiah, dasselbe neue Jerusalem gesehen haben mussten, konnte die Sekte die Zahl zwölf aus Ezechiel in ihrem Kommentar auf die Vision Jesaias übertragen.

Dass in den Rollen vom Toten Meer die „Einung" von Qumran als ein Bau, Tempel oder Stadt beschrieben wird, ist bereits aus anderen Quellen bekannt [2]). Hier werden offensichtlich die einzelnen Steingattungen des neuen Jerusalems als die Institutionen der Sekte gedeutet. Es ist leider unmöglich auszumachen, über welche Institutionen unser Text spricht, da sowohl unser Wissen über die Organisation der Sekte als auch der Text selbst lückenhaft sind. Wir können nicht einmal sagen, ob die dreimalige Erwähnung der zwölf auf ein einziges Gremium aus zwölf Männern oder auf mehrere derartige Gremien anspielt. Nach der Kriegsrolle (II: 1-3) wird es in der

---

[1]) Oder nach einer anderen Entzifferung „wie das Gericht".
[2]) Siehe O. BETZ, „Felsenmann und Felsengemeinde", *ZNW* 48, 1957, 49-77; D. FLUSSER, *The Dead Sea Sect and Pre-Pauline Christianity, Scripta Hierosolymitana* 4, 1958, 229-236. Siehe jetzt besonders B. Gärtner, The Temple and the Community in Qumran and the New Testament, Cambridge University Press 1965. Unser Fragment wird auf den Seiten 42-3, 78-9 behandelt.

Endzeit zwölf Priester, zwölf Vorsteher der Leviten und zwölf Stammeshäupter geben. Im Sektenkanon (VIII: 1) lesen wir von „zwölf
Männern und drei Priestern, vollkommen in allem, was offenbart
ist von dem ganzen Gesetz". Werden wir einmal wissen können, wie
diese Institutionen mit der dreimaligen Erwähnung der zwölf in unserem Text zusammenhängen?

Für unsere Untersuchung ist wichtig, dass in unserm Fragment
nicht nur dreimal die Zahl zwölf direkt oder indirekt erwähnt wird,
sondern dass auch von den Grundsteinen des neuen Jerusalems —
der Gemeinde gesprochen wird und eine Steingruppe mit den Häup-
tern der zwölf Stämme Israels gleichgesetzt wird, deren Namen ja
sowohl auf den Steinen der Brustplatte eingraviert waren, als auch
auf den zwölf Toren des neuen Jerusalems, wenn man so die Worte
Ezechiels in 48: 31 verstehen will. Dieselbe komplizierte Symbolik
finden wir in der Beschreibung des himmlischen Jerusalems in der
Offenbarung Johannis: „Und eine Mauer hat es gross und hoch, und
hat der Tore zwölf, und auf den Toren sind der Engel zwölf, und
Namen aufgeschrieben, die Namen der zwölf Stämme von den Söhnen
Israels. Gen Morgen sind drei Tore und gen Mitternacht drei Tore
und gen Mittag sind drei Tore und gen Abend sind drei Tore; und in
der Mauer der Stadt sind der Grundsteine zwölf, und darauf sind
zwölf Namen von des Lammes zwölf Aposteln". (21: 12-14). Und
weiter sagt der christliche Seher: „Die Grundsteine der Mauer um
die Stadt, sie sind mit allem köstlichen Gestein geschmückt" — und
diese einzelnen Edelsteine, welche die zwölf Grundsteine schmücken,
sind dieselben wie die Steine der Brustplatte des Hohepriesters, nur
in einer andern Ordnung. (Apk 21: 19-21). Dass die Grundsteine
mit diesen Edelsteinen nur geschmückt sind, scheint eine Abschwä-
chung einer ursprünglichen Gleichsetzung zu sein.

Sowohl in essenischen Fragment als auch in der Offenbarung
Johannis wird also das endzeitliche Jerusalem auf die Gemeinde
gedeutet: in beiden Texten wird von den Grundsteinen gesprochen,
und zwar in Verbindung mit den zwölf Steinen der Brustplatte des
Hohepriesters und mit dem Namen der zwölf Stämme Israels, und
diese Symbolik weist irgendwie auf ein Gremium von zwölf Männern
hin — in der Offenbarung sind es die zwölf Apostel. Wie ist diese
Verwandtschaft der zwei Texte zu erklären? Darf man annehmen,
dass die Offenbarung Johannis, die sonst vom essenischen Einfluss
ziemlich frei ist — zum Unterschied, z.B. vom Evangelium Johannis
— in diesem Punkt einem ausserchristlichen Einfluss ausgesetzt

war? Dies wird man jedoch wegen des verhältnismässig späten Datums der Apokalypse kaum annehmen dürfen. Obendrein ist zu bedenken, dass die Zwölf doch schon von Jesus eingesetzt worden sind und es deshalb kaum vorstellbar ist, dass ihre Ideologie erst im Zeitalter Domitians von einer essenischen Ideologie der Zwölf beeinflusst sein sollte. Dabei wird sich noch zeigen, dass man die symbolische Ideologie der Zwölf, die wir in der Offenbarung Johannis (und auch in dem essenischen Fragment) finden, zurück bis in die Tage Jesus verfolgen kann. Darum wird man annehmen müssen, dass bereits den zwölf Aposteln essenische Vorbilder vorangegangen sind und dass die Tradition in der Offenbarung Johannis eine im wahrsten Sinne des Wortes apostolische Tradition ist.

Dies kann auf Grund eines anderen Abschnittes der Offenbarung Johannis gezeigt werden, der auf derselben urchristlichen Überlieferung fusst. Johannes von Patmos schliesst den Brief an die Gemeinde von Philadelphia mit den Worten: „Der Überwinder, machen werde ich ihn zum Pfeiler in dem Tempel meines Gottes und er wird nie mehr von ihm weichen und schreiben werde ich auf ihn meines Gottes Namen, den Namen auch von meines Gottes Stadt, Jerusalems des neuen, das hernieder aus dem Himmel steigt von meinem Gott, und meinen neuen Namen (Apk 3: 12)". Die urchristliche Überlieferung über die Apostel, die wir auch aus der Schilderung des neuen Jerusalems kennen gelernt hatten, ist hier von dem Autor zu einer Anrede Christi an den einzelnen Gläubigen umgewandelt. Hier wie dort wird von einem neuen Jerusalem gesprochen, von einem Teil des Baues und von seiner Beschriftung. Der wichtigste Unterschied ist, dass hier im neuen Jerusalem der Tempel Gottes steht, wogegen nach der eigentlichen Schilderung des endzeitlichen Jerusalems es dort keinen Tempel geben wird, „denn Gott der Herr der Allbeherrscher, ihr Tempel ist er und das Lamm (Apk 21: 22)". Dass nach dieser Darstellung ein Tempel im neuen Jerusalem nicht vorhanden sein werde, ist gegen jüdische Erwartung [1]); die Parallelstelle (Apk 3:12) bewahrt also anscheinend in diesem Punkte die ursprüngliche, nicht tendenziös bearbeitete Überlieferung.

Ein anderer wichtiger Unterschied zwischen den zwei Parallelstellen in der Offenbarung Johannis ist, dass während im Kapitel 21 von den Grundsteinen mit den Namen der Apostel die Rede ist, im Kapitel 3 der Gläubige mit einem Pfeiler verglichen wird, auf dem

---

[1]) E. LOHMEYER, *Die Offenbarung des Johannes*, Tübingen 1953, S. 174.

Namen aufgeschrieben sind. Dies ist nicht eine willkürliche Änderung des Verfassers, denn das Symbol des Pfeilers gehört zu der urkirchlichen Überlieferung über die Apostel. Ein Zeuge für sie ist schon Paulus, der im Galaterbrief (2: 9) erzählt, er sei in Jerusalem Jakobus, Kephas und Johannes begegnet, „die da für Pfeiler galten". Und Klemens von Rom (5: 1-5) spricht von den tapferen Vorbildern seines Geschlechtes, von den „grössten und gerechtesten Pfeilern", von den guten Aposteln, und nennt Petrus und Paulus. Da sich gezeigt hat, dass Apk 3: 12 eine Bearbeitung der symbolischen Schilderung der Apostel ist, wird man annehmen müssen, dass die Bezeichnung „Pfeiler" in der Urgemeinde nicht nur eine Ehrenbezeichnung gewesen ist, sondern dass die Zwölf sowohl als Pfeiler des endzeitlichen Tempels als auch als Grundsteine des neuen Jerusalems symbolisch verstanden worden sind, wobei, wie wir ja auch aus anderen Stellen des Neuen Testaments wissen, der Tempel und das neue Jerusalem für das Urchristentum Symbole für die Kirche waren.

Eine Variante der apostolischen Überlieferung, die uns die Offenbarung Johannis bewahrt hat, finden wir im Epheserbrief (2: 19-22) wo wir lesen: „So seid ihr auch nicht mehr Fremdlinge und Beisassen, sondern ihr seid Mitbürger der Heiligen und Hausgenossen Gottes, aufgebaut auf den Grund der Apostel und Propheten, da er, Christus Jesus, der Eckstein ist, durch welchen der ganze Bau zusammengefügt ist und wächst zu einem heiligen Tempel im Herrn, durch welchen auch ihr aufgebaut werdet zur Behausung Gottes im Geist". Auch hier kommen die Symbole der Stadt und des Tempels vor und die Apostel sind die Grundsteine des Baues.

Nach Matthäus 16: 17-18 hat Jesus selbst einem von den Zwölf, Petrus dem Fels, verkündet, dass er auf diesem Felsen seine Gemeinde bauen will. Es hat sich gezeigt [1]), dass das ganze Bild in Mt 16: 18 mit der essenischen Ideologie verwandt ist. Wichtig ist auch, dass die Seligpreisung Petri, mit der das Logion beginnt, ihrer Form nach tief in der jüdischen Tradition verwurzelt ist: nicht nur ihr Wortlaut hat einen autentisch rabbinisch-hebräischen Klang, sondern auch dem Inhalt nach finden wir viele solche Seligpreisungen in der rabbinischen Literatur — eine solche ist auch in Lukas 11: 27 erhalten. In solchen jüdischen Lobsprüchen wird gewöhnlich die Mutter oder die Eltern des Gelobten erwähnt — darum wird anscheinend an unserer Stelle Petrus „bar Jona", der Sohn Jonas genannt. Wird

---

[1]) Siehe den Artikel von BETZ oben S. 136 Anm. 2.

man also das Logion, wenigstens in seiner Urform für echt halten müssen? Wenn dem so wäre, dann hat schon Jesus selbst auf einen von den Zwölf ein ähnliches Bild angewandt, wie wir es aus der späteren apostolischen Tradition kennengelernt haben: diese hat die Zwölf als Grundsteine der Gemeinde bezeichnet und Jesus hat nach Matthäus Petrus den Fels genannt ,auf dem die Gemeinde aufgebaut wird.

Wollen wir nun zu der Offenbarung Johannis zurückkehren. Wir haben gesehen, dass das Ende des Briefes an die Gemeinde von Philadelphia (Apk 3: 12) auf einer Überlieferung über die Apostel fusst. Wollen wir auch das Ende des nächsten siebenten Briefes an die Gemeinde von Laodicea betrachten: „Siehe, ich stehe vor der Tür und klopfe an; so einer höret meine Stimme und tut auf die Tür — eingehen werde ich zu ihm und Nachtmal halten werde ich mit ihm und er mit mir. Der Überwinder, geben werde ich ihm zu setzen sich zu mir, auf meinen Thron, wie ich auch überwunden habe und habe mich gesetzt zu meinem Vater, auf seinem Thron (Apk 3: 20-21)".

Auch hier ist eine Tradition über die Zwölf zu einer Anrede Christi an den einzelnen Gläubigen umgeformt. Das Jesuswort, auf dem die Worte der Offenbarung Johannis gegründet sind, ist uns sowohl in Mt 19: 28 als auch in Lk 22: 28-30 überliefert und meiner Ansicht nach kann uns die Offenbarung Johannis helfen, den ursprünglichen Wortlaut des Jesuswortes wiederherzustellen. Sowohl in der Offenbarung als auch in Lukas ist das Sitzen auf dem Thron mit dem eschatologischen Mal verbunden, darum gehörte Lk 22: 28-30a zum ursprünglichen Logion — siehe auch die Erwähnung des Vaters sowie in Lk als auch in Apk! Dagegen ist Lk 22: 30b gegenüber der Überlieferung in Matthäus abgekürzt: in der Offenbarung wird über das Sitzen mit Christus gesprochen und in Matthäus lesen wir, dass die Zwölf zusammen mit dem Menschensohn auf den Thronen sitzen werden. Darum wird das ursprüngliche Logion an die Zwölf annähernd so gelautet haben: „Doch ihr seid es, die bei mir in meinen Anfechtungen ausgeharrt haben [1]). Und ich vermache euch, wie mir mein Vater vermacht hat das Reich, dass ihr essen und trinken möget an meinem Tisch in meinem Reiche und wenn der Menschensohn sitzt auf dem Thron seiner Herrlichkeit, werdet auch

---

[1]) Vielleicht ist der ursprüngliche Wortlaut in Mt 19: 28a erhalten: „Wahrlich, ich sage euch, ihr, die mir folget".

ihr auf zwölf Thronen sitzen und richten die zwölf Stämme Israels" [1]).

Die meisten Forscher sehen in unserem Logion ein echtes Jesus-wort, denn die Verkündigung, dass die Apostel die zwölf Stämme Israels richten werden, hat einen echten Klang, da sie auf das Volk, mit dem Jesus verbunden war, ausgerichtet ist. Wichtig ist, dass auch in dem essenischen Fragment die Steine des neuen Jerusalems auf die Häupter der zwölf Stämme Israels gedeutet werden, aber die Verwandtschaft zwischen dem Jesuswort und dem essenischen Text geht noch weiter. Denn Jesus sagt nicht, dass die Apostel nur zu Stammeshäuptern der zwölf Stämme sein werden, er sagt, dass sie die Stämme richten werden [2]) — und wir haben ja gesehen, dass auch nach der apostolischen Überlieferung in der Offenbarung Johannis das Motiv des Richtens erkennbar wird, dass diese Überlieferung sich nicht auf die Feststellung beschränkt, dass auf den zwölf Toren des neuen Jerusalems „die Namen der zwölf Stämme von den Söhnen Israels" eingeschrieben sind (Apk 21: 12), sondern ausdrücklich bemerkt wird, dass die zwölf Grundsteine der Stadt mit den Namen der Apostel durch die zwölf Edelsteine geschmückt sind, welche auf der Brustplatte des Hohepriesters die Namen der zwölf Stämme getragen haben (Apk 21: 19-21) und damit die Gedankenverbindung

---

[1]) Eine spätere Entwicklung der Tradition von dem Menschensohn und dem Richten der zwölf Stämme finden wir in dem auch an sich wichtigen apokalyptischen Text über den Menschensohn im Testament Abrahams (ed. M. R. James, Cambridge 1892), kap. 12-13. Das Testament Abrahams wird von Vielen mit Recht für jüdisch gehalten; es ist, meiner Ansicht nach, überhaupt fraglich, ob das Buch wesentlich christlich bearbeitet ist. Die Bezeichnung ‚Menschensohn' wird dort wörtlich als der Sohn Adams verstanden. Der hohe Richter ist also Abel. Die Menschen werden nämlich nicht durch Gott, sondern durch einen Menschen gerichtet werden, und da alle Menschen von Adam stammen, werden sie durch seinen Sohn gerichtet werden. Im zweiten Gericht werden dann die zwölf Stämme Israels richten und im dritten Gericht Gott selbst. Der ursprüngliche Text über die zwölf Stämme ist nur in der besten Handschriften erhalten — die anderen Handschriften schieben hier natürlich die zwölf Apostel ein (die Varianten bei James, S. 53). Unser Text berichtet auch von zwei Engeln, einem zur Rechten und einem zur Linken des Menschensohnes, von denen der eine die Verdienste und der andere die Sünden aufschreibt. Vielleicht ist dies für die Bitte der Söhne des Zebedäus wichtig (Mt 20: 20-28; Mk 10: 35-45). Über diese Perikoppe siehe unten.

[2]) Dass die Gerechten am Endgericht teilnehmen werden, ist an sich ein bekanntes apokalyptisches Motiv, siehe z. B. Daniel 7: 22; Weisheit Salomos 3: 8 I. Kor: 6: 2 (vgl. 4: 8); BILLERBECK IV S. 1097, 1103-4, P. VOLZ, *Die Eschatologie der jüdischen Gemeinde*, Tübingen 1934, S. 275-6. Auch nach dem Habakukkommentar der Sekte (V, 4-6) „in die Hand Seiner Erwählten wird Gott das Gericht über alle Völker geben und durch ihre Anklage werden alle Frevler Seines Volkes für schuldig erklärt."

zu dem Gericht der Urim und Tummim geschaffen ist, die in der Brustplatte verwahrt waren. Auch in der typologischen Deutung der Steine des neuen Jerusalems in dem essenischen Fragment werden sowohl die Stammeshäupter Israels erwähnt, als auch die Steine der Stadt mit dem „Gericht der Urim und Tummim" in Verbindung gebracht. „Und du gibst in das Gewappen des Rechtsspruches die Urim und die Tummim, sie seien auf dem Herzen Aharons, wenn er kommt vor den Herrn. So trage Aharon den Rechtsspruch der Söhne Israels vor dem Herrn stetig" (Ex 28: 30). So werden in dem essenischen und in dem urchristlichen Text die Zwölf durch die Steine der Urim und Tummim symbolisiert, auf denen die Namen der zwölf Stämme eingeschrieben waren und die zum Rechtsspruch dienten. Darum konnte also Jesus gesagt haben, dass seine zwölf Apostel am Tage des Menschensohnes die zwölf Stämme Israels richten werden.

Es hat sich aber auch gezeigt, dass die Verkündigung Jesu an die Zwölf ursprünglich zu einer breiteren symbolischen Ideologie gehört hatte, die wir in der Offenbarung Johannis und in dem essenischen Fragment kennengelernt haben. In diesen beiden Texten hängt das Symbol der Steine der Urim und Tummim in dem Gewappen des Rechtsspruchs mit dem Symbol der Grundsteine des neuen Jerusalems zusammen. Es gehört also das Richten der Zwölf am Ende der Tage in demselben Rahmen wie die Vorstellung, dass die zwölf Apostel die Grundsteine der Kirche sind. Eine Variante dieses Symbols ist das Jesuswort über Petrus den Fels, auf dem die Gemeinde aufgebaut ist. Wie überraschend es auch zu sein scheint, es hat sich durch den Fund der Rollen vom Toten Meer jetzt gezeigt, dass das Jesuswort über die Apostel als eschatologische Richter und das Petruswort zu einem Vorstellungskreis der typologischen Deutung des neuen Jerusalems gehören, der schon vorchristlich-essenisch ist. Diese Deutung hat ihren Niederschlag im 21. Kapitel der Offenbarung Johannis gefunden. Hätte man den Mut gehabt, in den Worten der Apokalypse eine apostolische Tradition zu suchen und würde man aus der Angleichung der zwölf Grundsteine an die zwölf Edelsteine der Urim und Tummim, die zum Rechtsspruch dienten, den richtigen Schluss gezogen haben, dass das Jesuswort über das endzeitliche Richten der Apostel zu demselben Ideenkomplex gehört, wie das Symbol der Grundsteine, dann hätte man allerdings die Lösung auch ohne die Rollen vom Toten Meer finden können. Wichtig ist nicht nur, dass die Schilderung des neuen Jerusalems in der Offenbarung Johannis (Kap. 21) uns die Ideologie der Zwölf in ihrer Urform

erhalten hat, sondern auch dass der vorletzte und der letzte Brief der
Offenbarung mit zwei „apostolischen" Motiven schliessen, die hier
zu zwei Christusworten an den Gläubigen umgewandelt sind, die
im essenischen Fragment und im Kapitel 21 der Apokalypse verbunden sind, aber sonst im Neuen Testament selbstständig vorkommen, nämlich das Motiv der Grundsteine (in Apk 3: 12 kommt die
Variante des Pfeilers vor) und das Motiv der Gerichtssitzung (Apk
3: 20-21). Sollte man also auch sonst in der Offenbarung Johannis
nicht nur nach astralen und heidnisch-mythologischen Motiven
suchen, sondern die Erkenntnis ernst nehmen, dass die Offenbarung
Johannis eine Schöpfung aus palestinensischen Gedanken sei, unbe-
rührt von irgendwelcher „hellenistischen" Frömmigkeit [1])? Auch
unsere Ergebnisse haben gezeigt, dass die Offenbarung in der Überlieferung der jerusalemer Urgemeinde verwurzelt ist.

Wollen wir nun die bisherigen Ergebnisse in einer Tabelle zu-
sammenfassen:

Das essenische Fragment	*Offenbarung*	*Übrige Parallelen*
1) Das neue Jerusalem	1) Kap. 21: Das neue Jerusalem	1) Eph 2: 19: Die Stadt.
2) a. „Ich gründe dich in Saphire", die Deu- tung ist, dass sie die Gemeinschaft der Einung gegründet haben ... wie ein Saphir unter den Steinen	2) Zwölf Grundsteine mit den Namen der zwölf Apostel (Apk 21: 14, vgl. 3: 12).	2) Eph 2:20: „Aufgebant auf dem Grund der Apostel". Mt 16: 18: Die Gemeinde ist auf Petrus, dem Fels, auf- gebaut.
b) „Aus Rubin mache ich deine Zinnen", die Deutung geht auf die zwölf ...		
3) sie leuchten im Ge- richt der Urim und Tummim.	3) Apk 21: 19-20: Die Grundsteine-Urim und Tummim.	3-4) Mt 19: 28; Lk 22: 30 (vgl. Apk 3: 21): Die Zwölf werden die zwölf Stämme Israels richten.
4) „All deine Umfassung von Edelgestein", die Deutung geht auf die Stammeshäupter Is- raels.	4) Apk 21: 12: Die Na- men der zwölf Stäm- me auf den Toren Je- rusalems.	

---

[1]) LOHMEYER (s. oben, S. 137, Anm. 1)

Der Vergleich hat gezeigt, dass zwar die Offenbarung Johannis die vollsten Parallelen zu dem essenischen Fragment aufweist, aber aus den übrigen Stellen des Neuen Testaments wird klar, dass die breite Symbolik, die mit den zwölf Aposteln verbunden ist, ihren Niederschlag in Quellen gefunden hat, die viel älter als die Offenbarung Johannis sind. Das Jesuswort über die Apostel als eschatologische Richter der zwölf Stämme Israels wird für echt gehalten und das Petruswort ist anscheinend in seinem Kern auch ursprünglich. Aber auch wenn die Ursprünglichkeit der zwei Logien nicht sicher sein sollte, jedenfalls haben sie ihren Sitz im Leben der jerusalemer Urgemeinde, in dem Kreise der zwölf Apostel selbst. Das essenische Fragment hat gezeigt, dass die entwickelte, komplizierte Symbolik, die wir in der Offenbarung Johannis finden und derer Motive in zwei Jesusworten vorkommen, vorchristlich ist. Daraus wird man schliessen müssen, dass diese symbolische Ideologie der Zwölf ihren Eingang in die Gemeinde Jesu fand, als Jesus die Institution der Zwölf gegründet hat. Diese Ideologie wurde dann von den Zwölf und ihren Anhängern tradiert, bis sie ihren vollen Niederschlag in der Offenbarung Johannis gefunden hat.

Aus dem Gesagten folgt, dass Jesus die Körperschaft der zwölf Apostel nach essenischem Vorbild gegründet hat. Dass Jesus selbst die Zwölf berufen hat, ist schon daraus zu ersehen, dass nach seinem Tode, als Judas der Verräter ausgeschieden ist, man an seiner Stelle einen anderen Apostel gewählt hat, um die Zahl zwölf wieder voll zu machen (Apk 1: 15-26). Daraus folgt auch, dass die Zahl von Anfang an bedeutsam gewesen ist, wie man auch aus der Vergleichung der verschiedenen Listen der Zwölf folgern kann: in Einzelheiten sind die Listen verschieden, doch die Zahl steht fest. Am Anfang hat allerdings Jesus aus seinen Schülern einen inneren Kreis von fünf ausgesondert, wie wir aus den evangelischen Berichten schliessen können — diese Überlieferung ist auch dem Talmud bekannt (Sanh. 43a) [1]. Auch die Namen der Fünf wechseln in der Überlieferung: daraus folgt, dass auch hier die Zahl das Entscheidende gewesen ist. Jesus hat diese Zahl seines inneren Schülerkreises nach rabbinischen Vorbildern bestimmt, denn in der rabbinischen Literatur wird öfters von fünf Schülern oder fünf Ältesten berichtet [2]. Dann hat Jesus

---

[1] Siehe C. O. Dodd, *Historical Tradition in the Fourth Gospel*, Cambridge 1963, pp. 302-6.
[2] Awoth 2, 8, Jebamoth 62b vgl. Sanh. 14a, die fünf Weisen von Bene Berak in der Pessahaggadah, Tossefta Mikwaoth 7, 10, S. 660. Tossefta Tohoroth 9, 14, S. 670-1; jer. Bezah III 6; Moed katan 20a (nach dem Text im Buch Haeschkol);

diese Körperschaft erweitert — auch da war die Zahl entscheidend.
Wie wir gesehen haben, hat die Ideologie der Zwölf essenische
Vorbilder: man wird also annehmen müssen, dass essenische Einflüsse
mitgespielt haben, als Jesus seinen inneren Kreis von fünf auf zwölf
erweitert hat. Wir haben schon gesehen, dass in der essenischen Literatur — auch ausserhalb unseres Fragments — die Rede von einer
Einheit von zwölf Männern ist [1]); dies kann man kaum von der
rabbinischen Literatur sagen. Auch aus diesem Grunde ist also ein
essenischer Einfluss auf die Berufung der Zwölf wahrscheinlich.

Ist die Verwandtschaft des essenischen Fragmentes mit der Ideologie der Zwölf so zu erklären, dass eine essenische Institution mit
ihrem breiten ideologischen Rahmen auf Jesus direkt eingewirkt hat,
als er die Zwölf berufen hat, oder handelt es sich vielleicht um andere,
den Essenern verwandte Kreise, denen Jesus bei der Gründung der
Zwölf verpflichtet war? Wir wissen heute, dass Johannes der Täufer
zwar kein Essener war, aber dass er ihnen geistig verwandt war;
er hat Jesus getauft und zwischen seinen Schülern und der Gemeinschaft Jesus bestanden auch später wechselseitige Beziehungen. Und
Johannes der Täufer war es, der gesagt hat: „Traget euch nicht mit
der Einbildung zu sagen: Wir haben Abraham zum Vater: denn ich
sage euch, Gott kann aus diesen Steinen dem Abraham Kinder
aufrichten [2])" (Mt 3: 9; Lk 3: 8). Man sieht also, dass der Täufer
mit den essenischen Bild des Steinbaus für die Gemeinde der Erwählten Gottes vertraut war. Auch die Zahl zwölf musste für die Organisation seiner Gemeinde eine Bedeutung gehabt haben, denn wir
lesen in der Apostelgeschichte (19: 1-7) von zwölf Schülern in Ephesus, die auf die Taufe Johannis getauft worden sind. Zwei Motive
der urchristlichen Ideologie der Zwölf finden wir also auch im Kreise
Johannis des Täufers: die Zahl zwölf und das Symbol des Steinbaues.
Es besteht also eine Möglichkeit, dass Jesus die Institution der Zwölf
nicht direkt nach einem essenischen Vorbild gegründet hat, sondern
dass er von dem Täufer und seiner Gemeinde beeinflusst war.

Die Ideologie der Zwölf, wie wir sie aus der Offenbarung Johannis
und aus dem essenischen Fragment kennengelernt haben, war also

---

nach Soferim 1, 7 wurde sogar die Septuaginta von fünf Ältesten übersetzt.
Vgl. auch die fünf Männer mit Ezra im IV Ezra 14: 24 und die fünf Gefährten
des Baruch in der Baruch-Apokalypse I 5: 1. Für die Hinweise schulde ich Dank
meinem Freunde S. SAFRAI.

[1]) Siehe die Kriegsrolle II, 1-3; den Sektenkanon VIII, 1.

[2]) Einige Parallelen zu dieser Formel siehe A. SCHLATTER, *Der Evangelist Matthäus*, Stuttgart 1959, S. 74.

in ihren Hauptzügen vorchristlich; sie war an jene Institution der essenischen Gemeinde, oder vielleicht auch der Gemeinde des Täufers, gebunden, nach derer Vorbild Jesus die Körperschaft der Zwölf geschaffen hat. Aus der merkwürdigen Tatsache, dass die komplizierte und erhabene vorchristliche Symbolik wieder im vollen Lichte in einem so verhältnismässig späten Dokument wie die Offenbarung Johannis erscheint, ist zu schliessen, dass die zwölf Apostel, die natürlich die ideologische Bedeutung der essenischen Institution gekannt haben, nach derer Vorbild sie entstanden sind, diese Ideologie auch auf sich selbst bezogen haben. Auf dieser erhabenen Ideologie begründeten anscheinend die zwölf Apostel ihre Ansprüche auf die zentrale Funktion ihrer Institution sowohl in der göttlichen Weltordnung, als auch in der jerusalemer Urkirche. Wir haben gesehen, dass sich diese Ideologie wenigstens teilweise in zwei Jesusworten widerspiegelt: in dem Petruswort und in dem Wort über die Apostel als endzeitliche Richter der Stämme Israels. Auch wenn wir nicht ganz sicher sein können, dass diese zwei Logien Urworte Jesus sind, werden wir doch kaum annehmen können, dass Jesus das Kollegium der Zwölf nach einem Vorbild geschaffen hat, dessen Ideologie er nicht wenigstens in einem gewissen Masse bejaht hat. Einmal hat allerdings Jesus die Hoheitsansprüche der Apostel als eine Anmassung zurückgewiesen. Als die Söhne des Zebedäus, oder ihre Mutter, von Jesus begehrt haben, er möge ihnen gewähren, dass in seiner Herrlichkeit einer zur Rechten und einer zur Linken sitzen möge, antwortete er, dass das Sitzen zu seiner Rechten oder Linken zu verteilen nicht ihm zukomme, sondern es komme denen zu, welchen es bereitet sei (Mt 20: 20-28, Mk 10: 35-45). Dieser Ausspruch fusst auf derselben eschatologischen Vorstellung wie das Logion über das Sitzen der Apostel auf den zwölf Thronen, aber gleichzeitig besteht eine scharfe Spannung zwischen diesen zwei Jesusworten: die Worte an die Zwölf sind eine positive Zusage, wogegen Jesus den Aposteln Jakobus und Johannes erklärt, es stehe nicht ihm, sondern nur Gott zu, die Sitze im endzeitlichen Gericht zu bestimmen. Es scheint also, als ob Jesus einmal die essenische Anschauung, dass die,, Zwölf im Gericht der Urim und Tummin leuchten" werden, bejaht, dass zweite Mal aber abgelehnt hätte. Mir scheint es doch, dass wir aus dieser Spannung zwischen den zwei Jesusworten nicht folgern dürfen, dass eines von ihnen unecht wäre. Die Spannung lässt sich vielleicht durch dass Selbstbewusstsein Jesu erklären, das sowohl durch echte Demut als euch durch echtes Hoheitsgefühl gekennzeichnet ist. Jedenfalls weisen beide Jesusworte auf dieselbe eschatologische Hoffnung der Apostel. Jesus konnte also einmal diese Zuversicht bejahen und ein anderes Mal konnte er sie gedämpft haben. Gerade diese Spannung zwischen den zwei Jesusworten zeigt, dass an ein und dasselbe Bild angespielt wird, das den beiden Logien zugrunde liegt.

Die zwölf Apostel sind eigentlich die einzige „kirchliche" Institution der messianischen Gemeinschaft Jesus. Denn in dem charismatischen Bereich, „gibt es keine „Behörden", sondern nur charismatisch, im Umfang des Auftrags des Herrn und des eigenen Charisma, beauftragte Sendboten" [1]. Darum werden ja die Zwölf auch Apostel, Sendboten, genannt, aber bildeten doch unter den übrigen Aposteln eine ausgesonderte Gruppe [2]. Vielleicht wird man aber die Zwölf nicht nur charismatisch, sondern im tiefsten Sinne des Wortes kirchlich „ekklesiologisch" verstehen müssen, sowohl als eine Organisation, als auch eine eschatologisch-mythische Institution. Wir können ja diesen Aspekt der zwölf Apostel von seinen vorchristlichen Wurzeln über die Worte Jesu bis zu der Offenbarung Johannis verfolgen. Ist es ein Zufall, dass die drei Jesusworte, nämlich das Petruswort, das Jesuswort über die eschatologische Richtergewalt der Zwölf und das Wort an die Söhne des Zebedäus, für die man Parallelen im essenischen Fragment einerseits und in der Offenbarung Johannis andererseits finden kann, vielleicht die einzigen Worte Jesus sind, die von dem Hoheitsanspruch der Apostel handeln? Wurde vielleicht sonst der esoterische Aspekt des Sinnes der zwölf Apostel in der synoptischen Tradition teilweise verwischt? Dies sind Fragen, die durch das essenische Fragment geweckt worden sind und ihrer Beantwortung harren. Jedenfalls haben wir durch den neuen Text einiges über die urchristliche Ideologie der zwölf Apostel lernen können.

---

[1] Max WEBER, *Wirtschaft und Gesellschaft*, Köln-Berlin 1964, S. 180.

[2] Die beste Behandlung des Problems, findet man noch heute bei E. MEYER, *Ursprung und Anfänge des Christentums* I, 1924, pp. 264-299.

INITIATION ET MYSTÈRE DANS JOSEPH ET ASÉNETH

PAR

MARC PHILONENKO
Strasbourg

Le judaïsme de la Diaspora, et tout particulièrement le judaïsme de la Diaspora égyptienne, a-t-il permis que se développe en son sein un culte marqué par l'influence des cultes à mystères? La question n'est pas nouvelle. On a surtout cherché à la résoudre en partant de l'œuvre de Philon. En effet, la terminologie du philosophe alexandrin paraît souvent faire écho à la phraséologie des mystères [1]. Faut-il aller plus loin et découvrir dans quelques rares textes de Philon des allusions à des repas mystiques de caractère initiatique [2]? On le croirait volontiers, mais plus d'un critique rejette une telle interprétation et maintient que l'œuvre de Philon toute entière est ,,un mystère littéraire et non pas un mystère cultuel" [3].

Nous voudrions tenter d'éclairer ce problème difficile en apportant le témoignage d'un pseudépigraphe de l'Ancien Testament trop peu connu, *Joseph et Aséneth*, et que G. D. KILPATRICK a eu le mérite de sortir de l'oubli où il était longtemps tombé [4]. *Joseph et Aséneth* a été édité à deux reprises à la fin du siècle dernier, par P. BATIFFOL [5], puis par V. M. ISTRIN [6]. Ces deux éditions sont malheureusement

---

[1]) Cf. E. BRÉHIER, *Les idées philosophiques et religieuses de Philon d'Alexandrie* 3, Paris, 1950, p. 242-246.

[2]) Voir J. PASCHER, Η ΒΑΣΙΛΙΚΗ ΟΔΟΣ, *Der Königsweg zu Wiedergeburt und Vergottung bei Philon von Alexandreia*, Paderborn, 1931, p. 185-191 et surtout E. R. GOODENOUGH, *By Light, Light. The Mystic Gospel of Hellenistic Judaism*, New Haven, 1935, p. 8 et 259-262; *Jewish Symbols in the Greco-Roman Period*, New York, 1956, tome VI, p. 206-207.

[3]) H.-Ch. PUECH, *Revue de l'Histoire des religions*, 116, 1937, p. 99.

[4]) G. D. KILPATRICK, ,,The Last Supper", *The Expository Times* 64, 1952, p. 4-8.

[5]) P. BATIFFOL, ,,Le Livre de la Prière d'Aseneth" in *Studia Patristica* I-II, Paris, 1889-1890. Traduction anglaise de E. W. BROOKS, *Joseph and Aseneth*, London, 1918; traduction allemande de P. RIESSLER in *Altjüdisches Schrifttum ausserhalb der Bibel*, Augsburg, 1928, p. 497-538.

[6]) V. M. ISTRIN, *Apokriph ob Josiphje i Asenephje*, Trudy Slavjanskoj Komissii pri Imperat. Moskovskom Archeologiceskom Obscestvje, Moscou, 1898.

sans valeur critique et n'ont pu fournir que des fondements fragiles aux trop rares études consacrées à notre écrit [1]). Nous avons été amené à établir, en partant de nouveaux manuscrits, un texte grec plus sûr [2]) qui est à la base des quelques remarques qui vont suivre.

Le thème du roman de *Joseph et Aséneth* est tiré du texte de la Genèse. En Genèse 41 : 45, il est dit que Pharaon donna pour femme à Joseph Aséneth, la fille de Pentéphrès, le prêtre d'Héliopolis. Un tel mariage pouvait heurter des consciences juives scrupuleuses. Comment, en effet, Joseph, ce juif pieux, avait-il pu épouser une égyptienne?

---

[1]) Citons, entre autres contributions, K. KOHLER, article ,,Asenath" in *The Jewish Encyclopedia*, New York, 1902, tome II; E. SCHÜRER, *Geschichte des jüdischen Volkes im Zeitalter Jesu Christi* [4], Leipzig, 1909, tome III, p. 399-402; C. LUCERNA, *Asseneth*, Wien, 1921; V. APTOWITZER, *Asenath, The Wife of Joseph. A Haggadic Literary-Historical Study*, Hebrew Union College Annual I, 1924, p. 239-306; BOUSSET-GRESSMANN, *Die Religion des Judentums im späthellenistischen Zeitalter* [3], Tübingen 1926, p. 24; R. REITZENSTEIN, *Die hellenistischen Mysterienreligionen* [3], Leipzig, 1927, p. 248-249; *Die Vorgeschichte der christlichen Taufe*, Leipzig-Berlin, 1929, p. 120; P. BATIFFOL, *L'eucharistie, la présence réelle et la transsubstantiation* [10], Paris, 1930, p. 190, note 3; P. VOLZ, *Die Eschatologie der jüdischen Gemeinde im neutestamentlichen Zeitalter* [2], Tübingen, 1934, p. 50, 286, 388-389 et 408; H. PRIEBATSCH, *Die Josephgeschichte in der Weltliteratur*, Breslau, 1937; L. GINZBERG, *The Legends of the Jews* [7], Philadelphia, 1955, tome V, p. 374-375; J. JEREMIAS, ,,The Last Supper", *The Expository Times* 64, 1952, p. 91-92; *Die missionarische Aufgabe in der Mischehe*, Beihefte zur Zeitschrift für die Neutestamentliche Wissenschaft 21, Berlin, 1954, p. 255-260; W. NAUCK, ,,Die Tradition und Komposition der Areopagrede", *Zeitschrift für Theologie und Kirche* 53, 1956, p. 39; *Die Tradition und der Charakter des ersten Johannesbriefes*, Tübingen, 1957, p. 169-171; K. G. KUHN, ,,Repas cultuel essénien et cène chrétienne" in *Les manuscrits de la mer Morte*, Colloque de Strasbourg, 25-27 mai 1955, Paris, 1957, p. 75-92 repris dans K. STENDAHL, *The Scrolls and the New Testament*, London, 1958, p. 65-93, sous le titre *The Lord's Supper and the Communal Meal at Qumran*; H. SCHLIER, *Der Brief an die Epheser* [2], Düsseldorf, 1958, p. 275, note 4; O. BETZ, ,,Geistliche Schönheit" in *Festschrift für A. Köberle*, Hamburg, 1958, p. 71-86; J. JEREMIAS, *Die Kindertaufe in den ersten vier Jahrhunderten*, Göttingen, 1958, p. 39-41; *Die Abendmahlsworte Jesu* [3], Göttingen, 1960, p. 27-28; O. BETZ, *Offenbarung und Schriftforschung in der Qumransekte*, Tübingen, 1960, p. 96 et 137; M. BLACK, *The Scrolls and Christian Origins*, London, 1961, p. 151; A. ORBE, *La unción del Verbo*, Rome, 1961, p. 151; M. DELCOR, ,,Un roman d'amour d'origine thérapeute: le Livre de Joseph et Asénath", *Bulletin de littérature ecclésiastique* 63, 1962, p. 3-27; G. DELLING, ,,Partizipiale Gottesprädikationen in den Briefen des Neuen Testaments", *Studia Theologica* 17, 1963, p. 22-24, 29, note 1 et 31 note 4; A. JAUBERT, *La notion d'Alliance dans le judaïsme aux abords de l'ère chrétienne*, Paris, 1963, p. 360, note 24, 365, note 38 et 39, 398, note 65.

Par contre, l'article de Chr. BURCHARD, ,,Ei nach einem Ausdruck des Wissens oder Nichtwissens Joh. 9, 25, Act. 19, 2; I Cor. 1, 16, 7, 16", *Zeitschrift für die Neutestamentliche Wissenschaft* 52, 1961, p. 73-82 et sa thèse de doctorat, toujours inédite, *Untersuchungen zu ,,Joseph und Aseneth"*, Göttingen, 1961, reposent sur une étude personnelle de la tradition manuscrite.

[2]) On nous permettra de renvoyer à notre ouvrage à paraître: *Joseph et Aséneth, Introduction, texte critique, traduction et notes*.

Selon la tradition rabbinique, Aséneth était en réalité la fille de Dina violée par Sichem [1]) et que Putiphar avait recueillie. Joseph n'aurait donc pas épousé une égyptienne, comme une lecture naïve de la Genèse le laisserait croire, mais une femme qui était juive par sa mère [2]).

L'auteur de *Joseph et Aséneth* a connu cette explication, mais il l'écarte implicitement en faveur d'une autre interprétation. Selon lui, la fille du prêtre d'Héliopolis est bien une égyptienne, mais elle s'est convertie au judaïsme pour épouser Joseph. Mieux encore, son cas est exemplaire et elle peut être tenue pour la figure idéale du prosélyte.

Que l'on nous permette de résumer brièvement l'histoire de Joseph et de la belle Aséneth. La première des sept années de famine, Joseph fut envoyé par Pharaon ramasser le blé de tout le pays. Arrivé à Héliopolis, il rend visite au prêtre de la ville, Pentéphrès. Celui-ci a une fille du nom d'Aséneth qui est courtisée par de nombreux prétendants. Aséneth les dédaigne tous et, lorsque son père cherche à la convaincre d'épouser Joseph, elle refuse avec insolence. Mais quand Joseph apparaît, c'est le coup de foudre. La jeune fille s'avance pour embrasser Joseph, mais celui-ci la repousse en ces mots (8: 5-6): „Il ne convient pas à un homme pieux, qui bénit de sa bouche le Dieu vivant, et qui mange le pain béni de la vie, et qui boit la coupe bénie d'immortalité, et qui est oint de l'onction d'incorruptibilité, d'embrasser une femme étrangère, elle qui bénit de sa bouche des idoles mortes et muettes, et qui mange à leur table le pain d'étouffement, et qui boit de leurs libations la coupe de traîtrise, et qui est ointe de l'onction de perdition. Mais un homme pieux embrasse sa mère, et la sœur qui appartient à sa tribu et à sa famille, et la femme qui partage sa couche, elles qui bénissent de leurs bouches le Dieu vivant".

Le refus de Joseph, on le voit, est motivé par des raisons religieuses. Comment pourrait-il embrasser une femme dont la bouche est souillée par les idolothytes?

Il y a plus. Le texte reprend une formule ternaire, rythmée et liturgique que nous retrouvons ailleurs dans *Joseph et Aséneth* (15: 4):

> manger le pain de vie,
> boire la coupe d'immortalité,
> être oint de l'onction d'incorruptibilité.

---

[1]) Genèse 34: 2.
[2]) Sur cette légende, voir V. Aptowitzer, *art. cit.*

Cette formule ternaire suppose un repas qui comporte trois phases liturgiques distinctes, centrées la première sur le pain, la seconde sur la coupe, la troisième sur l'onction.

On a voulu rapprocher du repas de *Joseph et Aséneth* le repas sancré célébré par la communauté de Qoumrân [1]). De fait, les textes de Qoumrân révèlent l'ordonnance d'un repas communautaire qui avait pour préface une bénédiction prononcée sur le pain et le vin [2]). Toutefois, le rapprochement n'est pas pleinement satisfaisant, car il n'est jamais fait état dans les documents de Qoumrân d'une onction lors du repas [3]).

Un renvoi au repas des Thérapeutes n'est guère plus suggestif. En effet, la mention d'une onction en relation avec le repas est incertaine dans le traité de la *Vie Contemplative* [4]) et de plus, s'il est question d'une onction dans le texte du *De Vita*, cette onction précède le repas, elle ne le suit pas.

Un passage du *Testament de Lévi* (8: 4-5) mentionne bien une onction dans le cadre d'un repas dont les éléments sont le pain et le vin, mais ici encore cette onction précède le repas.

Quant aux textes gnostiques auxquels on pourrait songer, ils ne présentent que rarement la séquence pain-coupe-onction [5]) et à côté d'autres séquences [6]), si bien qu'il paraît difficile de leur accorder une valeur particulière.

Force est donc d'admettre que nous sommes en présence d'une pratique originale. L'histoire du repas juif, plus complexe qu'on ne l'admet d'ordinaire, s'enrichit d'une variante remarquable.

Comme l'a montré K. G. KUHN, la signification de ce repas est clairement révélée par les génitifs qui viennent qualifier le pain, la coupe et l'onction. Le pain est un pain de vie; la coupe est une coupe d'immortalité; l'onction est une onction d'incorruptibilité [7]). Ce que le juif pieux trouve dans ce repas, c'est ce que l'initié trouvait dans

---

[1]) K. G. KUHN, *Repas cultuel essénien . . .*, p. 88-91 et *The Lord's Supper . . .*, p. 74-77.

[2]) *Règle* 6, 4-5; *Règle annexe* 2, 18-22.

[3]) A noter de surcroit que les esséniens ont connu un curieux tabou de l'huile. Voir A. DUPONT-SOMMER, *Les écrits esséniens découverts près de la mer Morte* [2], Paris 1960, p. 170, note 5.

[4]) *De Vita* r 36. Cf. P. GEOLTRAIN, *Le traité de la Vie Contemplative de Philon d'Alexandrie*, Semitica X, Paris, 1960, p. 55.

[5]) *Evangile de Philippe* 123, 1 (éd. W. TILL, *Das Evangelium nach Philippos*, Berlin, 1963).

[6]) *Evangile de Philippe* 115, 27-29; 125, 3-6.

[7]) K. G. KUHN, *Repas cultuel essénien . . .*, p. 90 et *The Lord's Supper . . .*, p. 76-77.

les mystères: la „vie", l'„immortalité", l'„incorruptibilité". Quant aux „étrangers", c'est la mort qui les attend. Aséneth éclate en sanglots, mais Joseph ému de pitié prononce alors la prière suivante (8: 10-11):

> „Seigneur, Dieu de mon père Israël,
> Toi qui es le Très-Haut, le Fort,
> qui donnes la vie à l'univers,
> et qui appelles des ténèbres à la lumière,
> et de l'erreur à la vérité,
> et de la mort à la vie,
> Toi-même, Seigneur, donne la vie à cette vierge,
> et bénis-la,
> et renouvelle-la par ton Esprit,
> et reforme-la de ta main,
> et revifie-la de ta vie".

Cette prière est très instructive pour la signification à prêter au repas. A la formule ternaire pain-coupe-onction correspond ici et en 15: 4 une autre formule ternaire:

> renouvelle-la
> reforme-la
> revifie-la.

Cette rénovation, cette reformation, cette revification promise à Aséneth, c'est celle qui est promise à l'initié dans les cultes à mystères [1]. On notera que le parallélisme des deux formules ternaires laisse supposer que la rénovation est opérée par le pain, la reformation par la coupe, la revification par l'onction.

Nous avions laissé Aséneth à ses larmes, retrouvons-la maintenant. A la prière de Joseph elle répond par la pénitence et par le jeûne. Elle rejette les idoles et se réfugie auprès du Très-Haut. L'ange Michaël lui apparaît alors et lui dit (15: 4): „Voici, à partir d'aujourd'hui tu seras renouvelée, reformée et revifiée, et tu mangeras le pain de vie, et tu boieras la coupe d'immortalité, et tu seras ointe de l'onction d'incorruptibilité".

Cependant, dans notre roman, Aséneth ne mange pas le pain, ne boit pas la coupe et n'est pas ointe de l'onction, mais elle partage avec l'ange un mystérieux rayon de miel. La scène est si curieuse qu'il est nécessaire de la rapporter ici. Aséneth vient de proposer à

---

[1] R. REITZENSTEIN, *Die hellenistischen Mysterienreligionen* . . ., p. 262-263.

l'ange de préparer la table et d'apporter du pain et du vin. L'ange,
sans écarter expressément cette proposition, lui dit cependant (16: 1):
„Apporte-moi donc aussi un rayon de miel. „Aséneth n'a pas de miel
à la maison, mais — dit-elle — j'enverrai quelqu'un en chercher.
L'ange lui répond (16: 3-4): „Entre dans ta chambre et tu trouveras
un rayon de miel". „Aséneth-rapporte alors l'auteur — entra dans sa
chambre et trouva un rayon de miel posé sur la table, et le rayon
était blanc comme neige et plein de miel, et son parfum était comme
la senteur de la vie". Aséneth revient ensuite près de l'ange et lui
apporte le rayon de miel. L'ange bénit alors Aséneth et déclare (16: 7):
„Heureuse es-tu, Aséneth, car les mystères de Dieu t'ont été révélés;
heureux sont ceux qui s'attachent à Dieu par la repentance, car ils
mangeront de ce rayon. Car ce miel, ce sont les abeilles du paradis
de délices qui le font, et les anges de Dieu en mangent, et qui conque
en mangera ne mourra jamais."

Le Professeur KILPATRICK dans un remarquable article, en partie
consacré à *Joseph et Aséneth*, se borne à constater „qu'en fait Aséneth
ne partage pas le pain et le vin, mais un rayon de miel miraculeux" [1].
De son côté, le Professeur K. G. KUHN remarque: „l'expression
manger le pain béni de la vie et boire la coupe bénie de l'immortalité
est une formule stéréotypée qui n'a aucunement sa raison d'être
dans le récit lui-même. En effet, Aseneth ne reçoit ni pain ni coupe,
mais est nourrie d'un rayon de miel céleste" [2]. Il n'y aurait donc pas
de lien précis à établir entre le pain, la coupe et l'onction d'une part,
et le rayon de miel d'autre part. Une solution plus drastique consiste-
rait à reconnaître deux traditions liturgiques différentes qui vien-
draient s'entrecroiser dans notre roman. Ce serait clairement mettre
en lumière le problème posé, mais non point sans doute le résoudre.
Ne serait-il pas de meilleure méthode d'admettre que, lorsque l'auteur
a substitué le rayon de miel au pain, à la coupe et à l'onction, il obéis-
sait à une intention précise? Cette intention ne pourrions-nous pas
la retrouver? Il est permis de le penser.

Quel est ce gâteau de miel que l'ange fait miraculeusement apparaître sur la table d'Aséneth et dont les anges — nous dit-on — font
leur nourriture? La réponse est aisée: il ne peut s'agir que de la
manne [3]. Déjà, le livre de l'Exode (16: 31) reconnaît à la manne le
goût du miel. De plus, il est certain qu'à basse époque on a reconnu

---

[1] G. D. KILPATRICK, *art. cit.*, p. 5.
[2] K. G. KUHN, *Repas cultuel essénien* . . ., p. 90 et *The Lord's Supper* . . ., p. 75.
[3] Voir V. APTOWITZER, *art. cit.*, p. 282-283 et Chr. BURCHARD, *op. cit.*, p. 111.

dans la manne le pain des anges [1]). Cette interprétation est connue de la version des Septante où, au Psaume 78: 25, l'expression hébraïque לחם אבירים est rendue ἄρτος ἀγγέλων; on la trouve reprise dans la *Sagesse de Salomon* (16: 20).

Or, c'est au moment précis où Aséneth découvre sur sa table le rayon de miel que l'ange, tel un mystagogue, lui déclare (16: 7): „Heureuse es-tu Aséneth, car les mystères de Dieu t'ont été révélés." Là est la révélation initiatique, la mystérieuse leçon de l'ange: le pain de vie, c'est le pain des anges. Le lien entre la formule liturgique du pain, de la coupe et de l'onction et la découverte du rayon de miel est donc un lieu nécessaire. En faisant apparaître le rayon de miel céleste, l'ange dévoile à Aséneth le secret du mystère: celui qui participe ici-bas au repas sacré est déjà nourri de la manne céleste. „Il ne mourra jamais" (16: 8). Aséneth et tous les prosélytes qui la suivront passent donc ainsi des ténèbres à la lumière, de l'erreur à la vérité, de la mort à la vie. Ils sont appelés à l'immortalité.

Si l'exégèse qui vient d'être développée emporte la conviction, on admettra volontiers que certains conventicules juifs de la Diaspora ont célébré un repas sacré „mystérieux" et qu'ils ont présenté l'entrée dans la communauté juive comme une initiation au mystère.

---

[1]) Cf. L. GINZBERG, *op. cit.*, p. 236.

INITIATION, MYSTÈRES, GNOSE

(Pour l'histoire de la mystique dans le
paganisme gréco-oriental)

PAR

U. BIANCHI
Roma

Le but de cette contribution est d'étudier une série phénoménologique, qui est aussi bien un processus historique (non pas une „évolution"), et qui, tout en étant loin de monopoliser la phénoménologie et l'histoire de l'initiation [1]) et de la mystique sotériologique, a une place très remarquable dans le monde proche-oriental et grec.

a) Partant des *cultes de fécondité*, non ésotériques et non initiatiques, mais dont la vicissitude est finalisée par le renouveau saisonnier de la vie (dans l'intérêt du territoire et du peuple, et donc centré sur la personne du roi — bien que l'individu et les morts y soient intéressés aussi), rites type Tammuz (caractérisés par la lamentation, qui est l'aspect fort du cycle annuel, et qui est *précédée* — ou, du moins, n'est pas suivie — par le mariage sacré), on considère

b) les *mystères*, type Eleusis, où le moment saisonnier (naturiste-social) s'intègre à une très ancienne perspective „sotériologique" d'intérêt plus individuel [2]), initiatique et aussi ésoterique, une perspective — dans ces mystères — qui se déploie dans les enfers, où un sort spécial attend les initiés, qui ont familiarisé leur âme avec les dieux de là-bas. Une troisième forme

c) la *mystériosophie* (depuis le VIe siècle, jusqu'à la fin de l'antiquité païenne), interprète les données mystériques par le recours à une sophie qui est déjà une gnose, parce que la „vicissitude" de la vie féconde et du dieu mystérique est appliquée par elle à l'élément

---

[1]) Nous entendons par „initiation" l'accession rituelle d'un individu ou d'un groupe homogène dans un état, ou, plus spécifiquement, dans un corps sacralement qualifié et religieusement „autre"; l'initiation désacralisée ou même parodique en étant un épiphénomène.

[2]) Cette perspective appartient déjà aux cultures ethnologiques. Cfr. *infra*, p. 167, n. 1.

divin dans l'homme, ou à son âme divine (interprétation théo-anthro-
posophique du mythe de Dionysos démembré; spéculations mystiques
sur la *kathodos* de Koré-Persephone): dans cette forme mystique, le
schéma initiatique mort-vie concerne donc désormais un scénario
dualiste fondé sur l'opposition milieu divin/terre corps (ces derniers
étant identifiés aux enfers, à la geôle ou à la mort). Le sujet de la
vicissitude (du passage) est ici la substance divine, ou l'âme, l'âme
divine, et le moment cyclique, qui était définitif et sauveur dans les
rites de fécondité, est déclassé (se présentant comme métensomatose)
à deuxième moment (le moment douloureux, ,,de marge'' et aussi
de punition) de la vicissitude. Identifié avec le destin et la fécondité
(et — parfois — avec ses divinités respectives), ce cycle (roue de la
naissance) doit être surmonté par l'évasion finale hors de ce monde
qui est le sien, le monde de la fécondité, du destin, de la mort et de
la matière. Un exemple de cette mystériosophie, de cette pré-gnose,
est la réinterprétation du dionysisme qu'est l'orphisme. Finalement,
une quatrième forme,

d) la *gnose*, élimine les références mystériques (tout en élaborant
parfois un rituel magique) et identifie franchement la vicissitude
comme étant la vicissitude de l'âme divine, le *salvator salvandus*, en
fonction anthroposophique et dualiste.

Ce schéma quadruple, qui embrasse l'histoire du mysticisme païen
gréco-oriental, comme nous le disions, est loin de monopoliser la
phénoménologie et l'histoire de l',,initiation'' (au sens large du mot)
et de la mystique sotériologique. Pour ne rien dire des initiations des
peuples ethnologiques les plus anciens, les chasseurs (où la perspective de ces cérémonies est aussi bien individuelle que sociale —
tandis que le schéma des divinités ,,dema'' des planteurs peut inté-
resser le schéma sus-dit), il n'intéresse pas les religions bibliques,
où le ,,passage'' et la vicissitude sont fondés et justifiés par la conception monothéiste: leur idée n'est pas la vicissitude de la vie divine
féconde, ni de l'âme divine (des concepts qu'elles ne cessent de
combattre), mais la transcendance et la paternité de Dieu créateur, et
c'est justement sur cette dernière conception que la sotériologie
chrétienne inscrit le mystère du salut par l'incarnation du Fils de
Dieu.

La vicissitude

Le point de référence essentiel de cette recherche sera donc constitué par le concept de la *vicissitude* et de son protagoniste, la *vie divine*

dans la „nature" ou — respectivement — *l'âme divine.* Dans les rites de fertilité la vicissitude de la vie divine, et plus particulièrement du génie de la fertilité, est le centre du drame saisonnier d'intérêt collectif, joué par le roi; dans les mystères, cette vicissitude s'accompagne de références sotériologiques concernant l'au-delà individuel; dans les mouvements mystériosophiques, le moment saisonnier décline ou est interprété de façon allégorique, et le protagoniste de la grande vicissitude est l'âme, apparentée par son essence aux dieux: l'anticosmisme a déjà inférisé cette terre et sa fécondité, qui est maudite, douloureuse et mortifiante. Dans la gnose cela ne fait qu'atteindre son bout extrême. (Un autre courant, parallèle, souligne pourtant dans la mystériosophie, et — d'une certaine façon — même dans la gnose, le grand Tout, un *cosmos* vu sous l'aspect de l'Unité, de façon plus optimiste; et il est intéressant de voir ces deux attitudes — cosmosophique-totalisante et dualiste-anticosmique — combinées de façon parfois instable déjà avec Empédocle, Pythagore, qui selon la tradition parla le premier d'un „cosmos", Platon, la spéculation hermétique) [1].

Certes, il ne manque pas de savants qui en général concèdent trop à l'hypothèse pour admettre que les mystères grecs et hellénistiques, voire les rites orientaux à type tammuzéen [2], aient abrité une doctrine animologique, mystique et théologique bien arrêtée [3], voire

---

[1]) Cfr. *infra*, p. 160, n. 1.

[2]) Ces rites ne sauraient d'ailleurs être qualifiés par le *terminus technicus* de „mystères", dont le type reste Eleusis: si au moins l'ésotérisme est considéré (et il doit l'être) comme un élément essentiel des mystères. Les rites type Tammuz ont d'ailleurs en commun avec les mystères le rapport avec la „vicissitude" d'un dieu, en fonction saisonnière (ce qui n'implique pas nécessairement la „victoire" finale du dieu). Nous nous séparons ici de la définition d'ailleurs très sensible proposée par FOLLET, „Mystères", *Dictionn. de la Bible*, Supplément VI/1, col. 3. Pour ce qui est de l'aspect sotériologique, qui appartient aussi à la typologie des mystères, il est conditionné, dans les cultes de fertilité, par la nature même de ces cultes (voir *infra*).

[3]) A. MOORTGAT, *Tammuz. Der Unsterblichkeitsglaube in der Altorientalischen Bildkunst*, Berlin 1949, p. 79 s., parle d'une „renaissance" printanière du dieu et roi d'Uruk, qui aurait orienté les sumériens dans le sens d'une espérance au delà de la mort. A part les arguments que nous développons dans la suite, sur le sens de la perspective dumuzéenne, il faut rappeler que l'interprétation des monuments figurés dont MOORTGAT fait état a été contestée: cfr. F. R. KRAUS, in *Wiener Zeitschr. f. d. Kunde des Morgenl.* LII (1953), p. 38-80, et la contribution de FALKENSTEIN à la III Rencontre Assyriologique de Leyde (1952), *Compte Rendu*, Leiden 1954, p. 41 ss. Il faut admettre que l'Hadès sumérien connaissait aussi d'heureuses perspectives (cfr. le récit d'Enkidu, *Gilgam.* XII), mais le complexe devait être passablement morne. Cfr. KRAMER, *Genava* VIII, 5, p. 280.

voire qu'ils aient constitué les foyers d'une gnose. Il s'agit d'une
attitude qui doit être absolument écartée. Les documents autorisent
bien peu dans cette matière, et on a remarqué justement, depuis
LOBECK et ROHDE, ce que Aristote [1]) disait déjà fort bien: que les
mystères constituaient une expérience, bien plus qu'une doctrine;
de sorte que si les mystères, disons les mystères d'Eleusis, ont gardé
si bien leur secret, cela est arrivé surtout parce qu'il n'y avait pas
beaucoup à révéler. C'était surtout la parodie qui profanait le mystère.
Il n'en sera pas d'autant avec la mystériosophie, dont l'attitude sophique, mystico-idéologique, crystallise dans une „doctrine", dans une
sophie de l'âme en tant qu'élément divin. Bien plus, il faut se garder
des extravagances des milieux théosophiques, qui nous assurent
retrouver leurs doctrines sophiques déjà dans les cultes de l'Orient
ancien, non seulement de l'Egypte, mais aussi de la Mésopotamie.
Il faudra se garder d'autant plus attentivement de telles extrapolations
antihistoriques, que des connexions réelles seront effectivement à
retracer entre les cultes orientaux de fertilité, les mystères, la mystériosophie, la gnose.

*
* *

Le trait commun qui nous autorise à étudier les quatre phénomènes
distincts sus-mentionnés a) b) c) d) sous l'angle visuel d'un processus
historique réside dans le fait qu'il s'agit toujours d'un élément divin
qui est en vicissitude, qui — nécessité par une certaine contrainte
fatale, on dirait: connaturée ou cosmique — traverse une crise (une
mort, mieux une disparition ou une déchéance, voire une chute),
non nécessairement dans le sens éthique, mais bien dans le sens du
niveau: une absence, une période de „marge"; et puis se réintègre
à un état de présence qui, nous le verrons, est bien différent dans la
conception cyclique des rites de fertilité saisonnière et dans l'eschatologie „pneumatique" de la mystériosophie et de la gnose: tandis
que les deux issues, cyclicité et agrégation finale, se juxtaposent
encore dans le phénomène (que, inexactement, on dirait intermé-
diaire) des mystères.

Ces vicissitudes, de la vie divine dans la nature, ou de l'âme
divine à travers la nature et au delà d'elle, concernent l'homme, qui
participe — au moins par la célébration rituelle — avec ce quelque

---

[1]) TURCHI, *Fontes historiae mysteriorum*, Roma 1930, no. 87.

chose de divin dont on célèbre la vicissitude, ou — à la limite — s'en identifie. Naturellement, les limites et les formes de cette participation ou de cette identité sont à distinguer dans les différents cas: tandis que dans les rites dumuzéens il s'agit d'une participation surtout célébrative (mais, dans le cas du roi, au moins pour ce qui est du *hieros gamos*, réellement substitutive) à l'aventure du dieu [1]) (cela se vérifie encore, en partie, dans le drame éleusinien) [2]), dans la mystériosophie et dans la gnose la participation tend à se qualifier comme parenté naturelle et consubstantialité de l'âme divine, ou de l'âme pneumatique, avec les dieux, ou avec la Divinité, à la limite, dans le contexte du *salvator salvandus* [3]). (Les rites osiriens anticipant d'ailleurs, originairement par la voie de la médiation royale, une sympathie-identité du dieu et de son „initié"). Cette attitude mystique de *sympatheia* [4]), bien que se manifestant dans des formes si différentes, contraste de fond en comble avec une autre attitude qui se fait sentir puissamment dans la conception de la vie de l'Orient ancien (surtout en Mésopotamie) et de la Grèce classique: l'attitude „olympique" (homérique ou à la Gilgamesh), qui souligne au contraire l'impassibilité des dieux et l'éloignement respectif des dieux et des hommes, qui ont ἤθη et sorts tout à fait antithétiques: ῥεῖα ζώοντες les dieux éternels; destinés a la misère des maladies et, finalement, aux ombres mornes de l'Hadès et de l'Arallu les mortels [5]).

*
* *

Cette divergence si tranchée entre l'attitude mystique, „sympa-

---

[1]) Pour les textes relatifs au *hieros gamos* du roi sumérien, représentant Dumuzi, cfr. VAN DIJK, La fête du Nouvel An dans un texte de Šulgi, *Bibliotheca Orientalis* XI (1954), p. 83. KRAMER, „Cuneiform Studies and the History of Literature: The Sumerian Sacred Marriage Texts, *Proceedings of the American Philosophical Society* vol. 107, 6 (déc. 1963), p. 493-510. Le mariage du roi avec la déesse s'accomplissait au printemps, au commencement de l'année (cfr. le texte R. JESTIN, *Rev. d'Assyr.* XLIV, 51 ss. no. 1, FALKENSTEIN-VON SODEN, *Sumer. Hymnen und Gebete*, no. 18). Un texte publié par FALKENSTEIN, *Zeitschr. für Assyriol. NF XIV*, 1944, p. 105 ss., semble impliquer que ce mariage s'accomplissait au commencement de chaque mois. Cfr. aussi GURNEY, *op. infra cit.*

[2]) Les textes (d'ailleurs très discutés) dans TURCHI, nn. 125-136, surtout 130.

[3]) Pour ce terme, qui me semble ici plus spécifique que „Erlöster Erlöser", cfr. la discussion de C. COLPE, *Die religionsgeschichtliche Schule*, Göttingen 1961, p. 173 ss., avec laquelle nous ne sommes pas pourtant complètement d'accord.

[4]) Pour les limites où le sens de ce terme doit être entendu, cfr. notre discussion dans l'article „Saggezza olimpica e mistica eleusina nell'inno 'omerico' a Demetra, in *Studi e materiali di storia delle religioni*, XXXV (1964).

[5]) U. BIANCHI, art. cité à la n. précédente; id., Διὸς αἶσα, Roma 1953 (Studi pubblicati dall'Istituto ital. per la storia antica, XI), chap. I.

thisante", qui est commune de quelque façon aux rites de fertilité, aux mystères, à la mystériosophie et à la gnose, et l'attitude olympique, soulignant la séparation des milieux divin et humain, est fondamentale pour notre exposé; bien que l'attitude désenchantée sur cette vie et sur les destins humains joue aussi un rôle dans la dynamique interne de la pensée mystique, quand les rites saisonniers commenceront à fléchir devant les nouvelles expériences sotériologiques anticosmiques de la mystériosophie et de la gnose.

Les rites de fertilité. Dumuzi-Tammuz et Adonis

Les rites de fertilité de l'Orient ancien avaient évidemment une perspective „sotériologique", en tant qu'il s'agissait de garantir la survie du monde et d'empêcher qu'il sombrât dans la mort et l'inanition (comme il était arrivé exceptionnellement lors de l'absence d'Ishtar ou de l'éloignement de Déméter); mais il s'agit avant tout d'un salut social et collectif, sur le plan saisonnier.

Avec le rite de fécondité et fertilité, le pays (plutôt que la „nature" en général) est vivifié, avec tout ce qui vit dans le pays, où la vie se renouvelle (donc est „sauvée"). Le roi mésopotamien accomplit cela en représentant Dumuzi, le génie de la fertilité animale et agricole, et en célébrant (au nom et avec le nom de Dumuzi) le mariage sacré avec Inanna, la grande déesse féconde qui patronne le principe actif de la nature. Ce mariage s'accomplit au commencement du printemps, à la fête du Nouvel An, dans la „maison du roi", la „maison de la vie" [1]. La perspective sotériologique des rites de fertilité est saisonnière, donc cyclique, et tout porte à croire qu'elle comprenne aussi, comme issue du cycle (donc après le mariage sacré), la crise du dieu (son départ) et la lamentation, bien que les textes sus-mentionnés relatifs au mariage sacré du roi ne contiennent pas d'allusion à cette morne issue [2]. Le mois où le cycle se conclut serait alors le mois

---

[1] *Supra*, p. 158, n. 1. Comme le remarque VAN DIJK, *op. cit.*, p. 83 s., l'issue de ce mariage n'est pas la procréation d'un fils (dont onne parle pas), mais bien la fixation d'un heureux destin de la part de la déesse: donc une intéressante confirmation du rapport fertilité-vie de la nature-destinée.

[2] VAN DIJK, *op. cit.*, p. 88 distingue entre ces textes sumériens et les rituels récents. Dans les textes les plus anciens, „la fête se centre autour du mariage sacré"; dans le texte étudié en particulier par V.D. „il n'y a guère moyen de faire entrer le mime de l'humiliation du roi, de la mort de Dumuzi etc. „. . ." Partout il y a la joie sans dissonances". L'A. se demande si la signification de la fête n'ait donc changé avec le temps. Il en voit une indication dans le texte *Gilgamesh* VI, 44, que nous discutons dans la suite, et qui serait parodique du mariage rituel royal. (Voir aussi, dans un sens analogue, DE LIAGRE BÖHL, *Het Gilgamesj*

Tammuz le mois chaud, à l'occasion du solstice d'été, quand le cycle agricole se termine sous le rayons puissants du soleil (le sanglier). Or, dans ce cadre, la crise annuelle joue bien le rôle du moment dangereux qui doit être surmonté: mais ce „salut" arrive justement dans la répétition du cycle en tant que tel, qui, lui, constitue, dans la multiplicité de ses phases, la situation finale et définitive dans son alternance: en d'autres termes, le cycle annuel est en même temps vicissitude et „eschatologie", une eschatologie cyclique et saisonnière qui trouve dans son inlassable renouvellement son issue définitive et sa finalité [1]).

$$*$$
$$* \quad *$$

Il faut examiner de plus près ce *pattern*, et s'entendre sur le rôle que jouent les dieux protagonistes du drame saisonnier. On a trop parlé d'un Tammuz ou d'un Adonis que ressuscitent, et qui concluent triomphalement — par un hieros gamos — leur drame annuel. Les

---

Epos,[3] Paris-Amsterdam 1958, p. 145). Tout en renvoyant plus bas pour notre interprétation du refus polémique de Gilgamesh au mariage avec Inanna, nous remarquons ici que ce texte confirme que le sort de Dumuzi était lamentable déjà à l'époque ancienne. En outre, si l'épisode de la mort de l'époux divin était une accrétion postérieure, cela aurait signifié, bien plus qu'un changement de signification, l'accession d'un culte différent. De plus, tout en étant réservé pour ce qui est du *pattern* royal et de ses rapports (spécifiques et essentiels ou non) avec Dumuzi, on pourrait penser que l'humiliation du roi (tout comme l'humilité des dieux en deuil que Inanna visite après son retour des enfers) exempte ceux-ci de la mort, que Dumuzi *en personne* au contraire subit (et, à ce qu'il semble, pour toujours: cfr. *infra*), en connexion justement avec son refus du deuil (sur ce mythe, cfr. *infra*). Cette explication nous semble cohérente avec le fait, remarqué par GURNEY, *op. cit.*, que le *hieros gamos* concerne en général les dieux locaux, donc les rois locaux, tandis que la lamentation est typique (et donc originelle) pour Tammuz.

[1]) C'est justement ce type d'eschatologie que la mystériosophie et la gnose refuseront, bien que le processus éternel et réversible (élargi sur le plan cosmique) continue à jouer un rôle dans une cosmosophie parfois d'aspect optimiste, parfois d'aspect pessimiste et anticosmique (se rattachant par là à la pensée qui sera de la gnose): c'est le cas pour le *sphairos* d'Empédocle (cfr. aussi les deux mouvements contraires et alternatifs du monde dans le *Politique* platonicien). La guerre et l'harmonie des contraires est d'ailleurs le *topos* central de la spéculation présocratique, d'Héraclite à Parménide, avec des implications optimistes ou anticosmiques selon l'accentuation individuelle. Cfr. *infra* nos considérations à propos de l'idole adonique du Janicule, pour ce qui est des connexions entre le cycle saisonnier d'origine „dumuzéenne" et le cycle cosmique, type Aion, de la cosmosophie gréco-orientale. Pour ces aspects dans les présocratiques, cfr., de l'A., *La religione greca*, dans TACCHI-VENTURI, *Storia delle religioni*, 5e edit., Torino 1962, vol. II, p. 494 ss. et *Revue de l'histoire des religions*, t. 159 (1961) p. 43-45.

travaux récents de De Vaux [1]), Lambrechts [2]), Jacobsen [3]), Gurney [4]), Kramer [5]), et d'autres, mais déjà bien Baudissin — [6]), ont mis au clair ce concept, que c'est justement le pathétique, le deuil, *la lamentation*, qui règnent dans le milieu dumuzéen et adonique [7]). C'est bien le *départ*, l'absence du génie divin, bien plus que son retour, qui donne le ton général à ces cultes. Le retour (éventuel), la présence annuelle du dieu (qui pour Dumuzi se résout dans le rôle vicaire du roi) n'est en fonction que du cycle; tandis que son départ ,annoncé et qualifié même par la relative brièveté de son séjour terrestre, donne le ton à tout le cycle. Que l'on pense aussi aux ,,jardinets d'Adonis'', cette floraison destinée explicitement [8]) à la brièveté, par ceux mêmes qui la préparaient, et qui s'en défaisaient finalement en la jetant desséchée dans l'eau de la mer ou des sources, à la fin du bref séjour adonique. D'ailleurs, comme nous le disions, le mariage sacré, aussi bien dans le cas de Dumuzi que (on va le voir) dans celui d'Adonis, loin de couronner un retour à la vie, précède le départ, ne le suit pas: et cela pour cause [9]). A ces conclusions nous portent aussi les rapports entre l'amant divin et son amante, Inanna, Ishtar, Aphrodite. Tout en ne voulant pas identifier complètement des figures et des

---

[1]) ,,Sur quelques rapports entre Adonis et Osiris'', *Revue Biblique* 1933, p. 34.

[2]) ,,La ,,résurrection'' d'Adonis'', Mélanges Isidore Lévy *Annuaire Inst. Phil. et Hist. Orientales et Slaves* XIII (1953) Paris 1955, p. 216. Il nie que cette ,,résurrection'' soit ancienne et originale (dériverait d'Osiris). Voir aussi du même auteur, pour Attis, dans le *Bullet. Inst. hist. belge de Rome*, XXVII (1952), p. 141 ss. L'extension de l'invention joyeuse à Adonis et à Attis dériverait de spéculations tardives sur la palingénésie. D'ailleurs ni Adonis ni Attis ne sont liés avec le sort du mort dans l'audelà.

[3]) *History of Religions* I (1962), p. 189 ss. La thèse de Jacobsen *Journ. Near East. St.* XII (1953), p. 165, que le ,,pasteur'' Tammuz ait à voir avec le pouvoir vital du lait et avec la brève saison de celui-ci nous paraît trop particulière et se heurte aux connexions du *hieros gamos* de Dumuzi avec la fertilité agricole et animale, telles qu'elles ressortent des textes cités 158 n. 1 (si du moins ces connexions sont originelles; mais cette dernière question n'intéresse pas notre exposé).

[4]) ,,Tammuz Reconsidered: Some Recent Developments'', in *Journal of Semitic Studies*, VII (1962), p. 147 ss. Nous n'acceptons pas la thèse extrême de ce savant, que le dieu du mariage sacré et le Tammuz des lamentations ne sauraient être démontrés comme étant le même dieu.

[5]) *Studia Biblica et Orientalia* III (1959), 198 n. 1, et l'étude citée *supra*, p. 158 n. 1.

[6]) *Adonis und Esmun*.

[7]) Il ne s'agit pas, bien entendu, d'identifier complètement le culte de Dumuzi et celui d'Adonis, ni même ceux de Dumuzi et de Tammuz. (ni des différents personnages qui peuvent s'être fondus en eux). Mais les connexions générales et particulières ne sauraient être négligées.

[8]) Platon, *Phaidr.* 276B et d'autres font ressortir justement cet aspect. Cfr. De Vaux, *op. cit.*, p. 33 s., Lambrechts, p. 220.

[9]) Cfr. le texte de *Gilgamesh* et l'Idylle de Théocrite *infra* citt.

croyances qui ont existé dans un milieu cohérent mais complexe, et toujours en condensant l'exposé, nous attirons l'attention sur le fait que, même ici, on a trop parlé, et sûrement à tort, d'une Inanna, d'une Ishtar, qui vont dansles enfers sauver leur amant mort ou ravi. Si l'on considère le complexe des textes, on a l'impression que le cas soit exactement le contraire: voire que le séjour de Dumuzi aux enfers soit provoqué par la nécessité de la libération de la déesse. La partie ultérieure du mythe récemment publiée par KRAMER (d'après une tablette de Ur) le prouve [1]): elle se conclut sur la lamentation de Geshtinanna, la sœur de Dumuzi, pour le sort lamentable de celui-ci, que Inanna avait donné aux démons pour son rachat. D'ailleurs, on ne sait pas trop bien pourquoi la déesse était-elle allée dans les enfers [2]): peut-être, le fait que la déesse fait le voyage souterrain et en revient avec tant de périls pour elle et pour la stabilité de la nature, qui dépend de la présence *continuelle* (non pas alternative) de la déesse, n'est en fonction que de l'idée que dorénavant, *le danger surmonté une fois pour toutes, et l'ordre rétabli* (mieux: *fondé) sur le chaos* [3]), la place de la déesse — dont la maîtrise est à sa façon universelle — ne peut être que sur terre, ou mieux parmi les dieux toujours vivants; et que Dumuzi, au contraire, ne peut pas ne pas disparaître. Evidemment, la régularité saisonnière implique que la source divine de la fécondité reste „olympiquement" intacte et impassible (après un incident primordial qui faillit désorganiser le cosmos et mêler les morts aux vivants), tandis que le génie de la fécondité — plus „humain" qu'elle (et donc mortel) — ne peut être que présent-absent, au bénéfice du cycle, et comme garantie (le mythe sumérien disait: rachat) de l'impassibilité et de l'intacte puissance de la déesse, dont l'incident primordial ne devra plus se répéter.

Car le point est justement ici, que le *cycle, dans le rite de fertilité, est bon*, nécessaire et définitif, bien qu'il implique la mort, ou mieux l'absence, en fonction du retour, qui d'ailleurs ne peut être que temporaire. Ce retour évoque de lui-même, par nécessité psycholo-

---

[1]) KRAMER, 1963, p. 490-493. Le mythe raconté par le Ps. Apollodore 3, 14, 4, selon lequel Aphrodite avait donné en dépôt, dans une arche, le petit Adonis à Perséphone, aux enfers, pourrait indiquer, malgré le contexte, un dernier écho de l'idée que la grande déesse consigne son privilégié aux enfers p. 166, n. 3).

[2]) Pour en devenir la maîtresse (KRAMER, 1963, p. 491)? Certainement pas pour en faire revenir les morts (malgré KRAMER, l.c.): il s'agit ici seulement d'une menace de la déesse au concierge des enfers: ç'aurait signifié le chaos sur terre et la fin du royaume d'en-bas.

[3]) Cfr. la note précéd.

gique et objective, l'absence, le départ futur et imminent, donc la lamentation et le pathos, qui restent, comme nous le disions plus haut, le ton général, le mot dernier, le propre du cadre tammuzéen.

Cette interprétation des cultes tammuzéens et adoniques peut se réclamer de nombreux textes anciens et de bien des études modernes. Nous nous limitons à attirer ici l'attention sur un texte, qui, à propos de Dumuzi, est absolument formel. Il s'agit d'un passage de l'epos de Gilgamesh [1]). Quand Inanna a manifesté à ce héros — habillé en roi, donc avec allusion au *pattern* royal — le désir de l'épouser, Gilgamesh répond en refusant par ces mots: ,,Qui est donc que tu as aimé pour toujours''? Et puis il rappelle à la déesse tous ses époux, qui non seulement ont été nombreux, mais, surtout, ont reçu en connexion avec ses noces de lamentables destins: qu'il s'agisse d'animaux, accolés depuis lors à de lourdes labeurs, tel le cheval, qu'il s'agisse d'hommes, transformés en animaux. Or, Gilgamesh avait commencé la liste en rappelant Dumuzi, l'amant de la jeunesse d'Ishtar: ,,pour lui tu as disposé (destiné) la lamentation annuelle''. Voilà qui justifie la première réponse du héros: ,,tu es un palais qui écrase le vaillant''.

Ce texte est tranchant: la grande déesse, Inanna, ,,la plus trompeuse des femmes'' [2]), le pouvoir divin de la nature fertile, bénéfique et cruelle, qui flatte et qui tue, qui épouse et qui éloigne ses époux, capricieuse et monotone, est évidemment très cohérente à elle-même, et cela dans le cadre d'une vie naturelle et féconde, où la mort et la vie, le labeur et l'obtention mortifiante et défatigante des utilités quotidiennes, la désillusion même, sont les constitutifs de ce cycle qui, lui, représente une situation définitive et somme toute productive [3]). Dans ce cadre, le génie de la fécondité, l'époux et le parèdre de la déesse, dans ses connexions végétales non moins que pastorales, est lié à un sort pathétique [4]). Il est victime, mais (et JACOBSEN l'a mis en lumière dans une fine analyse psychologique) [5]) il est aussi le bien-aimé, le doux, le *toujours* désiré, l'objet d'un amour fait nécessairement

---

[1]) VI, 44.

[2]) Texte *ap.* KRAMER, 1963, obv., l. 14.

[3]) On pourrait comparer, d'un certain point de vue, l'épisode de la mérétrice qui introduit Enkidu dans la civilisation.

[4]) Même si Gilgamesh parodie le *pattern* du mariage royal selon l'interprétation de VAN DIJK et DE LIAGRE-BÖHL (*supra*, p. 159 n. 2), cela n'impliquerait pas une évolution ou décadence de ce rite, le sens fondamental du refus de Gilgamesh étant à chercher avant tout dans l'individu qui se pose la question de *sa* destinée humaine personnelle, que la grande déesse est loin de garantir, s'agisse-t-il du roi. Une version désacralisée du thème subsiste dans l'épisode de Kirké.

[5]) JACOBSEN 1962, cité à la p. 161 n. 3.

de nostalgie, d'attente, de satisfaction temporaire, d'absence. Or, ce sentiment de la présence-absence correspond assez à celui des femmes de l'Idylle XV de Théocrite. *Après* le mariage d'Aphrodite et d'Adonis on célèbre le départ de celui-ci: les femmes accompagnent Adonis à la mer et lui disent au revoir; elles l'attendront infailliblement pour l'année suivante [1]). Voilà d'ailleurs qui explique les mentions de quelques auteurs de la basse antiquité qui semblaient justifier l'idée d'une „résurrection" d'Adonis fermant le cycle [2]). L'attente confiante et sûre d'Adonis, qui n'est pas anéanti, mais qui sûrement reviendra, peut déjà être qualifié de présence: une présence dans l'absence, une présence qui s'identifie avec l'*annonce* (non pas la constatation!) qu'Adonis, malgré son départ, „vit" — c'est à dire, que le cycle continue —: or, c'est justement ceci, qu'il est „retrouvé", que dit l'annonce, et que disent les rares textes [3]) que l'on cite à propos de l'interprétation superficielle de la soi-disante résurrection finale du dieu [4]). Le texte

[1]) Vv. 131-146.

[2]) Lucian., *de Syria dea*, 6; Origen., *in Ezechiel*. 8, 14 — *P.G.* XIII, 797; (unde Hieronym., *in Ezechiel*. 8, 14 — *P.L.* XXV, 82); Cyrill., *in Isaiam* 18, 1, 2 — *P.G.* LXX, 440 (TURCHI, nn. 296, 298, 299, 300).

[3]) Lucian, l.c.: ζώειν τέ μιν μυθολογέουσι. Origène, ὡς ἀπὸ νεκρῶν ἀναστάντι ressent d'un vocabulaire chrétien (Jérôme: *et postea reviviscens* est plus anodin). Cyrille dit qu'Aphrodite avait *retrouvé* Adonis *aux enfers*, et que cette *nouvelle*, *annoncée* par Aphrodite après son retour de l'Hadès, arrêtait le deuil, et causait la participation collective des femmes aux manifestations de joie; quant aux particuliers du texte (d'intérêt rituel plus que mythographique) du Lucien, ils méritent d'être étudiés plus à fond, ce qui est impossible ici (Voir la n. suiv.). De plus, le fait que les femmes se coupaient la chevelure suggère à Lucien une comparaison avec l'usage d'Egypte, à l'occasion de la mort d'Apis: il voyait donc la fête dans une perspective funèbre. Or, ce particulier est donné par Lucien après la mention du deuil des femmes, l'annonce qu'Adonis vit et la phrase énigmatique ἐς τὸν ἠέρα πέμπουσι.

[4]) S. Cyrille (*op. cit.*, 441: cette partie n'est pas dans le recueil de TURCHI) parle d'une lettre qui était arrivée par mer, dans un vase, d'Alexandrie à Byblos, qui annonçait qu'Adonis avait été retrouvé; sur quoi les femmes de cette ville cessèrent le deuil. Mais probablement l'auteur s'est mépris, sur la base d'une interprétation erronée du texte d'Isaïe qu'il commente. Selon Lucien, *op. cit.*, 7, c'était une tête qui arrivait chaque année d'Egypte à Byblos. Mais la signification de l'expression κεφαλὴ βυβλίνη (qui devait être technique), dans le texte de Lucien, *op. cit.* 7, cause aussi un problème. Le scholiaste de Lucien (p. 187 Rabe) combine les deux données, interprétant ἐπιστολαί des LXX comme l'escorte qui était annuellement envoyée pour la tête. En tout cas, s'il y avait une tête, il s'en suivait qu'Adonis n'avait pu être retrouvé que dans l'Hadès, où il restait. Il faut naturellement se demander combien les mythes osiriens aient influencé ces conceptions sur le retour d'Adonis; il ne faut pas oublier que Origène (d'après lui Jérôme) et surtout Cyrille se réfèrent aux rites adoniques d'Alexandrie de leurs temps, et qu'Alexandrie est impliquée dans le récit de Lucien (et de Théocrite); de plus, selon Lucien, il y avait des Bybliens qui attribuaient ces fêtes à Osiris et il en trouve une confirmation dans l'épisode de la tête. Voir LAMBRECHTS, *op. cit.* p. 37 ss.

de Théocrite est formel: avec le douzième mois, donc pour quelques jours seulement, les Heures (donc la saison, le temps „saisonnier") ont ramené Adonis sur terre: une expression heureuse, qui définit exactement le sens et le dynamisme qui régit et meut le cycle adonique. A la fin du séjour, continue le poète, le dieu sera congédié, jusqu'à l'année suivante, quand il „viendra" [1]: il ne sera pas question, alors, ni de (re)naissance ni de résurrection, mais bien d'arrivée, et pour peu de temps.

Bion n'est pas moins clair, dans son *Epitaphe d'Adonis*, une analyse très sensible de l'ethos adonique. „Moi, malheureuse, je vis — Aphrodite gémit sur le cadavre —, je suis déesse et ne peux te suivre" (v. 52 ss.): paradoxalement, c'est le même rapport d'Inanna, déesse impérissable, avec Dumuzi, le héros mourant, — transposé dans un contexte et dans une sensibilité autant qu'il est possible autres. Adonis, *mort, continue* d'être beau (καλὸς νέκυς) [2]: son corps doit *encore* occuper son lit, bien que Perséphone, aux enfers, où il est maintenant, aille s'éprendre de lui. Voilà qui définit la nature du personnage et la situation, qui ne va pas être modifiée par une „résurrection". Le poète le dit clairement: „Il est jusqu'au Moïres qui rappellent Adonis de l'Hadès, par leur magie, mais il ne les entend pas; ce n'est pas qu'il ne veuille, c'est Koré qui ne le lâche pas. Cesse donc pour aujourd'hui tes sanglots, Kythérée ... tu aura encore une fois à pleurer, l'année qui viendra" (v. 96 ss.) [3].

En tout cas, ce qui est certain est que la fête du *hieros gamos* d'Adonis (dont seul Théocrite témoigne) ne couronne pas la vicissitude annuelle

---

[1] V. aussi le scholiaste *ad* vv. 103, 136, 143. Il n'est pas jusqu'à la vue d'Adonis sur le lit nuptial qui n'évoque aux visiteurs l'idée de sa mort: „lui, le trois fois aimé, qu'on aime même aux bords de l'Achéron" (v. 86). La signification de ce vers n'est donc pas seulement que Perséphone aimera Adonis dans l'Hadès; Adonis est le bien-aimé destiné à mourir (un ὠκύμορος à sa manière) et Aphrodite l'aime même mort (v. aussi Théocr., III, v. 48 et le texte de Bion, *infra* cit.): en quoi il y a pour le μονώτατος τῶν ἡρώων la prémisse du retour.

[2] V. 71. Cfr. la note précéd.

[3] LAMBRECHTS: „C'est dire clairement que la fête s'achève avec le deuil, et qu'on ne retrouvera Adonis que l'année suivante, et pour le pleurer encore". On s'étonne parfois que dans la fête de l'Idylle de Théocrite la „résurrection" du dieu fait défaut: mais l'au-revoir des femmes, qui expriment leur certitude que le dieu reviendra l'année suivante (et donc qu'il „vit", à sa manière) en tient parfaitement lieu. Nous pensons aussi à l'idole adonique du sanctuaire syrien du Janicule (Bianca M. FELLETTI MAJ, *Bullettino Comunale* LXXV (1953-55) p. 151 fig. 4): il est une momie, couché, mais ses yeux sont ouverts, et des œufs représentaient sur lui les symboles de la vie. Il est justement un dieu „mort" qui vit, et qui revient cycliquement, selon une *Weltanschauung* où le vieux cycle agraire est désormais le grand cycle cosmosophique de l'Aion (cfr. supra, p. 160 n. 1).

du dieu et le *pattern* rituel; elle en représente plutôt le premier acte qui suit immédiatement le retour. Le *gamos* de Dumuzi se réalisait dans la célébration printanière: dans le cas de la fête raccourcie qui, comme à Alexandrie, réunissait dans une période de deux jours tous les événements de l'histoire du dieu, le *gamos* du premier jour était accolé immédiatement, en été, à la fête du départ, que les femmes célébraient le matin suivant et qui correspondait, en Mésopotamie, à la célébration du mois Tammuz [1]).

Pour ce qui est du retour de Dumuzi-Tammuz, d'ailleurs, il n'est pas témoigné dans le mythe [2]): il s'agit plutôt d'un fait rituel, où d'ailleurs il ne concerne pas le dieu lui-même, mais sa présence efficace, réalisée par le roi qui le réprésente en en assumant le nom. On dirait même que le fait que Dumuzi, lui, ne quitte pas les enfers n'est que la contrepartie, le ,,rachat'', de la présence définitive d'Inanna parmi les immortels, au bénéfice de la vie (cfr. *supra*). Pour Adonis aussi, d'ailleurs, son retour est plutôt le fait du rite que du mythe: le meurtre d'Adonis par un sanglier reste l'épisode finale du mythe, qui fonde la lamentation. La coéxistence des deux aspects, a) acte final avec la mort du héros, b) cyclicité du rite et de la ,,présence'' de Dumuzi-Adonis, devrait être étudiée à part; nous constatons que les deux aspects confirment notre interprétation du cycle, qui culmine dans le pathétique, et nous renvoyons à notre étude citée p. 158 n. 4 sur la phénoménologie des mythes-rites saisonniers [3]).

---

[1]) Cela expliquerait pourquoi les fêtes d'Adonis sont attestées, selon les lieux et les textes, justement en été (*Realencycl.*, *s.v. Adonis*; en automne Ammian. Marc. 22, 9, 15: *annuo cursu completo Adonia*...?)

[2]) KRAMER, *Studia Biblica et Orientalia* III, p. 198 n. 1: The prevalent view that Dumuzi is resurrected every spring is quite without basis in fact. To judge from the available evidence ... the Sumerians believed that once Dumuzi had died, he ,,stayed dead'' in the Nether World and never ,,rose'' again. La ,,résurrection''[?] de Tammuz (avec la ,,résurrection'' de ceux qui célèbrent ses lamentations, ou des morts en général, qui flairent l'encens, dans la fête tammuzéenne) dont les derniers mots (problématiques) de la version *assyrienne* de la descente d'Ishtar ressemblent beaucoup à ce qui arrive justement dans une fête des morts, telles les Anthestéries ou les Parentalia: un retour éphémère; ou bien s'agit-il d'un soulagement des morts (ou de ceux qui ont célébré la lamentation) à la suite des rites funèbres tammuzéens. Tammuz à la porte d'Anu (dans le mythe d'Adapa) ne nous intéresse pas dans ce contexte: s'agissant d'un dieu, il ne faut pas s'étonner de le trouver dans ,,l'audelà'', surtout quand il s'agit d'un homme qui, comme Adapa, va y chercher quelque chose qui n'appartient pas à sa nature mortelle. D'ailleurs, Adapa, loin de féliciter Tammuz pour cette prétendue ,,assomption'', se procure sa faveur en rappelant par sa tenue de deuil que deux dieux, Tammuz et Gizzida, ont disparu du pays: justement ce qui arrivait à Tammuz.

[3]) Les deux aspects sont juxtaposés dans le récit du Ps-Apollodore, 3, 14, 4: présence alternative d' Adonis (sur le modèle du mythe de Koré) et sa mort finale

Des mystères à la mystériosophie

Nous voilà donc amenés à notre question finale, concernant les origines de la mystériosophie et de la gnose anticosmique. Dans les mystères type Eleusis le rite saisonnier exerce encore son influence puissante (pour le bien de la ville et de l'état), mais l'attention se dirige aussi puissamment vers une sotériologie individuelle, qui évidemment ne peut concerner que l'âme du myste (la résurrection des corps étant ici hors de cause). D'où la double appartenance des mystères: sotériologie naturiste, les rattachant aux cultes de fertilité saisonnière; sotériologie individuelle et initiatique, les rattachant aux initiations des peuples primitifs [1]).

Mais bientôt, déjà au siècle VIème, sinon plus tôt, le sort de l'âme commence à s'imposer davantage, en opposition à ce qui est du sort mortel du corps (nous nous référons toujours au monde mésopotamien et grec). La vicissitude de l'âme, qui, dans ce contexte historique, ne peut se conclure que dans un au-delà où le corps ne sera plus intéressé, se précise dans le sens dualiste, anti-somatique et en définitive anti-cosmique de la mystériosophie et de la gnose [2]). C'est le

par un sanglier. Un texte cité par KRAMER 1963, p. 515, semble faire allusion à des vicissitudes de Dumuzi dans le séjour infernal, où il est visité, pour une moitié de l'année, par sa sœur Geshtinanna, et, pour l'autre moitié, par un autre personnage.

[1]) Cfr. les mythes et les rites australiens cités par W. SCHMIDT, *Ursprung der Gottesidee*, III et IV, Münster, Westf. 1931 et 1935; R. PETTAZZONI, *Miti e leggende*, I, Torino 1948, p. 409-411, 414-416, et, plus en général, M. ELIADE, *Naissances mystiques*, Paris 1959. Des rapports avec les initiations du milieu agricole primitif pourraient être envisagés (Ad. E. JENSEN, *Mythes et cultes des peuples primitifs*, Paris 1954; id., *Das Weltbild einer frühen Kultur*, Stuttgart 1848, dont les comparaisons sur le thème du meurtre rituel ne sont pas toutes à retenir. Pour une comparaison avec Eleusis, K. KERÉNYI, „Paideuma", I (1938-40), p. 341 ss.

[2]) On a souligné depuis longtemps, dans les milieux des historiens des religions, mais aussi bien hors d'eux (que l'on songe à JASPERS), l'importance extrême de ce grand siècle, qui est le siècle de Pythagore et de l'orphisme naissant, d'Empédocle et des autres présocratiques, des Upanishads et de Bouddha, du Jina. Il s'agit de doctrines religieuses qui, bien qu'incarnées dans des milieux historiques très différents, n'en soulignent pas moins quelques aspects communs: la spéculation sur l'Un et la multiplicité, l'anticosmisme, le dualisme anthropologique, la fuite de la mort et du „cycle" des existences, l'intérêt cathartique, la métempsychose en fonction cathartique, l'abstentionnisme de type anticosmique, le penchant pour la révélation ésoterique, qui jaillit d'une „connaissance" ancienne, qui se prolonge dans une littérature consciemment pseudo-épigraph, ou le nom de l'„auteur" a la fonction d'une *sphragis*, le salut en tant que réintégration dans l'élément divin etc. Voilà autant de *topoi* de cette mystériosophie qui, en Grèce, s'exprime avec le grand mouvement „orphique", les hommes religieux (*theioi andres*) et les philosophes qui s'y rattachent (Pythagore et Platon étant les deux extrêmes, à mi-chemin entre la mystique et la philosophie): voilà, encore, autant

cas de l'orphisme, cette sophie dualiste et „spiritualiste" appliquée
au dionysisme, dont il semble représenter la réinterprétation critique,
qui continue et développe sa sotériologie, en lui donnant vraisemblablement des assises métaphysiques dualistes et anticosmiques.
L'orphisme critique dans le dionysisme tout ce qui a rapport avec le
sang et la fécondité, qui impliquent le cycle et la mort [1]); ce qui
était probablement le mythe initiatique de Dionysos et des Titans [2])
devient dans l'orphisme le récit d'un meurtre abominable, qui ne
cesse pourtant de conditionner la naissance et le sort futur de l'humanité, qui aura à se purifier de son contenu titanique [3]).

Cette réinterprétation orphique du dionysisme peut nous donner
un exemple de la façon de procéder d'autres courants mystériosophi-

---

de *topoi* du mouvement gnostique de la basse antiquité, un mouvement dont on
étudie depuis longtemps les origines dans les religions qui étaient ses contem-
poraines, mais dont on ne recherche pas assez la racine, justement, dans le grand
mouvement „spiritualiste", dualiste et anticosmique du VIème siècle avant J.-Chr.
Cela ne cesse de surprendre, quand on réfléchit au fait que déjà les anciens nous
ont indiqué la route, quand ils ont parlé, à leur manière, des connexions de la
pensée gnostique avec les philosophes de l'antiquité et nous ont laissé notice de
certaines évolutions ultérieures des systèmes gnostiques classiques (que l'on
pense au language tout à fait héracliféen du simonianisme postérieur etc.). Et
il faut lire les philologues et les historiens de la religion grecque pour retrouver
des remarques pertinentes sur certains aspects communs de l'orphisme et du
gnosticisme („attachement aux formes anciennes et traditionnelles de la pensée
mythique, joint au goût de la spéculation aventureuse": JEANMAIRE, *op. infra cit.*,
p. 400), auxquelles nous ajoutons la constatation que le caractère typiquement
livresque et pseudépigraphe de la tradition orphique anticipe les formes et les
raisons de la littérature gnostique, surtout apocalyptique: et que l'attribution
d'un „livre" à un personnage ancien, connu ou vénéré par tous, bien que particulièrement qualifié pour connaître des secrets mystiques, est typique, justement
dans son aspect, ,conventionnel", d'une „tradition" à type sophique, „gnostique",
soit dans l',,orphisme" soit dans la gnose. V. notre art. "Le problème des origines du gnosticisme", à paraître dans *Numen*, 1965.

[1]) Pour une attitude anti-mystérique, fondée sur la critique des présuppositions
naturistes des rites sanglants, cfr. Héraclite, frgg. 124, 125, 162, 127, 130 D) où
il critique les bacchants et les initiés, qui s'initient de façon impie aux mystères
usités parmi les hommes, qui chantent les chants des choses honteuses pour Dionysos *qui est le même que Hadès*, et qui se purifient (du sang de l'impiété) se conta-
minant encore avec le sang (des purifications).

[2]) JEANMAIRE, *Dionysos*, Paris 1951, p. 372 ss., 387 ss. Selon l'A., ce schéma
initiatique n'aurait pas de connexion originaire avec Dionysos: mais l'hypothèse
initiatique n'élimine pas la perspective mystérique dans le mythe dionysiaque,
le mystère étant, justement, un phénomène initiatique.

[3]) L'interprétation anthropologique et anthroposophique du mythe de Dionysos dévoré n'est pas attestée avant Olympiodore (KERN, *Orphicorum Fragmenta*,
no. 220), si la τιτανική φύσις dont Platon, *Leg.* III 701 B.C. ne s'y réfère pas
(mais cfr. aussi les textes dont KERN, *op. cit.*, Index III, p. 381, *s.v.* τιτάν).

ques par rapport à la vieille mythologie des mystères [1]); la gnose, elle, ira plus loin, en créant une autre mythologie, mais ne cessera d'utiliser des *topoi* semblables, dans le cadre des théories relatives au démiurge, où le vitalisme agressif et égotique de celui-ci rappellera les anciens dieux violents et féconds. Alors ces faits se produiront: le cycle de la fécondité et de la nature deviendra le "cycle" ou la „roue de la naissance", le κύκλος (ou le τροχός) τῆς γενέσεως [2]), auquel l'âme doit échapper, et ce bas monde et ce corps seront parifiés aux enfers où à une geôle.

Aux sources du gnosticisme: l'inférisation du cycle et de la nature.

Dans ce cadre gnostique (qui est déjà celui des mouvements mystériosophiques, comme l'orphisme), la nature, le cycle, la fécondité, la violence agressive et productrice des dieux et des déesses de la nature (en tant que γένεσις et φύσις) seront déclassés et inférisés: ils ne constitueront plus la situation finale, l'équilibre définitif, bénéfiquement alterne du cycle de la vie, mais tout cela appartiendra désormais au deuxième moment du „passage", de ce grand passage qu'est la vicissitude, le *descensus* et l'*ascensus* de l'âme divine. Celle-ci aura désormais pris la place du protagoniste, qui revenait dans les cultes de fertilité au génie de la vie divine de la nature: et, malgré le cadre anticosmique qu'elle intègre, elle dénoncera son héritage par son caractère vitaliste: que l'on pense au concept de ζωή dans les gnostiques, et à la gnose „simonienne" [3]).

---

[1]) Des procédès analogues, dans un contexte différent, plus philosophique, dans les Néoplatoniciens. Cfr. p. ex. KERN, *op. cit.*, nn. 211 ss., surtout 229 (citation néoplaton. des vues orphiques sur les mystères de Dionysos et de Koré).

[2]) KERN, no. 229. Cfr. p. ex. KERN, no. 32, c. 6: κύκλου δ'ἐξέπταν βαρυπενθέος ἀργαλέοιο (metr., lamelle de Thurii, IV-III s.av. J.-Chr.); 224: οὕνεκα ἀμειβομένη ψυχὴ κατὰ κύκλα χρόνοιο ἀνθρώπων ζώιοισι μετέρχεται ἄλλοθεν ἄλλοις.

[3]) Il est à remarquer que la déesse féconde, dont on affirme la tromperie (déjà depuis l'Inanna sumérienne — cfr. *supra*) et le caractère de hiérodule des dieux par des expressions qui — hors du contexte du culte de fécondité — seraient blasphématoires, prête par là-même au culte. Or, on doit remarquer que l'Hélène du simonianisme, Ennoia déchue, ne cesse pas d'être divine, et qu'on ne doit pas la blasphémer (Iren., *adv. haeres.* I, 23: *fuisse autem eam et in illa Helena, propter quam Troianum contractum est bellum; quapropter et Stesichorum per carmina maledicentem eam* (sic), *orbatum oculis* — le docétisme de la Palinodie du poète sicilien ne pouvant qu'avoir de la suggestion pour des gnostiques). Il est inutile de rappeler toute la discussion comparative sur la mythologie mésopotamienne et la mythologie gnostique (descente d'Inanna etc.), depuis ANZ, dont le petit travail, *Zur Frage n. d. Ursprung des Gnostizismus* (Leipzig 1897) est plus modéré que bien des autres travaux *religionsgeschichtlich* qui le suivirent. Il faut ajouter que le pendant naturiste de la Sophie gnostique déchue n'est pas surtout Inanna-Ishtar, mais bien son

Il arrive aussi que le cycle, qui était originairement le cycle saisonnier, se transforme désormais dans le cycle de la métensomatose, le cycle de l'âme prisonnière, le „moment de marge" de l'âme divine exilée, dont elle doit se libérer; et les dieux féconds auront leurs héritiers non seulement dans les dieux sabéens de Harran, mais bien dans les archontes et les démiurges de la gnose, ou dans les démons de la gnose mandéenne, continuant les noms et quelques attributions du panthéon babylonien.

Puisque nous avons mentionné les Mandéens, nous rappellerons finalement que cette conclusion était déjà annoncée dans une tendance implicite de la spiritualité mésopotamienne: le propos de Gilgamesh, qui se méfie d'Inanna, une fois rapporté à l'expérience de l'homme commun (non du favori de la déesse), est un propos qui manifeste somme toute une attitude de soupçon à l'égard de cette grande nature qui nous dépasse dans toutes les directions: „qui est-ce que tu as aimé pour toujours" [1])? Seulement, Gilgamesh préfère n'avoir pas d'illusions dangereuses et rester ce qu'il est; comme le mésopotamien, qui adore la vie, cette vie, pourtant si courte et menacée, accepte et respecte somme toute ses dieux féconds et violents, qui peuvent la lui prolonger, quitte à les transformer lentement en démons: la théo-démonologie mandéenne en sera l'aboutissement extrême [2]). En effet, le gnostique en viendra à cet extrême: il dévoilera

---

parèdre (v. *supra*): quand la nature sera inférisée, et qu'elle n'aura plus affaire à la vie, mais seulement à la mort, il en sera fini avec la déesse impassible (cfr. *supra*) qui engage son parèdre dans le cycle: la grande hypostase féminine dont, selon les systèmes gnostiques, le monde tire plus ou directement ses origines y sera engagée à son tour.

[1]) Cfr. la note précéd.

[2]) Naturellement, avec des influences occidentales. Il faut se rappeler que les „Sept" sont en Mésopotamie parfois des dieux (ou „un" dieu, Sibitti), bénéfiques ou maléfiques qu'ils se montrent, parfois les démons. Qu'on se rappelle aussi, dans ce contexte, d'autres sectes de cette région, tels les Yézidis, les „adorateurs du diable" (cfr., pour ces connexions, U. BIANCHI, *Il dualismo religioso*, Roma 1958, chap. II). L'Iran, à son tour, avait déjà démonisé depuis longtemps ses *daiva* violents: voilà un aspect a considérér, quand on étudie les possibles sources iraniennes du gnosticisme (nous nous permettons de renvoyer ici à nos contributions sur le concept de *darǝghō-xvadhāta* et sur le sacrifice-meurtre du taureau, resp. dans le *Unvala Memorial Volume* et le *J. J. Zarthoshti Madressa Centenary Volume*, à paraître). Pour ce qui est de l'autre aspect de la pensée mazdéenne, surtout post-gathique, qui pourrait entrer en ligne de compte ici (une ‚certaine' tendance à la consubstantialité lumineuse entre Ormazd, les Amahraspands et la création, qui n'élimine pourtant pas la personnalité du premier, ni des âmes; le concept d'une création descendante; la tendance aux hypostases célestes): *Zamān i Ohrmazd*, Torino 1958, p. 121 ss., *Rev. de l'hist. des relig.*, t. 159 (1961) p. 38-39 n. 1 et 33 n. 1.

la mystification et la tyrannie des dieux de ce monde. Quand, où et comment cela s'est produit? Le savoir, signifierait résoudre le problème des origines du gnosticisme. Ce qui importe ici est de remarquer que le scénario (et le drame) essentiel de la gnose est né, dans le Proche-Orient et en Grèce (dans cette dernière déjà avec la mystériosophie orphique), quand la perspective divine de la vie féconde a échoué, et que l'âme a aspiré à une sotériologie individuelle anti-cosmique, contre ce monde et ses dieux matériels, au delà du vieux pessimisme non racheté de l'individu mésopotamien et homérique [1]).

L'autre possibilité, alternative, n'est pas dans les perspectives du monde mésopotamien ou grec, ni de la mystériosophie ou de la gnose: je me réfère à la conception monothéiste, qui, déjà dans l'Ancien Testament et puis avec l'Eglise, n'a cessé de polémiser contre la divinisation de la nature et de son cycle, et, puis contre la divinisation de l'âme en vicissitude cyclique; elle n'a trouvé le salut que dans la grâce de Dieu, créateur et restaurateur des êtres humains, dans leur totalité psycho-somatique. Voilà qui fonde le propre de la conception biblique de Dieu, de l'homme, de l'âme, de la révélation, du salut, de la résurrection, de la connaissance religieuse, voire du mystère et de l'initiation. La divinisation de la nature et de l'âme est au contraire le présupposé de l'expérience mystique païenne, orientale et grecque, dont le gnosticisme (et, de leur manière le platonisme et le néoplatonisme) sont l'aboutissement extrême.

P.S. Le but de cette communication n'etait pas d'épuiser le thème de l'eschatologie individuelle en Mésopotamie, mais, plus spécifiquement, de comparer la structure du rite naturiste et les perspectives des mystères et du gnosticisme.

---

[1]) Sur le plan éthique, les deux attitudes gnostiques classiques découleront de cet anticosmisme: ou bien l'abstentionnisme de type anticosmique, ou bien le libertinisme qui se fait monde à ce monde. Parfois, les deux choses combinées selon des symbologies complexes et souvent étranges.

Pour quelques aspects structuraux communs du mythe naturiste des cultes de fertilité et du mythe psychique du gnosticisme (coëxistence des aspects prototypique et typique), cfr. *Studi e materiali di storia delle religioni*, XXXV (1964), p.p. 184, n. 20, et 192.

NEW TESTAMENT BAPTISM
AN EXTERNAL OR INTERNAL RITE?

BY

R. A. BARCLAY

Leeds

—"Now a discussion arose between John's disciples and a Jew over purifying." [1]) John 3: 25 RSV.

Nothing of the contents of this discussion is recorded. There is enough material in the Gospels to see what John's disciples were likely to say. What the Jew might say on his part can only be inferred from known Jewish practices, such as proselyte baptism, or that of such sects as the Essenes, of those of Qumran, assuming the Qumran, group fell within the Gospel period.

JOSEPHUS, however, may be indicating the general line of such a discussion when he refers to John the Baptist in his Antiquities of the Jews. He says that John was a good man, "he commanded the Jews to exercise virtue, as to righteousness towards one another, and piety towards God, and so to come together to baptism for that the baptism would be acceptable to him, if they made use of it, not in order to the putting away of some particular sins only, but for the purification of the body; supposing still that the soul was thoroughly purified beforehand by righteousness". [2])

Josephus appears to be defining the nature of the rite of baptism as to how far it is an external rite of water-purification of the body, and how far it has internal purification for the soul. [3])

According to Josephus the purified soul is the first step on the

---

[1]) C. K. BARRET "The reference is not to the baptism performed by John, or to that performed by Jesus, but to Jewish purification in general." *The Gospel according to S. John*, in loc.

[2]) Josephus, *Antiquities of the Jews*, Book VIII c. V para. 2 (WHITSON ed.). The reference follows the description of the defeat of Herod's army by Aretas, king of Arabia. „Now some of the Jews thought that the destruction of Herod's army came from God, and that justly ,as a punishment for what he did against John, that was called the Baptist, for Herod slew him."

[3]) E.g. "Create in me a clean heart, O God, and put a new and right spirit within me." Psalm 51: 10 RSV.

way to the purified body. The immersion of the body in water is the external rite with an internal pre-significance of the clean heart and the right spirit.

The question at once arises, why the external immersion should be required at all. Is it not sufficient that the internal state of 'righteousness' be achieved? What does the immersion, the baptism, *add* to this internal state?

The Manual of Discipline of the Qumran groups has a long section which is very definite that "No one is to go into water (lakes, river or baths are mentioned), in order to attain the purity of holy men. For men cannot be purified except they repent their evil". In the Manual there is no repudiation of waters of purification.[1]) The question again arises, what do the waters *add* to the state of the soul which is "in righteousness"?

We turn now to the Baptism of John. The preparatory condition *before* there can be water-purification in John's baptism is clearly related in the Gospels, or is it so clear? Let us look at the passages:

(*i*) *Mark* 1: 1-8: "John the baptizer appeared in the wilderness preaching a baptism of repentance for the forgiveness of sins".

The people were "baptized by him in the river Jordan, confessing their sins", v. 5., while John says, "I have baptized you with water but he (i.e. the 'mightier-than-I') will baptize you with the Holy Spirit". v. 8.

Presumably the state of repentance comes first; the act of confessing must be there with the repentance.

What did John see in the *water* addition? He is at pains to separate the water rite from what 'the mightier-than-I' will give as the *new* baptism—baptism with the Holy Spirit. This is definitely an addition to the repentance, confession and water-purification associated with John's rite.

(*ii*) *From Matt.* 3: 1-12 a further addition is given as a reason for repentance: "Repent, for the kingdom of heaven is at hand" v. 2. This is indeed *news* of the first order; never before was it said "the kingdom of heaven is at hand".

The condition of being within the kingdom, now near, was

---

[1]) Manual of Discipline ii, 25-iii, 12. trans. TH. GASTER "The Scriptures of the Dead Sea Sect", p. 52, 1957. e.g. 'Only by the submission of the soul to all the ordinances of God can his flesh be made clean. Only thus can it really be sanctified by waters of purification.' GASTER notes that the Manual is against the idea 'that the act of immersion can *by itself* absolve from sins'. p. 106.

repentance *before* the final approach which made the kingdom to be actually beside them.[1]

(*iii*) *Luke* 3: 1-17 in a further extended version of the Baptist's preaching underlines the place of repentance as issuing in revised modes of conduct in different walks of life.[2]

The Fourth Gospel differing in so many respects from the Synoptists differs here also.

John 1: 19-34 makes no reference to the baptism of repentance unto the remission of sins, nor to a baptism with fire, an addition of Matthew to the Marcan saying about the Holy Spirit, Matt. 3: 12. Instead the Baptist in John's Gospel witnesses to the *Person*, unknown to the people or to John himself at the first, but whom he can point out as the "Lamb of God" v. 29 "who takes away the sin of the world." This is a new designation of a new person. He then affirms "for this I came baptizing with water, that he might be revealed to Israel". v. 31.

(*i*) *Revealed* to Israel as the Lamb, presumably in the context of the sacrificial system of Israel; or, in the sense associated with the servant picture in Isaiah 53: 7, "like a lamb that is led to the slaughter".

(*ii*) *Revealed* to Israel as the baptizer "with the Holy Spirit". v. 33.[3]

(*iii*) *Revealed* to Israel as Son of God, for finally John says "I have seen and borne witness that this is the Son of God" v. 34.[4]

John the Baptist in his capacity of forerunner of Jesus was justified in trying to describe Jesus so that he could be recognised by his people. That is, recognition in His Special function in their religious history as the "Lamb slain"; in his special activity as the Giver of the

---

[1] Matthew extends his reference to baptism from 'the Mightier-than-I' by saying "He will baptize you with the Holy Spirit and *with fire*". The image of fire is linked with the harvest process of separating the wheat from the chaff. The chaff is burned with "unquenchable fire" v. 12—a process of separation under judgment.

[2] Luke 3: 17 e.g. tax-collectors and soldiers, both classes not beloved by the Jews. While the Jews were not to pride themselves on their racial descent from Abraham, and were not to fail in the exercise of practical charity.

[3] The baptism of Jesus was with water, and at that time John says "the Spirit descended" as a dove from heaven". v. 32., to identify Jesus as "he who baptizes with the Holy Spirit." v. 33.

[4] This last theme "Son of God" is elaborated in John c. 3 vv. 22-36 when John's own disciples come asking him about Jesus practising baptism, or rather having it practised by His disciples. John re-affirms the special nature of this new Person as Messiah. "I said I am not the Christ, but I have been sent before him." 3: 28.

Holy Spirit, in that same history which knew the power of the spirit of God; and finally, relating Jesus to the God of their history as God's Son.[1])

The association of this teaching with water-purification is made by John the Baptizer, though it might be thought that it could be dissociated from baptism without loss of meaning.[2])

We can ask the question here, into what community did John the Baptist initiate the baptized person? He names none. Modern scholarship has come to stress that the community is the new Messianic people of God, thus setting John's activity in a "great eschatological context".[3]) However this may be, the initiation was into a community with a new faith. Baptism was the external concomitant of this faith.

Yet this new faith was still based on the Old Testament faith that God forgave sins; that man should ever repent and confess his sins, accepting the free gift of God's forgiveness, because God exercised Hesedh, mercy, loving-kindness, to him that believed. The mode or manner in declaring this faith which should issue in moral righteousness was now intensified in the Coming One, 'the mightier-than-I', 'the Messiah" 'the Lamb of God', 'the Giver of the Holy Spirit' who could enable men to achieve the new life of the new community in a lively hope of the final consummation of the kingdom of heaven when all should come to believe in the Son of God.

This faith clearly required a 'metanoia', a change of mental and spiritual outlook, whether accompanied by waterpurification or not. How far it could be attached to, or contained in, the external rite depended on ingenuity in interpretation. And no attempt at this is

---

[1]) None of these were likely to be acceptable teaching. The Gospel of John is the narrative of how unacceptable they were.

[2]) Of course the Jews were familiar with their own proselyte baptism as were the Gentiles who had to submit to the entire ritual of initiation into the Jewish community of faith after instruction. This is not the place to discuss this question of proselyte baptism to that of John the Baptist. Though it is now generally agreed that it was in existence as a rite in early NT times, it was not until AD 65 that it was made obligatory for non-Jews to enter Judaism by this act of baptism-initiation.

[3]) Modern scholarship as represented e.g. in the World Council of Churches Commission on Faith and Order in its report "One Lord, One Baptism", 1960, has come to stress that "John's preaching and baptism had one sole aim; to gather the Messianic people, to make ready a people prepared", Luke 1: 17. Baptism is therefore "an act of reception into the new Messianic people of God. It did not have its meaning and purpose in itself, but in Him who was to come." John's activity was thus set „in a great eschatological context", which conditioned his baptism, which was not "merely a symbol of purification from sin which was the object of his preaching of repentance". p. 50 ff.

made in the Gospels, or indeed in the rest of New Testament for John's baptism.

The Baptism of Jesus: We now turn to the baptism of Jesus at the hands of John. Three times in the Synoptists we have a reference to what must have been the way in which Jesus viewed the origin of John's baptism. In reply to the Temple officials who questioned his authority, Jesus challenges them with the question, "Was the baptism of John from heaven or from men?" Mk. 11: 30; Matt. 21: 25; Luke 20: 4.[1]) They saw the dilemma and replied in self-defence "We do not know". Mk. 11: 33.

One must assume here that Jesus accepted John's baptism as *derived from heaven*, i.e. from God. It was a divine institution, and therefore required obedience from himself as being part of the will of God.

John, as is well known, questioned Jesus coming to him for baptism.[2]) Matthew gives details of the conversation with John. John wanted the role of the baptizer and the candidate for baptism to be reversed. Let Jesus baptize him![3]) Jesus' reply to this gives dominical authority for the rite of baptism (apart from any question about the closing words of Matthew's Gospel 28: 19). He declares its meaning for Himself. "Let it be so now; for thus it is fitting for us to fulfil all righteousness." Matt. 3: 15. "For us" (in the Greek 'hemin') clearly identifies Jesus with other people being baptized. How does Jesus think of himself as amongst the "us", (hemin), since John's baptism was linked with repentance and confession of sins?

In Old Testament theology 'sin' and 'righteousness' are classical contrasting conceptions.[4]) Within this Jewish context [5]) the signifi-

---

[1]) "Was the baptism of John from heaven or from men?" Mark 11: 30; Matt. 21:25; Luke 20: 4. If you answer that I will tell you about my authority. The Temple officials had to argue it out among themselves. They saw the dilemma; if it was from heaven then they would be challenged as to why they had not believed it, if it was from men, then they feared the people would attack them as John was reckoned to be a prophet. So they pleaded inability to answer. "We do not know" Mark 11: 33. So Jesus on his part replied then I am not speaking to you about my authority either. v. 34.

[2]) Mark begins his Gospel with the story, Mark 1: 4-11. cf. Mt. 3: 13-17, Luke 3: 21-22, John 1: 29-34.

[3]) Presumably because John viewed himself as in the category of sinners, and the Messiah as outside of these.   [4]) See for example Isaiah c. 59 vv. 15-17.

[5]) The sacrifices of the old order, still in practice in Jesus' time, the *right* sacrifices, required "The sacrifice acceptable to God is a broken spirit; a broken and a contrite heart, O God thou will not despise". Psalm 51: 17. This broken and contrite heart for sin is the prelude to the great sacrifice described at the end of the Psalm. They are corporate sacrifices, the plural is used, whether supplied by the individuals or through the temple arrangements.

cance of Jesus' revalation in regard to sin is made manifest. Himself sinless, *He had come to deal with sin.* [1]) His life-story really begins "in heaven" for He was "sent" by God [2]) This "sending" is meaningless unless the Godhead viewed sinners as "redeemable." In being "sent" He came sharing the sin of men, not by sinful action, but by being *one with them* (Emmanuel, God with us) in the full significance of sin in their soul's experience, its pathos, its tragedy and its guilt. In various ways Isaiah c. 53 had spoken of it. "The Lord has laid on him the iniquity of us all". Jesus entered into the corporate experience of men in regard to sin, 'sent' by God for this purpose, whatever the consequence might be for Himself.

But more important than just being sent by God, He took it upon Himself willingly, in identification and actually 'bearing', 'carrying' as a load, as the burden of His life, which he need not have carried in view of his origin. "It is fitting for us to fulfil all righteousness." To be righteous involved confession of sin in relation to and its effect upon Himself and God. To become 'righteous' involves the acknowledgement of God's forgiveness, though He did not require this for Himself. Further righteousness involved the acceptance of the will of God for us all. Jesus accepted that will in his Incarnation.

Righteousness, then, is the attitude towards the world problem of sin as that is seen in the biblical record. Man needs to be saved from sin; man is capable of redemption because of the righteousness of God which includes, is indeed manifested in, the forgiveness of sins. This is surely in keeping with John's baptism.

Secondly, in contrast with sin, as the old way of living, i.e. 'in sin', righteousness is the new way of living, i.e. is living rightly by God's will. For Jesus that will was known. "For I have come down from heaven, not to do my own will, but the will of him who sent me". John 6: 38.[3]) Jesus looks forward to the will of God being done. "Thy will be done on earth as it is in heaven." (Lord's prayer).

That Jesus puts the Father's will first, and not his own is declared

---

[1]) His life-story really begins in "heaven" for He was "sent" by God. See John's Gospel for this emphasis particularly.

[2]) John 6: 38; 7: 28; 8: 29; 12: 49; 14: 24, and "O righteous Father, the world has not known thee, but I have known thee; and these know that thou hast sent me". 17: 25.

[3]) This is in line with John the Baptist's demands. Whereas for the ordinary people at the baptism of John it might mean nothing more than ceasing to be extortioners like taxgatherers, or soldiers being less bloody, or Jews being less race-conscious, for Jesus it was commitment to fulfilling what had rightly been declared by Isaiah as the function of the Servant of Mankind.

in the crucial prayer in the Garden of Gethsemane, "My Father, if this cannot pass unless I drink it, thy will be done". Matt. 26:47. As the suffering servant of mankind He must reveal the will of God through suffering.

What has this understanding of the concept of 'righteousness' to do with external water-purification? The answer must be—nothing, except that Jesus makes this the first step in the new creation[1]) of man as a child of God.[2])

As we have already noted it seems likely that Jesus viewed the baptism of John as 'from heaven', and here at his own baptism there is acknowledgement by 'Heaven' in the voice that said "This is my beloved Son",[3]) the climax of the incident as recorded by Matthew. The Sonship of Jesus was declared and with it the way opened for the adoption of men as the sons of God the Father again.

Jesus' baptism is thus part of the divine revelation of God's own nature, as well as the explanation of His attitude to sin and forgiveness. By Jesus participating in the water-rite initiating the world into this revelation, he transforms the water-rite into a spiritual-rite. As it were, water-baptism was itself baptised with a new meaning. This was not purification in water as such, whether for bodily cleanliness or even spiritual symbolism for a 'metanoia', a new religious outlook. It was a personal comitment to the will of God.[4])

Jesus knew this involved his suffering, and he tried to make his disciples understand this on more than one occasion. He uses intensively the word "baptism" to describe what he anticipated. "I have a baptism to be baptized with; and how I am straitened till it be

---

[1]) As in Creation (Genesis c. 1) the Light came first to the world, so while the Spirit had brooded over the waters of chaos, God cleft these waters asunder to make Heaven and earth, the basis of "cosmos" under the Light.

[2]) Matthew 3: 17.

[3]) The World Council of Church Report on 'One Lord, One Baptism' regarding John's difficulty over baptizing Jesus says John could not reconcile it with his own conception of the Messiah; the idea that the Messiah should be baptized with the baptism of repentance for the remission of sins. The problem was solved by the voice from heaven Matt. 3:17; cf. Mark 1: 11; Luke 3: 22, and note their close connection with Isaiah 42: 1, i.e. not just the seal of messianic vocation, but to be the Messiah as the Isaianic Servant of the Lord. Hence Jesus as servant, as the only righteous one, was to enter vicariously into the 'sin of many', Isaiah 53: 12, to bear it as his own sin and so to make the many participate in his righteousness." It was also his consecration to suffering and to death. Only so was 'all righteousness' fulfilled." Matt. 3: 15.

[4]) Certainly no one at Jordan could anticipate Jesus' death and resurrection. To bring even his disciples to anticipate this proved impossible *until the events had taken place.*

accomplished." [1]) Luke 12: 50. In baptism one went down into the waters, was buried by them, and then one rose again from them.[2]) This analysis of baptism was later to receive classical expression from S. Paul.

In the event Jesus accepted the water-rite for Himself. It was his answer to the relationship of himself not only to what John was teaching, but to what He was to fulfil in regard to God's love for sinful men through his death and resurrection. In one sense the water meant nothing, but in another it meant everything, as the whole man, body, soul and spirit were dedicated, 'covenanted' to perform the will of God for the salvation of mankind.

Jesus appears to have considered the external rite of immersion essential. It ceased to be an "odd" ceremony or even a familiar one. It became an overwhelming necessity in the divine plan of declaring redemption. It was necessary above all to show that redemption signified purification in the midst of a sinful world, and *from* that world, in order to effect the will of God for His world. "Thy will be done on earth, as it is in heaven . . ." whatever heaven wills as best for earth. That includes Jesus' life in all its aspects.

I have spent time on the activity of John the Baptist and on Jesus' Baptism in relation to it,[3]) because that is the historical sequence of events regarding baptism, events which occupied a very short time, but which are basic to the New Testament; and also because in the Gospels there is a lack of description of other baptismal ceremonies which were undoubtedly held.

We now look briefly at episodes recorded in the book of the Acts which show how people came to water-baptism of the new faith. In this we shall indicate the kind of interpretation which appears to have been given to the rite.

---

[1]) Cf. Mark 10: 38-39; Matt. 20: 22 according to some mss. Baptism as plunging into the waters is a common metaphor for affliction and sorrow. E. F. SCOTT suggests this verse throws light on the way in which Jesus regarded baptism, and it helps to explain the origin of some of the ideas later associated with the Christian rite as we meet it in the Acts and Epistles. Jesus Himself may well have "first forged the link between the idea of 'baptism' and 'death'." vd. W. F. FLEMINGTON, *The New Testament Doctrine of Baptism*, p. 31-32.

[2]) From this it would appear that Jesus interpreted his baptism in relation to the will of God, which he knew and anticipated, that he must die and rise again.

[3]) John the Baptist may have thought that baptism in water would end with him, and be replaced by the baptism of the Spirit; there is no evidence that he did so teach; if he had he would have been open to criticism as to the use of water-baptism anyway.

The first group of baptismal incidents recorded in the Acts simply mention the performing of the ceremony after response to the preaching of Paul about the Lord. Lydia of Thyatira, Acts 16: 14-15; the jailor at Philippi, Acts 16: 33 ff; Crispus at Corinth, Acts 18: 8, cf. I Cor. 1: 14.

The second group I make suggests a certain *incompleteness* in the type of baptism received. First there is the incompleteness of John's baptism from the *Christian* point of view. Acts 19: 1-7 tells of Paul's visit to Ephesus. There some dozen people, disciples of John, who had been baptized according to John's rite, were ignorant of what John had been stressing about the baptism of the future, namely, that it involved belief in the One to Come who baptized with the Holy Spirit. So these disciples were *re-baptized* in the name of Jesus and became empowered by the Holy Spirit.

The next example is the baptism of Cornelius at Caesarea. This followed not only Peter's proclamation of Jesus as the one "anointed by God with the Holy Spirit and power" (Acts 10: 38), but the coming upon the audience of the *presence* of the Holy Spirit. Later Peter was to report in a defensive speech in Jerusalem "As I *began* to speak the Holy Spirit fell on them just as on us at the beginning" (Acts 11: 15-16) "and I remembered the word of the Lord, how he said, 'John baptized with water, but you shall be baptized with the Holy Spirit"—a paraphrase of a post-resurrection saying of Jesus as recorded in Acts 1: 5.

Scholarship has been concerned with the sequence here, since the Holy Spirit comes *before* the baptism, not along with it (accompanying it), nor *after* it, (as might be expected). We need not discuss this insoluble problem here. So far as our study is concerned we note that baptism stands out as *the external ceremony which has to be performed, whatever goes before*, whether proclamation and acceptance of Jesus as Lord, and, or, the gift of the Holy Spirit. The external rite highlights any or all of these.

In the next example there is again incompleteness. It is that of Philip's visit to Samaria (Acts 8: 12-13) where it is evident that the gift of the Spirit did not accompany the baptism. Men and women there had been baptized as a result of Philip's preaching about the Kingdom of God and the name of Jesus. It was the apostolic group at Jerusalem who felt it necessary to send Peter and John to Samaria expressly to presence the gift of the Holy Spirit by the laying on of hands upon those previously baptized. The baptism was apparently "valid", so far as it went as an external rite, but it was incomplete and so could be added to, if it was to be fully Christian. John had suggested this in his announcement that the prerogative of Jesus was to give the Holy Spirit. Jesus himself had indicated this too just before Pentecost. Acts 1:4-5.

The next example, that of the Ethiopian eunuch (Acts 8: 36 ff), has no reference to the gift of the Holy Spirit nor to the forgiveness of sins. It shows instead the external rite as declaratory of the nature of Christ. The eunuch anxious for baptism affirms to Philip "I believe that Jesus Christ is the Son of God". v. 37. Here was a declaration of faith; whatever he had believed previously about the meaning of Isaiah c. 53, he had now moved forward to the historic person of Jesus. He has an internal change in his outlook in biblical interpretation. His religion now contains a theological definition of the person of Jesus. Philip had evidently made Isaiah c. 53 a precise reference to Jesus as the Messiah, the Christ. So whether the theological definition "Son of God" is original to the text here or not, the eunuch's baptism is acknowledgement of the person of Christ in the sense that Christ is *in* his baptism.

The absence of reference to the forgiveness of sins and to the Holy Spirit contrasts with the powerful emphasis on both of these by Peter on the Day of Pentecost. "What shall we do?" cried the crowd after Peter preached. "Repent, and be baptized everyone of you in the name of Jesus Christ for the forgiveness of your sins; and you shall receive the gift of the Holy Spirit." Acts 2: 38.[1]) The people were expected to understand this from what they knew and had been told about Jesus. Forgiveness of sins by God was old teaching. It was *new* in being linked with Jesus. Receiving the Holy Spirit was also old teaching,[2]) but receiving the gift of the Holy Spirit consequent

---

[1]) Acts 2: 38. This verse is giving baptism as the guarantee of forgiveness. No doubt they were accustomed to the Old Testament teaching in the sacrificial system, which was still at this time in full swing in the Temple. Shortly, with the destruction of the temple, sacrifices would disappear from Jewish religious practice. In this system the forgiveness was guaranteed through the sacrifice, the inner assurance regarding this was a matter of faith, dependent on accepting a "word", whether that of the prophet or psalmist. Repentance was in any case the pre-requisite for bringing a sacrifice of whatever kind. There was certainly no justification for forgiveness unless there was consciousness of guilt as a pre-requisite.

[2]) Old Testament leaders had been specifically endowed with the Spirit of the Lord for their activities. There is no mention of the Spirit being associated with any ceremony. A man might be conscious of the Spirit of God as the Psalmist who prayed "take not thy holy spirit from me" Ps. 51: 11, but how he had received

to baptism, or at baptism, this was undoubtedly new teaching. The newness of the baptismal rite and its meaning was a genuine break in traditional religion.

The last example in this group is that of Paul's baptism, presumably at the hands of Ananias after Paul had recovered his sight. (Acts 9: 18). After the baptism Paul is reported as proclaiming Jesus in the synagogues of the Damascus area, as "the Son of God" and "proving" Jesus was the Christ, the Messiah. 9: 22. Here again is the theological conviction expressed as it was for the eunuch—Son of God, Messiah, Christ-Servant. Baptism incorporates this confession of faith. Whether *with* the baptism, or *after* it, or *before* it. The promise that Paul would be filled with the Holy Spirit was also given by Ananias, Acts 9:17, but it is not stated when it was given. So long as he manifested it, possessed it, was what mattered whenever it was given. Baptism as an external rite could carry a number of meanings expressing the new internal faith of the baptized person, so long as they were intimately connected with the name and person of Jesus.

It is this relationship of the external rite and the internal significance to which Paul was to give classical expression in his letter to the Romans. Whatever lustrations the Romans and the Greeks were familiar with in their variety of religions, Paul defines in Romans what *Christian baptism* is in all its fulness. In doing so he must base it on what happened to Jesus at the hands of men and by the will of God. Language could not express more clearly and definitely than Romans 6: 1-4 what was Paul's view. Karl BARTH in his commentary on Romans on 6: 3 says "Baptism is an occurrence belonging to the concrete world of religion." Here we would remind ourselves that it is the concrete world of the *Christian religion*.

The passage is worth reading in full. "What shall we say then? Are we to continue in sin that grace may abound? By no means! How can we who died to sin still live in it? Do you know that all of us who have been baptized into Christ Jesus were baptized into his death? We were buried therefore with him by baptism into death, so that as Christ was raised from the dead by the glory of the Father, we too might walk in newness of life." Romans 6: 1-4.

Of course these words could only have been written after the cross and the resurrection, and after these events had been considered and examined much as to their final significance. At no point earlier in the

---

this we do not know. The Spirit came and it went, Ps. 51: 10-12. He did not associate it *with the performance of sacrifices*. v. 17.

Gospels are they so linked in anticipation, though Jesus as we have seen did refer to the baptism and the cup to drink. Nor are they linked so in the examples of Gentile baptisms.

Is Paul super-imposing a symbolic meaning? Is he trying to make an external rite into an internal one of faith in the dogma of salvation which he proclaimed as being resident in the death and resurrection of Jesus? The symbolism is excellent. It gives a *new* meaning by Paul. The interpretation is neat and precise, to be accepted or rejected. The question however is the *reality* in the relationship between the external rite and the experience within the rite. Can it induce a considered acceptance of the dogma of this salvation, or can it act as a "shock" to impress the already convinced believer, and so indelibly impress it on his mind and heart, and be used as a 'witness' to the faith called Christianity?

On this view baptism could never be just an artistic symbolism. If it is symbolism at all, it is as some have suggested, of the type of the prophetic symbolism where the action and the meaning are one. Apart from the question of the type of symbolism, Paul is underlining baptism as an *event* in which the participant *was committed to a new and redeemed life*. "all of us who have been baptized"—that is the event for each, for all—a significant external water-purification act performed in one's life consciously and deliberately in faith to signify the soul's relationship to God, the Father, the Son and the Holy Spirit.

This short paper has been concerned only with the evidence of the New Testament event of baptism as an external or internal rite of initiation. Such questions as the mode of baptism by immersion or sprinkling, the relationship of the baptism of believers only or that of infant baptism to Church membership are not its concern. Its aim was to discover how far New Testament evidence showed that the external rite of water-purification was not separated or divorced from the inner rite of soul-purification. We believe we have been able to indicate that whatever form the soul-purification took in repentance, confession, reception of the Holy Spirit, proclamation of the nature of Jesus as Messiah (Christ) or Son of God, and the coming of the Messianic kingdom of God, this was incomplete without the act of baptism, the immersion in water. Finally that in the providence of God baptism was the obligatory concomitant to express the *new* relation of man with God in Christ.

JOHN THE BAPTIST
IN CHRISTIANIZED GNOSTICISM*

BY

LEANDER E. KECK

Vanderbilt University NASHVILLE, U.S.A.

Several preliminary remarks are in order. First, we must bear in mind that even though the new texts from Nag Hammadi are of inestimable value, for many forms of Christianized Gnosticism we are as dependent now as before on what its opponents (i.e., Irenaeus) report. This fact must continue to control all generalizations about Gnosticism and its development. This is as true for gnostic interpretations of John the Baptist as for any other theme. Second, in studying what gnostics thought about John, there is value in examining a relatively late document in which both the Christianization [1]) and the mythologization [2]) are far advanced, namely *Pistis Sophia*. From this vantage-point, we shall comment briefly on other gnostic treatments of John. We cannot be exhaustive; instead we shall be selective in the hope of being suggestive. Finally, in the canonical gospels the attitudes toward John are commonly regarded as accurate clues to the Evangelists' treatment of Jesus, a kind of index of their Christology. An underlying question for our theme is whether the gnostic treatment of John is also an accurate guide to their Christology, especially their soteriology.

---

* A paper delivered at the Study Conference on *Rites on Initiation* sponsored by the I.A.H.R. at Strasbourg, Sept. 17-22, 1964. The text is virtually that of the paper as presented; only the most important footnotes have been added.

[1]) The term "Christianization" presupposes the existence of non-Christian gnosis which is probably pre-Christian as well. Christian gnosticism reveals various degrees of Christian influence.

[2]) The term "mythologization" presupposes an increasing attention among gnostic writers to mythological details about the various aeons and their interrelationships. The Nag Hammadi texts reveal, in part, the existence of a Christianized Gnosticism in which such interests are surprisingly limited (*vide*, e.g., *Gospel of Truth*). At the same time, later texts, such as the Books of Jeû, are almost incomprehensible at points because of their preoccupation with speculative details.

I

Pistis Sophia is a complex, third-century work which uses older sources.[1]) Throughout its various strata (Chaps. 7, 60-62, 133, 135) we find references to John which form a fairly consistent interpretation. The work claims to be the teaching which Jesus revealed to his disciples after his ascension and return to earth. Only at this point did he disclose the truth about himself, often in the form of answers to questions from the disciples (a fairly common literary form, as the *Wisdom of Jesus Christ* reminds us again). The first question sets the stage for the entire book: "Where did you go and what is the meaning of the cosmic disturbance which occurred after you ascended?" Jesus gives a double answer: (1) He tells about his coming and going (Chaps. 6-8). Here the cosmological speculation stands in the background and serves to explain the historical phenomenon of Jesus in time-space. (2) The full gnosis reverses this proportion and emphasizes the cosmic and trans-cosmic mysteries that lie behind the earthly phenomena and sacraments. Here is found the elaborate myth of Pistis Sophia, her fall, her repentance by means of psalms, and her restoration. This is the bulk of the book. Significantly, John the Baptist appears at the beginning of the first answer and at the climax of the second. He stands at the beginning of the first because this is where he stands in the gospel tradition. He stands at the climax of the second because the entire mythological scheme of redemption for Pistis Sophia is a prototype of man's redemption. Therefore when Pistis Sophia completed her repentence, the Savior appeared, and this appearing has its earthly counterpart in the appearing of Jesus at the Jordan (Chap. 60-62). In the Third Book which deals with the gnostic ethic and salvation, there is no mention of John, though Book Four (perhaps the oldest material in the document) does mention him once more.

Having noted where *Pistis Sophia* speaks of John we can now ask what it says. The first and last mention of John take up the same point—the appearing of John as Elijah on the one hand and as the

---

[1]) The most recent critical edition is W. TILL's revision of C. SCHMIDT's *Koptisch-gnostische Schriften* (GCS 45) 1. Bd.: Die Pistis Sophia, Die Beiden Bücher des Jeu, Unbekanntes altgnostisches Werk. Berlin: Akademie-Verlag, 1954. The best English translation is that of G. R. S. MEAD, *Pistis Sophia*, London: John M. Watkins, 1921, from which the passages are quoted. For a discussion of the sources of *Pistis Sophia*, see C. SCHMIDT, *Gnostische Schriften in koptischer Sprache aus dem Codex Brucianus* (TU 8), Leipzig, 1892.

miraculously-conceived son of Elizabeth on the other. The problem
is how both of these can be true at the same time. The New Testament
does not deal with this question because it views John typologically
—that is, as an event of the same pattern in which God acted before.
Thus the story of John's birth echoes the birth-story of Samuel, the
anointer of the first King David, and the role of John is that of Elijah,
the lonely prophet of the wilderness who incurred the wrath of
Ahab and Jezebel just as John did that of Herod and Herodias;
besides, Elijah was expected at the End-time. This mode of thought
emphasizes certain parallels of persons and of divine action; it has no
interest in metaphysical problems because it is a sophisticated, *metaphorical* way of reading history. Allegorical interpretation, on the
other hand, especially as pursued in gnostic thought, puts precisely
the metaphysical question in the foreground. The historical event or
saying is merely a phenomenal code-word for the hidden, higher
truth. This is why *Pistis Sophia* must answer the question metaphy-
sically: How can John be Elijah, and how can Elijah be born of
Elizabeth? Again we find a double answer. First of all, the Savior
himself, before his own birth, provided the necessary metaphysical
composition of John. The Savior took a "power" from one of the
aeons and seeded into Elizabeth the potentiality of John's work so
"that he might be able to make proclamation before me and make
ready my way and baptize with the water of the forgiveness of sins".
In this way, it became possible for John to speak about a Savior who
came from outside time-space. Than an epistemological problem lies
in the background here is perfectly clear. In the next place, the Savior
found the soul of Elijah and had it transferred into Elizabeth's womb.
"So the power of the little Iao, who is in the midst, and the soul of
the prophet Elias, they are bound into the body of John the baptizer."
We may pause to observe that for our text, understanding history
and what was said in history requires knowledge of the pre-existent,
other-worldly essences which time-space makes obscure. Neither
the fact of John nor Jesus' words about him makes sense without
this knowledge, according to *Pistis Sophia*. This is why Jesus must
reveal the metaphysical nature of John as well as of himself. The key
to John, therefore, is what is literally "in him": the aeonic power
of little Iao and the soul of Elijah. Interestingly, our text uses John
1: 20 where the Baptist says, "I am not the Christ" but completely
ignores the next verse where he also says, "I am not Elijah".

We may now profitably compare *Pistis Sophia* with part of Heracleon's commentary on John [1]) insofar as Origen's quotation allow us to. In Fragment 5 Heracleon also deals with the problem of Elijah and John, but does not avoid the embarrassment offerred by the New Testament which reports on one page that John was Elijah and has him deny it on another. Heracleon solved the dilemma by saying that when Jesus called John a prophet and Elijah, he was not speaking about John himself, but about his externals, his circumstances (τὰ περὶ αὐτόν) but when Jesus said John was greater than any man yet born, he spoke of his inner meaning. Therefore, the question "Are you Elijah?" must be answered "No", for John is not his externals. Heracleon put it rhetorically: "When John was asked if he himself were the clothing [his externals] would he have answered, 'Yes'?" Apart from this exegetical subtlety, what catches our attention is that Heracleon's answer is precisely the opposite of that in *Pistis Sophia*. *Pistis Sophia* gave a metaphysical answer, metempsychosis, for the question, How can John be Elijah?, while Heracleon argued that one cannot say that John is Elijah but only that he assumed such externals.

But having raised the question of the being of John in contrast with his circumstances, Heracleon does not let the matter drop, for the gospel text compelled him to deal with it, since John identified himself as the voice crying in the wilderness. Here Heracleon resorted to metabasis. He worked with three characters: the Logos who is Jesus, the voice who is John, and the echo of the voice which is the prophets. He put it into an epigram: The voice becomes *logos*, the echo becomes voice. This means that the whole prophetic order was transformed into John's voice, while the voice itself (φωνή) became *lógos*, that is, was taken up into coherent discourse, was transformed from mere sound into speech. This redemption of John reflects the destiny of the Demiurge as Sagnard and Mouson [2]) rightly pointed out. For Heracleon, John represents the Demiurge and the psychics who can receive the benefits of the salvation brought by Christ. *Pistis Sophia*, on the other hand, said nothing about John and the Demiurge.

Returning to *Pistis Sophia*, we take up the climax of the myth. Pistis Sophia had been ejected from the pleroma and has now finished

---

[1]) For a full discussion of this theme, see J. Mouson, "Jean-Baptiste dans les fragments d'Heracleon," *Ephemerides Theologicae Lovanienses* 30 (1954), 301-22.

[2]) See F. M.-M. Sagnard, *Le gnose Valentinienne et de temoignage de S. Irénée*, Paris: Librare Philosophique J. Vrin, 1947, 492 f. and Mouson, *op. cit.*, 314.

her repentances and is ready for redemption. Now the First Mystery sent down a light-power from the highest realm and this joined another light-power emitted by the subjacent Savior. These light-powers met and became a great stream of light which saved Pistis Sophia. At Chap. 60, there begins a series of interpretations of this meeting, often using Scriptures, especially Psalm 84: 10 f.

> Grace and Truth met together
> Righteousness and Peace kissed each other
> Truth sprouted forth out of the earth
> And Righteousness looked down from heaven

There follow five interpretations of these lines. The first and fifth deal explicitly with gnostic mythology, while the second, third and fourth take up biblical texts that speak of Jesus. All five interpretations concentrate on the composition of the one who saves, giving the first and final words to mythology. John the Baptist is merely mentioned in the third interpretation. The meeting of Grace and Truth occurred at the Jordan, when Grace as the Spirit descended on Jesus as the Truth. The fourth interpretation is more interesting. The meeting of Grace and Truth occurred when the pregnant Mary met the pregnant Elizabeth. Besides, Grace as Jesus met Truth as John on the day of baptism; the very same meeting is mentioned in the next line of the Psalm which speaks of the kiss of Righteousness and Peace. However, the sprouting up of Truth from the earth refers to Jesus who was born of the earth-dweller, Mary, while the downward look of Righteousness refers to the aeonic Savior who in the form of Gabriel looked down upon Mary at the annunciation. The fifth interpretation refers to the epiphenomena of the baptism and does not mention John at all. What is the significance of this treatment of John? That the real center of attention is the composition of the Savior is clear, just as it obvious that the process was completed when Jesus was baptized. But the lustration as practised and preached by John is not at all significant. John's baptism was important because it was the occasion for what was pivotal, the completion of the Savior's being. In the "midrashic" use of the Psalm, the references to John show a concern to claim the Old Testament as a valid, though enigmatic, oracle pointing to Jesus.

This way of treating the Old Testament and its relation to John and Jesus differs from that of the Ophites describes by Irenaeus (*Adv. haer.* i 30). This group was fundamentally hostile to the Old

Testament. The Creator, Ialdabaoth, is regarded as a malign deity whose work, fortunately, is continually frustrated by his mother, Prunikos. The biblical Heilsgeschichte is interpreted as the story of this struggle. Ialdabaoth and his sons, the powers of the planets, each had his own Old Testament prophet through whom he was glorified among men. At the same time, above mother Prunikos was Sophia, who managed somehow to have these prophets speak also of the First Man, despite their relationship to Ialdabaoth. This means that a correct interpretation of the Old Testament requires one to distinguish those materials which relate to Ialdabaoth and his offspring from those which refer to Sophia above and her true gnosis. It is at this point that we pick up the trail of John the Baptist. Prunikos used the unsuspecting Ialdabaoth to emit two men in marvellous circumstances: John from the barren Elizabeth and Jesus from the Virgin Mary. This sets the stage for the salvation of Sophia, the female counter-part of Ialdabaoth. When Sophia asked for help, Prunikos sent down the aeonic Christ; when he came to Sophia they became bride and groom (just as the light powers met in *Pistis Sophia*). This bride-groom descended into Jesus at baptism and left before the crucifixion. What is the place of John the Baptist in this scheme? Three things are reported by Irenaeus. (a) Whereas Moses and the prophets were prophets of Ialdabaoth, John and Jesus are both discontinuous with the whole prophetic order. They are special emissions of Prunikos. John does not belong with the prophets. (b) There is no room here for John as Elijah, since Elijah is explicitly named as one of the prophets that belongs to Sabaoth, a son of Ialdabaoth. How the Ophites treated the New Testament tradition at this point Irenaeus did not report. (c) The actual mission of John is reported as follows:

> When the Sophia below recognized that her brother [Christ above] descended to her, she proclaimed his coming through John and prepared the baptism of repentance and made Jesus suitable in advance so that the descending Christ might find a pure vessel and so that through her son Ialdabaoth the Woman might be proclaimed by Christ.[1]

Here the heraldic work of John and the preparatory nature of his baptism are strictly traditional items. What is new is the report that

---

[1] Quoted from R. M. GRANT's translation in *Gnosticism*, New York: Harper & Row, 1961, 58.

John's baptism made Jesus suitable by purifying him. What the Church would later deal with by means of the doctrine of the Immaculate Conception, the Ophites dealt with in the baptism of Jesus: the man born in Ialdabaoth's sinful world must be made pure before he can receive the aeonic Savior. Baptism nullifies the effects of the cosmos on the body born within it, and presumably cancels the control of Ialdabaoth over it. Here the rite itself is important and is not simply the occasion for something else. A question remains, however, did the Ophites hold this view of John's baptism in general, and of gnostic lustrations as well, or was this view of John's rite limited to Jesus? Two things are clear in any case: a wedge has been driven between John and the Old Testament on the one hand, and the sacramental cleansing of John's rite is held on the other. Neither Heracleon nor *Pistis Sophia* took such positions.

As we return to *Pistis Sophia*, we take up its third discussion of John. In Chap. 133 Jesus expounds the need for all men to receive the mysteries so that they may be free from fate. At the climax of the discussion of his own work, Jesus explains John's preaching in a way that illumines his own mission:

> For this cause, therefore, hath John the Baptizer prophesied concerning me saying, "I indeed have baptized you with water unto repentance for forgiveness of your sins. He who cometh after me is stronger than me. Whose fan is in his hand, and he will purify his floor. The chaff indeed he will consume with unquenchable fire but the wheat he will gather into his barn." The power in John hath prophesied concerning me, knowing that I would bring the mysteries into the world and purify the sins of the sinners who shall have faith in me and hearken unto me and make them into refined light and lead them into the light.

This agrees with no gospel text completely, for it eliminates the reference to John's unworthiness and to the Coming One's baptizing with fire and spirit; moreover, it reverses the last two lines. As a result of these modifications, *Pistis Sophia* has no vestige of any early Christian polemic against John. More important, this rephrasing outlines four aspects of Jesus' work: (a) The coming of the Stronger One is the bringing of the mysteries into the world. Presumably Jesus is stronger because whereas John can offer only repentance for sins, Jesus offers release from fate through the mysteries. This is why the repentances of Pistis Sophia are directed to the Christian mysteries and not to the baptism of John. The New Testament understands the coming of the Stranger One as his coming upon the historical scene; *Pistis Sophia* understands it as his coming into the cosmos itself. (*b*) The purifying of the floor is fulfilled in Jesus' work of purifying believers. This is confirmed in Chap. 141 where Jesus says,

> Amen I say unto you: I have brought nothing into the world when I came save this fire, this water, this wine and this blood ... And the fire, the water and the wine are for the purification of the sins of the world.

Likewise, Chap. 125 reports that Jesus said,

> ... the mystery of them [i.e., the mystery of the baptisms] becometh a great, exceedingly violent, wise fire and it burneth up the sins and entereth into the soul secretly and consumeth all the sins which the counterfeiting spirit had made fast on to it.

(c) The burning of the chaff is the refining of the believing sinners. The writer(s) takes the purifying of the floor and the burning of the chaff to be virtually identical saving acts. By this means, the potentially destructive role of the Coming One, as John himself originally viewed it, is eliminated altogether. John's original message of judgment and grace is transformed into an undialectical announcement that the Savior will bring salvation by means of mysteries.

II

We may now draw some conclusions about the interpretation of John in *Pistis Sophia* and set them in the context of other, selected gnostic texts. We must, of course, forego the satisfaction of being able to examine all the material in the scope of this paper. (1) *Pistis Sophia* has no interest in John as such, nor in his message and its relation to his rite of initiation, nor in the power of his rite as such. At the same time, it is not embarrassed by the fact that the Savior was baptized by John, probably because John's baptism had already been stripped of its independent content.

(2) In *Pistis Sophia* there is no real attempt to relate Christian baptism or Gnostic Christian rites to that of John. We may put it tersely: Jesus did not receive the gnostic rites—he brought them. Therefore believers do not participate in Jesus' baptism but merely receive its benefits. Even

in the related Books of Jeû, in which sacraments play a key role and in which Jesus himself presides at the altar, there is no attempt to relate the baptism of Jesus and the ministry of John to the rites of initiation into the gnostic community. Likewise the Nag Hammadi *Gospel of Philip* discusses baptism in some detail and ignores John and his rite.[1]) In *Pistis Sophia*, the baptism which Jesus received was the occasion for the completion of the Savior. John's sacramental rite did not bring this about. The same conclusion is valid for Heracleon and for Christian gnostics generally. Only the Ophites saw the rite itself as contributing directly to the completion of the Savior.

(3) *Pistis Sophia* has no interest in the asceticism of John, nor in his disciples nor in his discipline, nor in Jesus' rejection of John's ethos, even though this treatise is itself concerned with such questions. This is also true of gnostic materials not mentioned here.[2]) In short, the historical questions connected with John are ignored entirely and attention is focused on the one moment when the careers of Jesus and John intersect, and even here attention is concentrated on Jesus. The only exception to this disinterest in John himself is the strange tradition of the Pseudo-Clementines (*Hom.* ii 23 f.), according to which John was a Hemerobaptist with thirty disciples, among whom were Simon Magus, Helen and Dositheus. This tradition makes John the source of Simonian gnosis and therefore the virtual opponent of Jesus. Whether or not this thread of legend was part of the lost *Kerygmata Petrou*, it surely rests ultimately on Samaritan syncretism's attempt to claim John as part of its opposition to Christianity.[3])

(4) Thus we are led to a fourth conclusion, that these gnostic materials (apart from the detail from the Pseudo-Clementines) offer

---

[1]) See, e.g., Par. 68, 81, 90, 95, and the discussions by E. SEGELBERG, "The Coptic-Gnostic Gospel according to Philip and its Sacramental System", *Numen* 7 (1960), 189 ff. and by R. McL. WILSON, *The Gospel of Philip*, New York: Harper & Row, 1962, 144.

[2]) In addition to other fragments of Heracleon (discussed by MOUSSON), we might profitably analyse the references to John in the Excerpts of Theodotus (especially Exc. 4 f.) and the Apocryphon of James from Nag Hammadi, in which the end of prophecy is dated from the beheading of John. This latter work is not yet published; for this brief report of its reference to John I am indebted to W. C. VAN UNNIK, *Newly Discovered Gnostic Writings*, trans. by Hubert HOSKINS (SBT 30), London: S.C.M. Press, 1960, 81 ff. and to the mention of it (in the discussion that followed the paper) by Dr. J. ZANDEE of Utrecht.

[3]) See also Kurt RUDOLF, *Die Mandäer*. Teil I: Prolegomena: Das Mandäerproblem, (FRLANT 74). Göttingen: Vandenhoeck & Ruprecht, 1960, 75. Most students and discussions of the problem are wary of assessing the historical worth of this tradition.

no independent information about John, despite the syncretistic character of his baptism and its relation to similar movements in the area. These gnostics apparently knew no more about John than what they could infer from our (not yet) canonical gospels. Though gnostics were not averse to developing legends in their own way to their own ends, they appear to have had no interest in doing so for John. Yet John was the one man who, according to the Fourth Gospel at any rate, clearly witnessed and understood the central mystery of gnostic Christology—the descent of the other-worldly power to the born Jesus. (The nature of the traditions about John the Baptist in heterodox Judaism and in Jewish Christianity [some of which was also gnosticized] is another problem.) There is a possible exception—an unnamed treatise, as yet unpublished, from Nag Hammadi, which treats the baptism of Jesus and the river Jordan.[1]) Therefore we keenly await the publication of this text. Yet even if it should emphasize precisely those things which are absent from the texts we have surveyed, it would only high-light the picture by its own contrasting light.

(5) Finally, the absence of independent traditions about John means that the gnostic interpretations of John are basically exegetical. It is because John is embedded in the gospel traditions and texts that he is discussed at all. Even here, we must remember that the Nag Hammadi *Gospel of Thomas* (Log. 52, 78) can use New Testament sayings which speak of John, and omit all reference to John. The question with which we began, namely whether in the gnostic materials the treatment of John could be regarded as an index to Christological concerns, may now be answered with a clear "No". Gnostic Christology, for all its limitations, was a vital and often exciting enterprise; the gnostic interpretation of John, however, is largely an attempt to make something out of a theologoumenon. In the last

---

[1]) According to DORESSE, this writing speaks of "the power who came to us upon the river Jordan—a sign which showed that the reign of the carnal generation was ended". This does not meant that John's baptism was viewed as a sacrament of release from fleshly existence, for the text also says "the river Jordan, this, to him, is the strength of the body—that is, the essence of pleasures; and the water of Jordan is the desire for carnal cohabitation." We are not surprised, then, to read that John is "the archon of the multitude" in contrast with the Son of Man. If these extracts are typical, then we are in the midst of an anti-Johannine, anti-Jewish milieu. Until the text is available, further comment is premature; hence we have not discussed this text in the body of the paper. See Jean DORESSE, *The Secret Books of the Egyptian Gnostics*, trans. by Philip MAIRET, London: Hollis & Carter, 1960, 219 f.

analysis, even the subtle *Pistis Sophia* gets no farther than this. It remains to be seen whether the text from Nag Hammadi will do better. Be that as it may, the treatments of John show an attempt to come to terms with the Christian tradition. It is important that we see that this is precisely what the Christianization of Gnosticism meant. In this way, even our negative conclusion has positive value.

CONDITIONS OF MEMBERSHIP OF
THE ISLAMIC COMMUNITY

BY

W. MONTGOMERY WATT
Edinburg

In recent times occidental scholars of Islam seem to have paid little attention to the question of how a man becomes a Muslim and what conditions he must fulfil in order to remain a member of the Islamic community. The fullest relevant article in the *Shorter Encyclopaedia of Islam* appears to be that on "Murtadd" (apostate); and even this is more concerned with the treatment to be given to the proved apostate than with the essential marks of apostasy.

Any investigation of the conditions of membership of the Islamic community must begin with the lifetime of Muḥammad. The evidence for this, however, in the Qur'ān and the Traditions is notoriously difficult to deal with, since the precise reference of a Qur'ānic phrase is often doubtful, while the antiquity of many Traditions is questioned. In a short paper like the present the best that can be done is to state in a general way what appears to have been the position in the years from 622 to 632. Two different matters are relevant in this connection, one more applicable to groups and the other to individuals. The first is the performing of *ṣalāt* and payment of *zakāt*, and the second is the repetition of the *shahāda* or confession of faith. *Ṣalāt* and *zakāt* occur frequently in the Qur'ān in conjunction with one another, and the context suggests that these are essential marks of membership of the community that followed Muḥammad or one of the earlier prophets. These marks of membership, however, belong to groups rather than to individuals. The performing of the *ṣalāt* or worship is normally a communal activity; and the collectors of *ṣadaqāt*, of whom we hear in the accounts of Muḥammad's administration, who were presumably dealing with what is called *zakāt* in the Qur'ān, were sent to tribes or subdivisions of tribes. It also appears that in the wars of the Ridda or Apostasy in the reign of Abū-Bakr the act tantamount to a declaration of war was the refusal of a tribe to make the customary money payments to the caliph in Medina. Thus everything points to a specific requirement of *ṣalāt* and *zakāt* by Muḥammad from his allies, though the precise requirement may have varied from group to group. The fact that the obligation lay on groups and not on individuals is in accordance with the fact that under Muḥammad and for some time afterwards the Islamic state was conceived not as a body of individuals but as a federation of tribes and smaller groups. At a later date, indeed, the performance of the *ṣalāt* by an individual apostate was sometimes taken as a sign that he had repented of his apostasy; but this is not at variance with what has been said about the communal character of the obligation of *ṣalāt*.

The other condition for membership of the community—and apparently a more individualistic one—was the repetition of the *shahāda* or confession of faith, "there is no god but God, Muḥammad is the messenger of God". This is attested in Tradition. A pagan Arab, proscribed by Muḥammad at the conquest of Mecca, managed to avoid execution by making his way secretly into Muḥammad's presence and, before he could be arrested, repeating the *shahāda*. The precise wording of the *shahāda* is not found in the Qur'ān, though it may be said to be implied. The first half of the *shahāda*, however, occurs many times (if we include slight variants), though not as a formula to be repeated; and it is therefore worth considering the possibility that at an early period the first clause of the *shahāda* was used by itself as a confession of faith. On the other hand, it would seem on general grounds that there was little need, so long as Muḥammad was alive, for a precise formula to denote the moment at which an individual became a Muslim; an individual convert would normally make some act of personal loyalty to Muḥammad, and of the adequacy of this the latter himself would be the judge. The need for a formula would only be felt towards the year 700 when many individual *dhimmīs* began to make profession of Islam; and this is all that the Traditional material can be taken to demonstrate, although it may contain some genuine reminiscences of the period before 632. While there may thus be some doubt about the earliest use of the *shahāda* as a mark of conversion, Muslims were certainly characterized from the beginning by belief in the oneness of God and in the prophethood of Muḥammad.

A fresh condition of membership of the community was introduced by the Khārijites about the time of the civil war between

'Alī and Mu'āwiya (656-61). Their assertion was that the *ṣāḥib kabīra*, the man who has committed a grave sin, is excluded from the community. This point had immediate relevance to the questions raised by the assassination of the caliph 'Uthmān in 656, but it came to be treated in a completely general way. It implies that, in order to remain a member of the community, a man must not fall below a certain standard of moral conduct. The community thus becomes a "community of saints". At first sight this insistence on the avoidance of major sins might seem to be an individualistic matter; but the context of ideas in which the Khārijites made their assertion was communalistic. They spoke of the community of Muslims as "the people of Paradise" (*ahl al-janna*); and the reason for the exclusion of the grave sinner from the community must have been that his sin, since it merited Hell, imperilled the status of the whole community as "people of Paradise". Their thinking was thus close to the communalistic attitude of the first point mentioned. When it came to the realities of politics, Khārijism in its pure form soon proved completely impracticable as the basis of an actual state, and was gradually modified. Something of this principle of the Khārijites was taken over by the Mu'tazilites, though their view was essentially a compromise. They held that the grave sinner went to Hell and therefore did not belong to "the people of Paradise", but they did not demand his exclusion from the this-worldly political community.

The first opponents of the Khārijites were the Shī'ites, who, in contrast to the Khārijite insistence on the community as divinely-founded, emphasized the importance of the divinely-guided leader. In the course of time, however, many Muslims who were not Shī'ites opposed the Khārijite principle of the exclusion of the grave sinner from the community. These Muslims were called Murji'ites, but this was only a nickname given by critics, and indicates a tendency or attitude and not a close-knit sect. Some extreme exponents of this Murji'ite tendency went so far as to affirm that "along with *īmān* sin does no harm"; that is to say, when a man is a *mu'min*—believer, member of the community—the commission of a sin does not lead to his exclusion from Paradise. This extreme Murji'ite view was not widely accepted, however, for it was realized that it seriously belittled the difference between uprightness of life and moral depravity. Even those Murji'ites, however, who rejected this extreme view, agreed that grave sin did not lead to a man's exclusion from the community. At the same time they considered the difference between righteousness and wickedness important, and held that sin would be punished either in this world or the next.

The formulations of the Murji'ites led to discussions of another aspect of the question, namely, that connected with the idea of *īmān*. This word is usually translated "faith", but the connotations of the European words "faith", "foi", "Glaube", are not appropriate to the Islamic context. It seems best here not merely to avoid the translation but also to think of *īmān* primarily as "that which makes men *mū'minūn*"; and we remember that *mu'minūn* or "believers" is the commonest appellation in the Qur'ān of the followers of Muḥammad. It is membership of the community that comes first; and then subsequently Muslim thinkers may discuss what is essential to membership. This is basically what they are doing when they discuss the nature of *īmān*. The aspect of *īmān* to which most of the Murji'ites gave prominence was the acceptance of intellectual contents. This aspect is found already, indeed, in the group of Traditions to the effect that *īmān* is *īmān* in God, his angels, his book, his messengers and the final resurrection. The precise content, however, was not a frequent subject of discussion for the Murji'ites with one another or with opponents, while such discussion of contents (articles of belief) as took place among later theologians was not closely linked with the question of membership of the community.

One important line of development of the conception of *īmān* as the acceptance of intellectual contents is to be found in the works of the Ḥanafites or followers of Abū-Ḥanīfa, including the Māturīdites. Abū-Ḥanīfa is often called a Murji'ite, though he exhibited the Murji'ite tendency in a moderate form which was not heretical, but was in fact incorporated into the central Sunnite position. The Ḥanafites, starting from the conception of *īmān* as the acceptance of doctrines, emphasized the point that the outward profession of the doctrines with the tongue was not sufficient; there must also be inner acceptance in the heart. The doctrines to be professed are seldom mentioned explicitly; they were doubtless either those of the *shahāda* or of the Tradition about *īmān* mentioned above. The difficulty of deciding which doctrines were essential does not seem to have been felt by the Ḥanafites for several centuries. This disregard of problems about particular doctrines was in line with the Ḥanafite assertion that *īmān* is indivisible, that is to say, it was not the acceptance (external and internal) of articles of belief as separate items, but the acceptance of the doctrinal position of the community as a totality. Presumably a man who held some belief seriously at variance with the general position of the community would be excluded from it. This, however, did not affect the main point, namely, that a man was either a member of the community or he was not; there was no third possibility, and there were no differences between members in respect of their membership, even though they might differ in piety and in uprightness of life. In accordance with this set of ideas the Ḥanafites held that *īmān* could neither increase nor decrease, and this assertion came to be a mark of the distinctive Ḥanafite position.

A slightly different conception of *īmān* underlies the other main stream of theological thought in the central body of Sunnites, that of the Ashʿarites. For this school mere acceptance of doctrines, even when both internal and external, was not sufficient for membership of the community; there must also be action. If the inhabitants of an island pronounced the *shahāda* at intervals but otherwise observed none of the religious duties known as "the pillars of Islam", one could hardly call them a community of Muslims. With such thoughts in mind the Ashʿarites insisted that *īmān* must include action as well as outward profession and inward acceptance. They might be said to be generalizing from the earlier conception of *ṣalāt* and *zakāt* as marks of an Islamic community, whereas the Ḥanafites were developing the *shahāda*. The consequence of introducing action into the conception of *īmān*, however, was that, since men's observance of religious duties varied, they differed in respect of *īmān*; and thus it came to be a distinctive feature of the Ashʿarite position in contrast to the Ḥanafite that *īmān* could increase and decrease.

Another matter prominent in the early discussions was the ultimate fate of the grave sinner. The problem, as already hinted, was to avoid excluding the grave sinner from the community (as the Khārijites had done), and yet not to belittle the difference between the upright man and the sinner. Al-Ashʿarī himself tended to a rigorous moral outlook; he accepted the doctrine of Muḥammad's power of intercession for sinful members of his community on the Last Day, but he would not go beyond asserting that this power existed and that it would be exercised on behalf of *some* Muslim sinners, but not necessarily on behalf of all. This left open the possibility that some Muslims might be eternally in Hell. On the whole, however, the theologians of the central Sunnite body tended to the view that all Muslims who remained Muslims would eventually be in Paradise, though they would be punished for their sins. The punishment might be on earth or in Hell, but, if the latter, it would be for a limited period only. Thus the Islamic community was a *firqa nājiya* or "saving sect", membership of which led certainly to Paradise.

The same general picture is gained by considering what, from the central Sunnite position, leads to exclusion from the community. In general it may be said that exclusion is due to *shirk* or *kufr*. The term *shirk* was originally applied to idolatry or polytheism, but, strictly speaking, it is the association of any other being in the worship and service due to God alone. In effect it is denial in word or deed of the first phrase of the *shahāda*. *Kufr* is less easy to define. It is that which characterizes non-Muslims or rather opponents of the Islamic community, and also that which changes a Muslim into an opponent of the community. Any article of belief or any activity which was felt to indicate that a man had broken away from the Islamic community would be an instance of *kufr*. This shows how it came to be regarded as a less serious offence to drink wine than to assert that wine-drinking was licit; the former was merely an individual fault, for which a man would be punished and then pardoned, whereas the second was the denial of a basic rule of the community. To say that, because a man holds a false article of belief, he is in a state of *kufr* is not contrary to the Ḥanafite conception of *īmān* as indivisible, since to hold a contrary belief on some important matter is tantamount to a rejection of the Islamic community. The ulema had the power to decide when a view was erroneous to the extent of constituting *kufr*, but according to al-Ghazālī they abused this power and applied the label of *kufr* to minor deviations.

The conclusion of this investigation is that there is more communalistic thinking in Islam than is usually realized. It is often remarked that the Islamic community is thought of as a tribe or "super-tribe", and this is relevant in the present connection, for it appears that for most Muslims membership of the community is by birth. It is noteworthy that most of the early Khārijites held that the children of *mu'minūn* went to Paradise and those of *kāfirūn* to Hell. For non-Muslims, of course, the pronouncing of the *shahāda* could be regarded as marking entrance into the Islamic community; but Islam has never boasted about conversions, and has sometimes passed them over in complete silence. The norm is the community propagating itself by natural reproduction. Moreover, as in the case of a tribe or natural community, the essentials of membership are not clearly formulated. A man ceases to be a member if he does something which the general body of Muslims feel to be incompatible with membership. Usually this will be something which aligns him with a rival community; but the point to notice is that the ultimate criterion is the "feeling" of the general body of Muslims, this "feeling" which is formalized in the conception of *ijmā'* or consensus. From time to time theologians have drawn up elaborate lists of the essentials of membership of the Islamic community, but these lists have never been accepted by the consensus and have therefore never been effective. This very dominance of the *ijmā'* or consensus is further evidence of the deep communalism or communal solidarity of Islam, of which another aspect is the absence of any rite of initiation.

THE INITIATION CEREMONY OF THE BEKTASHIS

BY

HELMER RINGGREN
Åbo

The aim of this paper is not to offer any new and startling solutions of the problems of Bektashi initiation, nor to unveil any of the secrets of this order of dervishes, but only to provide the study conference with some concrete material for the discussion of some of the general questions connected with the rites of initiation.

Being a real order with closed membership, the Bektashis naturally had a very elaborate initiation ceremony. The ritual of this ceremony is found in the so-called *erkan-name*'s, or ritual-books, which exist in a great number of handwritten copies. John BIRGE, who wrote the most comprehensive book on the Bektashis *The Bektashi Order of Dervishes*, London 1937), had in his collection four such books of varying size and completeness. Recent Turkish books on the Bektashis seem to have used other, partly different copies. The account of the initiation ceremony given by Tevfik OYTAN in his *Bektaşiliğin içyüzü* (Istanbul, 1948-9) and by Kemal SAMANCIĞIL in his *Bektaşilik tarihi* (Istanbul, 1945) differ to some extent both in the order of the items and in the wording of the songs and prayers from the one given by BIRGE. Another account, naturally not quite as exact, is given in Yakup KADRI's novel *Nur Baba* (of which there is an excellent German translation by A.-M. SCHIMMEL, *Falter und Flamme*). It is hard to tell whether or not this difference depends on local or individual variations in the ritual, for since the Turkish writers do not specify their sources we know neither the provenance nor the exactitude of their data.

BIRGE's account of the initiation, or *aynicem* (the derivation of the word is not clear), seems to be complete and is based on his four *erkannames*, which are now kept in the library of the Hartford Seminary Foundation, Hartford, Conn. But it is almost exclusively descriptive and makes no real attempt at a historical or functional analysis, and some interpretative details of the ritual are merely recorded.

The ceremony takes place in the main room, or sacred hall, of the

monastery, the *meydan evi*, In this room, opposite the entrance door
with its threshold (which is very important!), is a throne, the *tahti
Muhammet*, consisting of three steps and holding twelve or more
candles (therefore often called also *çırağlık*, or place of candles). The
twelve candles seem to symbolize the twelve imams; a special, tall
candle called "the candle of the law" (*kanun çırağı*) has three wicks
symbolizing God, Muhammad, and Ali. To the left, in front of the
throne, there is a sheepskin, or *post*, for the *baba* (leader of the monastery) or *mürşit*. Around the room there are other sheepskins, four or
twelve, named for various leaders of Bektashism, and in addition
one for the *rehber*, or guide. "The position in the exact centre of the
meydan is always called *Dar-i Mansur* or simply *Dar*, the 'gallows of
Mansur al-Hallaj'. Standing in this place is therefore symbolic of life
for principle in memory of the death of the one who said *enelhak*,
'I am reality' ". (BIRGE, *op. cit.* p. 180).

The symbolism of all this is important. The threshold marks the
borderline between the profane and the sacred (ELIADE): the *meydan*
is the sacred place, and the candidate to be initiated enters the realm
of the sacred. In this holy place the holy ones of the past are present:
the imams and the great figures of Bektashi history. In view of the
importance ascribed to the tradition or succession of teachers in
Muslim mysticism, this is highly significant. The candidate is brought
into the presence of the whole Bektashi tradition, to share the fellowship of the *erenler* (initiated) and saints of the past.

The ceremony takes place in the evening, or night. Earlier that
same day he has brought a ram to the *tekke* (monastery) for sacrifice.
Theoretically, the *tiğbent*, or rope belt, to be used in the initiation
should be made from the wool of this ram.

In the evening, while the members are gathering in the *meydan*,
the candidate, called *talip*, i.e. seeker, is being prepared for the
initiation in an adjoining room by the *rehber*, or guide. He takes off his
shoes and takes the ablution (*abdest*); during the ablution the *rehber*
recites a number of *tercemans*, or prayers, in which the meaning of the
purification is expounded: he washes his hands in order to be freed
from all the prohibited things to which he has stretched his hands
before; he rinses his mouth in order to cleanse it from all falsehood
and fault that may have issued from it; he rinses his nose to cleanse it
from whatever forbidden things he has smelt; he washes his face in
order to be absolved from every shameful thing; his feet in order to
be cleansed from every instance of having walked in rebellious and

mistaken paths; while he wipes his head and ears he wishes to be absolved from every unreasonable thing which is counter to the religious law, and further, while wiping his face, from all the acts of disobedience which he has committed. KADRI adds that this ablution differed from the ordinary ablutions in so far as it was effective for ever. The meaning is quite clear: it is the complete removal of all that is sinful and unclean and that belongs to his former life.

The guide and the candidate now approach the door of the *meydan* and do proper reverence to the threshold, kissing it etc. The guide says: "O opener of doors'" and the *mürşit* replies: "Verily we have opened to thee a manifest victory (or, door)" (Kor. 48: 1). Then the *talip* is lead into the *meydan*. Bowing repeatedly, both advance toward the *mürşit*, who now speaks and gives the following so-called advice to the candidate:

O Seeker, you wish to enter the way of Muhammad Ali ... But this way is difficult, this way is the way of reproach, it is sharper than the sword [this way is a shirt of fire]. Afterward your enemies will be many. Afterward there will be no value in repentance, for the brothers have said: Come not, come not, turn not, turn not; the property of him who comes, the soul of him who turns. Will you keep and carry out the advice and council of the brothers?

The *talip* anwers: "God, yes, by God". Here we have obviously a piece of instruction and warning, leading up to the question "Are you willing"? and the answer.

The *mürşit* now turns to the *çırağçı* (the one who lights the candles) and says: "Brother, brethren, arise, in accordance with the rites of Muhammad Ali, awaken the candle of this soul". The *çırağçı* then lights his *delil* (candle-lighter) from the candle of the law and lights all the other candles. One of the formulae recited says: "The light of Muhammad is born from Ali, the sun and the moon. Let us also receive a particle of it." Finally he lights the candle of the initiate, reciting a special prayer "in the name of the King", and then, in the *dar*: ". . . since we have lighted the candle of glory, for the love of God . . . may it burn, be burnt, until the assembling of the judgment. . .". Two more prayers follow, after which the *mürşit* asks the *rehber* to be the necessary guide to this soul who is seeking the way; the *rehber* promises to do so and takes the candidate outside the room.

At this point KADRI describes how the *rehber* brings a thin, white rope, obviously the *tiğbent*, puts it around the candidate's waist, winds part of it round his neck and fastens one end on his thumb and takes the other one himself; SAMANCIĞIL says that the candidate is now lead like a sacrificial sheep into the *meydan*. The same author also says that he is wrapped in a shroud like a corpse, but none of the other sources mention anything about this.

Now the guide and the seeker again enter the *meydan*. (KADRI mentions only *one* entrance; OYTAN combines the ceremonies of the first and the second entrance into one.) Then, standing in the middle, the *dar*, the guide recites the prayer:

Standing in the courtyard of Reality myself,
being the dust of the convent, my face is prostration and worship,
my word being whatever is thy command, to the King in gene-
   rosity,
I have stood waiting, my eye looking for the answer giving
   permission.

Then, after a salutation, the *rehber* addresses the *mürşit*: ". . . with his head bare, with bare feet, his neck tied, crawling on his face, we have here a male lamb sacrifice by the name of so and so, who wishes the approval of the brethren to make the married man's confession. What is the order of the *mürşit*? Shall we present him?" The *mürşit* places the question before those present, who give their consent. (KADRI has a different wording, but the gist of the question is the same. OYTAN also has different words, *op. cit.*, p. 174).

The *rehber* then surrenders the *talip* to the *mürşit*, by requiring the *talip* to take hold of the *mürşit*'s skirt. The *talip* kneels; the *mürşit* takes him by the right hand and recites a formula; then he whispers into his right ear the following instruction (*telkin*):

a) Confession of sins: I ask pardon of God for every crime which I have committed intentionally or unintentionally, secretly or openly. And I repent of the sin which I know, and of the sin which I do not know.

b) Creed: And I testify that there is no God except God, He is one and has no partners; and I testify that Muhammad is His slave and His apostle; and I testify that the commander of the faithful is Ali, the Saint of God . . . (some Shi'ite and Bektashi particulars follow).

c) instruction: Know that our lords, the twelve imams are one light with God, have faith . . . do not lie, do not eat forbidden things, do not be a slave to lust, do not practise hate, pride, envy, anger, enmity, back-biting ... behave with caution, give honour to your inferior, give respect to your superior, wherever you look, behold the Divine Reality, do not look upon anything as separate from or other than Reality, be sincere in your confession, know that Reality is present in you ... Knowing this, have faith.

It is interesting that the simple moral rules gradually lead up to a statement of the radical secret of Bektashism, namely the "Oneness of existence" and the presence of Reality in man.

Then the *mürşit* takes the *tac*, the headpiece of the Bektashis, recites a prayer, in which mention is made of the ascension of Muhammad and the greatness of God—the connection with the *tac* is not clear —and after the prayer he puts the *tac* on the head of the *talip*, takes the *tiğbent* (belt) and ties it around the waist of the *talip*, saying: "O ye who believe, be patient ... and be firm and fear God" (Kor. 3: 200), adding a reference to God's greatness and oneness. Then he takes the hand of the *talip* and reminds him of the importance of his oath of fealty and asks him: "Have you accepted the faith which you have confessed in the Face of God, and the counsel, and the advice?" The question is repeated three times, and each time answered by yes.

The putting on of the *tac* and the oath of promise form the central part of the ceremony. The Bektashis often refer to it as "offering one's head" In a collection of poems by the present leader of the Bektashis in Turkey, we find the following allusion to the initiation:

To the sword I gave my neck for the love of those who attain Reality.
I received the light from the candle for the love of those who give light.
I died before my death for the love of those who show the truth.
In the convent of a Saint I became a sacrifice.

These lines show the symbolism of the initiation: sacrifice, death, receiving of light.

Returning to the ceremony, we find the *rehber* reciting a *terceman*, which, *int. al.*, contains the following words:

Praise be to God that I have become a real slave of God.
From the soul and by the tongue with love (I have become) the servant of the Family of the Mantle.
Departing from the way of darkness, I have put foot on the straight path.

> I have awakened from the sleep of indifference, I have opened the
> eye of my soul.

This is another interpretation of what has taken place: a complete
break with the past and the beginning of something entirely new.

After another prayer, there follows some instruction concerning
the *posts* and other things in the *meydan* and their symbolical meaning:
the *talip* is now a member of the order and is taught their secrets.

After this the *talip* is seated in his place, the *rehber* and the *mürşit*
recite a passage each—of less interest—whereafter the candle-lighter
is asked to take the cup with the drink (whether it is raki or not, is
uncertain); he does so, and serves the drink to all. Again, the meaning
is obvious: the Seeker is now a member of the order and enjoys the
full fellowship of the community.

Finally the candle-lighter sweeps the room—an interesting parallel
to the custom in the daily service of the Egyptian temples, aiming
obviously at the removal of everything that is unclean from the holy
room—and a prayer brings the formal service to a close. "The re-
mainder of the evening is spent in a social way, both food and drink
being passed around. The drink is served in a formal way" by a
cupbearer, a second cupbearer offers food, *meze*, and a third one
follows offering a napkin. Then those who wish rise for the dance,
sema.

I am aware that several approaches are possible in the analysis of
this ritual. We might apply a historical method and try to find out
the origin of the various elements of the ritual and to trace the historical growth of the ceremony. I am almost convinced, for instance,
that there is some connection between the *tiğbent* and the *kusti* of the
Parsis. At one point of the ritual there is a sprinkling of rose-water—
left out in the description above as being not essential—the structure
of which strongly reminds you of a description of some part of the
Orthodox Christian liturgy. Is there any connection here? Turkish
scholars are eager to point out similarities with shamanistic rituals
in order to carry the Bektashi traditions back to pre-Islamic Turkish
culture, but much of this seems somewhat doubtful.

On the other hand it is possible that some confusion or lack of
logic in the ritual may be explained as the result of continuous growth
and revision which has spoiled an original, simple pattern.

It seems however that a phenomenological or a functional approach
would be more profitable for the topic of this study conference. I

have given some hints in this direction previously in this paper, and I should like to add a few remarks.

It is fairly easy to apply to this ceremony the pattern set up by A. VAN GENNEP for a *rite de passage*, although it must be admitted that the middle part, "marge" is not very clearly discernible. The initial element of *separation* is quite clear, and so are the items that mark the *integration* of the *talip* into his new life as an *eren*, into the fellowship of the initiates, *erenler*, "those who have attained". I should like to suggest that we could also use the terms of modern sociology and describe the rite of passage as the ritualization of a change of status or role. This would narrow down the range of phenomena included in the term and lead to the exclusion of some of the rites that VAN GENNEP was inclined to count as rites of passage, as for instance the New Year ceremonies. The gain would be a much clearer definition of the category. The functional interpretation would not be affected in our case. The *aynicem* marks the transition from the role of an ordinary believer to that of a Bektashi, the initiate's separation from his old life and his integration into the fellowship of the *erenler*.

This means that we should have to reckon with at least two types of initiation ceremonies, the tribal initiation of socalled primitive people on one hand, and the initiation of secret societies at a different level of culture on the other. It is quite obvious that the Bektashi ceremony belongs to the latter type. It seems to me that VAN GENNEP's pattern is valid at least for this type.

LA SIGNIFICATION PSYCHOLOGIQUE
DE L'ÉSOTÉRISME

PAR

EDMOND ROCHEDIEU
Genève

Il convient tout d'abord de bien préciser les termes employés en indiquant ce que nous entendons par „la signification psychologique de l'ésotérisme". En effet il s'agira d'une étude inspirée par les recherches récentes sur la psychologie de l'homme en société, sans négliger pour autant d'autres problèmes psychologiques, entre autres celui de l'angoisse. Jusqu'au moment où furent inaugurées ces recherches psychologiques sur l'homme en société, la psychologie s'était intéressée avant tout à l'homme individuel, partant de la présupposition, qui semblait aller de soi, que les observations faites sur un individu à un moment donné de son histoire, à condition qu'elles fussent menées selon les règles d'une méthode rigoureusement scientifique, devaient être valables non seulement pour le même individu pris à d'autres époques de son évolution, mais également pour l'ensemble des êtres humains normaux.

Encore à la fin du siècle dernier et au début du XXe siècle, seuls quelques précurseurs — un Gabriel TARDE, un Gustave LE BON — s'étaient préoccupés des modifications qu'un changement d'environnement peut apporter dans la conduite des individus.

Cependant, depuis une trentaine d'années, plusieurs psychologues ont systématiquement développé une *psychologie de l'homme en société*, désignant par ce terme une discipline nouvelle qui trouve sa place à mi-chemin entre la psychologie classique, penchée sur l'individu et définissant ce qu'elle entend par *fait psychologique*, puis formulant des *lois psychologiques* auxquelles obéissent tous les hommes, et la sociologie qu'intéressent les phénomènes sociologiques toujours fonctions du groupe social.

Si nous résumons en quelques thèses les résultats obtenus, nous pourrions dire que cette *psychologie de l'homme en société* revêt actuellement 3 aspects: 1) une *psychologie collective*, dans laquelle le collectif prend le pas sur l'individu, où la pression du groupe exerce une telle influence sur l'individu que celui-ci ne peut s'y soustraire; 2) une *psychologie sociale* qui montre, à l'opposé, l'action exercée par l'individu sur la société, certains individus marquant de leur personnalité toute une époque, toute une civilisation, toute une religion, d'autres individus n'ayant qu'une part infinement modeste aux transformations du groupe auquel ils appartiennent, bien que toujours il faille compter avec cette influence individuelle; 3) une *psychologie différentielle de groupe* où l'accent est mis sur les particularités et les traits communs des ensembles humains, certains comportements appartenant en propre à tels groupes et créant un style de vie particulier à certains milieux, si bien que l'individu, passant d'un groupe à l'autre, modifie sa conduite et s'adapte aux habitudes psycho-sociales des différents groupes.

Or l'ésotérisme, s'il concerne indiscutablement des individus, se présente également sous l'aspect d'un groupe religieux à caractère spécifique, dont les traits d'ailleurs peuvent varier d'une forme d'ésotérisme à une autre. Dès lors, n'allons-nous pas retrouver, en étudiant l'ésotérisme, les trois aspects de la psychologie de l'homme vivant en société, mais cette fois-ci au niveau de la religion, à savoir: 1) une *psychologie collective de l'ésotérisme* où la pression du groupe ésotérique façonne l'individu et commande sa conduite; 2) une *psychologie sociale de l'ésotérisme* dans laquelle certaines personnalités s'affirmeront et contribueront à l'édification puis à la transformation du groupe ésotérique; 3) une *psychologie différentielle de l'ésotérisme* qui met en lumière ses lois propres, ses habitudes, ses coutumes, ses réactions spécifiques, tout un ensemble de données psychologiques qui nuanceront le groupe ésotérique et l'opposeront à l'exotérisme?

Quels sont alors ces traits caractéristiques, à la fois sociaux et individuels, qui donnent à l'ésotérisme sa physionomie particulière? Un certain nombre d'élements nous ont paru se dégager dans cet éclairage spécial de l'observation psychologique, que nous avons groupés sous 9 rubriques différentes, non pas qu'une pareille énumération soit exhaustive, mais simplement parce qu'en précisant ces traits il nous est possible d'en contrôler l'exactitude. Facilement on s'illusionne soi-même sur ce que l'on croit observer et je sens bien tout le risque que comporte l'emploi d'une méthode psychologique pour la compréhension des faits historiques.

D'une façon générale nous constatons que l'ésotérisme, quels qu'en soient d'ailleurs la forme ou l'environnement culturel, adopte les sentiments et l'attitude propres aux *minorités*, sentiments et attitude que complèteront certains comportements plus spécifiquement religieux. Ainsi donc ce sera la psychologie du groupe minoritaire qui à tout propos marquera l'ésotérisme. Ceci posé, que voyons-nous?

1) — Le groupe ésotérique se réfère le plus souvent au message spirituel que lui a laissé un maître particulièrement vénéré, *un inspirateur historique ou mythique*, dont les paroles, réservées aux adeptes, affirment l'existence de valeurs spirituelles cachées ou méconnues du grand nombre. Que ce message ait été transmis directement aux initiés par le fondateur du groupe ésotérique ou qu'il leur soit parvenu du fond des âges comme un héritage précieux et lointain, toujours est-il que des liens affectifs profonds existent entre cette personnalité inspiratrice et les initiés qui bénéficient de son message.

2) — Dès lors surgissent une série de problèmes étroitement en rapport avec la vie communautaire. En premier lieu apparaissent des *interactions psychiques* entre les membres du groupe, entre les initiés dont les sentiments, même les plus secrets, exercent une influence réciproque. Et ces interactions psychiques sont d'autant plus efficaces que la dimension du groupe est restreinte: les initiés d'une vaste secte subissent moins que ceux d'un petit clan fermé les contre-coups émotionnels des angoisses qui agitent certains de ses membres, et d'autre part les fidèles triés avec soin, et donc peu nombreux, d'un groupe particulièrement imperméable aux influences étrangères, vivent intensément les espérances qu'ils partagent. Toutefois l'exiguïté même du groupe ésotérique encourageant les échanges, chacun des membres ayant toute facilité d'entrer en contact avec ses co-équipiers, cette collaboration en vase clos a souvent pour conséquence la subite apparition de disputes qui n'éclateraient pas dans une société plus nombreuse où les oppositions personnelles se compenseraient. Dès lors — et c'est le deuxième trait de l'ésotérisme en connexion avec la vie communautaire de minorité — des *divisions intérieures* vont surgir qui se traduiront par la formation de sous-groupes, dont certains prendront leur indépendance. Enfin — troisième conséquence des vicissitudes que connaissent les minorités — les *restrictions à la liberté individuelle*, qui normalement devraient être librement et joyeusement acceptées par tous ceux qui se rattachent à une minorité distincte de la masse, vont de plus en plus exiger des contrôles et des sanctions. Si bien que des exclusions seront prononcées, au nom même des principes et des vérités que l'on prétend sauvegarder, alors

qu'en réalité les vrais motifs de ces sévérités seront souvent des incompatibilités personnelles que l'on se garde d'avouer.

3) — Toutes les minorités sociales, du fait qu'elles doivent se défendre pour subsister, sont *créatrices de personnalités*. Tel sera le cas dans les milieux ésotériques où l'ambiance permettra à bien des êtres, jusqu'alors repliés sur eux-mêmes ou écrasés par la vie, de trouver l'occasion de s'épanouir et d'entrevoir des horizons insoupçonnés.

4) — Pourtant le respect dû à la personnalité en tant que telle sera aisément sacrifié: *sans pitié à l'égard des dissidents*, n'admettant pas parmi les initiés des vues nouvelles en désaccord avec l'enseignement qui leur a été donné ou des comportements autres que ceux qui leur ont été enseignés, les groupes ésotériques ne se soucient guère, lorsqu'il s'agit de conserver la pureté de la tradition initiatique, d'être équitable envers chacun; la loi d'amour, affirmée comme principe de base, ne joue que pour les „initiés" et, parmi ceux-ci, qu'à l'égard de ceux qui demeurent strictement fidèles à l'initiation reçue.

5) — Le développement et l'expansion des groupes ésotériques rencontrent des obstacles qui exigent, pour être surmontés, des ressources nouvelles. Non seulement l'initiation se fera progressivement, mais une stricte *hiérarchie* s'imposera dès que le groupe grandit.

6) — Pourtant, si les préoccupations institutionnelles caractérisent souvent le groupe ésotérique — et nous pourrions parler dans ce cas de la pression du collectif sur l'individu, donc de *psychologie collective* — on doit bien constater que les initiés, de leur côté, attirent souvent à l'ésotérisme par la simple intuition qu'ils ont des réalités spirituelles, invisibles à l'homme du commun, par le sens direct qu'ils possèdent d'une spiritualité que précisément l'ésotérisme leur a révélée — et dans ce cas nous pourrions parler d'un phénomène de *psychologie sociale*, puisque c'est l'individu qui agit sur le milieu et le transforme.

7) — De sorte qu'on est en droit d'affirmer que l'ésotérisme agit comme un antidote au „processus de masse", à cette „massification" qui menace l'individu lorsque la collectivité le domine, commandant ses pensées, ses sentiments et sa volonté.

Si la discipline interne propre à tout ésotérisme tend à exclure les dissidents, il faut bien reconnaître d'autre part que le fait même d'avoir été initié à la connaissance d'un salut *libère de la contrainte du milieu* et détend du même coup les pressions impersonnelles qui menacent la vie intime de la personne.

8) — La sagesse ésotérique, par sa prétention de révéler la vraie nature de l'homme et le sens profond de la destinée, *apaise l'angoisse*

secrète suscitée par le sentiment d'une totale impuissance accompagnée de l'appréhension d'un danger inconnu. Les initiés ne se sentent plus des profanes sans force et sans ressources devant un péril qu'ils ne parviendraient pas à préciser; ils ont au contraire la certitude de posséder la connaissance qui leur permettra de faire face victorieusement à toutes les menaces imprévues, dans cette vie comme dans l'au-delà. Ils sont membres d'une communauté d'êtres élus, mis à part, différents de la masse qui se perd.

9) — Comme le notait C. G. Jung en un raccourci saisissant: „Tous les enseignements ésotériques cherchent à appréhender ce qui se déroule dans la psyché sans qu'on en puisse rien apercevoir, et tous les ésotérismes revendiquent pour eux-mêmes la suprême autorité".

INITIATION AND THE PARADOX OF POWER
A SOCIOLOGICAL APPROACH

BY

E. M. MENDELSON
London

While initiation is a very rich phenomenon for the history of religion or comparative religion, social anthropology finds it to be an elusive one. It seems to be so much tied to the intimate development of individuals that it is hard to say exactly in what way it is a part of any given social structure or organisation. The classic way of handling the matter is to talk of *rites de passage*, which are especially characteristic of simple societies. At certain selected moments in the life-cycle, society puts all members of a particular age through an initiatic process. Sociological stress is usually laid on those things the age-group learns which will make them better members of their society, and the function of initiation is related to this socializing process. This seems to me to miss out certain very important factors. In the first place, the achievement of maturity in any individual or group is a continuous process whose study is sacrificed to the discontinuity of social convenience. Yet many initiations teach an individual that social recognition at particular moments is unimportant when compared with the ceaseless process of self-improvement. More important still, it would seem that the sufferings and abstinences which are imposed on initiatic candidates have a function which is not merely that of making them better members of society. They are ambiguous, it seems to me, in that they are also teaching the individual to rely upon himself when society, as it must inevitably do at times, fails him.

It is one of the weaknesses of sociology—the reverse side, of course, of its strength—that it rarely includes within itself the means of studying anyone's escape from society. It is not sufficient, however, to leave such matters to Psychology, for they, in turn, react back upon the texture of society and culture in very marked ways. One can, if one wishes, say that, in initiation, society *also* teaches its members how to do without it and talk of a function of initiation in the promotion of self-reliance. I prefer myself to look a little further afield.

Great progress has been made in recent years by the French anthropological school under Lévi-Strauss in the theory of reciprocity. Briefly, the idea is that society is created and maintained through a complex network of exchanges—mainly of goods, women and language—between men, so that everyone is so dependent upon someone else for his vital needs that no escape from social life is possible. Age-old taboos, such as those against incest or the consumption of totemic foods, can be reduced to simple terms by saying that the hoarding of one's own goods or women damages social life by short-circuiting it: obviously independent strands of wool lying side by side are a very different matter from these same strands knit into a pattern. Nor need we be primitives or peasants to know that any desire on our part to "get away from it all" is immediately frustrated by the vision of our complex and irremediable entanglement in networks of family, friendship, business and so forth.

I want to argue that the importance of initiation, in its broadest aspect, lies in that it offers a way out of reciprocity. The stress, in initiation, is always laid upon self-improvement, self-enhancement, self-completion: it is always something that is being *added* to the initiate and, if anything is substracted from him by abstinences or sufferings, it is only as a first stage so that something greater, more important, may ultimately be gained. In the last resort no initiation known to us leaves an individual less powerful than he was before. If, in the initiations of simple societies, the stress is usually laid on gaining socially valuable powers, this is not necessarily so in the higher forms of initiation where total power, total knowledge or any other form of completeness will enable the successful candidate to be entirely himself, living in perhaps, but not dependent upon, society.

In his book on *Kingship*, Hocart, adopting a diffusionist approach, proposes that various forms of improvement are modelled on kingship. Rituals connected with marriage, the establishment of officials and initiation itself, he argues, must all have been based on the coronation of kings. But I have argued elsewhere that the human capacity for symbolization is limited by its obligation to utilize the brute matter of life as we know it. When we look at these rites we must conclude that it is not the initiate who is like a king but rather a king who is like an initiate. The image or symbol of the complete power which characterizes the initiate is taken from the human field where it can be found: that is, in the kingship, the supreme power on earth, or even, in the godhead, the supreme elsewhere. I cannot develop this here but may point to the fact that it is the king who normally commits what we might call "crimes against reciprocity": it is he who has more goods than any one else and more women and it is he, where incest is committed, who usually commits it. It is also he whose person is so sacred that it is hedged around by all sorts of privacies often pushed to great lengths so that the sacred king cannot touch the earth, communicate with lesser beings and so forth. The reason for all this is, normally, that the king must be outside society to a certain extent in that he has to serve as a link between it and para-social forces. Thus everything happens as if the king is self-reciprocating: he renders a cult to himself, he marries his own blood, his goods are so taboo that no one inferior can touch them; he is enprisoned in a kind of self-sufficient solitude of which we get echoes as late as in Shakespeare and which is the most exalted characteristic of the ideal initiate. It should be clear, I hope, that I am not arguing with Hocart on a matter of historical priority, but rather on a logical one. Moreover it should be clear to everyone that the initiate and the king, or chief, or leader, in most simple societies are, in any case, one and the same person.

Some years ago, my master Prof. Paul Lévy wrote a study of Buddhism as an initiatic system and I have recently had an opportunity to look at some of these problems in the context of a field study of Burmese Buddhism done in 1958 and 1959. Professor Lévy concentrated on ordination into the *Sangha* as an initiatic rite; I attempted to see the whole complex continuum of Burmese religion, including what is popularly known as "Animism", in the light of initiatic theory. Now it seems to me that the overwhelming Buddhist concern with self-improvement makes of this religion a crucial field of research for our concerns. Long ago Prince Siddhartha had the choice of becoming either a king or a Buddha and the implications of his choice still find echoes in modern Buddhist countries.

A sociologist in S.E. Asia has considerable problems in locating the social context of Buddhism. Basically things have progressed very little beyond the simple *Sangha-dayaka* relationship where the representatives of the religion are fed and kept by laymen in a more or less one-to-one relationship. Everyone, right up to and including the king, is a *dayaka*, that is an inferior, to the monk. The order of monks is not a church; monks associate together on a voluntary basis for a number of purposes but the Order can in no sense be called a corporate body, with its own treasures, possessions, rights and regulations etc. Individuals go in and come out of the *Sangha* more or less as they please. The *Sangha* is not a sine qua non of any ritual beyond the simple feeding and upkeep; it is nice to have monks about but it is not necessary. Monks are not priests with a vital part to play in man-God relationships. In such a context the normal weapons of sociology seem curiously inadequate, and it is certainly difficult to say what the monks *are for*, what is their social function.

If, instead of concentrating on reciprocity alone, we concentrate on the tension between reciprocity and anti-reciprocity, however, we find a much richer situation. The influence of Buddhism has been such in Burma that it is not impossible to think of the Burman as a man whose main idea is to achieve autonomy, whose main ideal is to leave society behind him. Both psychologists and political scientists have recently illustrated this theme, an extremely important one which must not be hidden by the superficial trappings of so-called modern democracy in Burma. We reach the conclusion, in terms of my present concern, that the monk is there to serve as a model of non-reciprocity: he is the person who, within *Vinaya* limits, always receives and never gives: a material illustration of his own perpetual drive to self-enhancement.

Now it has been said that Buddhism is such a non-worldly religion that it cannot exist without other forms of religion, such as "Animism", spirit-cults and what have you, to deal with the urgent matters confronting man in this world. This is true to some extent though the very long symbiosis of Buddhism and local religions genuinely precludes one from being able to say what is Buddhist and what is not in the prevailing mixture. I have therefore preferred to avoid the view which sees different parts of Burmese religious life as discontinuous and to attempt an overall view of the phenomena found in the field.

We are all familiar with the Buddhist stress on self-enhancement, differing only from other initiatic systems in that, at the very apex of the process involved, the self itself explodes into non-self, or rather something which is no longer either self or non-self. We are perhaps less familiar with a stress of great sociological importance, namely that placed upon the different levels of awareness of the doctrine characteristic of the people who approach it at different times and in different places. This is not an all-or-nothing system, one in which all individuals are equally outside salvation until, upon joining a church, they acquire the means of salvation. In the latter case we have a kind of discontinuous, once and for all initiation which various rituals may from time to time confirm; in the case of Buddhism we have a continuous initiation in which the process of self-improvement goes forward (and backwards, of course) not only in one lifetime but over several. Readings from the Canonical Texts give me the impression that, virtually from the beginning Buddhism was regarded as a teaching to which various people would come in various frames of mind. Thus it is not true that an "animist" cannot be a Buddhist; he is merely a Buddhist with incomplete or imperfect knowledge of the doctrine. The notion of perfecting one's knowledge of the doctrine, is of course, found in all religions and is not exclusively Buddhist. But we only have to look, at the popular level, at the Heaven-Hell dichotomy in all its forms, or the God-Satan dichotomy, to see that, for practical purposes involving the mass of men, we have here a very real difference indeed.

The primary instrument of Buddhist self-enhancement is, of course, meditation. Essentially, this is a process of looking at the world and concluding, after examining all its aspects, that it is not worth the having. One after the other various forms of attachment are sloughed off together with the reciprocal action which they imply. One of the main revelations of this examination is that these various attachments which, because of their variability seem to be organized in some kind of hierarchy of desirable and undesirable, are, in reality, not various, diverse or more or less important but—since they all spring from one root—similar, identical or, in other words, exactly as valuable or as not valuable as any other. Eventually, in some Schools, the meditator may discover that all these attachments are the mere shadow-play of mind, thus drawing into himself all the different aspects of the world and leaving only the task of putting an end to himself. We thus have three stages: the first we may call self-other reciprocity; the second self-self reciprocity; the third wipes out reciprocity altogether, and can be termed non-reciprocity.

Now in the Buddhist system no less than in others there is temptation. The meditator is warned that, along the way, the very arduous and lengthy way be it said, he will encounter experiences which, far from quitting him of attachment will in fact add momentarily to his attachments. This is because there are two branches of mental development, *Samatha*, the way of Tranquility, and *Vipassanā*, the way of Insight, which should be pursued side by side. If I have understood this matter correctly, the attainment of *Samatha* can lead to inbalances and the meditator be tempted by the powers that *Samatha* offers as if they were of special value. These powers are straightforwardly magical and include invisibility, unorthodox locomotion under the earth and in the sky, changing form, entering another body and so forth. The Buddhist texts are aware of these possibilities but they can be no more than a false goal.

In keeping with the theory that a lower level of sophistication will always tend to materialize things which the higher level accepts as merely symbolic—a theory to which Professor ELIADE has made the most notable contributions—the average Burman, in his religious quest, will remain very largely at the level of self-self reciprocity and consider the acquisition of the powers I have mentioned as the highest good. This means, ultimately, that for the mass of people, it is not levels of sophistication or comprehension of the doctrine that determine the religious hierarchy but levels of power. I have pointed out elsewhere that that which does most to confuse and mask the essential difference between the two is that, on the one hand, we remain within an initiatic process all the time with upward progress through hierarchical levels of attainment and, on the other hand, both ways demand that certain goods and enjoyments should be abstained from so that greater progress may be made. The *difference* is that the lower man will consider abstinence as a means of acquiring more power; only the higher man, the world-renouncer, will understand that abstention is an aim in itself: "that at the highest point of development the sum of power gained will automatically turn back into the comprehension that will destroy it". At the same time it is important to notice that this does not mean a lack of self-awareness on the part of the person who finds himself to have an inferior knowledge of the doctrine. One will often hear in Burma that such and such a meditational practice or such and such an abstinence is too difficult and furthermore that, to claim it falsely, would lead to madness since magical power strikes back at the sorcerer's apprentice. The general acceptance of the whole Buddhist frame of reference means that everyone recognizes that the *Sangha* is at the very top of the scale, at least symbolically, and I often have the impression that the *dayaka* supports the monk so that he shall do what he, as layman, as shackled by reciprocity, cannot do. In the end, as everywhere else in the sociology of religion, we return to the fact that while religious effort tends towards a state of non-reciprocity in its initiatic forms, realism here as elsewhere determines the limits to which theoretical absolute freedom is bound by relative freedom in practice. But the loose structure of Burmese religion and society does permit a wide latitude of claims made by a person on one particular rung of the ladder to those *beneath* him and the field is very much open to a plurality of small sects each dependent on a charismatic leader and each as short-lived as he.

This is not the place to develop the significance of such a situation for our understanding of Burmese contemporary life, especially politics. Here I have wanted to do something much more general. Whether or not other disciplines have achieved a more balanced view of initiation, it remains that my discipline, social anthropology, has continued to regard initiation as something sporadically connected with the education of youthful members of society into the ways of their society and working in the direction of making them better members of that society. Basically, this is not very different from education and it seems to miss everything that is particularly religious about the phenomenon in question. By looking at a case in which the *whole religion* seems to be an initiatic system I have wanted to modify the current assumption that once we have dealt with *rites de passage* we have done with the topic of initiation. A sociologist can, I suppose, inisist that Burmese religion, whatever we may call it, does in fact fit in with Burmese society and that, if the Burmese desire is to escape from society, then their religion certainly trains them for that. It still remains to show how we can, in every case, suppose that initiation trains one to be a fully-functioning member of society when the value of society and functioning therein is questioned by at least one system we know of. One other anthropologist, working with higher religions, seems to have come to similar conclusions: I refer to Louis DUMONT's article on "Le renoncement dans les religions de l'Inde".

One final point. It is not too far fetched to say that the overiding preoccupation of the social anthropologist today is with social control: that is who, in any given society, has the say over whom. Most of our sociological studies deal with subordination and super-ordination of individuals or groups in relation to each other and there has been serious discussion recently (in the Lévi-Straussian articles on dualism and triadism) as to whether social equality is ever possible at all in any form of society. The various forms of initiation reviewed here, ranging from primitive *rites de passage* to higher religions, seem to echo the basic concern with power which is characteristic of all social life. It may be that by stressing self-enhancement and by tending towards the abolition of reciprocity and dependence, initiation creates for the human spirit a place in which the question of power is no longer posed. Certainly the Burmese progress is one from an "animist" stage of being possessed by spirits, through one in which one possesses spirits and controls ever more important and powerful ones to a final "Buddhist" stage in which the necessity of being possessed or possessing is no longer a valid question. For the true paradox of power is, surely, that when everything is yours nothing is any longer yours, when you have become everything, a complete totality, nothing can be above or below anything else. Whether this is pure escapism or whether it is something which responds very deeply to a basic problem of human existence it is certainly not for our disciplines to judge. But that does not mean that they can afford to disregard it altogether.

INITIATION ET HISTOIRE

PAR

A. BRELICH
Roma

Des recherches particulières que je suis en train de conduire depuis quelques années, m'ont mis en face de nombreux problèmes généraux qui concernent le sujet de notre colloque. Je crois que pour en aborder quelques-uns, il est inévitable de vous indiquer, en bref, la nature et le but de mes recherches: nous en gagnerons un point de départ pratique.

Je dirai tout de suite que le thème de ces recherches est loin d'être nouveau: sans vouloir remonter à la découverte même des faits — les analogies apparemment surprénantes entre certains rituels grecs et les rites d'initiation des peuples que nous appelons conventionelle-ment 'primitifs', analogies remarquées bien avant Andrew LANG par le missionnaire LAFITAU — et sans vouloir refaire l'histoire des interprétations données à ces faits, toujours sporadiquement, par les savants depuis la fin du siècle dernier jusqu'à nos jours, je rappelerai seulement qu'en 1939 Henri JEANMAIRE, dans son gros volume *Couroï et Courètes* a étudié organiquement la question dans son en-semble, question que, six ans après, George THOMSON a reprise dans un chapitre de son volume sur *Eschyle et Athènes*.

Or, tout en admirant la richesse et la profondeur du travail de JEAN-MAIRE et la clarté des pages de THOMSON, je ne crois pas être le seul, entre nous, à éprouver, vis-à-vis de ces œuvres, la sensation de n'en être pas complètement satisfait. J'essayerai de montrer que cette sensation est justifiée par l'insuffisante rigueur méthodologique dont ces travaux se ressentent. Je laisserai de côté le chapitre de THOMSON, trop bref pour n'être pas schématique et incomplet, et je me bornerai à illustrer le procédé de JEANMAIRE, non, bien entendu, dans ses interprétations de détails où argumentations brillantes, intuitions et fantaisies ne se mêlent que trop souvent, mais seulement dans la structure fondamentale de son œuvre. Après avoir fait remarquer certaines particularités de l'organisation sociale homérique et, en générale, archaïque, par exemple la différentiation par âges des fonctions, qui lui rappellent, justement, des institutions analogues des sociétés illettrées H. JEANMAIRE passe en revue un grand nombre de rituels initiatiques africains. Successivement, à la lumière de la structure et des motifs les plus répandus de ces rituels, il analyse des institutions sociales, des rites et des mythes grecs, dans les quels on retrouve les motifs, les éléments formels, les séquences plus caractéristiques des initiations africaines.

Il est hors de doute que les recherches contenues dans le volume sont extrèmement intéressantes: même là où elles n'emportent pas la conviction du lecteur, elles sont toujours suggestives et stimulantes Mais en ce moment-ci ce ne sont pas les interprétations de détails qui retiendront notre attention; ce sont les questions de principe. Il faut que nous nous demandions, quels sont les *buts* et quels sont les *postulats* d'une recherche de ce genre-là.

Quant aux buts, ils semblent, somme toute, assez pauvres: il s'agit de démontrer que dans la civilisation de la Grèce classique il existaient des traces résiduelles de l'institution initiatique connue chez les peuples primitifs. En cela, JEANMAIRE ne s'écarte pas de ses prédécesseurs. Or, une conclusion semblable peut paraître assez banale: on sait, depuis au moins un siècle, que toute civilisation conserve des héritages primitifs. D'un autre côté, on pourrait dire qu'il ne s'agit même pas d'un résultat, mais bien d'un point de départ: en effet, à partir de cette constatation, on pourrait poser le problème, d'où viennent ces héritages préhistoriques de la civilisation grecquex? en quelle mésure, par exemple, ils dépendent du composant indo-européen, en quelle mesure du composant méditerranéen de l'hellénisme? quel est le rôle des Doriens dans leur conservation? Mais ce sont des problèmes que JEANMAIRE ne se pose pas.

Quant aux postulats de ses recherches, il y en a un que nous devons examiner de plus près. Pour le formuler dans les termes les plus simples, il s'agit de la conviction que l'initiation est un phénomène typiquement *primitif*, tandis que dans les civilisations dites 'supérieures' on ne pourrait constater que les 'résidus', les 'survivances' de cette institution primitive. Comme vous le verrez un peu plus loin, je finirai par n'être pas trop éloigné de cette opinion, mais à condition d'en rectifier les termes. Pour le moment — et précisément en vue de ces rectifications — je préfère soulever une objection d'un autre ordre: d'autant plus, que le postulat de JEANMAIRE, n'étant pas suffisamment clair, y prête le flanc.

On pourrait, en effet, commencer par dire: comment et pourquoi
l'initiation devrait être un phénomène par excellence 'primitif'?
Parmi ses exemples africains, JEANMAIRE mentionne des initiations à
des sociétés secrètes: or, de sociétés secrètes, avec les rites d'admission
relatifs, on en connait suffisamment dans les civilisations supérieures,
même dans celles des temps modernes et contemporains: il n'y a
aucune raison d'y voir une institution exclusivement primitive.

A ce point, toutefois, il me paraît nécessaire de nous mettre d'accord
sur l'emploi du terme ,initiation'.

Une analyse phénoménologique ou, si vous voulez, structurelle,
de *tous* les phénomènes que nous sommes habitués à désigner — soit
dans le langage courant, soit dans la terminologie scientifique —
par le terme 'initiation', ne peut qu'aboutir à la constatation d'une
identité substantielle qui est sous-jacente à toute leur variété. A quel
point les initiations tribales, les initiations aux sociétés secrètes, aux
mystères, aux métiers, les initiations sacerdotales, chamaniques,
guerrières etc., sont caractérisées par les mêmes formes et par la
même structure, on peut bien le voir dans le brillant volume de
M. ELIADE sur les *Naissanses mystiques*, où l'esprit pénétrant de l'auteur ne s'arrête pas devant les simples parallélismes formels, mais
il part à la recherche de leur raison d'être: l'auteur montre que dans
tous les cas particuliers il s'agit d'une nouvelle naissance de l'individu
initié, précedée par une décomposition de sa personnalité, par sa
re-immersion dans un état chaotique, et suivie par son intégration
à un niveau supérieur de l'existence. Des analyses de ce genre-là ne
sont pas seulement justifiées sur le plan de leurs finalités; elles sont
sans doute très utiles aussi pour l'interprétation de nombreux détails
du phénomène étudié.

Au point de vue historique, cependant, ce genre de recherches ne
donnent pas beaucoup de fruits. Essayons de les appliquer, par
exemple, au problème concret que nous avons choisi comme notre
point de départ. Si nous constatons, comme il est inévitable, que
l'initiation aux mystères grecs a exactement la même structure que
toutes les autres initiations, primitives ou modernes, la question des
origines des mystères grecs s'évanouira du même coup. Elle ne se
pose même plus, comme ne se posent plus les questions relatives à
tous les autres phénomènes et institutions grecs dont JEANMAIRE
recherchait l'origine dans l'institution initiatique primitive. En vérité,
la méthode phénoménologique ne nous conduit qu'à découvrir des
variantes d'un seul phénomène, abstraction faite de toute dimension

historique: elle s'explique sur un plan horizontal, en ignorant l'existence du plan verticale des développements et des transformations, qui est celui de l'histoire. Pourtant, les plus modestes connaissances historiques nous mettent en état de constater que les différentes 'variantes' phénoménologiques du 'théme' initiatique ne se trouvent pas, l'une à côté de l'autre, dans toutes les civilisations; que, par exemple, les institutions comme celle des mystères grecs ou hellénistiques ou comme celle de l'initiation aux différents métiers sont totalement absentes de la civilisation d'une société qui vit exclusivement de la chasse et de la cuillette, tandis que cette dernière société peut bien cultiver l'initiation tribale qui, à son tour, n'existe pas dans les sociétés organisées en forme d'état et, en général, dans les civilisations 'supérieures'. Or, c'est seulement à l'aide de ces connaissances historiques élémentaires — et, *a fortiori* de celles plus détaillées — qu'on peut poser le problème des rapports historiques entre les phénomènes structurellement analogues. Tout en appréciant les analyses phénoménologiques qui décèlent le *pattern* unique sous-jacent à une grande variété de formations historiques, j'insiste sur le fait que si elles sont conduites unilatéralement, elles risquent de méconnaître le contexte historique.

Nos efforts scientifiques, à mon avis, ne devraient pas viser à confondre, mais bien a distinguer et à préciser les significations à donner aux termes dont nous nous servons; ne pas les élargir au point de rendre inutile toute définition, mais bien les restreindre pour pouvoir nous en servir dans des raisonnements sans équivoque.

Pour reprendre le fil de mon propos, je repète que la question des rapports historiques entre certaines institutions grecques et les rites d'initiation primitifs ne se pose même pas, si non à la condition de préciser mieux le sens de ce dernier terme. Aussi longtemps que nous considérons les phénomènes grecs comme des variantes atemporelles d'un thème initiatique, général et vague, le problème historique ne se pose même pas. Si, au contraire, nous observons avec soin et attention, le phénomène initiatique dans les civilisations les plus reculées dans le temps, et si nous remarquons que, dans le monde grec, les phénomènes de forme analogue présentent, tout de même, des différences spécifiques susceptibles d'être définies, nous sommes à même de faire une confrontation historique.

Il est vrai que nous ne vivons plus à l'époque de TYLOR et de cet évolutionnisme qui identifiait, de façon simpliste, la civilisation primitive avec la civilisation préhistorique; on sait, aujourd'hui, qu'il y a de nombreuses et différentes civilisations 'primitives', comme il y avait de nombreuses et différentes civilisations préhistoriques, et on ne trouve pas une seule, parmi les premières, qui soit identique à une seule des secondes. Il reste, toutefois, indiscutable que les civilisations que nous sommes habitué à appeler 'supérieures' constituent un type de civilisation tout récent — il n'y en a pas de plus vieille de soixante siècles — et bien nettement caractérisé par une large convergence de facteurs techniques, économiques, sociaux et intellectuels, comme l'agriculture portée sur une grande échelle, l'urbanisation, la spécialisation dans les métiers, l'écriture, etc., etc. C'est seulement par rapport à ce type particulier de civilisation que nous pouvons rapprocher, malgré leurs différences évidentes, les civilisations primitives actuelles et celles de la préhistoire. Mais on verra toute à l'heure que cela peut être suffisant pour permettre des interprétations historiques.

Reprenant, pour un instant, mon propos sur les interprétations purement phénoménologiques ou structurelles des rites d'initiation — comme celles que nous offre le volume de M. Eliade — je voudrais fair l'observation suivante: on a vu que ces interprétations donnent un sens très large au terme 'initiation'; mais il me semble que pour être consequentes avec elles-mêmes, elles devraient élargir encore plus le sens du terme, jusqu'à le faire coïncider avec celui de 'rites de passage'; en effet, l'objet de tout rite de passage se désintègre dans ses qualités pour se réintégrer à un niveau différent. Or, on sait, depuis A. van Gennep, que l'initiation — dans toutes les significations qu'on voudra attribuer à ce terme — est un rite de passage; mais voudrions-nous dire par là que tous les rites de passage sont des initiations? Pourtant, non seulement les caractères structurels, mais aussi les éléments purement formels sont largement identiques dans tous les rites de passage, y compris les diverses espèces de 'initiation': se couper les cheveux, pleurer, changer de vêtements ou de nom, observer des abstinences, etc., sont des motifs qu'on retrouve dans les rites de passage les plus divers: dans les initiations comme dans les rites funèbres, nuptiaux, de guérison ou de purification.

Or, si nous préferons le chemin des distinctions à celui des confusions, nous devons nous demander si, malgré toutes les analogies structurelles et toutes les formes rituelles interchangeables, il existe des critères qui permettent de distinguer un rite de passage d'un autre. Ce qui est certain, c'est qu'indépendamment de nos analyses scientifiques, personne ne confondra un mariage avec des funérailles. Mais quand, plaisanterie mise à part, nous nous demandons où est la différence entre ces deux rites, nous ne la trouverons ni dans leur structure fondamentale, ni dans les détails rituels extrèmement variables, fluides et interchangeables: nous la trouverons simplement dans les *fonctions* différentes des deux rites. Tous les deux rites, sans doute, font dépasser une condition précédente et font accéder à une condition nouvelle: la différence est seulement que le rite nuptial conduit de la situation de célibataire à l'état conjugal, le rite funèbre de l'appartenance au monde des vivants à l'état de mort.

Or, c'est précisément le critère — la différence des fonctions — qui permet de faire un peu d'ordre dans le champ des rites disparates qu'on est habitué à appeler avec le terme unique de 'initiation'. Entre ces rites, en effet, malgré toutes les analogies formelles, il y a des différences aussi évidentes que celles qui distinguent les noces des funérailles. Qu'on compare, par exemple, l'initiation chamanique qui transforme un individu ordinaire en un individu exceptionnel, avec l'initiation tribale par la quelle on devient précisément un individu ordinaire, en dépassant la condition d'un être amorphe et dépourvu de tout état social.

Parmi tous les rites que nous appelons initiatiques, celui de l'initiation tribale ou, si l'on veut, clanique — de toute façon, l'admission rituelle d'un individu aux conditions normales du groupe social, — semble être, à la lumière de l'ethnologie comparée, le plus ancien et le plus répandu: il est connu et pratiqué par d'innombrables peuples primitifs de tous les continents et de tous les archipels, aussi bien qu'à tous les niveaux ethnologiques, à commencer par les civilisations dites de la 'chasse inférieure.'

Bien que ce rite ait été étudié à plusieurs reprises par des savants illustres, de SCHURTZ, WEBSTER et VAN GENNEP à JENSEN, HAEKEL, ELIADE, etc., il ne sera pas inutile en souligner certains traits moins connus et souvent négligés. Par exemple, dans la littérature scientifique, même dans celle contemporaine, on trouve souvent que l'initiation tribale est appelée un rite de puberté, et elle est incluse parmi les rites du cycle de la vie individuelle. Il y a sans doute de rites de puberté, censés conférer aux adolescents les capacités sexuelles normales de l'adulte: mais ces rites peuvent se célébrer dans le milieu de la famille et n'exigent aucune intervention publique. Tout au contraire, l'initiation est organisée par la communauté qui oblige les jeunes gens et les jeunes filles à s'y soumettre; elle peut conférer rituellement aussi les capacités sexuelles, parce qu'elle confère aux novices toutes les capacités attendues d'un membre normal du groupe sociale; mais, en premier lieu, il s'agit de leur conférer le *statut* social de membre responsable de la communauté. Il en résulte que le protagoniste actif du rite, la partie principalement intéressée, n'est pas l'individu, mais bien la société qui, sous peine de s'éteindre avec la mort des anciens, a besoin d'accueillir toujours de nouveaux éléments, en les transformant conformément à ses exigences.

Or, il est clair que ce type d'initiation, en vertu de sa fonction précise, est à l'abri de toute confusion avec des autres rites que d'habitude on appelle 'initiations': rite public et obligatoire pour tous les individus admissibles, il se distingue des initiationes aux sociétés secrètes, aux mystères, aux métiers comme il se distingue des initiations royales, sacerdotales ou chamaniques.

Si je ne me trompe, personne n'a étudié encore organiquement la question de savoir pourquoi ce type d'initiation, si répandu dans le monde ethnologique, est — à une exception près que je rappelerai sous peu — totalement absent des civilisations supérieures antiques et modernes, tandis que d'autres espèces d'initiation peuvent s'y rencontrer. Ici et à présent, je ne peux proposer à votre attention que deux des facteurs susceptibles de créer cette situation: le premier est que, dans les civilisations supérieures, la communauté est organisée dans la forme de l'état, où une minorité dirigeante enlève une grande partie de la responsabilité active aux individus ordinaires, tandis que dans la société tribale les membres adultes participent plus directement à la chose publique; le second, qu'au niveau primitif tous les individus adultes du même sexe sont plus ou moins capables des mêmes activités fondamentales, tandis que la spécialisation poussée qui se produit dans les civilisations supérieures abolit l'homogénéité de la société et par conséquent, la forme unique que la société pourrait imprimer à ses nouveaux adeptes.

Toutefois — on n'a pas manqué de le remarquer — l'institution initiatique n'a pas disparu des civilisations supérieures, sans y laisser des traces. S'agit-il, alors, des survivances inertes, des éléments pétrifiés d'époques plus anciennes dans le corps vivant d'un monde nouveau? En tel cas, les recherches consisteraient en un travail d'antiquaire, plus que d'historien. Mais si nous supposons que les mêmes besoins qui ont donné naissance à l'institution au niveau primitif, continuent, partiellement, à agir aussi dans les conditions nouvelles de la civilisation supérieure et que cette civilisation nouvelle les satisfait à sa façon, avec des institutions nouvelles mais qui absorbent ce qui est utilisable des formes anciennes, alors notre recherche devient à la fois plus intéressante historiquement et plus complexe, plus délicate.

Il ne s'agira plus de mettre en évidence les ressemblances formelles entre tel rite grec et les rites d'initiation primitifs, méthode illusoire, puisque — comme je viens de le dire — il n'y a aucun élément formel des rites initiatiques qui ne se retrouve également dans d'autres rites de passage. Cela ne vaut pas seulement pour la coupe des cheveux, pour la plainte rituelle, pour les abstinences, la flagellation, le travestissement, la ségrégation, le symbolisme sexuel, etc., etc.: même certains détails rituels dont on aurait probablement raison de soupçonner les origines dans les initiations tribales — telle la circoncision ou l'emploi rituel du rhombe — se sont introduits, dès l'époque préhistorique, en d'autres types de rite. Le seul contrôle valable pour la supposition qu'une institution d'une civilisation supérieure dépend historiquement des initiations primitives, est de rechercher si elle reponde, dans les nouvelles conditions et conformément aux nouvelles exigences, aux fonctions fondamentales des initiations primitives.

*

*   *

Comme le but de ma communication n'était pas d'anticiper les resultats de mes recherches sur certains faits grecs, mais de montrer, seulement, la nécessité de distinctions précises, d'une terminologie nuancée et d'une méthode historique moins superficielle que celle qui jusq'à présent a été employée dans le domaine de mes recherches, je pourrais terminer ici. Mais je crains que ce que j'ai dit ne puisse sembler quelque peu abstrait, si je n'ajoutais pas, très rapidement, au moins quelques exemples.

J'ai dit qu',,à une exception près" l'initiation de type primitif disparait des civilisations supérieures. Or, l'exception se trouve précisément dans la Grèce antique, dans certaines régions ou, mieux, certains états culturellement conservateurs du monde grec, comme Sparte et les *poleis* crétoises, où l'*agoge* des jeunes gens ne maintient pas seulement plusieurs formes bien connues des initiations tribales, mais encore leur fonction originelle: c'est la communauté qui oblige les jeunes gens à passer une longue période, divisée en étapes selon les âges successifs, dans un isolement collectif, avec des restrictions particulières, en leur imposant aussi des épreuves caractéristiques. Sans avoir subi cette 'initiation', on ne devenait pas citoyen, on ne

partageait ni les droits ni les devoirs de ceux qui, à Sparte, s'appelaient
'les égaux' (*homoioi*). Une analyse plus approfondie de l'institution
spartiate peut jeter quelque lumière aussi sur certains éléments qui ne
peuvent dépendre que de l'orientation nouvelle de la civilisation
supérieure grecque: par exemple, l'insertion de certain rites initiatiques, comme la flagellation, dans des cultes polythéistes permanents,
comme celui d'Artémis-Orthia. En effet, la civilisation hellénique,
malgré ses différences regionales et ses stratifications, conserve son
unité fondemantale: entre les institutions conservatrices de Sparte
et celles, progressistes, par exemple, d'Athènes il n'y a pas de rupture,
mais une infinité de passages bien nuancés. Or, si à Sparte nous
trouvons l'initiation primitive presqu'inaltérée, à côté de la quelle
et en connexion avec la quelle, on voit émerger des formes nouvelles,
dans les états plus innovateurs on ne trouvera plus d'initiation, mais
ces formes nouvelles, plus développées, qui n'accompagnent plus les
rites primitifs, mais les remplacent. Dans toute la Grèce on trouvera,
par exemple, des cultes, surtout des fêtes qui, avec le rôle qu'y jouent
les jeunes gens ou les vierges — souvent un nombre limité d'eux qui
représentent symboliquement leur classe d'âge — et avec le caractère
de renouvellement de la collectivité, revèlent leur dépendance historique de l'institution primitive.

Mais quell'est, alors, — pourrait-on demander — la place historique
des *mystères* grecs? Trois traits précis montrent avec toute évidence
que la fonction fondamentale des initiations tribales est totalement
absente des mystères: l'initiation n'est pas obligatoire; elle n'est pas
séparée pour les deux sexes; elle est ouverte à tous les âges. Pourtant,
il n'y a peut-être pas une autre institution grecque qui suit aussi
fidèlement, dans ses formes, le *pattern* de l'initiation primitive. La
solution du problème n'est pas, malgré tout, trop difficile, à condition
de nous nous rappeler que la fonction fondamentale des initiations
tribales — la fonction qui permet de les distinguer de tous les autres
rites apparemment semblables — n'est pas, tout de même, leur fonction unique. Nous avons vu que le protagoniste actif des initiations
tribales est la communauté; elle est l'intéressée numéro un; mais
cela ne signifie pas que l'individu qui subit l'initiation, n'y soit pas
personnellement intéressé lui aussi: sans être initié, en effet, il resterait
exclu de la vie normale de la société. Il y a plus: en entrant dans le
corps social, l'individu y trouve protection, et sûreté. Cette sensation
de sécurité que l'individu acquiert par l'initiation, s'exprime, chez
un grand nombre de peuples primitifs, en des formes qui, pour la

logique — mais seulement pour la logique — dépassent sa signification originaire: on dit que l'initiation garantit la santé, la défense contre la sorcellerie, et même un destin favorable dans l'autre monde. Il s'agit de besoins qui, quand les initiations tribales tombent en désuetude, ne trouvent pas facilement satisfaction. On crée alors des rites semblables qui, n'ayant plus de fonctions publiques, perdent les caractéristiques qui en dépendaient, mais conservent et développent les formes utiles à l'individu.

Je m'arrête ici: si j'ai réussi à vous montrer comment le respect des distinctions peut conduire à des résultats d'intérêt historique, j'ai atteint mon but.

RELIGION ALS EINWEIHUNG

VON

ANTON ANTWEILER
Münster

Selbst wer nur wenig von Religion kennt und sich kaum um sie
kümmert, weiß, wie vielgestaltig sie gewesen ist und heute noch ist.
Selbst wer festzustellen glaubt oder sogar davon überzeugt ist, daß
die Religion zurückfällt und überwunden werden muß, kann sich
dessen nicht erwehren, daß er wenigstens gelegentlich über sie
nachdenkt.

Von dem Aufbau der Gesellschaft, von der Berufsgliederung, von
der Wissenschaft, von der Kunst, von der Kleidung, Ernährung,
Bestattungsform her läßt sich Religion darstellen und beurteilen.
Doch von alledem sei nichts gewählt, sondern die Religion werde
vielmehr betrachtet, sofern sie Einweihung ist.

Um davor bewahrt zu bleiben, Ungeeignetes zu verwenden oder
Wichtiges zu übersehen oder Falsches miteinander zu verknüpfen,
ist es angemessen, von einer konkreten Form der Religion auszugehen,
wofür der Katholizismus gewählt sei, was nicht nur deswegen nahe-
liegt, weil ich mich zu ihm bekenne, sondern sich auch deswegen
empfiehlt, weil er mindestens reich und breit, vielleicht auch tief
und hoch ist.

Was unter Religion als Einweihung verstanden werden kann,
wird noch deutlicher, wenn man den Eingeweihten mit dem Nichteingeweihten, den Religiösen mit dem Unreligiösen vergleicht.
Danach wird es um so leichter, die Religion als Leben, als Einweihung
in das „Leben in Fülle" (Jh. 10: 10) zu schildern.

EINLEITUNG

Einweihen heißt, durch Wort, Handlung, Erlebnis jemanden in
etwas feierlich einführen, was ihm aus eigener Kraft nicht zugänglich, aber für ihn lebensnotwendig ist.

Dieses Lebensnotwendige kann absolut oder relativ sein. Als

absolut darf es bezeichnet werden, wenn es dasjenige meint, ohne
das einer nicht leben kann: atmen, essen, schlafen, wohnen, wozu
man auch das Zeugen rechnen darf, wenn man nicht nur an den
einzelnen, sondern an die Menschheit denkt, ohne überdies der Frage
nachzugehen, ob und inwieweit ein einzelner überhaupt Mensch sein
oder auch nur werden kann. Relativ notwendig ist das, was man
benötigt, wenn man eine Aufgabe zu erfüllen hat, was meistens
dadurch geschieht, daß man ein Amt beansprucht oder auferlegt
bekommt. Das gilt für alle Führer: ob zu Gott hin oder durch Wald
und Gebirge oder über See oder im Kriege oder bei der Anlage einer
Siedlung.

Jedenfalls ist es, von einer bestimmten Stufe der Entwicklung ab,
die sehr früh liegt, nicht selbstverständlich, daß jeder alles kann oder
alles zu werden selbst lernt. Er muß eingewiesen werden, was um so
feierlicher geschieht, je weniger Bereiche man hat, in die man eingewiesen werden kann. Noch heute kennen wir das bei den Bäckern,
Buchbindern, Seefahrern, Piloten, Schülern und Studenten. Selbst
wenn diese Bräuche zum Ulk abgesunken sind, so bewahren sie nicht
nur uraltes Gut, oder Brauchtum, sondern lassen sie auch erkennen,
daß auch wir heute noch immer dafür ansprechbar sind.

Nimmt man Einweihen im religiösen Sinn, so bedeutet es, in den
gottnahen Bereich einführen oder sogar mit Gott verbinden. Wie
vielfältig das nach Form, Schicht und Geschichte sein kann, soll
nunmehr am Katholizismus verdeutlicht werden. Freilich wird es
nicht möglich sein, bei jeder Zeremonie anzugeben, von wem, wann,
wo, weshalb und wozu sie eingeführt wurde; das ist noch nicht
genügend klargestellt. Doch auch ohnedem wird erkennbar, daß die
einzelnen Weiheformen erst allmählich gewachsen sind.

DER KATHOLIZISMUS

Im Katholizismus gibt es eine zweifache Form der Einweihung:
die Sakramente und die Weihen. Wenn man sich über sie einen Überblick verschafft hat, kann man beide unter einem allgemeinen Ge-
sichtspunkt betrachten und zusammenfassend bewerten.

1. Die Sakramente. Seit dem 13. Jh. kennt die katholische Kirche
sieben Sakramente, definiert als äußere Zeichen einer inneren Gnade.

Als grundlegendes Sakrament gilt die Taufe. Sie ist es, die aus
dem „Menschen" den „Christen" macht, als Bad durch Tod zur
Wiedergeburt (Röm 6: 3). Was als Sterben und Auferstehung in der
Vegetation Jahr um Jahr erkennbar ist, was in vielen Mythen als

Weg für Götter und Menschen geschildert und gedeutet wird, wird
über die Anschaulichkeit des Bildes hinaus durch den Vollzug von
Priester und Gläubigem zur erhebenden und formenden Kraft.
Derjenige, der mit Christus verbunden zu werden verlangt, muß mit
diesem Christus sterben, im Wasser, wie Jesus bei der Taufe (Mt 3: 16)
und im Blut, wie Jesus am Kreuz als Sühneopfer (Rö 3: 25) für die
Gerechtigkeit (Rö 5: 9). Wasser und Blut symbolisieren gleichermaßen
das Untertauchen aus dieser Welt hinweg in den Tod, in das Nicht-
seiende, in das Verwerfliche. Das Auftauchen macht deutlich, daß
der „Abgestorbene" zu neuem Leben aufersteht, in das Licht, in das
Leben hinein. Denn das hat er ja vorher begehrt: den Glauben, der
zum ewigen Leben hinüberträgt. Um dieses Untertauchen — heute
meist zum Übergießen vereinfacht, wozu wiederum statt „lebendigen",
fließenden Wassers stehendes benutzt wird — haben sich viele Zeichen
geordnet, die das Neue und Wunderbare sinnenfällig machen sollen.

Jeder kann wiedergeboren werden, aber er muß sich darum bemü-
hen, er muß sich zur Kirche hin begeben, geistig und körperlich. An
der Kirchentür wird er empfangen und über sein Anliegen befragt.
Man macht ihm deutlich, wie gefährdet er ist: er wird angeblasen,
damit der Satan ausfahre und seine Fesseln zerbrochen werden; er
erhält als erste Nahrung Salz, Zeichen der Reinigung und Erhaltung;
ihm wird Erkenntnis, Wahrheit und heilige Lehre versprochen, und
dann erst wird er feierlich, im Schutze priesterlicher Gewandung, in
das Kirchengebäude zum Taufstein geleitet. Noch einmal wird der
Satan beschworen, der Täufling mit Speichel des Priesters gesäubert
und geschützt; Brust, Nacken und Kopf werden stellvertretend für
die Sinnesorgane und den Leib gesalbt und dann wird das Wasser
übergegossen, während die Taufworte gesprochen werden. Ein neues
Kleid und ein neuer Name machen ihm deutlich, daß das Leben
radikal geändert wurde, und die Kerze mahnt ihn, das Licht des
neuen Lebens zu hüten, es insbesondere nicht durch Sünde zu ver-
dunkeln oder zu verlöschen.

Die Gläubigen bilden innerlich eine Gemeinschaft, in die hinein
der Täufling nun aufgenommen ist, die sich auch äußerlich abgrenzt.
Wird ein Erwachsener getauft, so hat er feierlich dem Heidentum
oder dem Judentum oder dem Islam oder der Sekte, der er bislang
angehörte, abzusagen. Er gehört jetzt zur Kirche, die als Gottesgemeinschaft jede Stammes- oder Staats- oder Menschheitsgemein-
schaft übersteigt, wenn auch nicht immer ausschließt oder aufhebt. Wie
stark diese Gemeinschaft sich zu schützen bestrebt und für notwendig

hält, kann man aus dem Eid entnehmen, den ein Bischof oder Abt vor der Weihe zu leisten hat, in dem der Schutz der Kirche in die Person des Papstes hinein konzentriert ist. Auch der König kann erst geweiht werden, wenn kirchliche Zeugen versichern: „wir wissen und glauben, daß er der Kirche Gottes würdig und für sie nützlich ist, zugleich auch in bezug auf die Herrschaft über dieses Reich", für das er geweiht werden soll.

Das Leben, das die Taufe vermittelt, ist neu, so neu, daß das vorherige Leben eigentlich keines war, sondern Gefangenschaft in den Fesseln des Satans und Blindheit in der Nacht oder Befleckung im Schmutz der Sünde. Das neue Leben ist das eigentliche, licht, frei, aber verpflichtend, weil verlierbar, und gefährdet, weil übermenschlich und göttlich. —

Die Eucharistie nährt und schützt dieses neue Leben, so wie jedes Leben genährt und geschützt werden muß und jedes Lebendige nur die ihm zugeordnete Nahrung erträgt. Die Gottesspeise, Jesu Fleisch und Blut, schützt vor dem bösen Feind, der alles, was er kann, daransetzt, um die Gottesgemeinschaft zu zerstören und das Gottesleben zu vernichten. Sie ist Nahrung zum ewigen Leben, sie macht die Empfangenden „gleichen Leibes und gleichen Blutes mit Christus" (Cyrill v. Jerus., Myst. Kat. 4:1). Sie muß ehrfürchtig behandelt und empfangen werden; deshalb wurde schon bald und streng gefordert, vor ihrem Empfang nüchtern und enthaltsam zu sein. Als Speise ist sie nur dem Gläubigen erkennbar, und Jahrhunderte hindurch war die Feier des heiligen Mahles sorgfältig gehütetes Geheimnis, in das der Täufling erst nach der Taufe endgültig eingeweiht wurde. Eines Leibes mit Christus, mit Gott zu sein: das war und ist das neue Leben.

Die Firmung läßt erkennen, daß der Wiedergeborene die Erde nicht verließ. Er muß das neue Leben Gottes im irdischen Leben der Menschen bewähren. Dazu wurde er, als erwachsener Täufling, sogleich nach der Taufe gestärkt, wird er, als kindlicher Täufling, erst befähigt, wenn er die Lebens- und Geschlechtsreife erlangt hat. Er wird geprüft, aber von den harten Erprobungen im außerchristlichen Raum ist nur der gelinde Backenstreich übriggeblieben, den der Bischof erteilt. Auch die Binde um die Stirn deutet nur noch schwach an, daß man sich ganz in Gottes Gemeinschaft begibt, und dies, daß der Firmling den Fuß auf den rechten Fuß des Paten setzen soll, läßt erkennen, wie eng die Gemeinschaft der Gläubigen auch eine solche des täglichen Lebens und leiblichen Zusammenhangs sein soll.

Verheißen und verliehen wird dem Firmling die Gabe der Weisheit und des Verstandes, des Rates und der Stärke, der Wahrheit und der Frömmigkeit und der Furcht des Herrn: Gaben, die deutlich machen, wie sehr das neue Leben eines des Geistes, der Innerlichkeit, der Gottesverbundenheit sein soll — ein wahrhaft neues Leben jenseits des Leibes, des Pompes, der Menschen oder gar des Teufels, und dennoch jederzeit auf dieser Erde sichtbar und prüfbar.

Wurde die Taufe mit Wasser und in Blut gespendet, so die Firmung im Feuer, in der Glut des Geistes, in der Helle des Lichtes Gottes. —

Die Ehe ist auch für den Christen eine, für die meisten sogar die Hoch-Zeit des Lebens; sie vollzieht sich nicht wie der Aufgang und Untergang der Sonne, wie das Aufsteigen und Niederfallen des Wassers, wie das Wehen des Windes und das Wogen des Meeres. Die Ehe gehört in den Naturbereich des Werdens und Vergehens, ist aber über ihn hinausgehoben, weil sie für den Christen eine sittliche Leistung und ein religiöser Dienst ist.

Die Ehe ist ein Abbild dessen, wie sich Christus zu der Kirche verhält (Eph 5: 22-27). Man kann in diesem Verhältnis das uralte Bild von der Hochzeit des Himmels mit der Erde erkennen. Aber selbst wenn dieses auf die Auffassung von Paulus eingewirkt haben sollte, so will es doch mehr als dieses sein. Es will darauf hinweisen, daß Mann und Frau nicht als einzelne handeln; daß sie nicht dem Kreislauf der Natur verfallen sind; daß ihre Beziehung nicht vergänglich und nur körperlich ist; daß sie vielmehr einem Geschehen eingeordnet sind, das mit der Erschaffung der Welt grundgelegt und durch die Wirksamkeit Jesu erneuert, gefestigt und erhoben wurde; daß sie einen Dienst vor Gott tun, wenn sie der menschlichen Gemeinschaft dienen und daß diese Gemeinschaft nur in Gott und mit Gott beständig und segensreich sein kann.

Damit wird die Ehe zur Teilhabe an der Schöpfermacht Gottes. Weil die Ehe leicht dahin mißverstanden werden kann, nur ein Naturvorgang zu sein, für den der Mensch nicht verantwortlich zu sein braucht, deswegen bedarf sie dessen, begriffen und durchleuchtet zu werden, um dem Menschen bewußt zu machen, daß er in ihr das Geheimnis des Lebens erfährt, ja, darüber verfügt. Sie soll den Menschen mit Gott verbinden und dadurch lebendig machen.

Das wird als so stark empfunden, daß auch bei der Jungfrauenweihe die entscheidende Frage ist: „wollt ihr gesegnet und geweiht und unserem Herrn Jesus Christus, des Höchsten Gottes Sohn, angelobt werden ?"

So also ist die Ehe Einweihung in das Innere des Lebens, irdisch und überirdisch. —

Die Beichte ist notwendig, weil das christliche Leben, wie alles Leben, verletzlich ist, was wieder darauf beruht, daß der Mensch nicht verläßlich ist. Er bedarf dessen, geheilt zu werden, nicht nur mit Binden und Pflastern und Salben, sondern mit Verständnis, Kraft, Hoffnung und Glaube. Die Sünde zerstört das Heile, ja, kann den Menschen nur mit dem Heilen und Höheren verlocken, und je mehr sie es getan hat, um so mehr verlangt er danach, geheilt zu werden, unverletztlich zu sein und das Heile zu bewahren. Daß Jesus damals die Sünden vergeben hat, setzt sich in dem fort, was Er Seiner Kirche als Vollmacht gegeben hat: Sünden zu vergeben, den Menschen zurechtzurücken und wieder auf Gott hin auszurichten.

Aber noch mehr: durch den Sturz wird der Mensch auf die Höhe aufmerksam. Er bemerkt, daß oberhalb dessen, woraus er gestürzt war, etwas ist, das er bis dahin nicht bemerkte; er wird inne, daß eine noch höhere Kraft noch besser hochhält, als es die durch die Sünde verlorene getan hat, und so leitet die Beichte dazu an, über die Heilung des Verletzten hinaus den Sinn auf das Höhere zu richten, emporzusteigen, besser zu werden, Gott näher zu kommen und mit den Menschen enger verbunden zu sein. Die Beichte drängt darauf hin, das Leben zu konzentrieren. —

Die Priester- und Bischofsweihe geht darauf zurück, daß die Menschen ungleich sind, was auch weder durch Taufe noch durch Firmung, weder durch Eucharistie noch durch Beichte aufgehoben wird. Wenn aber die Menschen ungleich sind, müssen sie sich ordnen, und wenn sie sich ordnen, bedarf es solcher ,welche auf die Ordnung hinweisen, in sie einweisen und sie überwachen. Das ist das Amt des Bischofs, des Episkopos, des „Aufsehers". Weil, was in dieses Amt fällt, zu umfänglich wurde, wurde es aufgeteilt und verschiedenen Stufen von Amtsträgern zugewiesen.

Keines dieser Ämter aber wählt man sich oder beansprucht es gar. Man muß darin von der Gemeinde, tätig in ihrem Leiter, eingewiesen werden, wie jedesmal auch die Gemeinde befragt wird, wenn das angestrebt wird und geschehen soll. Selbst unscheinbare Ämter und untergeordnete Dienste bedürfen der anerkannten Einweisung. Das beginnt mit den Aufgaben des Türhüters, setzt sich fort in denen des

Vorlesers und Dämonenaustreibers und vollendet sich in der Weihe des Altardieners.

Über diesen niederen Weihen stehen die höheren, die nur im Anschluß an jene erteilt werden können. Der Subdiakon soll Gott dienen, die Keuschheit wahren, beim Kirchendienst helfen. Waren bei den niederen Weihen die Aufgaben genau festlegbar, so sind sie nunmehr solche, die das ganze Leben ausfüllen: Gottesdienst in Keuschheit für die Kirche. Wieder genauer sind die Aufgaben des Diakon umschrieben: Hilfe beim eucharistischen Dienst, bei der Taufe, bei der Predigt. Der Priester, als der verhältnismäßig selbständige Helfer des Bischofs, soll opfern, segnen, führen, lehren, taufen und gehorchen. Mit dieser letzten Pflicht soll gewährleistet sein, daß der Dienst in größerem Rahmen reibungslos verläuft, festgelegt vom Bischof.

Der Bischof soll richten, auslegen, weihen, opfern, taufen, firmen. Betont steht an der Spitze, daß er richten und auslegen soll, für Ordnung sorgen im sichbaren Bereich von Besitz und Macht und Recht, und im unsichtbaren des Glaubens. Daß er eine Schlüsselstellung innehat, wird erkennbar, vielleicht sogar erschreckend und beinahe abstoßend erkennbar an dem Eid und Versprechen, die er vor der Weihe feierlich abzulegen hat. Die vielerlei Zeremonien der Weihe, Niederwerfung, Handauflegung, Tragen des Meßbuches, Ölung und Binde um die Stirn machen sinnenfällig, wie sehr er seinem Amt verbunden und ihm ausschließlich zugehörig ist. Was für ihn Leben ist, wird ihm nur durch die Einweihung als Einweisung zugänglich und handbar. —

Die Krankenölung will hervorheben und erlebbar machen, daß auch die Krankheit zum Leben gehört, aber nicht als ein mechanischer Vorgang, sondern als ein Vollzug, der zum Leben gehört, wenigstens zu diesem gebrechlichen, vorläufigen, unzulänglichen, bedrohten Leben. Man fällt nicht einfach auf das Lager hin, man unterwirft sich nicht dem Schmerz wie man es beim Regen tut, sondern man soll sich darauf besinnen, daß auch die Krankheit ein Weg zum Leben in Gott ist. Der ganze Mensch ist krank, der ganze Mensch soll gestärkt und getröstet werden. So werden Auge und Ohr, Nase und Mund, Hand und Fuß gesalbt, nicht nur, um die Krankheit zu vertreiben, sondern auch, um darauf hinzuweisen, daß alle diese Organe Werkzeuge der Sünde sein konnten, aber solche des heilen Lebens werden und sein sollen.

Der Kranke gehört fast noch mehr als der Gesunde Gott zu.

2. Die Weihen. Erst allmähhlich haben sich die sieben Sakramente als besondere Formen der Einweihung herausgebildet, bis im 13. Jh. ihre Zahl und Eigenart feststand. Damit aber war nicht unmöglich gemacht, daß sich andere Formen der Weihe entwickelten, die zwar minderen Ranges, aber nicht weniger wichtig und feierlich waren, ja manchmal sogar augenfälliger und prunkvoller wurden.

Diese Weihen beziehen sich auf Ämter, die innerhalb der christlichen Gemeinschaft und Gesellschaft wichtig wurden. Sie haben sich, wie die Ämter, allmählich entwickelt und bezeugen die Stufung der Gesellschaft, das Gewicht der Amtsträger und die Auffassung von einem geordneten Leben.

Zu ihnen gehören die Weihen von Abt und Äbtissin, welche Ämter nicht nur innerhalb der Klostergemeinschaft wichtig waren, die bestimmte Formen der Vergesellschaftung und Sicherung darstellten, sondern auch außerhalb des Klosters im Reichsverband und als Landesfürsten, die über beträchtlichen Grundbesitz, großen Heerbann und weitreichenden Kultureinfluß verfügten, durch Bauten und Schulen.

Von König und Königin wurde als erstes gefordert, daß sie der Kirche nützlich seien, woran erkennbar wird, wie stark das Leben in alle Schichten hinein von der Forderung reinen Glaubens geprägt werden sollte.

Die Jungfrauen und Krieger dürfen zusammen genannt werden, weil sie die Kämpfer für die Kirche waren und sein sollten: die einen durch Gebet und Entsagung, die anderen durch Schwert und Hingabe.

Allen Weihen war gemeinsam die eindringliche Pracht der Worte und Gebärden und die feierliche Überreichung des Kleides und der Würdezeichen des Amtes. Nur, wer berufen und bestätigt ist, ist amtsfähig, und keiner ist es von sich aus.

3. Die Segnungen. Wie die Sakramente durch die Weihen, so wurden die Weihen durch die Segnungen ergänzt. Sie sind als minderen Ranges schon an der einfachen Form der Spendung erkennbar, und daraus, daß jeder Priester sie spenden kann. Sie umranken den Alltag in vielfältiger Form, und man kann kaum sagen, daß sie ihn entsprechend durchdringen und bestimmen, wie es die Sakramente und Weihe wenigstens anstreben und beanspruchen.

Es gibt Segnungen für Almen, Archive, Arzneien, Autos; für Büchereien, Bienen, Bier, Brot, Brücke, Brunnen, Butter; für Druckerei; für Eier, Eisenbahn, Ernte; für Felder, Feuerspritze, Fischerboot, Flugzeug, Fuhrwerk; für Gewänder, Geflügelfleisch, Glocken, Gold,

Gürtel; für Hafer, Haus, gegen Heuschrecken, für Hochöfen; für Kalkofen, Käse, Kerzen, Kinder, Krankenwäsche, Kreide, Kuchen; für Lamm und Lilie; für Maschinen, gegen Mäuse, für Mühlen, Münzen, Myrrhe; für Palm, Pferde, Pilger; für Ring, Rosen, Rosenkranz; für Saaten, Schrift, Schnüre, Schule, Seidenraupen, Seismographen, Speck, Stall; für Telegraphen, Tragbahren, Trauben; gegen Überschwemmung und Ungeziefer; für Vereinsfahne, Wein, Weingärten, Wohnzimmer, gegen Würmer; für Ziegelei und Zweige.

Man erkennt: was immer dem Menschen wichtig wird, soll von Gott her gebilligt, geschützt, gefördert werden; und was immer dem Menschen schädlich wird, soll von Gott her gebannt und unschädlich gemacht werden.

4. Einordnen und Vergleichen. Überblickt man die Sakramente, die Weihen und die Segnungen, so ergibt sich, daß der katholische Christ dessen bedarf, eingeweiht zu werden, um das Leben insgesamt und in seinen wichtigen Teilen oder Stufen zu erfahren und betätigen zu können.

Die Sakramente entsprechen ihrem Wort: sie sind Mittel zur Heiligung dessen, der sie empfängt, wobei mit Heiligung das Heil-sein der ganzen Person während des ganzen Lebens gemeint ist, aber auch nur des Lebens: es gibt kein Sakrament des Todes oder des Sterbenden.

Hineingehoben wird man in das neue Leben durch die Taufe. Sie soll Tod und Wiedergeburt nicht nur sein, sondern auch erlebt machen. Damit ist das Eigentliche und Entscheidende getan. Seit man aber dazu überging, die Kinder zu taufen, konnte zwar die Handlung an dem Kinde vorgenommen werden; es konnte aber weder erleben, was geschah, noch beschließen, sich zu entscheiden. Das kann und soll später nachgeholt werden; aber weder wird besonders darauf gedrängt, noch wird es überprüft, so daß, wer die Entscheidung für das neue Leben unterläßt, doch als ihm zugehörig betrachtet wird.

Die Firmung soll die Lebens- und Geschlechtsreife bestätigen und bewirken und stellt insofern die Vollendung der Taufe dar. Je mehr aber der junge Mensch gezwungen wird, sich auszubilden und weit über die Jahre der beginnenden Geschlechtsreife hinaus noch lernen muß und in jederlei Hinsicht abhängig ist, um so weniger kann die Firmung ihn dessen bewußt machen, daß er erwachsen sein oder möglichst bald werden soll, daß er auf eigenen Füßen zu stehen und in allem für sich verantwortlich zu sein hat. Wissenschaft, Rat,

Stärke sind ihm fremd, und es geschieht leicht, daß Frömmigkeit und Furcht des Herrn ihm fremd bleiben, weil man den Geist nicht teilen kann. Selbst wenn er vom Feuer ergriffen und durchglüht ist, wird es ihm in den seltensten Fällen gelingen, danach zu leben, weil er in zu vielem sich nach anderen zu richten hat, die sich weniger auf Geist und Liebe als auf Recht und Macht berufen.

Die Ehe kann kaum der Aufgabe genügen, die ganze hohe Zeit des Lebens zu umspannen. Zu sehr ist das Tun für das tägliche Brot aus der Familie herausgewandert, so daß weder Frau noch Kind sehen, was der Vater für sie tut, aber auch der Vater nicht erlebt, was Frau und Kind erfüllt oder erschüttert. Die Familie steht nicht in sich selbst, und sie mag noch so gesund sein, es hilft ihr nichts, wenn andere Familien und Gruppen, besonders der Staat, versagen. Das Spiel des Himmels mit der Erde ist unfeierlich, geschäftlich und gemein geworden, und das Erlebnis des Ganzen zerbricht an der Ausplünderung des Menschlichen.

Die Krankheit ist heute weniger etwas, was der Mensch als sich zugehörig betrachtet, ein sittlicher Vorgang, als vielmehr etwas, wofür der Arzt und die pharmazeutische Industrie zuständig ist, zumal die Sorge um die Kosten auf Kasse und Staat abgewälzt sind.

Die kirchlichen Ämter sind nur noch kirchliche. Die Kirche verfügt nicht mehr, weder nach Geist noch nach Gesetz, über das Gemeinwesen; nicht mehr über Wissenschaft und Forschung, über Schule und Erziehung, über Bauten und Kunst. Sie weist nicht mehr die Wege in die Zukunft; ihre Ämter sind für den Alltag belanglos.

Die Beichte ist nicht mehr der Sturz in Gottes Barmherzigkeit und Liebe, nicht mehr das Erwachen aus dem Tode bei lebendigem Leibe, das man nur selten erleben kann, sondern mit in den Erziehungs- und Lenkungsplan eingebaut. Weit mehr noch ist sie abgelöst durch die Psychologie in all ihren Sparten und Stufen, traktabel und nicht mehr Gnade.

Die Eucharistie, Gott als Speise, sollte den Gläubigen in Gott einbeziehen, bei einem Festmahl, das unvergeßlich sein sollte, wie das Mahl Christi mit Seinen Jüngern. Es ist nicht abzuschätzen, wie sich das vervielfältigte eucharistische Mahl auswirkt. Aber es bleibt das Anliegen unverändert: mit Gott verbunden zu werden und zu bleiben, sich zu stärken und zu verbinden mit solchen, die gleichen Glaubens sind.

Die Einweihung, grundsätzlich in der Taufe vollzogen, verteilt sich über die entscheidenden Zeiten und Stufen des Lebens hinweg und soll es ganz umgreifen. Dabei bedient sie sich des Zeigens, Handelns und Sprechens. Gezeigt wird die Eucharistie, werden die Symbole des Glaubens, des Amtes und der Macht, und gezeigt auch, bei der Taufe, das Glaubensbekenntnis und Herrengebet. Als Handeln bieten sich dar das Tauchen oder Übergießen, das Hauchen und der Backenstreich, das Salben und Kleiden. Gesprochen wird, um zu belehren, zu befehlen, zu formen.

Die Farben sind wichtig und bedeutungsvoll: weiß und schwarz, rot und grün, violett und rosa.

Mutproben werden verlangt, wenn auch nur selten und manchmal leicht: das Fasten vor den Weihen und vor dem Osterfest mit dem Herrenmahl, die Nüchternheit vor der Eucharistiefeier, der Backenstreich bei der Firmung und die Bindung bei der Priester- und Bischofsweihe.

Alledem, was die Kirche zur Einweihung vollzieht, liegt zugrunde, daß sie neues Leben vermittelt. Dieser Gedanke, mehr dieser Glaube und diese Überzeugung sind so alt wie die Kirche. Die neue Lehre in Macht rühmte man von Jesus (Mk 1: 27); den neuen Bund stiftete Jesus (Lk 22: 20), nachdem Er das neue Gebot der Liebe gegeben hatte (Jh 13: 34). Als neues Geschöpf pries Paulus den Getauften (2 Kor 5: 17), so daß er zu einem neuen Menschen wurde (Eph 2: 15). Bei der Abtsweihe wird das eindringlich verdeutlicht: „der Herr ziehe dir den alten Menschen, samt seinen Handlungen, aus; der Herr bekleide dich mit dem neuen Menschen, der nach Gott in wahrer Gerechtigkeit und Heiligkeit geschaffen ist". Diese Worte lassen keinen Zweifel daran, daß Auskleiden und Ankleiden nicht mehr als ein Bild für das sein sollen, was als nur vor Gott geschehend für die Menschen unsichtbar ist und bleiben muß.

Gerade darum ist die Kleidung so bedeutungsvoll, bei Taufe und Weihe, bei Krönung und Gelübde.

5. Zusammenfassung. Die Einweihung will den ganzen Menschen ergreifen und das ganze Leben umfassen, das den Tod nur noch leiblich kennt, weil es in Gott einbezogen ist und immer währt.

So, wie der Katholizismus die Einweihung entwickelt hat und heute noch übt, entspricht sie einfacher Lebens- und Herrsch-form, übersichtlich und leicht handlich: mit solchen, die zur Kirche gehören, und solchen, die es nicht tun; mit Vorstehern, die für alles zuständig sind; mit Herrschern und Königen, denen man nahe ist; mit Heiligen, die sich aus dem Leben zurückziehen und dennoch zum Ganzen gehören. Dieser Bereich wird von den Sakramenten und

Weihen umfaßt. Als das Leben sich aufgliederte, folgte man ihm mit Segnungen.

Die Segnungen aber sind nicht so gewichtig, daß sie als notwendige Einweihung vor Gott und den Menschen und einem Beruf empfunden würden. Man denke an den Arzt, was an Verantwortung ihm obliegt; an die Forscher, die sich im Dienst der Wahrheit verzehren; an die Lehrer, welche das unübersehbare Wissen übersichtlich und handlich zu machen versuchen; unter den Forschern besonders an die Biologen und Astronomen, beide mit schwindelerregenden Erkenntnissen; an die Techniker und Wirtschaftler, deren Kühnheit schon fast selbstverständlich geworden ist; an die Beamten, deren Verläßlichkeit die Bedingung unseres komplizierten Lebens ist.

Man begreift, daß die Einweihung durch die Kirche, wie sie heute noch weitgehend üblich ist, unwirksam geworden ist, weil sie aus dem Erlebnisfeld der Menschen gerückt ist, und man begreift, daß die Kirche sich auf ihre Aufgabe besinnt, allen Menschen, auch den heutigen, die Einweihung in das ganze Leben zu geben, nach der alle verlangen, auch in Sünde und durch Schmutz hindurch. Und man begreift endlich, daß keine Einweihung jemals eine unveränderliche Form finden kann, sondern, wie das Leben, veränderlich sein muß.

DER UNRELIGIÖSE

Am Katholizismus kann man sich verdeutlichen, was Einweihung in das Leben ist oder wenigstens sein kann. Das Gleiche kann man auch dadurch erreichen, daß man vom Gegenteil ausgeht, daß man zusieht, wie derjenige ist, der nicht eingeweiht ist. Und wenn der Eingeweihte als religiös gilt, so ist umgekehrt der Nicht-eingeweihte unreligiös.

Man kann einwenden, daß es nicht berechtigt ist, den Katholizismus, als Abstraktum, zu vergleichen mit dem Unreligiösen, als Konkretum. Man müsse verlangen, den Katholiken mit dem Unreligiösen zu vergleichen. Doch das wäre schwierig, wenn nicht unmöglich. Denn der Katholik ist immer nur einer, der einer bestimmten Zeit zugehört. Ein solcher kann nie alles das an sich verwirklichen oder verdeutlichen, was als zum Katholizismus zugehörig betrachtet wird. Er kann weder alle Sakramente, noch alle Weihen, noch alle Segnungen erhalten, kann also nicht darbieten, was zum Katholizismus gehört. Man müßte also, um möglichst wenig zu unterschlagen, von vielen Katholiken sprechen, und das kommt auf das gleiche hinaus, als wenn man vom Katholizismus spricht und ihm alles zuordnet, was ihm zugehört.

Umgekehrt ist es mit dem Unreligiösen. Der Katholizismus, obwohl Abstraktum, bietet sich immerhin als Gebilde dar, das man feststellen kann, weil er sich als Gesellschaft oder gesellschaftsbestimmend darbietet. Die Unreligiosität dagegen ist nicht organisiert. Sie ist nicht nur, wie der Katholizismus, weitläufig, sondern verschwommen, unfaßbar, manchmal sogar den Katholizismus durchdringend. Der Unreligiöse dagegen ist ein Mensch, den man sieht, mit dem man sprechen kann, der vielleicht herausfordert. Geht man durch, in welch verschiedenen Formen der Unreligiöse sich darbieten kann, so hat man einen Überblick über die Unreligiosität, also etwas Entsprechendes wie den Katholizismus.

Es ist also nicht abwegig, sondern förderlich, dem Katholizismus den Unreligiösen entgegenzustellen, und es sei in der Absicht versucht, den Sinn der Einweihung deutlicher zu machen.

Der „Unreligiöse" ist als Bezeichnung unscharf. Er kann genauer bestimmt werden als der Nicht-eingeweihte, als der sich Ausschließende, als der Nicht-zugelassene oder Nicht-berufene und als der Gleichgültige.

1. Der Nicht-eingeweihte. Er kann überhaupt nicht oder teilweise nicht eingeweiht werden oder sein. Überhaupt nicht eingeweiht ist, wer von dem Gott oder den Göttern nichts weiß; wer die zugehörigen Gläubigen als Gemeinschaft nicht kennt oder anerkennt; wer die geforderte Lebensart nicht betätigt oder billigt; wer den Glauben an diesen Gott oder diese Götter für überflüssig, für quälerisch, für einschränkend, für herabsetzend hält; wer andere Regeln des Verhaltens für nützlicher oder gar keine für sinnvoller hält. Ein solcher muß dem Gläubigen als gottlos gelten, auch dann, wenn der Gottlose sich nach anderen Göttern richtet. Er ist nicht eingeweiht, er verfehlt den Gott in diesem und in jenem Leben, er ist uneingeweiht, er ist unreligiös, er ist mindestens, verloren wenn nicht verdammt.

Teilweise nicht eingeweiht und deswegen unreligiös kann auch derjenige sein, der nur einen Teil des als Norm gefaßten Glaubens anerkennt: der Sektierer. Er ist nicht zur Erkenntnis der Wahrheit gekommen (2 Tim 2: 4), er wurde nicht erleuchtet oder hat die Erleuchtung nicht angenommen; er ist verfinstert (Eph 4: 18), verhärtet (Mk 6: 52), verschlossen (Mt 23: 13), verwerflich (1 Kor 9: 27) und verworfen (Mt 8: 12). Die Geschichte umrissener Glaubenssysteme bietet viele Beispiele dafür, wie viele Uneingeweihte,

Unreligiöse, Gottlose es geben kann: die christologischen und trinitarischen Streitigkeiten im Christentum, die Auseinandersetzungen zwischen Judentum und Christentum, zwischen Christentum und Islam und innerhalb des Islam. Wer nicht eingeweiht ist, faßt es nicht, und umgekehrt: wer es nicht faßt, kann nicht eingeweiht werden.

Ob überhaupt nicht oder teilweise nicht eingeweiht: ein solcher verfehlt den Weg und damit das Leben und damit das Eigentliche, wofür er da ist.

2. Der sich Ausschließende: Als unreligiös gilt, wer sich ausschließt, entweder von vornherein oder nachträglich.

Von vornherein schließt sich aus, wer sich weigert, für Anderes, Neues, Höheres offen zu sein; wer sicher ist, in seiner Lebensform das Endgültige, das Sichere, das Unumstößliche gefunden zu haben; wer es ablehnt, sich mit dem zu befassen, was andere als sinnvoll, als notwendig, als erhebend und heiligend betrachten und betätigen; wer es als unsinnig betrachtet, über mehr nachzudenken als über das, was das Greifbare nahelegt oder fordert. Es mag sogar sein, daß der Verstockte insgeheim anerkennt, er könnte doch nicht in allem recht haben und der andere ihm durch den Glauben überlegen sein. Aber dann um so mehr weigert er sich, verhärtet er sich, verstockt er sich. Er will nicht belehrt, er will nicht bekehrt werden.

Möglich ist aber auch, daß einer sich erst nachträglich ausschließt. Er hat zu einer Glaubensgemeinschaft gehört, er hat sie anerkannt, er hat in ihr innerlich gelebt. Aber dann ging ihm auf, daß er eingeengt wurde, daß er sich nicht ausweiten konnte, daß der Acker ohne Saat und die Saat ohne Nahrung blieb. Dann hat er sich losgesagt, nicht leichtsinnig, sondern schmerzlich, aber losgesagt, weil er das Leben nicht so weit und hoch und tief empfand, als er es forderte und vor sich und vor den Menschen und vor Gott fordern mußte. Er hat sich aus dem, was ihm geläufig, was ihm sogar lieb war, ausgeschlossen, um sich nicht dem Leben zu versagen, das vor ihm stand und in ihm drängte.

Beide, der von vornherein und der nachträglich sich Ausschließende, gelten denen als unreligiös, von denen sie sich ausschließen. Sie sind Verlorene, die das Leben weggeworfen haben. Es braucht nicht verspielt worden zu sein, wie es der verlorene Sohn getan hat. Aber es ist verloren. Es ist die Bekehrung zum Unglauben, wie sie Romain Rolland im Jean Christophe (L'Adolescent) geschildert hat. Immer freilich muß man sich darüber klar sein, daß, als ausgeschlossen zu gelten, nur möglich ist in bezug auf eine Gemeinschaft, die sich als Norm betrachtet und betrachten muß.

3. Der Nicht-zugelassene. Als unreligiös, als nicht eingeweiht gilt auch, wer nicht zugelassen wird, wer nicht berufen ist, sei es, daß er unzulänglich ausgestattet ist, sei es, daß er zu klein ist, sei es, daß er anders geformt ist.

Wie immer man Religion auffassen mag, das leistet sie immer oder soll und will sie wenigstens leisten, einen Halt zu geben. Dieser Halt ist möglich, weil die Religion den Gläubigen in ein Ganzes einordnet, aus dem er nicht herausfallen kann. Die Formen der Religion unterscheiden sich dadurch, daß sie dieses Ganze verschieden bestimmen und daß der Halt verschieden verläßlich ist. Damit man sich aber halten kann, ist es notwendig, daß man Organe hat, mit denen man anderes ergreifen kann, so wie das Bild eine Öse haben muß, damit es an einem Nagen aufgehängt werden kann. Wer dies entbehrt, ist unzulänglich ausgestattet; er ist weder imstande, sich mit Menschen zu verbinden, noch imstande, sich mit Gott zu vereinigen. Er kann nicht in die Gemeinschaft der Gläubigen aufgenommen werden, so wie diese ihren Gott verehren. Unabhängig davon ist die andere Frage, ob einer nicht dadurch, daß er da ist, schon in Gott, in der Welt, in die Menschen eingebettet ist. Auch um diese Frage geht es nicht, sondern darum, ob jemand, über diese allgemeine Einbettung hinaus imstande ist, eine besondere oder erhöhte oder verfeinerte Form der Einbettung anzunehmen oder aufzunehmen, die in dem besonderen Fall als die geforderte Form der Religion angesehen wird.

Geht man von dieser besonderen Form aus, dann versteht man, wieso gesagt werden kann, daß einer nicht berufen ist. Damit ist eben dieses gemeint, daß er nicht genügend ausgestattet ist, um sich dem einzufügen, was als Religion betrachtet und gefordert wird.

Es mag aber auch sein, daß einer zwar einen Halt in einem Ganzen hat, daß aber dieser Bereich zu klein ist, als daß er als hinreichend anerkannt werden könnte. Wer nur Berliner sein will, es also ablehnt, darüber hinaus etwas anderes zu sein, kann nicht als Deutscher, schon gar nicht als Europäer gelten, als nur in dem Sinne, daß er innerhalb Deutschlands und innerhalb Europas da ist, was aber nicht hinreicht, um ihm die Gesinnung zu geben, die er haben muß, um im vollen Sinn als Deutscher und als Europäer zu gelten. So auch werden im religiösen Bereich viele als nicht zugelassen oder als nicht berufen betrachtet, deren Bereich zu eng ist, so etwa die „Wilden" oder „Primitiven" zu den „Hoch"religionen, wie sie sich gern bezeichnen. Jahrhundertelang hat man missioniert, überzeugt, man müsse den anderen Gott und Religion überhaupt erst bringen.

Als nicht zugelassen gilt auch, wer zwar religiös, aber anders geformt ist als derjenige, der anerkennen oder zulassen soll. Die Fremdheit oder Feindschaft zwischen Dörfern oder Städten oder Ländern ist oft genug eine solche zwischen den zugehörigen Göttern. Es kann sein, daß diese Götterfeindschaft nur die Menschenfeindschaft tarnen oder rechtfertigen soll. Es kann aber auch sein, daß in dieser Feindschaft sich der Unterschied im Grundgefühl des Lebens auswirkt und eben damit bekundet, daß keiner aus seinem Beziehungsbereich heraustreten und sich in den des anderen hineindenken kann. Sogar im katholischen Spanien ist das zwischen den Dörfern mit ihrer Mutter-Gottes-Verehrung bis auf den heutigen Tag wirksam.

Den Nicht-zugelassenen als nicht berufen zu bezeichnen, beruht darauf, daß man weiß, daß letztlich keiner dafür verantwortlich ist, daß er so ist, wie er ist; daß, wie er ausgestattet ist, davon abhängt, als was und zu was er berufen ist, und das geht letztlich immer und nur von Gott aus. Das schließt nicht aus, daß es Menschen gibt, die beanspruchen oder sich anmaßen, darüber zu urteilen, ob einer berufen ist, und daß dieser Urteil kleingeistig, engherzig, überheblich und ungerecht sein kann. Dennoch lebt auch dieser Mißbrauch davon, daß jeder Mensch weiß und jedem zugesteht, sich nicht selbst ausgestattet zu haben. Unabhängig davon ist dies, ob jemand seine Ausstattung in rechter Weise benutzt und ausgewertet, sich also würdig gemacht hat, zugelassen zu werden, weil er auch in diesem Sinne berufen ist.

4. Der Gleichgültige ist entweder wertfrei oder Augenblicksmensch. Als wertfrei gelte, wem es nur darauf ankommt, was greifbar oder genießbar ist, zu erleben. Weder kümmert es ihn, ob etwas wahr oder gelogen, richtig oder falsch, ehrenhaft oder verwerflich, würdig oder würdelos ist, noch auch, ob es vor dem Urteil der Menschen oder Gottes, vor dem Entscheid des Gewissens und der Verantwortung bestehen kann. Treue und Anstand, gute Sitte und stillschweigende Verabredung zählen nicht. Nur das Zählbare, Vorweisbare, Aufhäufbare gelten. Ihn schiert es nicht, daß ein anderer an Himmel und Hölle, an Jenseits und Vergeltung, an Gott oder Götter, an Aufstieg oder Abstieg, an einmaliges oder mehrmaliges Leben glaubt. Ihn kümmert es höchstens insofern, als er auch das in seine Rechnung einbeziehen kann, nicht aber insofern, als er es

berücksichtigt, achtet und anerkennt. Werte sind nur Worte, die er den Mißratenen, Erfolglosen, Untätigen, Schwächlingen und Lügnern überläßt. Er selbst hält sich an Tatsachen, für die er stellvertretend Zahlen gelten läßt, hinter denen er aber immer die Tatsachen spürt und wägt. Was Kirchen, Propheten, Heilige sagen, berührt ihn nicht, belustigt ihn höchstens. Es ist ihm gleichgültig, in dem Sinne, als ob es nicht sei und wirke.

Der Augenblicksmensch ist eine Sonderform des Wertfreien. Er kann sich von ihm dadurch unterscheiden, daß er zwar Werte anerkennt. Aber er ist mit ihm dadurch gleich, daß er diese Werte nicht als dauernd, als verbindend, als verbindlich anerkennt. Er lebt dem, was ihm gerade beifällt oder einfällt: dem Schönen, Guten, Wahren; dem Erbarmen und der Begeisterung; dem Tun und dem Faulenzen; dem Großartigen und dem Gemeinen. Aber er will nicht derjenige sein, in dem das alles aufeinander bezogen, zueinander geordnet und voneinander getrennt ist, mit gleichbleibender Beziehung oder Bindung. Er will immer nur derjenige sein, in dem sich gerade das abspielt, was gespielt wird — mehr nicht.

Für den Gleichgültigen gibt es keinen Gott und keinen Nächsten, keine Liebe und keine Reue, keinen Aufblick und keinen Ausblick. Religion ist bestenfalls ein Wort, das er kennt, und Religiosität eines Menschen kümmert ihn so wenig wie die Frage, ob der Sirius eine Atmosphäre hat. Er braucht nicht in das Leben eingeweiht zu werden; was er davon kennen muß, weiß er ohnehin oder erfährt er da, wo er es braucht.

5. Zusammenfassung. Der Unreligiöse ist derjenige, dem etwas fehlt. Es mag sein, daß er bei sich selbst keinen Mangel verspürt, aber andere gibt es, die überzeugt sind, daß sein Leben größer sein könnte, daß es das aber nicht ist, weil er nicht in dieses größere Leben eingeführt wurde. Es kann auch sein, daß er diesen Mangel selbst verspürt, darunter leidet, ihn auszugleichen versucht und eben damit bestätigt, daß ihm etwas vorenthalten ist oder wird, wonach er verlangt, was er aber aus eigener Kraft nicht erreichen kann.

Wenn man am Katholizismus ablesen kann, was Religion sein kann und sein will, so am Unreligiösen das Gleiche, nur von der anderen Seite her, nicht von der konvexen, erfüllten, sonder von der konklaven, leeren.

DAS LEBEN IN FÜLLE

Es gibt keine bessere Beschreibung, vielleicht sogar Definition der

Religion, als diejenige, die Jesus gab, als er vom „Leben in Fülle"
(Jh 10: 10) sprach, obwohl Er gewiß weder die Religion beschreiben
noch sie definieren, sondern „nur" das Neue Seines Lebens, Seines
Gebotes, Seines Reiches schildern wollte.

Dieses Wort aber kann dazu helfen, sich über Grund und Ursprung, über Kern und Auswirkung der Religion, also nicht nur
des Christentums, zu vergewissern. Wenn es für die Religion gilt,
dann um so mehr für das Christentum, und wenn für das Christentum,
so nur deswegen, weil es in höchstem Sinne Religion sein will.

1. Grund und Ursprung. Der Mensch fühlt sich hilflos, preis-
gegeben dem, daß er da ist; daß er von innen her bedroht ist, durch
Hunger, Durst, Müdigkeit, Krankheit, Hoffnungslosigkeit; daß er
von außen her bedroht ist, durch Pflanzen und Tiere, durch fallende
Bäume und Felsen, durch Höhlen und Schluchten, durch Wasser und
Hitze, durch Freunde so gut wie durch Feinde. Je mehr er erwacht
und erfährt und weiß, um so deutlicher wird ihm, wie gefährdet er ist:
durch Eiszeiten, durch Kontinentverschiebungen, durch Sonnen-
ausbrüche, durch Sternbildungen, durch Energieverschwendung,
durch die Nichtumkehrbarkeit aller für ihn wichtigen Vorgänge.
Dagegen sucht er Schutz, bei sich, indem er vor-sieht und vor-sorgt;
bei anderen, indem er sich mit Gleichgesinnten zusammenschließt;
bei der Natur, indem er sich einfügt und auf sie lauscht; am meisten
aber, weil alles das unzulänglich ist, bei den Göttern, bei Gott, bei
jenen Wesen, die alles tragen, alles wissen, alles können. An sie wendet
er sich, ihnen opfert er, vieles, auch Liebes; mit ihnen will er verbunden sein, bei ihnen fühlt er sich sicher.

Das kann man auch vom Gegenteil her belegen. Der Volksmund
weiß: Not lehrt beten — wenn er auch nichts darüber sagt, ob Not
nur beten lehrt und nicht auch fluchen und lästern, und nichts darüber,
ob immer beten und nicht auch verzweifeln und verstummen. Als
ein Kind einmal gefragt wurde, warum es und seine Geschwister und
Eltern nicht mehr zur Kirche gingen, antwortete es rasch, unbe-
schwert und sicher: „Uns geht es jetzt gut; mein Vater verdient so
viel, daß wir nicht mehr zur Kirche zu gehen brauchen". Wer sich
geschützt weiß, verliert das Gefühl dafür, daß er, schon als Mensch,
ungesichert ist, und damit den Anzeiger dafür, ob und wie sehr er
religiös ist. Darin kann man auch den Grund dafür erblicken, daß in
manchen Gemeinschaften, die sich religiös nennen und für welche
die Religion Grund und Anspruch ihres Daseins bedeutet, eben
diese Religion nicht mehr spürbar und lebendig ist, weil sie unter

dem Gewirre des täglichen Treibens und unter der Last der augenfälligen Pflichten versteckt und unwirksam geworden ist. Der langsame Niedergang vieler Klöster und Klostergruppen macht das auch im großen deutlich und veranlaßt, über den Sinn der Religion und über das Recht dieser Gemeinschaften nachzudenken, oft genug zum Segen für die Religion und die Gemeinschaft, sei es für letztere auch nur, um sie verschwinden zu machen. Der Mensch erträgt es nicht, sich darüber zu täuschen, daß er gefährdet und deswegen hilflos ist.

Dieses Bewußtsein, gefährdet zu sein, verläßt den Menschen nie. Selbst wenn er sich einmal gesichert und geborgen erlebt, so weiß er doch, wie vergänglich und wie trügerisch das sein kann. Er braucht die Religion, um sich gegen den Untergang, mindestens um sich gegen den Niedergang zu schützen. Er verspürt weniger die Mächte, die von außen an ihm nagen, als vielmehr die Kräfte, die ihn innerlich zermürben. Er weiß sich von der Sünde durchsetzt, daß von Jugend auf das Trachten seines Herzens böse ist (1 Mos 8: 21), er traut sich selbst nicht über den Weg. Deswegen richtet er Dämme und Schranken auf, als Versprechen und Gelübde. Deswegen sucht er Halt an Geboten und Gesetzen. Deswegen verlangt er nach Führung und Rat. Was der einzelne erlebt, braucht er dem anderen nicht anzuvertrauen: wo Menschen sich begegnen, wissen sie um diese Gefährdung von innen her und richten sie sich danach, ohne viel darüber sprechen zu müssen oder es klarzu bestätigen. Wo immer Menschen sich versammeln, mehr noch, wo sie sich anhäufen, verlangen sie danach, geführt zu werden, damit sie davor bewahrt bleiben, sich mehr zu schädigen, als sie es ohnehin tun.

Oft und gern und weithin zu Recht führen die Menschen die Gefährdung darauf zurück, daß es nichts Beständiges gibt. Sie suchen die Dauer im Wechsel. Sie brauchen jemanden, der nicht einschläft und aufwacht, der nicht müde wird und Erholung braucht, der nicht erst nachdenken muß, wenn er plant, der nicht fürchten muß, die Sonne könne einmal nicht aufgehen, die Sterne könnten einmal fallen und die Weltenflut alles ertränken. Die Menschen verlangen nach einem, der über Jahre und Jahrtausende gebietet, der mit den Sternen spielt und dennoch niemanden vergißt, niemanden verlacht, niemanden verwirft. Sie brauchen einen Ort der Ruhe, der nicht auf Zeit, der auf immer, der für alle, der in höchster Weise gilt, und sie finden ihn bei Gott, in Gott, als Gott.

So gründet Religion darin und entspringt sie daraus, daß der

Mensch der Gesellschaft bedarf, um bestehen zu können, wenn es um Brot und Wohnung, um Arbeit und Spiel geht; der Gemeinschaft, wenn er Nähe sucht, als Treue, Liebe, Verläßlichkeit; der Einweisung in die Welt, die er in bestimmter Weise erlebt, verarbeitet, mit Händen und Herz und Kopf. Das alles ist ihm Religion, und, was er als Ganzes ungenau und ungreifbar erlebt, wird ihm zu eigen und wird ihm bewußt, indem er allmählich in diese Welt hineinwächst, dadurch, daß er tut, was ihm diejenigen sagen, die ihn führen, und über das nachdenkt, wenn und wie sie die Welt deuten. So macht er den Weg von außen nach innen: von der Gesellschaft über die Gemeinschaft in die Welt hinein, bis hin zu sich selbst, indem er beginnt, Herr über seine Handlungen zu werden, was wieder dazu führt und voraussetzt, daß er Herr über seine Gedanken wird, die aus seinen Empfindungen aufsteigen und ihn das Wunder des Daseins innerhalb eines Ganzen, innerhalb eines Geistes erleben lassen.

Dieses, daß der Mensch sich gegen seine Hilflosigkeit schützt, indem er religiös ist und wird, hat aber auch sein Gegenbild. Um sich des Schutzes zu versichern, schafft er sich Zeichen, an denen er ablesen kann, daß er geschützt ist: Bauten, Kleidung, Gesellschaftsformen, besonders Machtstufen, Handlungen. Diese schützen ihn, legen ihn aber auch fest, das heißt, schließen andere Bauten, andere Kleidung, andere Gesellschaftsformen, andere Handlungen aus. So kann man die Religion auch definieren als die Gesamtheit der Hemmungen, die einer als verbindlich und die zu verletzen er als schädlich oder tödlich erachtet. Was man als Tabu im engeren oder weiteren Sinn kennt, macht augenfällig, was gemeint ist. Übernimmt man diese Hemmungen, ohne deren Sinn zu kennen, vor allem ohne das Gegenstück zu kennen, dem sie entgegengesetzt sind, dann wird der Schutz zur Beklemmung, dann wird die Religion die Ausflucht der Gehemmten, die sich nicht zutrauen zu leben, zu wagen, frei zu sein, anders zu werden; die ängstlich darauf beharren, daß weder Wort noch Gebärde, weder Bau noch Kleidung, weder Rang noch Anrede geändert werden, die darin, daß dieses unveränderlich bleibt, das Zeichen dafür erkennen, daß nicht nur Gott unveränderlich ist, sondern daß Er auch unveränderlich die Gläubigen unveränderlich erhält. Wie stark das Tabu-erlebnis sein kann, weiß man aus all den Fällen, in denen es mißbraucht wurde, also nicht im Dienste der Menschen vor Gott, sondern zum Nutzen einiger Machthaber gebraucht wurde. Das kann dahin führen, ganze Volksschichten niederzuhalten oder auszuschließen, sei es ausdrücklich, wie im indischen Kastenwesen, sei es unausgesprochen wie in Europa, wogegen sich die Bewegung der „Proletärs" erhob — wie sie sich damals nannten — und wo noch im 20. Jahrhundert die Arbeiter sich oft genug dem Priester gegenüber rühmten, sie wollten nicht religiös sein, weil sie „aufgeklärt" seien, also der Hemmungen enthoben, die man unberechtigterweise auf sie gestülpt hatte.

2. Der Kern. Versucht man, den Kern dessen zu finden, um den sich alles legt oder an den sich alles hält, was man religiös nennt, so kann man ihn als Allgefühl kennzeichnen, als ein Gefühl für alles, was dem einzelnen erreichbar ist, unter Dingen und Menschen, unter Irdischem und Außerirdischem. Weil unter diesem, was leicht zugänglich ist, als selbstverständlich angesehen wird, kommt es leich dazu, daß man unter religiös nur das Außergewöhnliche und unter dem Außerirdischen nur das Göttliche, nur Gott versteht. Aber unübersehbar ist, was trotzdem auch an Irdischem als religiös, als gottdurchtränkt betrachtet und behandelt wird, vom Wasser bis zum Wind, vom Stein bis zum Berg, von der Krankheit bis zur Überkraft, vom Häßlichsten bis zum Schönsten, ja vom Bösen bis zum Besten. In diesem Gefühl für alles, was wirkt, was also wirksam ist, sammelt sich und von ihm aus wird gespeist, was als Bedürfnis nach Hilfe, nach Geborgenheit, nach Erlösung, nach Steigerung den Menschen durchdringt und antreibt. Gerade dies, daß er danach verlangt, erlöst und erhoben zu werden, läßt ja erkennen, wie wenig er sich mit dem begnügt, was ihm zuhanden ist; wie sehr er danach verlangt, ausgeweitet, bereichert, erhoben, kurz, geheiligt zu werden. HENNEMANN hat dieses Allgefühl treffend beschrieben: „Die Religion kann man als vorbegriffliches Erleben der Innentiefen der Wirklichkeit bezeichnen, das dann später die Philosophie mit dem Begriff erfaßt" [1]), wobei man unter Philosophie ebenso Wissenschaft wie Theologie als mit eingeschlossen betrachten darf. Religion ist Lebensgefühl und dessen Ausdruck insgesamt, nicht als aufgegliedert wie andere Erlebnis- und Bewältigungsformen, etwa Kunst oder Wissenschaft; als dauernd, nicht vergänglich wie Mode jeglicher Art — obwohl auch der Mode nicht unzugänglich; als aufrichtig, nicht geheuchelt wie manchmal Freundlichkeit, Christlichkeit, Arbeitsamkeit — obwohl auch der Heuchelei nicht immer abhold in denen, die sich religiös nennen.

---

[1]) HENNEMANN Gerhard, *Naturwissenschaft und Religion*, Berlin 1963, 129 (Erfahrung und Denken, Bd. 11).

Weil auf das Ganze hin empfunden, ist Religion Halt vom Ganzen her. Davon mußte schon gesprochen werden, als vom Grund und Ursprung der Religion gehandelt wurde. Jetzt ist noch einmal darauf hinzuweisen, weil sich gerade darin der Sinn der Religion erschöpft. Alles andere ist immer nur Teil, als Gebiet, als Kraft, als Anliegen, als Betätigung, und Religion ist wahrlich nicht frei davon, aufgeteilt und zersplittert zu werden. Das aber ändert nichts daran, daß man sich damit an der Religion vergeht. Sie will das Ganze, und sie will das Ganze als Halt für den Gläubigen, für den Religiösen, für den Menschen. Dieses Ganze kann verschieden groß, verschieden gewichtig, verschieden personhaft gedacht werden. Es führt aber immer letztlich auf ein Geheimnis zurück, das, wenn es auch als Person gedacht, erlebt und angebetet wird, dennoch unsagbar, undenkbar, ungreifbar bleibt: „Gott wohnt in unzugänglichem Licht" (1 Tim 6: 16) und ist „verzehrendes Feuer" (Hebr 12: 29), obwohl Er Leben ist und Leben gibt.

Weil Religion das Ganze umfaßt, deswegen auch den Ursprung des Daseins für jeden einzelnen. Je mehr man sich dessen bewußt war, mit dem, was man tat, an den Urgrund heranzureichen, um so mehr war diese Tätigkeit dem Gott vorbehalten und durfte nur in dessen Auftrag ausgeführt werden. Dazu mußten besondere Menschen bestellt sein, deren Tun gottnah, heilig war. Heilig war so das Säen, das Landvermessen, das Bauen, besonders der Brücken, von woher heute noch die katholischen Bischöfe pontifices heißen, das Schreiben, das Lehren, das Zeugen neuen Lebens, sei es körperlich, sei es geistlich, wie ja vielfach die Priester Väter heißen und die Götter die Stammväter der Menschen sind, besonders derjenigen, die sich in besonderem Sinne als Menschen betrachten, der Adeligen und der Könige.

Religion ist eben das Urverhalten des Menschen, sowohl in bezug auf den Ursprung, soweit er ihn erkennt und erlebt, als auch in bezug auf die Kräfte, die er verspürt und betätigen will, als auch in bezug auf das Ziel, das er erstrebt, sofern er auf es hingetrieben oder von ihm angezogen wird. In der Religion ist der Mensch unverstellt und unverfälscht, obwohl er oft genug sich selbst und den Menschen und den Göttern etwas vorzumachen versucht, wovon er aber sehr wohl weiß, daß er es tut und eigentlich unterlassen müßte, da er es sich als schuldhaft anrechnen muß.

Im gleichen Sinn ist Religion Rückgriff auf die Primitivität, im guten wie im schlechten verstanden. Im guten, sofern der Religiöse sich auf den Ursprung, auf den Urgrund, auf das Urerlebnis besinnt und nichts anderes will, als alles dieses erleben und ausleben; im schlechten Sinne, sofern der Religiöse leicht geneigt und oft versucht ist, sich mit dem Primitiven zu begnügen, es also zu unterlassen, das Keimhafte wachsen zu machen oder wenigstens wachsen zu lassen; sich damit zu begnügen, nur andeutungsweise zu denken und zu tun, was genauer, sorgfältiger, feiner gedacht und getan werden müßte; die klobige Art des Benehmens, die große Form der Frömmigkeit, die ungeschlachte Art des Redens, die schmutzige Weise des Wohnens ist öfter für „Heilige" kennzeichnend, als es ihrem Amt und ihrem Glauben dienlich sein kann.

Wieder anders und doch wieder als Gleiches kann man die Religion als die Einheit der wirksamen Kräfte im Menschen bezeichnen. Vielerlei kann der einzelne, noch mehr vielerlei können die einzelnen, wenn sie sich zusammentun. Was sie leisten, indem sie sehen, hören, schmecken, gehen, laufen, schwimmen; indem sie schnitzen, schmieden, bauen; indem sie kochen, schneidern, malen; indem sie sprechen, dichten, mahnen; indem sie denken, sinnen, träumen; indem sie klettern, graben, tauchen, fliegen: alles ist bewundernswert und beträchtlich aufeinander abgestimmt. Dennoch fällt es oft genug auseinander, zwischen den Menschen — man nennt es Kampf und Krieg; und innerhalb des einzelnen — man nennt es Unfrieden oder Gespaltensein. Erst wenn das vielerlei zusammengefaßt wird oder erst, wenn man sich wenigstens bemüht, es zusammenzufassen, fühlt sich der Mensch gesammelt oder versammelt, erfüllt und ausgewogen, belastet und entlastet zugleich. Erst wenn viele sich einem Ziel zuordnen, das über sie hinausliegt, in dem sie sich wenigstens im Jenseits begegnen wollen, können sie darauf vertrauen, daß sie friedlich leben, ohne fürchten zu müssen, daß sie in Trägheit und Schmutz verkommen. Darauf, daß Religion Einheit sein will, beruht es, daß der Gedanke der Einheit gerade im religiösen Denken und Erleben unausrottbar ist: nicht nur, daß nur ein Glaube der wahre sein kann; nicht nur, daß nur ein Gott als der eigentliche geglaubt, verkündet und verteidigt wird; sondern auch, daß man den Unterschied zwischen Mensch und Mensch, zwischen Leib und Geist, zwischen Ding und Ding, zwischen Welt und Gott aufhebt und behauptet, alle seien nur Eines, und was als vieles erscheine, sei eben nur Schein und nicht Wirklichkeit. Nie wird es gelingen, diese Einheit nachzuweisen, aber immer wird es wahr sein, daß alles Wirkliche zusammen nur ein Eines sein kann, abgesetzt gegen das Nichts, das nur als

Ganzes oder Widerspruch zu der Einheit alles Seienden denkbar ist. Erst innerhalb dieses einen Seienden ist es sinnvoll, zwischen Gott und Welt, großer Welt und kleiner Erde und auf der Erde zwischen den vielen Dingen und Vorgängen zu unterscheiden, womit Alltag und Wissenschaft sich befassen. Aber das zu tun, ist nur sinnvoll, wenn alles Getrennte letztlich doch nur eines ist.

Wenn Religion Kern ist, dann ist sie, wie jeder Kern, verborgen. Darauf beruht es, daß Religiöses so oft esoterisch ist; daß schon dieses, in das Religiöse, in das eigentliche Leben aufgenommen zu werden, geheim ist, nur nach langer Vorbereitung zulässig und nur nach harter Prüfung möglich; daß die verbindenden Handlungen und verpflichtenden Zeichen geheim gehalten werden; daß man das Geheimnis nicht ausspricht und nur zögernd, wenn überhaupt, in Bildern darstellt; daß man sich bemüht, niemanden erkennen zu lassen, was man im Tiefsten denkt; daß man sich vor Gott verschleiert und ihm nur im Kämmerlein (Mt 6: 6) begegnen will. Was Geheimnis insgesamt ist, das Dasein, das Leben, das Denken, das Verlangen, die Liebe, das wird in der Religion als eines erfaßt und erlebt, und unter nichts leidet der Religiöse mehr als darunter, daß er dieses eine zersplittern muß, und sei es auch nur der Zeit nach, indem er nie imstande ist, alles zugleich zu sein, was er ist, und zugleich zu tun, was er kann, sondern auf ein ganzes Leben, das lang sein kann, und auf eine breite Fläche, die unabsehbar, auseinanderziehen und verteilen muß.

Die Religion ist der Bereich des Ganzen und Kernhaften, des Tiefen und Einheitlichen, nach Zustand und Auswirkung.

3. Auswirkung. Religion gehört zum Menschen. Der Mensch lebt, indem er sich auswirkt. Es ist also einsichtig, daß Religion sich auswirken kann und muß. Von dem vielen, an dem das ablesbar wird, sei nur einiges erwähnt.

Weil Religion sich auf das Ganze bezieht, das Ganze aber aus Teilen besteht, muß das Teil seinen Platz im Ganzen haben. Das leistet, für den Menschen, die Religion. Sie weist ihm den Platz zu, auf dem er zu stehen, oder, wenn das als zu statisch erscheinen sollte, sie weist ihm den Weg zu, den er zu gehen hat. Das bezieht sich zunächst auf das, was er zu tun und zu lassen hat, wenn er aufsteht oder schlafen geht, wenn er arbeitet oder ruht, wenn er anderen begegnet oder sich von ihnen trennt, wenn er zornig oder gelassen ist, wenn er dem Bösen begegnet oder ausweicht, wenn er das Gute sucht oder vermeidet, wenn er das Ende bedenkt oder wegschiebt. Über alles das belehrt zu werden, ist wichtig. Es schwebt aber im Leeren oder fällt ins unabsehbare, wenn unterlassen wird, die Welt mit allem, was in ihr ist und vorgeht, verständlich zu machen. Das tut die Religion: „im Anfang erschuf Gott den Himmel und die Erde" (1 Mos 1: 1); „im Anfang war das Wort" (Jh 1: 1). So lehrt das Christentum. Anderswo ist der Ur-ozean oder die Ur-meditation oder das Ur-ei oder die Urbegegnung zwischen Mann und Frau übermenschlichen Maßes oder was immer an Bildern man für geeignet gehalten hat, um zu verdeutlichen, warum es eine Welt gibt, weshalb in ihr Menschen sind, was diese Menschen sollen. Das letzte ist es, worauf es ankommt: der Mensch soll wissen, was er zu tun hat, weil er weiß, wo er ist und — vor allem — was er ist: ein Glied Gottes, ein Gedanke Gottes, ein Werk Gottes, ein Kind Gottes.

Die Religion will in die Ordnung einweisen, die zu achten ist, wenn anders der Mensch will bestehen können. Diese Ordnung macht sich dem Menschen am ehesten als Gesundheit spürbar. Diese ist die Harmonie zwischen Organen und Vorgängen, und so kann man die Religion als den Willen zur Gesundheit auffassen, mindestens sagen, daß sie sich als Wille zur Gesundheit auswirkt. Das erkennt man an den Geboten zum Fasten, zur Jahres- und Wocheneinteilung, an der Verteilung der Feste, an der Regelung der Ehe und Erziehung, an der Mahnung zur Arbeit und Ruhe. Mehr noch bemüht sich die Religion um die Gesundheit der Seele. Die Religion warnt vor dem Bösen, vor der Sünde, vor der Versuchung, vor der Begehrlichkeit; sie warnt vor den Fallstricken, die man sich selbst überwirft, mehr, als vor denen, die andere auswerfen. Sie leitet an, die Gefühle zu lenken, oft so sehr, daß sie ausgelöscht oder verfälscht werden; leitet an, die Gedanken zu zähmen, damit sie nicht überschlagen und verfilzen; leitet an, die Träume, die Wünsche, die Sehnsüchte zu bewältigen, damit sie weder sich nur verflüchtigen noch auch den Sinn für das Echte verfälschen. Sie will, daß der Instinkt unverletzt bleibe, die Quelle, aus der sich das Leben erneuert und an der es sich erfrischt. Wenn Religion instinktlos wird, ist sie verloren, ob nun der Instinkt genannt werde das Gotteserlebnis oder das Weltgefühl oder das Würdebewußtzein oder der Ordnungssinn, das ist gleichgültig. Ob eine Form der Religion noch instinktsicher ist, kann man an ihren Gebeten und Predigten — oder wie man das nennen mag — erkennen, auch an der Weise, ob und wie sie für sich wirbt — wobei es offenbleibe, in welcher Weise die Religion zu werben, zu missionieren das Recht und die Pflicht habe.

Nimmt man das alles zusammen, so darf man auch sagen: Religion ist Sorgfalt im Umgang mit der Wirklichkeit. Weder mit sich selbst noch mit seinem Besitz, weder mit den Menschen noch mit deren Dingen, weder mit seinen Gedanken noch seinen Gefühlen, weder mit seinen Organen noch mit deren Vollzügen, weder mit der Gesinnung noch mit der Wertung der anderen darf man leichtsinnig umgehen. Was man in jedem Gottesdienst sehen kann, wofern er einer ist, daß man behutsam mit Geräten, Gebärden, Worten umgeht, sollte verbindlich für alles sein, was man tagsüber tut. Man versteht es, weshalb jede Form der Religion auf Erziehung solchen Wert legt: keiner verhält sich „von selbst" richtig; jeder muß angeleitet werden, damit er nicht, indem er sich selbst vernachlässigt, andere schädigt, und umgekehrt, indem er andere schädigt, sich selbst verdirbt. Weder aber soll man sorgfältig sein, weil man sich selbst liebt, noch sorgfältig, weil man die anderen nicht verderben will, sondern deswegen, weil alle, die Menschen, die Dinge, die Vorgänge, das eine große Ganze bilden, das keiner versteht, das jeder nur ehrfürchtig wahrnehmen, handhaben und wertschätzen kann.

Das alles mag als schwierig, als fast undurchführbar erscheinen, und nach allem Anschein ist es das auch bis heute gewesen. Das braucht aber nicht immer so zu bleiben, und darf es auch nicht. Überdies ist es nicht so schwer, wie es erscheinen mag. Es gibt einen Anzeiger für das Richtige, den E. SÄNGER, der Raketenforscher, genau und klar gekennzeichnet hat. „Die Menschenseele enthält einen sicheren Kompaß, ihren Träger auf den richtigen Lebenshöchstwert und damit auf seinen richtigen Rang hinzuweisen: das Glücksempfinden. Der Mensch ist glücklich, der seinen angeborenen und durch seine ganze Anlage bestimmten alltäglichen Lebenshöchstwert klar erkannt hat und diesem voll leben kann" [1]. Wir sind noch weit davon entfernt, sowohl diesen Lebenshöchstwert zu erkennen, als auch davon, den erkannten zu befolgen. Wir behelfen uns derweil mit Geboten und Verboten, mit Grenzen und Schranken, mit Drohungen und Strafen. Wir sollten dazu kommen, einzusehen, daß das unwürdig ist; daß wir uns damit erniedrigen; daß wir dadurch den Lebenssinn verfehlen. Wir sollten auf das hören lernen, was das Wirkliche sagt, „auf Gott horchen", wie die alten geistlichen Lehrer sagten und die neuen besser verdeutlichen und einprägen sollten, als sie es tun. Wir sollten freier werden, indem wir uns mehr und

---

[1] E. SÄNGER, in: *Der Übermensch*, hrsg. v. E. BENZ, Zürich, 1961, 419.420.

endgültig an das Eigentliche binden. Wir sollten wissen und betätigen, daß uns nichts besseres geschehen kann, als glücklich zu sein. Dieser Kompaß ist verläßlich, wenn wir ihn zu lesen verstehen, und wer ihn zu lesen versteht, wird ihn auch befolgen.

4. Zusammenfassung. Religion entspringt dem, daß der Mensch nicht nur mechanisch und biologisch bestimmt sein will. Das bezeichnet zugleich, was sie zu leisten hat: als Gesamtheit der Grundgefühle das Leben erfüllen. Sie wurzelt in und besteht aus Angst und Vertrauen, Verlorenheit und Geborgenheit, Hingabe und Gegenwehr, Macht und Unterwerfung, Verehrung und Abstoßung, Erlösung und Vernichtung.

Anders: Religion ist Beziehungserlebnis der Ordnung. Unreligiös ist, wer ungeordnet ist, in sich, zur Welt, vor und in Gott. Er weiß nicht, oder wenn, er lebt nicht danach, daß Leben nur in Ordnung gedeihen kann, wobei es durchaus strittig sein kann, was der einzelne als Ordnung auffaßt: nicht aufgehoben wird dadurch, daß eine Ordnung sowohl vorgegeben als auch anzustreben ist.

Dieser Ordnung begegnet der Mensch zunächst in seiner Umwelt, in den Dingen und Menschen; diese führen ihn zu der Ordnung, die über den Menschen hinausgreift und als von Gott gesetzt erkannt und geachtet wird. Erst zuletzt erkennt der Mensch, daß die Ordnung auch innerhalb seiner zu gelten hat und dort am schwersten zu finden, zu halten, zu fördern, zu vergeistigen ist. Zu der Ordnung wird er zunächst von außen her hingeführt; er bejaht sie aber sehr bald, weil er wahrnimmt, wie sehr er auf sie eingestimmt ist und wie sehr er nach ihr verlangt, auch dann, wenn die seine von der der anderen abweicht. Insofern ist der Mensch von Natur aus religiös und bedarf keines Lehrers. Weil aber die Ordnung fast immer weiter greift, als der einzelne erfassen und bewältigen kann, ist er darauf angewiesen, von anderen eingeführt zu werden, und das ist, wenn es feierlich geschieht, die Einweihung, die allen Formen der Religion eigentümlich ist.

Dieser Einweihung, die durch andere geschieht, liegt zuvor diejenige Einweihung, die darin besteht, daß man dem Sein und Leben, dem Fordern und Warnen, dem Entbehren und Verlangen begegnet, sich selbst und den Menschen und Gott, dem Geheimnis des Daseins, dessen innezuwerden das Höchste für den Menschen darstellt. Das Dasein erweist sich nicht als hart und steif, sondern als weich und beweglich, als lebendig und immer wieder neu, als bezaubernd und berauschend, als erschreckend und verderbend — wenn man sich nicht einfügt und wenn man nicht eingeweiht ist.

Nur wenige sind es, welche den Weg allein suchen, weder das Dunkel noch das Licht fürchten, dem Guten und Bösen begegnen, sich selbst und dem Mitmenschen und dem Gott; welche die Weihe unmittelbar von Gott empfangen, wie Johannes und Jesus und in geringerem Maß die Künder des Ewigen, von denen die Menschen erfahren, als wie groß sie von Gott her gedacht sind und wie gering ihre Neigung ist, dem zu entsprechen.

Weil Religion Einweihung in das Leben ist, ist sie zugleich Zustand und Vorgang. Zustand der Einordnung in das, worin sich der einzelne Mensch vorfindet, und Vorgang als Hinwendung zu dem Ordnungssystem, das zwar vorgegeben, aber noch nicht erreicht ist. Weil den Menschen weitaus am meisten das beansprucht, was er noch nicht erreicht hat und ist, deswegen wird Religion fast ausschließlich als Vorgang definiert. Man sollte aber nicht übersehen, daß auch in einer Welt, die vollendet ist, christlich: nach der Parusie, Religion sein wird, und zwar als der Zustand der Ordnung, wie sie von Gott gewollt ist und gehalten wird, mit der inneren Zustimmung aller, als Einstimmung in das Ganze des Wirklichen und Geistigen. Die Hochform des Geistigen können wir Menschen uns kaum anders denn als Person vorstellen, und so vollendet sich für viele der Gottesbegriff im Personbegriff. Sofern damit gemeint ist, daß es eine Mitte gibt, die um sich weiß, alles aufeinander bezieht und werthaft durchdringt, wird dieser Personbegriff uneingeschränkt vom Göttlichen ausgesagt werden dürfen. Sofern aber Person als Ich-wesen begrenzt ist, muß man fordern, daß diese Personauffassung von Gott ferngehalten wird, so wie es alle diejenigen inbrünstig tun, die sich dagegen wenden, daß man den Unbegrenzten einenge, den Unendlichen umfange, den Undenkbaren begreifen könne.

Nimmt man Religion als Vorgang, so läßt sie sich bestimmen oder wenigstens beschreiben als Hinwendung zum letzt-erreichbaren Ordnungssystem, als bewußte Einordnung in die gesamte Wirklichkeit, als Wissen um Sein und Sinn, als Geneigtheit und Wille zu Forderung und Leistung. Nimmt man den Personbegriff, sofern er tragbar ist, hinzu, kann man Religion bestimmen als Zuwendung des Menschen zur personhaften Weltmitte, die gleichermaßen Ursprung und Halt und Ziel ist.

So heißt religiös sein, eingeweiht in das Leben zu sein, sich als

Glied und Werkzeug Gottes oder des Geistes oder des Ganzen zu wissen und zu erleben und zu betätigen.

Von dieser Einweihung sind alle anderen nur schwacher Abglanz und zaghafte Andeutung, wie der funkelnde Tautropfen von der Sonne.

EINWEIHUNG UND SPIRITUELLE NACHFOLGE

VON

MATTHIAS VERENO
Salzburg

Der Tod ist das „Urphänomen" aller Religion — und damit auch der Nachfolge als Verwirklichung der Religion im konkreten Leben, gewissermaßen in der „Horizontalen", ebenso wie der Initiation als deren Verwirklichung in der „Vertikalen". Von Platon ist das Wort überliefert: τελευτᾶν τελεῖσθαι, Sterben heißt initiiert werden. Τελεῖσθαι aber kommt von τέλος, „Ende", und so heißt es „vollendet werden", nämlich als Mensch. Der Mensch ist gegenüber dem Tier wesentlich durch sein anderes Verhältnis zum Tode gekennzeichnet. Nur er kennt Totenbestattung und Totengedenken. Für diese Aussage ist es unerheblich, ob es etwa der prähistorischen Forschung gelinge, eindeutig festzustellen, daß es in grauer Vorzeit Wesen gegeben habe, welche biologisch den späteren „Menschen" sehr ähnlich sahen und dennoch ihre Toten einfach liegen ließen. Es geht hier um die Wesensbestimmung des Menschen. „Tiere" kümmern sich um ihre Verstorbenen höchstens insoweit, als sie die Kadaver aus der Nähe der Lebenden wegschaffen (z.B. Bienen und Ameisen und, wie man sagt, Elefanten). „Menschen" treffen in der einen oder anderen Weise Vorsorge für das Tot-*sein* des Verstorbenen. Grenzfälle, die als solche umso lehrreicher sind, wären, daß man den Körper des Verstorbenen scheinbar unversorgt verwesen läßt, aber seiner Seele gedenkt, oder daß man in rein negativer Einstellung gegenüber dem Toten aus Angst vor schadenbringender Wiederkehr den Leichnam fesselt. Auch hier gilt die Sorge dem Zustand des Tot-seins. Und diese Sorge bezeugt das Bewußtsein, daß das Leben nicht mit dem Zerfall der physischen Leiblichkeit endet, daß das Wesen des Menschen nicht identisch ist mit der sichtbaren Tätigkeit seines individuellen Organismus. Solches nun ist „religiöses" Bewußtsein. Und wenn die Scholastiker den Menschen als *animal rationale* bestimmt haben, so möchte ich — wohl wissend, daß alle

„Definitionen" das Wesen nicht zur Gänze erfassen können — die Bezeichnung als *animal religiosum* für noch treffender halten.

Wo immer es Totenbestattung und Totengedenken gibt, gibt es Religion, d.h. bewußte Teilhabe an einem über-physischen, „jenseitigen" Leben. Dieses „andere" Leben beginnt nicht mit dem physischen Tot, „nachdem" das physisch-biologische Leben endete — sonst könnte man ja nicht von „weiter"-leben sprechen, wie es doch überall geschieht.

Es geht hierbei nicht um die Frage, ob man dieses Leben in einem individuellen Sinn verstehe, ob man ein unvergängliches „Ich" annehme oder leugne usw. Wir sprechen hier primär nicht vom Menschen, der lebt, sondern vom Leben, daran der Mensch (in welcher Gestalt auch immer) teilhat. In der Totenbestattung wird die Überzeugung bekundet, daß, während ein Aspekt des Lebens im Tod sein Ende findet, ein anderer Aspekt des Lebens gleichwohl weiterbestehe. Die Frage nach der Identität der Persönlichkeit oder Individualität steht in einem ganz anderen Zusammenhang. Das physisch-biologische Leben setzt sich fort in der Generationenfolge, ungeachtet der wechselnden Individualität. Wenn der Enkel dem Grab des Ahns Ehrfurcht erweist, so gibt er damit dem Bewußtsein Ausdruck, daß das „Leben" des Ahns nicht nur in seinem, des Enkels physischen Organismus weiterwähre, sondern auch noch in einer anderen Weise, und daß er, der Enkel, auch mit diesem „anderen" Leben des Ahns in geheimnisvoller Beziehung stehe. So wie das organische Leben des Enkels sein eigenes, individuelles ist und doch zugleich der Ahn organisch-biologisch in ihm lebt, so ist auch das „andere" Leben des Ahns zugleich das „andere" Leben des Enkels. Ahn und Enkel leben also in übersinnlicher gemeinsamer Teilhabe am anderen, „jenseitigen" Leben, das je nach der Kulturstufe in mehr oder weniger sinnlichen Gleichnissen erfahren bzw. vorgestellt wird.

Die griechische Sprache kennt zwei verschiedene Worte für „Leben": βίος und ζωή. Tatsächlich können beide Aspekte des „Lebens" als gesonderte Wirklichkeiten betrachtet werden, weil sie nicht mit Notwendigkeit zusammenfallen bzw. „parallellaufen". Es kann „künstlich" Verwandtschaft gestiftet werden — in der Ehe, in Blutsbrüderschaft und Adoption, in Gastfreundschaft, Vertrag, Staatengründung usw. Die „künstlichen Mittel", welche den Übertritt in eine neue „Lebens-Gemeinschaft" ermöglichen, sind rituelle Akte, kultische Zeremonien.

Kultische — d.h. aber: religiöse — Handlungen setzen also dort ein, wo für das Bewußtsein biologisches und über-biologisches, diesseitiges und jenseitiges Leben auseinandertreten. Wo die ursprüngliche Einheit beider Sphären zu zerbrechen droht, sollen sie eine neue Einheit stiften. Dies geschieht, indem jeweils der biologische Aspekt zugunsten des über-biologischen hintangesetzt, ja durch diesen außer Kraft gesetzt wird. Die neue Einheit wird zur neuen „Natur" — und damit auch zur Grundlage neuer Spaltung und neuer Versöhnung „von oben her". Diese Funktion bleibt dem religiösen Tun auf allen Stufen, die die Entwicklung des menschlichen Bewußtseins im Lauf der Jahrtausende gewonnen hat. Es kann also das religiöse Tun nicht „objektiv" an irgendeine Seins-Sphäre gebunden und mit ihr gleichgesetzt werden. Es ist, auf welcher Stufe auch immer, *Mittlung* zwischen zwei auseinandergetretenen Sphären; und jeweils wird deren eine vom Bewußtsein als „Natur", die andere als „Übernatur" erfahren.

Die Urerfahrung dieser Krisis — um nicht zu sagen: Katastrophe — des Bewußtseins, des Auseinanderfallens der Einheit und Ganzheit des Lebens, ist zweifellos der physische Tod. Dieser aber unterscheidet sich wesentlich von allen anderen „Spaltungs-Situationen", in denen kultisch-religiöses Handeln notwendig wird.

1. Er ist nicht nur eine einmalig-momentane Zäsur, die, nachdem sie mit Hilfe sakraler Handlungen überwunden ist, eine neue Lebensganzheit ermöglicht. Nach der Zäsur des Sterbens bleibt die Lücke des Tot-seins. Deshalb bedarf es nicht nur der „Übergangsriten", sondern einer unablässig währenden „Versöhnung" — was der Mensch von sich aus nicht leisten kann.

2. In anderen Fällen des Auseinandertretens beider Sphären ist dies mit einer willentlichen Entscheidung, einem absichtlichen Tun des Menschen verbunden. Die Krise des Todes ist absolut (d.h. wörtlich: „losgelöst") in dem Sinne, daß hier ein Geschehen überhand nimmt, das in keinem Verhältnis zu menschlicher Verursachung steht und dem (eben darum) auch kein menschliches Tun — als Widerstand, „Gegengift" oder Heilung — gewachsen ist.

Das Zerreißen der Einheit des Lebens im Bewußtsein ist die Voraussetzung aller „Religion", ja die fundamentale Gegebenheit des spezifisch menschlichen Bewußtseins schlechthin. Doch die Weise der Zerreißung, die im Tode geschieht, ist nicht nur graduell, sondern wesensmäßig tiefergreifend als alle anderen, weil *stricte verbo* nicht wiedergutzumachen. Darum kann auch Totschlag grundsätzlich nicht, wie andere Übertretungen, durch rituelle Handlungen, sondern nur durch den Tod gesühnt werden. (Wenn es Ersatzleistungen wie etwa Wergeld gibt, so bedeuten diese nicht eigentlich Ausgleich, „Versöhnung" des Totschlages, sondern Rückkauf des verwirkten eigenen Lebens bzw. des Lebens eines Sippenangehörigen oder der Gemeinschaft als solcher.)

Das Sterben ist die große „Sühne", Riten sind die kleinen Versöhnungen und Entsühnungen. Die Zeremonie versöhnt aktiv aktive Übertretung. Sie ist *objektives* Tun, Handeln aus den Zusammenhängen einer überindividuellen Ebene, um anderes Handeln, das auf der niedrigeren Ebene schuldhaft ist, weil es den Widerstreit zwischen beiden Ebenen aufreißt, auszugleichen bzw. aufzuheben.

Sterben dagegen ist der in höchsten Grade *subjektive* Aspekt, insofern der Mensch die Liquidation alter Zusammenhänge bewußt erleidet, um sich geläutert und entsühnt in neuen Zusammenhängen wiederzufinden. Hier gibt es nichts Vorherwißbares, nichts Gekonntes, nichts Objektives. Weil hier vom Subjekt, das dieses, den Tod, erleidet, etwas erfahren wird, das nicht, wie seine Aktivität, aus ihm selber erklärt werden kann, noch aus Objekten, so ist Sterben das Mysterium κατ' ἐξοχήν, dessen äußerer Aspekt jeweils mehr oder minder „objektive" Handlungen und Zeichen sein mögen.

„Sterben" bezeichnet hier ein Prinzip, das weit über den biologisch-physischen Tod hinaus wirksam ist. Es handelt sich um die Selbsterfahrung des Bewußtseins in seiner reinen Passivität — also jenseits dessen, daß es Träger, Grund und Zeuge unserer Akte ist. Solches Selbst-Bewußtsein ist aber etwas höchst Geheimnisvolles, etwas, was eigentlich die Grenzen der menschlichen Verfassung als solcher sprengt. Denn „menschlich" ist es, hinter jedem Geschehen einen Täter, einen Urheber zu gewahren. Auch in diesem besonderen Sinne ist die Todeserfahrung die Schwelle aller Religion, daß, wenn auch noch dieses äußerste Geschehen seinen Täter haben soll (das Geschehen des *Sterbens*, nicht etwa das des Totschlages als solchen), grundsätzlich nur ein über-menschlicher, ein göttlicher *auctor* in Frage kommt.

Zwischen dem subjektiven Leiden des Sterbens und dem objektiven Tun des Ritus bestehen nun mannigfache Beziehungen.

Wir sahen schon, daß das „andere" Leben, welches wir geradezu als das „Ahnen-Leben" bezeichnen können, in einem ganz bestimmten Sinne überindividuell ist. Jede organisch zusammengefaßte Gruppe — und damit auch jeder ihr angehörende Einzelne — steht in Verbindung mit „jenseitigen" Einflüssen besonderer Art, die gleichsam ihr psychisch-spirituelles Milieu bilden, ja ihr Leben ermöglichen. Die Harmonie dieses Lebens kann durch die „Geister" (wenn dieser Ausdruck hier, ohne sich mit näherer Erläuterung aufzuhalten, gebraucht werden darf) eines anderen Milieus empfindlich gestört, ja bedroht werden. Die Gruppen, die hier in Rede stehen, sind „Lebens-Gemeinschaften" nicht nur im Sinne gleichartiger Lebensführung ihrer Mitglieder, sondern in dem Sinne, daß alle gemeinsam dasselbe Leben besitzen oder an ihm teilhaben. Wer in eine neue Gemeinschaft eintritt, sei es Familie, Stamm oder Orden, muß rituell aus der alten Lebensgemeinschaft herausgelöst und in die neue eingegliedert werden. (Hieran erinnerten noch die Aufnahme-Zeremonien der Zünfte und Gilden, die ja nach bruderschaftlichem Vorbild organisiert waren.) Er muß einem Leben absterben, um einem anderen neugeboren zu werden. Hier wird der Doppelaspekt des Ritus besonders unmittelbar abschaulich: Er ist nicht nur — als das haben wir ihn zuvor betrachtet — aktive Sühne der Übertretung, sondern auch symbolischer Ausdruck von Tod und Wiedergeburt.

Solches gilt natürlich umso mehr, wenn bzw. in dem Grade als der Einweihungsritus nicht einen „horizontalen" Übertritt, sondern einen „vertikalen" Fortschritt zum Ausdruck bringt. In beiden Fällen handelt es sich um den Versuch, objektives Tun und subjektives Sterben miteinander zu verbinden. Es erscheint dann konsequent, wenn in höheren Einweihungen die Initiierten gelehrt werden, die genau festgelegten kultischen Handlungen — und nicht minder auch die formulierten Lehren — als Äußerlichkeiten anzusehen und in dem Maß, als das Bewußtsein mehr und mehr dieser Stützen und Hilfen entraten kann, sich auf den inneren Vorgang als auf das Wesentliche zu konzentrieren. Es handelt sich hier um ein in mystisch-esoterischen Zirkeln und Orden weit verbreitetes Prinzip; und es ist bekannt, daß es in der Praxis immer wieder zu Mißbräuchen und Ausartungen geführt hat — indem Menschen in größerem Maße das Äusserlich-Objektive für sich außer Kraft setzten, als sie durch inneren Tod und Wiedergeburt, d.h. durch bewußt erlittenes Reifen, dazu „berechtigt" gewesen wären.

Gegenüber der hier drohenden Gefahr des Libertinismus und einer „pneumatischen" Willkür, die für jede Gesellschaft gefährlicher ist als die gewöhnliche, äußerliche Willkür und Gewalttätigkeit, versuchen die Vertreter des Kultes ihr Recht zu behaupten. Dabei müssen sie keineswegs das Prinzip der inneren Erafhrung, der Bewußtseinswandlung verneinen. Vielmehr erscheint dieses in den höheren Religionsformen überall selbstverständlich und grundsätzlich anerkannt, wenn es auch durch die äußere Praxis für eine einfältigere Anschauung oft schwer zu erkennen ist. So lehrt etwa die Katholische Kirche, daß das Buß-Sakrament, um zu seiner objektiven Wirkung zu kommen, der „aufrichtigen Reue" (also der inneren Erfahrung und Umkehr) notwendig bedürfe, daß aber umgekehrt, im Falle kein Priester zu erreichen ist, die Erweckung aufrichtiger Reue genüge, um die objektive Gnadenwirkung des Sakramentes herbeizuführen — allerdings bedarf es dann der sogenannten „vollkommenen" oder Liebes-Reue, d.h. des im eigentlichen Sinne *pneumatischen* Vollzuges. Die Ablehnung der pseudo-pneumatischen These, es handle sich bei den Kulthandlungen nur um „exoterische" Formen, die für den „Wissenden" gegenstandslos würden, — die Ablehnung dieser These bedeutet nicht, daß hier die äußere Handlung über die innere Erfahrung gestellt werde, sondern nur, daß man an dem Prinzip der *Kult*handlung festhalte. Sobald das *opus operatum* dem *opus operantis* weicht, gibt es weder Kult noch Ritus, sondern nur subjektive Ethik bzw. letztlich unwesentliches Ornament.

Auch die Brahmanen haben an der Idee der objektiven Wirkung ihrer Kulthandlungen festgehalten, ohne deshalb das Prinzip der inneren Erfahrung (des „Sterbens") zu verleugnen. Aber gerade sie haben mit bewundernswerter Konsequenz das Problem zu Ende gedacht. Man anerkannte keineswegs einen Vorrang des subjektiven Tuns vor dem objektiven, aber man räumte die Möglichkeit ein, daß eine innere Erfahrung jenen äußersten Grad der Totalität und Ausschließlichkeit erreiche, wo sie reine Passivität werden muß: Der *jîvanmukta*, der „Lebend-Erlöste", der dem Bereich alles objektiven Handelns (alles Rituals und damit aller gesellschaftlichen Bezüge) entwachsen ist, kann — zumindest in der Sphäre irdischmenschlicher Zusammenhänge — *nichts tun*; sein scheinbares Tun ist ja kein *karman*, kein „Werk". Von ihm sagt Shankara: „Einer, der im Wachen, als wäre er im tiefen Schlafe, keine Zweiheit sieht, auch wenn er sie sieht, und der nicht mehr handelt, auch wenn er handelt" [1].

---

[1] Upadeshasâhasrî 10, 13, Vedântasâra 234, zitiert bei H. v. GLASENAPP; *Der Stufenweg zum Göttlichen*, Baden-Baden 1948, S. 60.

Alles Ritual, das nicht eine innere Umwandlung des Menschen begleitet, ist Bannung von Kräften einer äußeren Natur und in diesem Sinne Magie. Der Kultpriester der höchststehenden Religion ebenso wie der Medizinmann der primitivsten ist entweder Hierophant, Mystagoge oder „Magier", d.h. Exorzist.

Ist das Ziel der bannenden Zeremonie (der Magie) Erhaltung bzw. Regeneration des Bestehenden, Heilung der Natur, Verteidigung der Gesellschaft gegen von außen kommende, wahrhaft „negative" Mächte, so dient die Kulthandlung, die an innere Umwandlung, an bewußtes Sterben und Wieder-auferstehen gebunden ist, dem geistigen Fortschritt des Einzelnen wie der Gemeinschaft, der Verwirklichung (d.h. dem Zur-Wirkung-bringen) immer höherer Bewußtseinsstufen auf der Ebene des konkreten, des geschichtlichen Daseins. Nur durch die Verbindung von objektiven, durch Konvention festgelegten Zeichen (wozu nicht nur Kulthandlung und -bild, sondern auch die heilige Lehre gehört) und innerer Erfahrung, d.h. Sterben und Wiedergeburt, kann das eigentliche Prinzip aller geistigen Traditionsbildung und damit auch aller religiösen „Nachfolge" zu suchen sein. Es ist bemerkenswert, daß in den höheren Religionen der Kult seinen Schwerpunkt auf die Riten, die mit innerem Tod und Bewußtseinswandlung verbunden sind, verlegt, wogegen das bannende, exorzistische Element vergleichsweise zurück tritt.

Die Nachfolge ist die Fortpflanzung jenes Lebens, das der Zäsur, der Begrenzung durch den physisch-biologischen Tod nicht unterworfen ist. Auch an diesem anderen Leben, ebenso wie am organisch-individuellen, hat der Mensch unmittelbar und selbstverständlich teil. Das organische Leben bekundet sich durch körperliche Bewegung und erhält bzw. erneuert sich durch Ernährung (Stoffwechsel). Für die Fortpflanzung aber bedarf es 1. eines nicht ohne weiteres gegebenen Vermögens, 2. eines durch dieses ermöglichten willentlichen Aktes. Die Reife zum im biologischen Sinn ganz „seienden", selbständigen Menschen ist das Ergebnis organischer Entwicklung; Krankheit (hier also Impotenz) ist entweder Steckenbleiben auf einer unreifen Entwicklungsstufe oder Rückfall, Abfall vom organischen Voll- und Ganz-sein. In dieser Entwicklung gibt es Krisen, die wohl als Gleichnisse des am Ende des individuellorganischen Lebens stehenden Todes aufgefaßt werden können — als Kundgebung und Wirkung dieser Todes-Grenze innerhalb des Lebens. Die einscheidendste Krise des organischen Lebens ist eben jene, die der Fortpflanzungsreife vorausgeht, die Pubertät.

Die Befähigung zur Weitergabe jenes über-biologischen Lebens, dessen eigentliche Wirklichkeit der Begrenzung durch das Sterben des Organismus entrückt ist, „jenseits" dieses Sterbens liegt, muß demnach durch eine „Reife" erreicht werden, welche nicht nur den „Tod" der Pubertätskrise, sondern die Überwindung jenes Todes, der dessen Ur-Wirklichkeit ist, des Todes, der das biologische Leben als solches insgesamt begrenzt, zur Voraussetzung hat. Mit anderen Worten: Volle Verfügung über die „Funktionen" des über-biologischen Lebens hat, wer dem biologischen Leben *gestorben* ist. Daß solches möglich ist — nämlich während der Dauer des biologischen Lebens-, ist ein Beweis, daß es sich bei den „verschiedenen" Leben nicht um eine zeitliche Aufeinanderfolge, sondern um eine Überschichtung, besser: Ineinanderfügung und Durchdringung handelt. Nichtsdestoweniger, ja gerade deswegen ist der „Mysterientod" deutlich von der Entwicklungskrise zu unterscheiden: Er muß von einem im eigentlichen Sinne spirituellen Element bewirkt und geführt, auf dieses muß er gerichtet sein. Das Spirituell-„Übernatürliche" wirkt in doppelter Weise:

1. manifestiert es sich in einem äußeren Aspekt — der objektiv-konventionellen Handlung, der Weihe- oder Initiations-zeremonie;

2. aber in einem inneren Aspekt — einer höheren Stufe der Bewußtheit.

In der biologischen Entwicklungskrise ist das Bewußtsein weitgehend in dem Vorgang selber befangen; der Mensch kann ihn nicht „von außen" betrachten, er *weiß* nicht, was ihm, was mit ihm geschieht. In dem „Tod", der die Voraussetzung für die Fähigkeit, das andere, höhere Leben fortzupflanzen, ist, muß das Bewußtsein in gewisser Weise distanziert sein, um den Vorgang als solchen wahrzunehmen (was nicht heißt, daß der Mensch sich begrifflich-reflex „Gedanken" darüber machen müsse). Das deutsche Wort „Erfahren" faßt die Bedeutungen von „Erleiden" und „erkennen" zusammen. Wenn aber in Mysterientod und Einweihung das Bewußtsein solchermaßen von den reinen, inneren Vorgängen gesondert sein kann und muß, so schließt dieses die *Freiheit* gegenüber solchem Geschehen ein. Das Reif-werden für die Fortpflanzungsordnung des über-biologischen Lebens geschieht nicht von selbst, es ist vielmehr mit einem bewußten *Eintreten* in diese Ordnung verbunden. Nicht nur die Umwandlung, welche der organischen (physischen und psychischen) Entwicklungskrise entspricht, wird bewußt vollzogen, sondern auch die Vorbereitung dazu. Meist wird sie in Form eines

Unterrichtes erfolgen — so wie heute noch Ehe- oder Konfirmanden-Unterricht.

Wir können in dem über-biologischen Leben zwei Tendenzen unterscheiden, insofern seine Richtung der des biologischen Lebens zuwiderläuft oder mit ihr parallel geht, aber auf höherer Ebene — wobei wir uns freilich der Vorläufigkeit und Gleichnishaftigkeit solcher Bilder bewußt bleiben müssen. Die zweitgenannte ist die schöpferische, die erstgenannte die asketische Tendenz. Jene ist stärker auf die Gemeinschaft bezogen, diese stärker auf den Einzelnen. Jene zielt — im geistigen Umkreis der Hochreligionen — auf Erlösung *der* Welt, diese auf Erlösung *von* der Welt. Jeder inspirierte Impuls, der der Menschheit auf ihrem geschichtlichen Weg eine neue Richtung weist, bedeutet, daß das Bewußtsein des Verhältnisses zwischen Welt und Transzendenz eine Änderung erfahre. Aber in *jedem* Bewußtsein eines Verhältnisses der Welt zur Transzendenz sind notwendigerweise beide erwähnten Richtungen oder Pole wirksam.

Es kann darum auch nie einfachhin nur die eine oder die andere Nachfolge-Richtung geben. Nicht nur sind in jeder Religion, vor allem in jedem hochreligiösen System, beide Tendenzen enthalten, sondern dies gilt auch für jeden einzelnen, individuellen und augenblicklichen Nachfolge-Akt. Das andere, das spirituelle Leben ist eben überhaupt nicht in angemessener Weise als eine Linie vorzustellen, welche der Linie des biologischen Lebens parallel liefe — in dieser oder in jener Richtung. Es kann nur als eine höhere *Dimension* verstanden werden, welche die niedrigere Dimension sowohl ermöglicht als auch aufhebt (nämlich im Auswirken ihrer Eigengesetzlichkeit). Der *âtman* bzw. das *nirvâna* heben den *saṁsâra* auf, aber sie können auch als Ermöglichung seiner Manifestation verstanden werden. Die ζωὴ αἰώνιος ist, nicht nur lebendig in der Manifestation des natürlichen Lebens sondern sie setzt auch dessen Eigengesetzlichkeit außer Kraft. Besser als das Bild zweier Parallelen wäre also, um den Dimensionsunterschied im Verhältnis der beiden „Leben" zueinander anzudeuten, das Bild des Rechten Winkels.

Τελευτᾶν τελεῖσθαι — jeder Dimensionswechsel ist ein „Tod"; jedes Sterben ist ein Dimensionswechsel. Die niedrigere Dimension, die bisher „etwas" war, wird „nichts", ist der Grenzwert Null vom Standpunkt der neuen Dimension. Jedes Eintreten in eine spirituelle Nachfolge ist eine Initiation, ein Mysterientod, d.h. ein Dimensionswechsel im Bewußtsein.

Und damit gewahren wir die Unzulänglichkeit auch des eben gegebenen Bildes des Rechten Winkels. Es gibt ja viele „Initiationen", viele „Tode". Rituelle Esoterik hat die Zahl der Initiationen verschieden festgesetzt. Doch da es sich um innere Vorgänge handelt, können sie von solch äußerer Fixierung nicht in objektiv-verbindlicher Weise definiert, d.h. „begrenzt" werden. Das Bild des Rechten Winkel drückt nur aus, daß einer Linie, die in ihrer von Anfang an gegebenen Ebene bleibt, eine andere gegenübersteht, welche in ihrer Bewegung dauernd neue Ebenen gewinnt. Was aber, in optischer Veranschaulichung, als Unterschied zweier Ebenen bezeichnet wird, bedeutet eigentlich den Unterschied zweier Dimensionen. Wollten wir in der Senkrechten des Rechten Winkels wiederum einen Rechten Winkel anbringen, und dann wieder einen, usw., so würden wir in die Bereiche einer schlechterdings unanschaulichen, aber auch begrifflich unfaßlichen Vieldimensionalität geraten.

Und so bleibt denn das Einzige, worauf wir die große *complexio oppositorum* (die Vereinigung der Gegensätze) zurück führen können, welche für unser Bewußtsein das Verhältnis der Welt zur Transzendenz darstellt, das Mysterium des Todes — jenes Todes, der im Osten wie in Westen der Beginn und die Pforte aller lebendigen Religion ist [1]).

---

[1]) Vgl. zu Vorstehendem VERENO, *Das Wesen der spirituellen Nachfolge*. Eine vergleichende Betrachtung unter besonderer Berücksichtigung der großen Erlösungsreligionen des Ostens und Westens. KAIROS — *Religionswissenschaftliche Studien* (Nr. 2), Otto Müller Verlag, Salzburg 1965.

DAS FASTEN ALS INITIATIONSRITUS

VON

PETER GERLITZ

Bremerhaven

Im allgemeinen ist man der Ansicht, die Nahrungsaskese stelle nur ein apotropäisch-kathartisches Phänomen innerhalb der Religionsgeschichte dar und habe keine eigentlich kultische Funktion. Diese Ansicht muss aber sofort korrigiert werden, wenn wir das Fasten unter dem Aspekt der *Initiation* betrachten. Hier tritt es nämlich aus dem typischen Rahmen des Askese heraus und wird Mittel zum Zweck.

Neben den Hauptfastenpraktiken in der Religionsgeschichte, die sich im Laufe der Zeit zu kultisch nachvollziehbaren Riten entwickelt haben, wie z.B. das Trauerfasten oder das grosse kollektive Ritual des jüdischen Versöhnungsfestes (jôm hakippûrîm), der christlichen Quadragesima (τεσσαρακοστή) und des islamischen Fastenmonats Ramaḍān, lassen sich drei Typen feststellen, die dem Fasten den Charakter eines Vorbereitungsaktes für die Initiation verleihen. Natürlich stellt die Nahrungsaskese nur einen Teilaspekt in Bezug auf die Initiation dar; sie bedingt sie aber wesentlich; ja, in einigen Fällen ist sie sogar eine der Voraussetzungen für die Initiation.

(1) Der erste Typus hat noch eine apotropäisch-magische Funktion und kann als *jejunium praeparationis* bezeichnet werden. Da der Mensch in seiner Ganzheit, also als Leib und Seele, sich im Spannungsfeld dämonischer Kräfte befindet, steht er in ständiger Gefahr. Jeden Augenblick kann die böse Macht in ihn eindringen und die Kommunikation mit den guten, wohlgesinnten Geistern zunichte machen. Wenn die dämonischen Mächte Unheil anrichten und den Menschen schädigen, so wird dadurch nicht nur der Zustand der kultischen ἀγνεία gestört, sondern auch die Verbindung mit der Gottheit unterbrochen. Die Gottheit will aber den kultisch *reinen* Menschen. Deshalb muss der Mensch bemüht sein, dem Bösen eine möglichst geringe Angriffsfläche zu bieten, um so die Gefahr auf ein Mindest-

mass zu beschränken [1]). Auch von der Nahrung gehen bestimmte Kraftwirkungen aus, die leibliche oder seelische Schäden verursachen können. Das Fasten nun vermag neben anderen asketischen Übungen Unreines fernzuhalten, die eigenen Kräfte zu vergrössern und sogar in die Ekstase zu führen [2]). Atharvavēda V, 29, 6-8 gibt die Anweisung, dass bei heiligen Anlässen gefastet werden solle, damit die Dämonen nicht in den essenden Menschen einschlüpfen können. Und Plutarch [3]) meint sogar, dass die Fastenriten „δαιμόνων δὲ φαύλων ἀποτροπῆς ἕνεκα" begangen würden. Als Begründung wird einfach angegeben: Wenn die Dämonen nichts zu essen bekommen, dann verlassen sie den ungastlichen Körper [4]). Auf diese Weise erfolgt eine Tabuisierung.

Zahlreich sind nun die Beispiele, in denen das Fasten oder ein Teilfasten (semijejunium, die partielle Nahrungsaskese oder die Enthaltung von gewissen Speisen) eines von mehreren asketischen Phänomenen beim *Pubertätsritus* ist. So gehört für die Indianerstämme im nordwestlichen Waldgebiet Südamerikas etwa (Otomaken, Saliva, Tikuna und Konibo) das Fasten zur Vorbereitung für die Beschneidung [5]). Bei den australischen Encounterbaistämmen schleppen die Männer die Knaben an einen entfernten Ort, wo sie neben anderen Zeremonien auch 3 Tage und 3 Nächte fasten müssen [6]). W. SCHMIDT [7]) berichtet, dass die Knaben der Yuki-Indianer im Herbst durch Holzlöcher in das Tanzhaus hereingelassen werden, wo sie bis zum Frühjahr eingesperrt bleiben. Dabei müssen sie zunächst 4 Tage lang fasten und dürfen die übrige Zeit nur karge Nahrung zu sich nehmen. Während dieser Klausur werden sie vom Häuptling unterrichtet. Aber auch nach der Klausur besteht für sie ein einjähriges Abstinenzgebot für Fleisch und Fisch. Auch der Stamm der Yamana auf dem Feuerland führt ein ausserordentliches Fasten als Vorbereitung für die Jugendweihe durch[8]) Als Begründung für derartiges Fasten wird hier — wie bei anderen Mannbarkeitsriten

---

[1]) Siehe hierzu P. GERLITZ, *Das Fasten im religionsgeschichtlichen Vergleich*, philos. Diss., Erlangen 1954 (Masch. schr.), p. 7.

[2]) *Archiv Religionswiss.* XIV, 267.

[3]) *De Defectu Oraculorum* 417 C (ed. Bernardakis, 1889 ff./III, 88); vgl. F. J. DÖLGER, *Antike und Christentum* III, Münster 1932, p. 160 f.

[4]) *Pseudoclementinische Homilien* IX, 10 (*MPG* II, 248 f.).

[5]) BUSCHAN, *Illustrierte Völkerkunde* I, 2. ed., Stuttgart 1922, 267.

[6]) Vgl. auch FRAZER, *The Golden Bough*, London 1919-22, 3. ed., III, 205 ff.

[7]) *Ursprung der Gottesidee*, Münster 1912-52, V, 2, 66; vgl. p. 19.

[8]) W. SCHMIDT, *l.c.*, II, 2, 616; vgl. Pater KOPPERS, *Unter Feuerland-Indianern*, Stuttgart 1924, 41-100.

— die Härteprobe genannt; d.h. die Jugendlichen sollen abgehärtet
werden für den Fall, dass das Trinkwasser knapp wird oder Hungers-
nöte ausbrechen [1]). Aber damit hat man bereits dem Mythus eine
rationalisierende Interpretation gegeben. Tatsächlich wird hier die
Verbindung von *Initiation* und *Vision* so stark, dass man geradezu
von einem „Erfasten" der Gnade sprechen muss. D.h.: Mit dem neuen
Lebensabschnitt, der Mannbarkeit, tritt der Initiand zugleich auch in
das Stadium einer tieferen Einsicht in die Dinge ein. Es folgt eine Art
Horizonterweiterung in numinoser Hinsicht. Möglicherweise kommt
die naive Vorstellung hinzu, dass der Initiand durch sein Fasten einen
hilflosen Eindruck machen möchte, um damit Mitleid bei der Gottheit zu erregen. Wichtiger aber scheint die Erklärung zu sein, dass
ein fastender Mensch, der den irdischen Bereich durch Fasten und
Gebet eine Weile hinter sich gelassen hat, aufnahmebereit wird für die
Weisungen der Gottheit. So z.B. erklärt sich das Fasten nach der
Aufnahmezeremonie als Brahmanenschüler: Der Schüler muss
stehend und schweigend den Rest des Tages verbringen und darf
zunächst 3 Tage lang nichts Gesalzenes essen. Sodann, ehe ihm ein
als heilig geltender Teil des Lehrplanes übergeben wird, muss er
„mit verbundenen Augen, schweigend, sich 3 Tage lang bzw. einen
Tag und eine Nacht lang der Speise enthalten" [2]). Hier wird bereits
die Nähe zu anderen Initiationsriten, z.B. zum frühchristlichen
Taufexorzismus und zur prophetischen Nahrungsaskese, deutlich:
Man erwartet visionäre Erlebnisse, die während der Zeit des Hun-
gerns über den Gläubigen kommen sollen.

(2) Der zweite Typus des Fastens vor der eigentlichen Initiation
kann als *jejunium sacramentale* bezeichnet werden. Es wird sowohl
vor der Taufe als auch vor dem (ersten) Sakramentsempfang geübt.
Vor der *Taufe*, insofern sie im Grunde einen Initiationsritus darstellt.

Im Tauffasten, dem jejunium baptismum, begegnen sich sowohl der
apotropäisch-kathartische wie der präparative Typus des Fastens. Es
ist bezeichnend, dass gerade die Nahrungsaskese einen notwendigen
Bestandteil des Taufexorzismus darstellt. So ging beispielsweise
dem Taurobolium, das an den Mysten des phrygischen Attis vollzogen wurde, eine Speiseenthaltung in der Form der νηστεία voran [3]).

---

[1]) W. Schmidt, *l.c.*, VI, 2, 132. 135. 359.

[2]) [1]) Gobhila III, 10, 45. 47 und III, 2, 37; siehe auch H. Oldenberg,
Die Religion des Veda, 4. ed., 1923, 411.

[3]) Dazu vor allen Dingen R. Arbesmann, Das Fasten bei den Griechen und
Römern", in: RVV XXI, 1. Heft, Giessen 1929.

Dieses antike Taufsakrament diente dem Ziele, alle Schuld abzu-
waschen und die Wiedergeburt zu vollziehen. Dabei spielte das
Fasten eine hervorragende Rolle. Denn beim Empfang des Sakramentes müssen die Dämonen durch einen intensiven Exorzismus
vertrieben werden. Das Heilige darf nicht gefährdet sein.

Genau die gleiche Vorstellung finden wir bei *Gregor von Nazianz*,
wenn er bezüglich der christlichen Taufe sagt [1]): Jede sündigende
Seele und jede Seele des Ungetauften ist von bösen Geistern bewohnt.
Bei der Taufe jedoch irrt der Dämon unbehaust umher. — Es wird
deshalb deutlich, warum aus Furcht vor den umherirrenden Dämonen gefastet werden muss — und natürlich auch sexuelle Ent-
haltsamkeit geübt werden muss: die Taufe ist ja ein Geist mitteilender
Ritus (Handauflegung!), und das heisst, dass der Heilige Geist da
nicht Wohnung nehmen kann, wo die Dämonen zuhause sind. Der
Täufling müsse ja sonst befürchten, dass diese Dämonen mit ins
Taufbad steigen [2])! Ursprünglich war man der Meinung, dass die
Taufe *selber* die Dämonenaustreibung vornähme. Das ist ja auch ihr
eigentlicher Sinn.

Aber im Laufe der Zeit muss sich *vor* der Taufe ein besonderer
Exorzismus, zu dem neben Nachtwachen und sexueller Askese, Busse
und Reue, vor allem das Fasten gehörte, eingeschoben haben [3]).
Der erste Beleg für ein Tauffasten findet sich wohl Didache 7, 4; dort
wird nämlich verlangt, dass sowohl Täufer wie Täufling ein Fasten
vor der Submersion durchzumachen haben. Als Dauer werden ein
bis zwei Tage genannt, bei den Ebioniten sogar drei bis zehn Tage [4]).
Schon Justin der Märtyrer aber greift die neutestamentliche Tauf-
praxis wieder auf und spricht nicht mehr von den Dämonen, sondern
von den Sünden, die „ausgetrieben" werden müssen [5]): Die Baptizan-
den sollen angehalten werden, Gebete zu verrichten und unter Fasten
Gott um Verzeihung für ihre früheren Sünden zu bitten . . . Mittler-
weile war es üblich geworden, fast ausschliesslich an Passah zu taufen,
und so wurde auch das Fasten der Täuflinge zu einer Vorbereitung
auf diesen Tag hin [6]), ja, verschmolz geradezu mit der österlichen

---

[1]) *Oratio* 40 *in Sanctum Baptismum*, cp. 35 (MPG 36, 409); vgl. Cyprian, *De lapsis* 25 etc.
[2]) CLEMENS, *Excerpta ex script. Theodoti* 84, ed. STÄHLIN, GCS 3, 132.
[3]) Dazu der Vf. *l.c.*, p. 109.
[4]) *Pseudoclementin. Homilien* III, 73; XI, 33.
[5]) JUSTIN, *Apologie* I, 61, 2.
[6]) GREGOR, *Orat* 40, 31 (MPG 36, 401 f.).

Quadragesima [1]), in der so wie so gefastet wurde. Erstmalig wird für das Tauffasten auch eine Erklärung aus dem Bereich der Ekstase gegeben. Tertullian sagt De jejunio 8 [2]): Das Fasten rufe den heiligen Geist herab.

Um 400 muss die Nahrungsaskese im Westen fester Bestandteil des Taufritus gewesen sein, denn Augustin sagt De fide et operibus VI, 8 [3]): „si per ipsos dies quibus eandem gratiam percepturi suis nominibus datis abstinentia ieiuniis, exorcismisque purgantur". Unmittelbar *vor* der Taufe wurden den Katechumenen dann die sogenannten Exorzismusspeisen Brot, Salz und Wasser (oder Öl) gereicht [4]). Schon F. Jos. DÖLGER [5]) hat darauf hingewiesen, dass auch diese aus der Fastenpraxis abzuleiten sind: Brot und Wasser reinigen die Seelen, Salz gilt als Dämonen vertreibendes Mittel. — Erst der Getaufte durfte das Fasten durch den Genuss von Milch und das Zaubermittel Honig brechen [6]).

Auch in späterer Zeit wurde von heidnischen Taufbewerbern eine lange Fastenzeit verlangt, bevor sie zur Taufe zugelassen wurden. So berichtet *Socrates Ecclesiasticus* [7]), dass noch um 440 ein gallischer Bischof an 3000 burgundischen Soldaten, die gegen die Hunnen kämpfen sollten, die Taufe erst dann vollzog, nachdem diese 7 Tage lang gefastet hatten!

Im Book of Common Prayer findet sich übrigens die Angabe [8]), dass sich auch heute noch in der anglikanischen Kirche erwachsene Taufkandidaten durch Fasten und Gebet auf die Taufe vorzubereiten hätten. Vom Charakter des eigentlichen jejunium baptismum ist jetzt natürlich nichts mehr zu spüren.

Zu dem Phänomen des jejunium sacramentale gehört nun aber auch das *Fasten vor dem Opfermahl* bzw. vor dem Empfang der Eucharistie. Der Sinn einer solchen Nahrungsaskese besteht offenbar darin, dass man sich einerseits mit einem gefüllten Magen nicht der Gottheit nähern möchte und andererseits bestrebt ist, das Opferfleisch rein und unvermengt in den Magen zu bekommen. Das Heilige muss unbedingt vom Profanen abgegrenzt werden. So ist z.B. bekannt, dass

---

[1]) CYRILL, *In praefat.*, cp. 4.
[2]) CSEL 20, 284.
[3]) CSEL 41, 43.
[4]) *Ägyptische Kirchenordnung*, cp. 48 u. 50 (FUNK, *Didasc.* II, 113=can. 20).
[5]) *Der Exorzismus im altchristlichen Taufritual*, Paderborn 1909, p. 88.
[6]) TERTULLIAN, *De corona*, cp. 3.
[7]) *Historia Ecclesiastica* VII, 30 (ed. HUSSEY, Oxford 1860).
[8]) Vgl. *Encyclop. of Religion and Ethics* (ed. HASTINGS, 1908 ff.) V, 770.

südamerikanische und afrikanische Naturvölker sogar Brech- und Abführmittel anwenden, um die heiligen Speisen gegenüber den profanen abzuwehren und sich deren volle Wirkungskraft zu sichern [1] Das Fasten vor dem Opfermahl wird also als eine Art Purgativ gebraucht, welches die kultische Reinheit und damit die Urverbundenheit mit der Gottheit wieder herstellen soll. Die unheilvolle Macht muss ausgestossen und die heilvolle angeeignet werden [2].

Auch hier geht es letzten Endes um die Vorbereitung auf eine Kommunikation zwischen Gott und Mensch, welche sich in der Speisegemeinschaft vollzieht. Es handelt sich dabei insofern um eine Art Initiationsritus, als es um eine Hineinnahme des Fastenden in den Bereich der Gottheit geht. Man fastet solange, bis die heilige Mahlfeier das Speisetabu löst. So setzt z.B. das Trinken des Kykeon-Trunkes (ein Mischtrank aus Gerste) anlässlich der eleusinischen Mysterien eine 9-tägige Nahrungsaskese voraus, die erst mit den Worten des Mysten: „ἐνήστευσα, ἔπιον τὸν κυκεῶνα" gebrochen ist [3].

Auch vor den Kommunionsfeiern der Eingeborenen der Pentecost-Inseln (Neuhebriden), an denen der Kavatrunk gereicht wird, fastet man [4]. desgleichen enthielten sich die alten Mexikaner vor dem Genusse des berühmten Sakraments des Huitzilopochtli einen Tag lang der Speise [5]. Ältere Forscher wie W. R. SMITH [6] erklären das Fasten als "primarily nothing more than a preparation for sacramental eating of the holy flesh".

In die Kategorie des Fastens vor einem für den weiteren Lebensweg entscheidenden Sakrament aber gehört auch die *vedischa Dīkshā*, die Weihe des Opferers, welche vor dem Somaopfer stattfindet. Die Verabreichung dieses Sakraments gilt als das Zeichen einer Neugeburt. Dabei sollen die Opfernden sogar „gegen die Gefahr der heiligen Substanzen und Potenzen" geschützt werden [7]. Bei der Dīkshā wird der Opferer gebadet, gesalbt, geschoren und setzt sich am Opferfeuer nieder. Eine der zur Weihe gehörenden Observanzen ist die Herbeiführung der völligen physischen Erschöpfung mit dem sogenannten

---

[1] FRAZER, *l.c.*, V, 2, 73. 75 ff. 83 f.; vgl. KAHLE in *ARW* 12 (1909), p. 145 f.
[2] Dazu Fritz BAMMEL, *Das heilige Mahl im Glauben der Völker*, Gütersloh 1950, 181.
[3] *Homerici Hymni* (ed. ALLEN, 1911), 47; NAUCK, *Eleusis*, Berlin 1922, p. 227 ff.; Karl KERÉNYI, *Die Mysterien von Eleusis*, Zürich 1962, p. 72.
[4] *Reallexikon der Vorgeschichte*, Berlin 1924 ff. (EBERT), III, 192, Art. Fasten.
[5] *Enc. of Rel. and Ethics* V, 761.
[6] *Religion of Semites*, London 1894, 2. ed., p. 434; siehe Vf. *l.c.*, p. 112.
[7] CHANTEPIE *Lehrbuch* II, 49.

„Atemfasten". Dadurch werden ekstatische Zustände herbeigeführt [1]). Als Mittel werden Schweigen und Fasten benutzt. Nach dem Šatapatha-Brāhmana IX, 5, 1, 1 ff. IX, 5, 1, 6 bilden sogar Fasten und Erschöpfung und die Behinderung der Atmungsorgane die Hauptelemente der Dīkshā, bis sich die ekstatische Verzückung in der stammelnden Sprache des Mysten ankündigt.

Schliesslich gehört in diesen Zusammenhang auch das Fasten vor der *christlichen Eucharistie*, das jejunium eucharisticum. Da es sich bei der christlichen Eucharistie nicht um ein blosses Teilnehmen an der Opfermahlzeit handelt, sondern um ein tatsächliches Vorhandensein der Gottheit *in* dieser Mahlzeit, wird das Numinose an diesem Phänomen um ein Vielfaches gesteigert. Nun muss man aber wissen, dass im Christentum schon ein Fasten aus Trauer um den Tod Christi (am Karfreitag) und ein Fasten als Vorbereitung auf die Osterzeit (die Quadragesima) üblich war. Dazu tritt jetzt ein Fasten vor dem Empfang der Eucharistie. Besonders streng ist man bei der Einhaltung gerade dieser Praxis dann gewesen, wenn es sich um eine „Erstkommunion" handelte, also um einen Ritus der Initiation.

Zu der Reinigungs- und Busszeremonie, die der Kommunion vorangeht, gehört es, dass der Leib und das Blut nüchtern — und das heisst: bevor man profane Nahrung zu sich genommen hat! — empfangen werden muss. Die Geschichte dieser Einrichtung geht ins dritte Jahrhundert oder gar noch weiter zurück [2]). Die Kommunion wurde oft sehr spät abends gefeiert, damit die Leute bis dahin fasteten; erst das heilige Mahl konnte das Fasten brechen [3]). Der Canon 29 des 3. Konzils von Nicäa [4]) scheint das Kommunionsfasten endgültig zum Gesetz erhoben zu haben. Es heisst dort: „placuit ut sacramenta altaris non nisi a jejuniis hominibus celebrentur" [5]). Auch *Augustin* kennt den Brauch und hält ihn für eine weltweite Verpflichtung [6]), weil es die Ehre eines derartigen Sakraments einfach erfordere, dass der Leib des Herrn *vor* der profanen Speise in den Mund eines Christen gelange! Die römisch-katholische Kirche legte noch bis vor kurzem Wert darauf, dass das eucharistische

---

[1]) Vgl. H. OLDENBERG, *Veda*, p. 398 ff.; das Vaitānasūtra des Atharvaveda 1, 13 (ed. CALAND, Amsterdam 1910, p. 2).
[2]) BASILIUS, *Homil. de jejunio* I, 6, 8 (MPG 31, 163 ff.) u. CHRYSOSTOMUS, *Hom.* 27 *in* I *Cor.* erwähnen sie.
[3]) Vgl. das Konzil zu Saragossa (380), bei 3 *Mansi*, 634.
[4]) HARDUIN, tom. I, fol. 964.
[5]) Vgl. Vf., *l.c.*, p. 117.
[6]) Epist. 54 ad Januar. 6, 8.

Nüchternheitsgebot von Mitternacht an bis zur Messe eingehalten wurde [1]). Neuerdings ist das Gebot zwar gemildert und erlaubt noch 3 Stunden vor der Kommunion feste Speise und 1 Stunde vor der Kommunion Flüssigkeit [2]). Auch verschiedene protestantische Kirchenordnungen empfehlen ein sogenanntes „jejunium praevium ex voto", das die Konfirmanden vor ihrer Einsegnung und die Ordinanden vor ihrer Ordination beobachten sollen [3]). Damit sind wir wieder bei der ursprünglichen Bedeutung des jejunium eucharisticum: Es soll den Initianden auf den neuen Lebensabschnitt, der durch ein Gelübde eingeleitet wird, vorbereiten und ihn so der Kraft der Gottheit teilhaftig werden lassen [4]).

Zum jejunium sacramentale gehört auch das *jejunium ordinationis*, das christliche Weihefasten. Da im Grunde die Priesterweihe eine Initiation ist, kommt dem ihr vorangehenden Fasten auch der Charakter eines Initiationsritus zu. Dabei handelt es sich um die einzige christliche Fastenpraxis, für die aus dem NT ein Beleg erbracht werden kann, nämlich Acta 13, 1-4. Saulus und Barnabas werden ausgesondert, wobei sie und die Gemeinde diesen Gottesdienst mit einem Fasten begehen. Übrigens fastete dabei auch der Ordinierende und empfängt so — nämlich auf solche Weise von den schädlichen Dämonen befreit — den heiligen Geist, welchen er durch Handauflegung weiterreichen kann [5]). Mit eben diesem Ritus wie in der Apostelgeschichte wird das Ordinationsfasten langsam zum festen Vorbereitungsritus in der christlichen Gemeinde. Bereits unter Leo dem Grossen werden die Ordinationen von Bischöfen, Priestern und Diakonen vor versammelter Gemeinde unter allgemeinem Fasten (jejuniis et a jejunantibus) vorgenommen [6]). Schliesslich wählte man die *Quatember* als Ordinationstermin; denn „sie waren Fast- und Busstage im eminenten Sinn, die ganze Gemeinde versammelte sich, wie sonst selten, in der Kirche" [7]). Die dämonischen Mächte, welche die Weihe hätten verhindern können, waren gebannt.

---

[1]) Vgl. die Apostolische Konstitution „Christus dominus" vom 6. 1. 1953.

[2]) Wasser bricht die Nüchternheit nicht.   [3]) Vf. *l.c.*, p. 118.

[4]) Die Sitte, nicht nur mit nüchternem Magen das Sakrament zu empfangen, sondern *nach* dem Empfang diese Nüchternheit noch eine ganze Zeit lang beizubehalten, wurde bis ins späte Mittelalter hinein geübt (*Thomas v. Aquin*, Summa theol. III, q. 80, art. 8 ad 6 (ed. Paris 1895, tom. V, 495 ff.).

[5]) Siehe Vf. Das Fasten, p. 119.

[6]) Leo an Dioskur von Alex (MPL 54, 625).

[7]) L. Fischer, *Die kirchlichen Quatember, Veröffentlichungen aus dem kirchenhistorischen Seminar in München*, IV. Reihe, Nr. 3, München 1914, p. 109. 110.

Noch heute finden Priesterweihen sowohl in der römisch-katholischen als auch in der anglikanischen Kirche mit Vorliebe an den Quatembersamstagen statt [1]), — ganz gewiss, ohne zu wissen, dass man einst an diesen Tagen nur deshalb ordinieren durfte, weil man vorher gefastet hatte und — von den Dämonen unbehelligt und bussfertig — den Weiheakt vollziehen durfte.

(3) Der dritte Typus des Fastens als Ritus der Initiation ist das ekstatische Phänomen des *Visionsfastens*, das als „*jejunium ecstaticum*" oder „*jejunium propheticum*" bezeichnet werden kann. Es stellt einen präparativen Faktor von höchster religionsgeschichtlicher Relevanz dar. Über die Ursachen, die von der Nahrungsaskese ausgehen und bei den Asketen visionäre Wirkungen hervorrufen, sind wir uns weithin im klaren. Es handelt sich um ganz bestimmte physiologische Vorgänge, die den Menschen in einen Zustand der äusseren und inneren Freiheit von den Dingen und damit „in die Nähe der Gottheit" versetzen. Wer nüchtern ist und gar fastet, der weist eine weit grössere religiöse Konzentration und eine weit grössere Intensität des Glaubens auf, als jemand, der den Genüssen dieser Welt verfallen ist [2]). Wer fastet, wird zu innerer Versenkung angeregt, von Träumen und Visionen heimgesucht [3]) oder gar in ekstatische Zustände getrieben, „in denen er sich von übersinnlicher Macht erfüllt zu werden glaubt" [4]). Der durch die Entsagung geschwächte Organismus mag dabei eine gewisse psychische Reizbarkeit zeigen und so „zur Phantasietätigkeit beitragen", wie allgemein angenommen wird [5]).

Was uns aber in diesem Zusammenhang beschäftigt, ist die Tatsache, dass hier *beim ekstatischen Fasten Weg und Auftrag des homo religiosus beginnen*. Es handelt sich also ausschliesslich um ein Fasten für Mystiker und Propheten, die sich auf die Verkündigung ihres Evangeliums vorbereiten. *Insofern wird die Initiation zur Voraussetzung für die Inspiration.*

Fast alle Schamanen und Seher haben ihren Auftrag mit einem ekstatischen Fasten begonnen. Nahezu alle Propheten und Stifter der großen Religionen haben denselben Weg beschritten: als Visionäre

---

[1]) Hierher gehört auch der Samstag vor dem Passionssonntag Judica.
[2]) E. HEUN, *Das Fasten als Erlebnis und Geschehnis*, Frankfurt/M. 1953, gibt Beispiele genug, welche die bessere Konzentration, das intensivere Denkvermögen und die stärkere geistige Leistungsfähigkeit des Fastenden preisen.
[3]) ANKERMANN, in Chantepie, Lehrbuch I, 160.
[4]) KONOW, in Chantepie II, 82.
[5]) Z. B. H. STRATHMANN, *Geschichte der frühchristlichen Askese* I, Leipzig 1914, p. 79.

wollten sie in die Ungegenständlichkeit der Gottheit eindringen und ihre Offenbarung hervorrufen oder sogar erzwingen. Das Fasten wird damit zur unmittelbaren Voraussetzung für die Offenbarung.

Im Bereich der Naturreligionen ist es in der Regel der Schamane oder der Zauberpriester, welcher aufgrund langer Fastenperioden übernatürliche Kräfte erhält und in die Zukunft zu schauen vermag [1]. Aber auch für den einfachen Stammesangehörigen ist es eine Selbstverständlichkeit, daß ein gefüllter Magen keine geheimen Dinge sehen kann. Der Fastende jedoch sieht als Jäger den zukünftigen Jagderfolg, der Gatte seine baldige Vaterschaft usw. Bei den Algonkin-Indianern ist es üblich, daß anläßlich des Pubertätsritus der Knabe oder das Mädchen, von einer älteren Frau begleitet, in die Einsamkeit geht und sich strenger Fasten unterzieht; dadurch werden Träume erzwungen, in denen sich der Schutzgeist dem Schützling offenbart [2]. Bezeichnend sind die anklagenden Worte eines Angehörigen des Yaganstammes (Feuerland) der den Grund für das Fehlen guter Medizinmänner im guten Essen der Christen sieht, das sich seine Stammesgenossen ebenfalls angewöhnt haben: „Davon werden Körper und Geist schwerfällig, die Träume aber kommen nicht mehr so lebhaft und häufig" [3].

Das Fasten um Visionen oder Offenbarungen kommt in allen Kulturkreisen vor. Rgveda VIII, 59, 6 heißt es, daß aus der vom tapas, der Askese, erfüllten Seele der Traum geboren und „die tapasgeborene, zu den Göttern dringende Rede". Den vedischen Theologen wird sogar gesagt [4]: „Das ist das ganze tapas, das Nichtessen".

Auch im *Judentum* finden sich seit alter Zeit ekstatische Fastenriten. So heisst es beispielsweise von Esra, dass er 7 Tage lang fastete, bis er die Vision erhält [5]. 4. Esra 5, 13 wird gesagt: „Wenn du noch mehr betest und wie heute weinst und 7 Tage lang fastest (צום) wirst du aufs neue Dinge erfahren, die grösser sind als diese". Auch in der Baruch-Apokalypse erfolgt die ekstatische Eingebung erst nach längeren Fasten [6]. Baruch geht nach der Eroberung Jerusalems zu Jeremia: . . .„ und wir zerrissen unsere Kleider und weinten und

---

[1] W. Schmidt, *Ursprung der Gottesidee*, 3. Teil, VIII, 735, vgl. 722. 725. 726 u. X, 611.

[2] Buschan, *Illustrierte Völkerkunde* I, 2. ed. 1922, p. 108.

[3] Nach P. M. Gusinde, 4. Reise zum Feuerlandstamm der Yagan, in: *Anthropos* XVI/XVII (1921/22) p. 973.

[4] *Śatapatha Brāhmana* IX, 5, 1, 6.

[5] 4. Esra 5, 20 f. 31.

[6] Syr. Bar. Apok. 9, 2-10, 1; vgl. 12, 5; 43, 3.

trauerten 7 Tage lang . . ., und nach 7 Tagen kam das Wort Gottes über mich". Von Rabbi Jehoshua ben Levi wird berichtet, er habe eine lange Zeit gefastet, damit Elia ihm endlich wieder erschiene [1]).

Bei den Griechen waren es hauptsächlich die Orakelstätten, an welchen Visions- und Offenbarungsfasten geübt wurden. So schrieb etwa das Ritual dem Propheten des klarischen Apoll vor dem Übermitteln des Orakelspruchs ein vierundzwanzigstündiges vollständiges Fasten, ein „jejunium plenum" vor. Erst dann durfte der Prophet das heilige Quellwasser trinken, welches bei ihm den ἐνθουσιασμός verursachte [2]).

Im numinosen Bezirk, in dem man auf die Offenbarung wartete, galt aber als eine der wichtigsten Voraussetzungen *die Inkubation*. Die Hauptsache war dort das Liegen, die absolute Ruhe, der Traumschlaf, aber als mittelbarer Zweck muss doch auch das Fasten angesehen werden [3]). Der Fastende will sich dabei von den in ihm hausenden Dämonen reinigen, um dadurch der visionären Erleuchtung Zutritt zu verschaffen [4]). Die Absicht ist also zunächst eine apotropäische.

Jedoch können die antiken Propheten und Priester immer nur als Übermittler der Gottesoffenbarung angesehen werden, als „Funktionen" also, welche immer wieder von neuem göttliche Botschaften und Urteile in Empfang nehmen und weitergeben. Es gibt nun aber in den vier grossen Religionen Beispiele *einmaliger* ekstatischer Nahrungsaskese. Hier wird das Fasten — neben anderen Exerzitien — ein notwendiger, einmaliger Akt zur Erlangung göttlicher Offenbarungen. Damit betreten die Fastenden gewissermassen Neuland; mit anderen Worten: hier beginnt ihre neue Existenz. Der Ort, den das Fasten im Leben des Propheten oder Mystikers einnimmt, ist also der Ort der Entscheidung.

Nun mag man natürlich die Frage stellen, ob das Offenbarungsfasten der Religionsstifter überhaupt in den Bereich der Initiation gehört. Gehört zur Initiation nicht doch mindestens eine zweite

---

[1]) Jer. Terumot 8, 4 fol. 32 b (WÜNSCHE, *Der jerusalemische Talmud in seinen haggadischen Bestandteilen*, Zürich 1880, p. 71); vgl. Vf. *l.c.*, p. 134.

[2]) JAMBLICHOS, *De mysteriis* III, 11 (ed. PARTHEY, p. 125).

[3]) DEUBNER, *De incubatione capita quattuor*, Leipzig 1910, p. 14 f. Ähnliches geschieht z.B. noch heute beim iᶜtikāf, einem in Sure 2, 183 erwähnten Brauch im Islam, der darin besteht, dass man sich für eine bestimmte Zeit lang in eine Moschee begibt, sich von der Aussenwelt mit ihren Zerstreuungen absondert und fastet (siehe WENSINCK/KRAMERS, *Handwörterbuch des Islam*, Leiden 1941, p. 234).

[4]) RE, ed. PAULY-WISSOWA, *Art. incubatio*, Sp. 1259.

Person, die den Vorgang aktiv steuert? Gehört zum Initianden nicht notwendigerweise der Initiator? Diese Frage ist wohl nur scheinbar berechtigt; denn entweder darf man diese zweite Person in der Gottheit sehen, die die Initiation veranlasst, oder aber die Initiation als Indienstnahme für einen neuen Lebensabschnitt ist bereits substituiert im Ritus selbst; in unserem Falle im Akt des Fastens [1]). Ausschliesslich als Substituierung ist die Initiation etwa in der buddhistischen Offenbarung gegeben.

Schon das Beispiel des *Buddha* bestätigt uns diese Annahme. Es gab eine Zeit, und zwar *vor* seiner eigentlichen Erleuchtung unter dem bodhirukkha, in der sich Buddha sechs Jahre lang, bis zum völligen Zusammenbruch, der grossen Anspannung, dem mahāpadhāna, unterzogen hat. Diese Methode war vermutlich jainistischer Art [2]). Im Majjhima Nikāya, Abschnitt 36 [3]), wird geschildert, wie sich der Gautama auf seiner Suche nach dem Heil bei Uruvelā niederlässt und asketische Übungen beginnt: Meditationen, Atemanhalten und strenges Fasten. Die Zunge gegen den Gaumen gepresst, wartet er auf den Augenblick der Erleuchtung. Aber der kommt nicht. Die Kasteiungen schwächten ihn derart, dass er einem schwarzen Schatten glich und der „dunkle Gautama" genannt wurde, heisst es. Es wird ihm nur die Erkenntnis zuteil, dass derartige Askese nicht zur Erleuchtung führen kann [4]). Da nimmt er wieder Nahrung zu sich, und seine fünf asketischen Begleiter wenden sich unwillig ab von ihm mit den Worten: „Üppig ist der Asket Gautama geworden, von geistigem Ringen abgeirrt, in Üppigkeit verfallen [5]). Aber nachdem Buddha das strenge Fasten aufgegeben hatte und die Erleuchtung unter dem Bo-Baume eingetreten war, verweilte er dennoch sieben Tage lang [6]) — in ein gelbes Gewand gehüllt, die Almosenschale in der Hand — in seiner bisherigen Lage „mit gekreuzten Beinen", wie es heisst, das Glück der Erlösung geniessend, seinen Geist auf die Verkettung von Ursachen und Wirkungen richtend —

---

[1]) Sie ist aber ferner substituiert in der Taufe, in der Ordination und ebenso im Visionsvorgang, im Offenbarungsgeschehen.

[2]) Konow in *Chantepie de la Saussaye* II, 106.

[3]) ed. der Pāli Text Society, London 1887-1902; vgl. auch M. Winternitz, *Der ältere Buddhismus nach Texten des Tipiṭaka*, (Religionsgeschichtl. Lesebuch, Heft 11), Tübingen 1929, p. 7 ff.

[4]) Vgl. Winternitz, *l.c.*, p. 7 ff.

[5]) Winternitz, *l.c.*, p. 9.

[6]) *Edm.* Hardy, *Der Buddhismus nach älteren Pāliwerken*, Münster 1926, 3. ed., p. 41. Nach einigen Traditionen sollen es sogar 4 mal 7, 7 mal 7 oder gar 7 mal 7 mal 7 Tage gewesen sein (Oldenberg, *Buddha*, 10.-12. ed., Berlin 1923, p. 116).

und fastete. Jetzt tritt also das Fasten *nach* seiner Erleuchtung ein. Erst dann zieht er zur Verkündigung des Evangeliums aus. Zwei Kaufleute reichen ihm die erste Nahrung [1]). Der Offenbarungsempfang und sein Eintritt in eine neue Existenz geht also u.a. auf sein Fasten zurück.

Noch deutlicher begegnet uns das Fasten als Auftakt zur prophetischen Berufung in Israel. Der erste, der im AT das *jejunium revelationis* übt, ist *Mose*, bevor er auf dem Sinai das Gesetz empfängt: Ex 34, 28 (cf. Dt 9, 9). Erst nach der langen Zeit von 40 Tagen und 40 Nächten erfolgt Offenbarung und Inspiration. Durch sein Fasten macht sich also Mose für das göttliche Offenbarungswort bereit. Er befähigt sich selbst zur Aufnahme des Numinosen. Wer himmlische Speise empfangen will, hat den Genuss der profanen Speise zu unterlassen. Gressmann sagt [2]) (wohl im Blick auf Philos Ausführungen Vita Mos. II, 68 f./Cohn-Wendland): Das Fasten „macht die Natur des Menschen heilig, sodass Mose das Übernatürlich-Heilige in sich aufnehmen kann". Wie Mose, so erscheint auch dem *Elia* Jahwe erst dann auf dem Horeb, nachdem er sich ein 40-tägiges Fasten auferlegt hat [3]). Ähnlich geht es *Daniel*, bevor ihm im dritten Jahre des Königs Kyrus eine Offenbarung zuteil wird [4]). Er muss sich einer schweren Askese unterziehen. Die Stelle lautet: „Damals verbrachte ich drei volle Tage in Trauer; wohlschmeckende Speise ass ich nicht. Fleisch und Wein kamen nicht in meinen Mund (es handelt sich wohl um eine Abstinenz), und ich salbte mich nicht . . . Am 24. des ersten Monats befand ich mich am Ufer des grossen Flusses . . . Als ich aufsah, und um mich blickte, da stand ein Mann da, in leinene Gewänder gekleidet . . ." Vers 12: „Und er sprach zu mir: „fürchte dich nicht, Daniel, denn vom ersten Tage an, da du dich kasteit hast vor deinem Gott, sind deine Worte erhört worden . . ."" So bereitet sich also der Seher durch anhaltende Nahrungsaskese auf Vision und Auftrag vor.

Den prophetisch-messianischen Typus des Fastens finden wir in der Versuchungsgeschichte Jesu, Matth. 4. *Jesus* erhält seine Berufung zum Christus und damit zum Empfang der Offenbarung erst, nachdem er — in Analogie zu Mose — 40 Tage und 40 Nächte gefastet hat.

---

[1]) OLDENBERG, *Buddha*, p. 116.

[2]) In *RGG* I, 2. ed., Art. Askese im AT, Sp. 575.

[3]) 1. Könige 19, 7 ff. Unerklärlich bleibt die Tatsache, dass von einem Offenbarungsfasten der grossen Propheten des AT nirgends die Rede ist. Nirgends wird berichtet, dass sie vor ihrer Berufung gefastet hätten. Wie kommt das? Und wie lässt sich das begründen?

[4]) Daniel 10, 2 ff., vgl. 9, 3.

Will man in der *Taufe Jesu*, die ja *vor* der Versuchung stattfand, nur
den Auftakt zu seiner Berufung sehen, so findet man in der Versuchungsgeschichte die eigentliche Bewährungsprobe zum künftigen
Heilshandeln des Messias vor. Bei beiden Phänomenen, Taufe und
Versuchung, handelt es sich um Initiationen für eine neue, von Gott
geoffenbarte Existenz. „Fastend bereitet sich Jesus auf die Bewährung
der ihm verliehenen messianischen Würde und Macht" vor [1]. „Als
ein vom Geist Ergriffener lebt Jesus in einer Welt, für die andere
als die irdischen Lebensbedingungen gelten" [2]. Die νῆστις Jesu
gehört zweifellos zu diesen nicht mehr irdischen Lebensbedingungen.

Es ist bezeichnend, dass die Versuchung des Satans *nach* Ablauf
der 40 Tage und Nächte erfolgt, denn ὕστερον ἐπείνασεν. Die
Angriffsmöglichkeit des Bösen ist gerade dann am grössten, wenn der
Prophet oder Asket auf dem Wendepunkt zum neuen Leben steht,
also eine Art körperlich-seelisches Vakuum eingetreten ist; und das
ist unmittelbar vor dem Empfang der Offenbarung der Fall. Christus
übersteht dieses Moment allerhöchster Gefahr und bewährt sich darin.
Darum wird ihm der Auftrag erteilt, sein Evangelium in die Welt zu
tragen. Sofort *nach* der Bewährungsprobe heisst es (Vers 11), dass ihn
der Satan verliess und die Engel zu ihm traten. Und das bedeutet,
dass der ganze Inhalt des Evangeliums nun zusammengefasst werden
kann in dem einen Satz (Vers 17): μετανοεῖτε ἤγγικεν γὰρ ἡ βασιλεία
τῶν οὐρανῶν.

Schliesslich muss auch *Muḥammad* genannt werden, der das Fasten
$\left(\text{ازصوم}^{50} \text{ صَام}\right)$ von als besondere Form der Enkratie wählte, die ihm
die Offenbarung des Qur'ān und damit den Auftrag zu seinem
prophetischen Amt ermöglichte. Bei der Nahrungsaskese anlässlich
der Herabsendung des Qur'ān muss es sich um ein ekstatisches
Phänomen gehandelt haben.

Durch den Fastenmonat *Ramaḍān* ist der Verzicht auf Speise
und Trank für den Islam eine durchaus bekannte Erscheinung, die
bis in vorislamische Zeit zurückgeht [3]. Vom Propheten selbst wird
überliefert, dass er erklärt habe, er besässe durch das Fasten eine
stärkere prophetische Macht, da dieses eine göttliche Unterstützung
für ihn bedeute [4]. Genaue Angaben über das Visionsfasten Muḥammads können nicht gemacht werden, jedoch berichtet *Ibn Hišam*

---

[1] BEHM, im *Theol. Wörterbuch*, ed. Kittel, Bd. IV, p. 932, Art. νηστεύω, νῆστις
[2] BEHM, *l.c.*, Fr. BÜCHSEL, *Der Geist Gottes im NT*, Gütersloh 1926, p. 172.
[3] Siehe Vf. *l.c.*, p. 48 ff.
[4] AL-BUḤĀRI, *Kitab ṣawm*, bāb 20, 48-50 (ed. KREHL), Leiden 1862-68.

(gest. 834) in seiner Muḥammad-Biographie [1]), dass sich der Prophet in der *lailat al-qadr*, der heiligen Nacht, auf dem Berge Hīra aufgehalten und sich dort die Herabsendung des Qur'ān geradezu „erfastet" habe. Diese Nachricht wird bestätigt durch Sure 2, 181 [2]), wonach die lailat al-qadr der Zeitpunkt im Monat Ramaḍān gewesen zu sein scheint, auf den hin gefastet wurde. Die lailat al-qadr ist nach Sure 97, 1 die Nacht, in der der Qur'ān herabgesandt wurde („Wir haben ihn /den Qur'ān/ in der Nacht der Bestimmung hinabgesandt"). Nun bleibt freilich unerklärlich, weshalb die Muslime ausgerechnet wegen der Qur'ānsendung *fasten* sollten; den Jahrestag der Offenbarung konnte man doch festlicher begehen! Aber seltsamerweise ist der Sinaiaufenthalt des Mose und die Theophanie zur Zeit der Einführung der Ramaḍānfasten ein häufiger Bezugspunkt in der Predigt des Propheten gewesen [3]). Danach würde also die Berufung des „Propheten" Muḥammad mit der Berufung des „Propheten" Mose in Zusammenhang stehen. Ja, Muḥammad hatte diese Parallelität ganz bewusst angestrebt, auch, was die Praxis seines Visionsfastens betrift. Hinzu tritt aber noch eine weitere Beobachtung: Es steht fest, dass die lailat al-qadr nicht in die vor dem Jahre 2 d.H. noch gebräuchliche Fastenzeit des Monats Muḥarram fiel, sondern im Jahre der Qur'ān-Offenbarung in einen vollständig „neutralen" Monat, eben in den Monat Ramaḍān [4]).

Weil an einem bestimmten Tage des Ramaḍān der Qur'ān herabgesandt wurde, darum sollte man fasten! Damit ist sicher, dass Fasten und Offenbarung auch im Islam in einem ursächlichen Zusammenhang zueinander stehen. Der Ekstatiker Muḥammad hatte, bevor ihm in der lailat al-qadr die Offenbarung der Heiligen Schrift zuteil wurde — wie Mose vor dem Empfang des Gesetzes auf dem Sinai und wie Jesus vor seinem Verkündigungsauftrag in der Wüste — ein *jejunium propheticum* durchgeführt. Da die Qur'ān-Offenbarung aus mehreren Einzeloffenbarungen bestand [5]), muss man sogar mit mehreren jejunia prophetica zu rechnen haben, ähnlich dem 4. Esra

---

[1]) Im Auszug abgedruckt in der Chrestomathie von BRÜNNOW-FISCHER, p. 40 f.

[2]) Medinensisch; in den mekkanischen Suren kommt das Fasten nur Sure 19, 27 vor; siehe WENSINCK/KRAMERS, *Handwörterbuch des Islam*, Sp. 650 (ṣawm).

[3]) So Sure 2, 48. 50. 60. 61. 86. 87; 7, 138-153; 20, 84-97. Dazu F. GOITEIN, Die Entstehung des Ramaḍāns, in: *Zeitschr. „Der Islam"*, XVIII, Heft 3/4, Berlin u. Leipzig 1929, p. 189 ff.

[4]) Vgl. *Sure* 2, 181.

[5]) Vgl. *Handwörterbuch des Islam*, Art. Ḳur'ān, bes. p. 345-355.

und der syrischen Baruch-Apokalypse. Als Zeitpunkt der Initiation darf aber die lailat al-qadr gelten, in welcher der Prophet den eigentlichen Fastenritus vollzog, um in einen neuen Existenzabschnitt einzutreten.

Der genaue Zeitpunkt der lailat al-qadr lässt sich nicht mehr feststellen; eine der letzten 5 ungeraden Nächte muss damit gemeint sein. Darum werden noch heute alle 10 Tage, unter welchen sich diese Nacht verbirgt, von den Muslimen mit besonders harter Askese verbracht [1]). Das Fasten im Ramaḍān wird damit zugleich als Erinnerung an Muḥammads Fasten um seine erste Vision begangen.

Prophetische wie mystische Religionsstifter haben also in gleicher Weise das ekstatische Visionsfasten als den Beginn eines völlig neuen Lebensabschnittes verstanden, eben im Sinne eines Initiationsritus. Empfang und Verkündigung der Botschaft vom Heil waren nur möglich auf Grund dieser körperlichen und seelischen Askese.

Abschliessend sei bemerkt, dass im Grunde alle drei hier vorgetragenen Typen, die für das Fasten als Initiationsritus konstitutiv geworden sind, miteinander in Verbindung stehen und einander bedingen, sodass einer aus dem anderen hervorgeht. Der apotropäisch-magische Typus des jejunium praeparationis darf als Vorstufe für das Tauf- und Opfermahlfasten sowie für die Nahrungsaskese anlässlich der Priesterordination, also des jejunium sacramentale, angesehen werden. Und dieses wiederum ist die Voraussetzung für das ekstatische Phänomen des Visions- und Offenbarungsfastens geworden, das wir jenunium propheticum genannt haben. *Sämtlichen* Typen des Fastens aber ist *ein* Merkmal gemeinsam: das ist der Wille zur Kommunikation mit der Gottheit. Damit wird das Fasten, obwohl ein Phänomen am Rande der Religionsgeschichte, zu einem wichtigen und unentbehrlichen Element im Bereich der Initiationsriten.

---

[1]) MUḤAMMAD ALĪ, *Manual of Ḥadīth*, Lahore um 1951, p. 506. Vgl. Rudi PARET, *Mohammed und der Koran*, Urban-Bücher, Stuttgart 1957, p. 43. Für das Fasten in der Gegenwart siehe Pierre RANDOT, *Der Islam und die Mohammedaner von heute*, aus dem Franz. von M. A. v. FRANZ, Stuttgart 1963, p. 124 ff.

SOME REFLECTIONS ON THE RITES OF INITIATION
(in the light of the papers presented at Strasburg)

BY

GEO WIDENGREN
Uppsala

I think it may be useful if we reflect for a while on what has been said and discussed during the charming days we have spent here at Strasburg. I could not possibly be present at the reading of *all* the papers; that was a sheer physical impossibility; but I have tried to gain some impression of all the contributions, though I cannot mention in this place every single paper.

1. First of all we should note that some papers were devoted to methodological and terminological questions. To every regular reader of the "Studi e materiali dell'historia dei religioni" it is obvious that such problems attract much attention in Italy—perhaps more than elsewhere.[1] It is not only useful but even necessary to be clear on what methods and terms you make use of in a special study or a special line of research. E.g. the question was raised by Dr. ZANDEE whether the term *rite de passage* (first introduced by VAN GENNEP in 1909) is still an appropriate, and therefore serviceable and useful term. At any rate it has been used many times during these days, but it may be that on the whole we are all of us a little too fond of so-called scientific slogans. In this special case, however, I should like to plead for the use of the term *rite de passage*, for it really sums up in the shortest possible way some special and very common traits in ritual actions.

As to method, it is evident that you *must* start with some idea of what method you are going to use. On the other hand I imagine that many, perhaps most of us have found that the material itself in the course of our investigation necessitates several, often rather drastic changes in our method. We are simply forced to regroup, rearrange,

---

[1] Prof. BRELICH kindly explained this fact to me. According to him it is due to the influence of R. PETTAZZONI upon his pupils, who inherited from their teacher this special interest into questions of method.

rewrite our material, in accordance with the new method we eventually found more suitable, because better adapted to facts. When we have finished our work and printed it then we discover what method has been applied by us. And very often we also discover what changes in method should have been introduced—but which we were not able to find out at the time of our actual work. Abstract discussions about method could be carried on infinitely, without leading anywhere. I think it characteristic too that prof. BRELICH's methodological and terminological questions were based on his own basic research work on initiation ceremonies, and that their value depends on that very circumstance.

2. Some other papers tried to analyze and value the so to speak inner, "esoteric" aspect of initiation or to emphasize what spiritual values may have been associated with such rites in the minds of the believers. In this case the phenomenological, the sociological or the psychological points of view dominated the treatment of the problem. I may mention here the interesting paper read by prof. Rochedien on esoteric religion as well as the very pertinent questions put forward in the discussion by Prof. Scholem.

First of all it seems necessary to give a satisfactory definition of "esoterism". In this concrete case I am all for terminological strictness because it is quite obvious that this term "esoterism" is taken in too many meanings. Then we may ask e.g. "under what circumstances does a movement develop into a group, possessed of esoteric knowledge"? The answer to this question evidently depends a) on external factors=sociological circumstances b) on internal factors=psychological circumstances. Because Manichaeism was mentioned in the discussion I allow myself a few words on a phenomenon that I have made a study of for many years.[1] Manichaeism cannot from its beginnings be called an "esoterism", because its founder went forth with the claim to be a propagator of a world religion. Seldom do we meet with such a missionary zeal as in Mani's religion.

Further, we distinguish in Manichaean religion one group of initiated, the *electi*, and another of non-initiated, the *auditores*, but the difference is not dependent on various degrees of knowledge, of religious insight, *but* on various religious practices. Seemingly the

---

[1] Cf. WIDENGREN, *The Great Vohu Manah*, 1945; *Mesopotamian Elements*, 1946; *Mani und der Manichaïsmus*, 1961; English transl. to be published 1965 by WEIDENFELD and NICHOLSON.

same holds true in the case of Buddhism, from where Mani most probably took over his type of organization.

Manichaeism in most places developed into a kind of "esoterism", but at least in one country, the Uigur kingdom, it was the state religion. Now, I cannot see how we could call a state religion an "esoteric" religion without using "esoteric" in another sense than that usually given to it. On the other hand, when Manichaeism was relegated to an existence as an underground movement it is quite obvious that it acquired some of the traits characteristic of an "esoteric" type of religion. But that was evidently more so when Manichaeism, in order to be tolerated, leaned heavily on the dominating type of religion: e.g. Christianity, Islam, and Buddhism. Then Manichaeism could claim to be the "esoteric" aspect of the dominant religion, to provide the true, "esoteric" knowledge of this religion into which it promised to initiate its adherents.[1])

As to sociological aspects, such were presented by Prof. Mendelsohn in a highly instructive and persuasive paper,[2]) especially important because presented by an expert in sociology who is moreover possessed of a fieldworker's knowledge of his subject. However, his paper leaves me uncertain in some crucial points, and I should like to read and digest it before venturing any assessment of its ultimate importance for the History of Religions.

3. Finally, the majority of papers read during our study-conference tries to give a substantial and accurate description of rites of initiation or of some special problem connected with such ceremonies. These papers accordingly possessed a more or less accentuated historical character. It may be of some use to see what religions were covered by these contributions. As far as I can make out these religions were those of:

the Far East
Buddhism
India
Iran
Nomadic peoples of Asia
Egypt

---

[1]) As Prof. BLEEKER did after the lecture, I should like to stress our gratitude for the stimulating paper read by Prof. ROCHEDIEU. Too little of the psychological treatment of problems is generally presented at our congresses.

[2]) *Initiation and the Paradox of power: a sociological interpretation.*

Israelites and Jews
Christianity
Greece
Islam
Ancient America
Africa
and other illiterate peoples.

I have not been able to discover that Rome, the Nordic-Teutonic peoples, or the peoples of the ancient Near East were the subject of any treatment, though of course they may have been mentioned in some of the papers I was unable to listen to.

Now, we should be very grateful for the fact that Indian religion, Buddhism, and Islam were so extremely well represented here by highly competent scholars. For many years the danger has been imminent that especially Buddhism and Islam would altogether disappear from the disciplins of the History of Religions; this would of course mean a complete disintegration of the History of Religions. For us in I.A.H.R. it is all-important to keep in contact with the special fields of our study and I gather that the new interest taken in the present position of the great world-religions will serve that purpose. At any rate I should like to express my thanks to the scholars occupied with Islamic, Buddhist, and Indian studies who went to Strasburg. That does not of course mean that we are less grateful for all other valuable contributions; but they come from fields generally well represented at our meetings.

On the other hand it is highly regrettable that the religions just mentioned (those of Rome, Teutonic peoples, and the Ancient Near East) were not treated here. Nordic-Teutonic religion is still represented by some outstanding scholars, though mostly belonging to an older generation. As to the ancient Near East, one has the impression that it has lost much of the interest it used to attract from scholars, and this in spite of the fact that its importance cannot be said to have diminished. In former days much of the actual interest was perhaps too much dependent on theological as well as anti-theological viewpoints. The Ancient Near East was studied far too much with an eye to its importance for the historical interpretation of the Bible. From our point of view we could say: more because of its importance for Israelite-Jewish and Christian religions than for its own sake. Well, the comparative view is still important, and generally speaking at least, we historians are able to treat the questions of origin of such and such a myth or such and such a rite occurring in Jewish or Christian religion in a more dispassionate atmosphere than was the case in the days of the Bible-Babel discussion. But I have in mind the great importance the religions of ancient Egypt and Mesopotamia have acquired in our day as representatives of religions in very old high-cultures. When it comes to the description of the more remote stages of the history of religions we must more and more recur to the oldest religions in the world from the strictly chronological point of view, thus the Egyptian and Mesopotamian culture areas. Hence their renewed importance both for history and phenomenology.

4. And now I pass over to some remarks originally made more or less as marginal notes while listening to some of the papers contributed to our symposium.

A recurring trait in the preparations of initiation is fasting. In his paper on this topic Dr. GERLITZ tried to establish 3 types of fasting as an integrated part of initiatory rites.[1] Leaving aside here the proposed typology, which I find very interesting though partly somewhat problematic, I should like to emphasize above all the preparatory character of fasting in connection with initiation. This quality was stressed by Prof. Kerényi in his fascinating lecture on the Eleusinian mysteries [2] where he analyzed the mental state of the participants as brought about by fasting—coupled with the use of intoxicating drugs.

In the tribal ceremonies fasting, as is well known, actually occupies a prominent place [3], and the same holds true of shaman initiations where fasting is the necessary condition for the initiated shaman's spiritual experiences.[4] All this is well known.

Fasting as an act of preparation for initiation into the mysteries is also mentioned in the classical description of such an initiation as left by Apuleius when he tells us how Lucius, during a thrice-repeated ten-day period, had to abstain from the flesh of animals and from wine (*Metamorphos.* XI 23, 28, 30) before being initiated into the Isis mysteries.

Here again Christian ritual has the same characteristic trait, for

---

[1]) Cf. GERLITZ, *Das Fasten als Initiationsritus.*
[2]) Cf. KERÉNYI, *Die Voraussetzungen der Einweihung in Eleusis.*
[3]) Cf. *ERE V*, 759, 761 f.
[4]) HARVA, *Die religiösen Vorstellungen der altaischen Völker*, 1938, p. 488; Eliade, *Le chamanisme*, 1951, p. 91; Stadling, *Shamanismen* i Norra Asien, 1912, p. 53.

there fasting was observed for one or two days by the candidates before their baptism, according to *Didache* VII 4. Early Christian writers, such as Justin (*Apology* I 61) and Tertullian (*De baptismo*, 20) also mention this practice. The *Canons* of Hippolytus actually prescribe this pre-baptismal fasting (XIX 106, 105-52) and the same is the case in other church orders.[1]

5. I should like to dwell at some length on the didactic element of initiation ceremonies, for although this element is very important it is not always given due attention. In this case, too, the connection with the ceremonies of tribal initiation is easily discernible.

The hierophant acts as a teacher, preparing the neophyte for some time before his initiation. Here again the story of Lucius' initiation into the Isis mysteries is highly characteristic. Prof. Bleeker in his introductory lecture referred to the report given by Apuleius in his Metamorphos. XI, but otherwise this famous chapter in the novel of Apuleius does not seem to have been the subject of special interest during our symposium. It is, however, a model of initiation into mysteries of the Hellenistic-Roman period. From a psychological point of view we should note how by the use of highly refined methods the neophyte is held back from initiation until his eagerness has brought his expectations to a climax of intensity, XI 21-23.

The didactic element hinted at in Apuleius XI 19, 21-22 f. every-where plays a very considerable role in an initiation marked by a religious character. It should not be overlooked that the same holds true also of tribal initiations of a mixed social and religious type.[2]

Take also e.g. Christian baptism. At a very early date we find how an initiation in the form of a catechism was used to prepare the baptizand for his baptism.[3] The oldest extant specimen is actually based on Jewish patterns, for post-exilic Judaism knew the proselyte baptism as a kind of initiation into the Jewish community of such people as were born outside the Jewish nation.[4] The prescriptions found in the Dead Sea Scrolls have confirmed the statement given by Josephus (*Bellum* II, VIII 7) concerning the obligations to be fulfilled by the neophyte, who underwent a kind of baptism as his

---

[1] Cf. *ERE* V, 768.

[2] Cf. HEILER, *Erscheinungsformen und Wesen der Religion*, 1961, p. 436 n. 17 with references to literature.

[3] Cf. *RGG*[3] III, 1179 with references to literature.

[4] Cf. KLEIN, *Der älteste christliche Katechismus*, 1909; Audet, *La Didachè*, 1958, p. 188 f.

initiatory ceremony. During two years preceding his initiation he was instructed in the secrets of the community of the Essenes.[1])

In this connection I should like to refer to the stimulating paper "Die Berufung der Zwölf und eine Rolle vom Toten Meer" read by Prof. Flusser. Unfortunately the text, a *pesher*, published by Allegro (*JBL* LXXVII/1958, p. 220 f.) is very fragmentary, and for that reason I can well understand the scepticism expressed by prof. Scholem after the lecture. On the other hand, of course, it is healthy to be presented with provocative ideas; they force us to check things and to rethink.

Such catechisms are to be met with also in other religions e.g. in Zoroastrianism, but I shall return to this phenomenon in another connection (cf. below section 11). In this place I should like to point out the very strong didactic element in Bektashi initiation ceremonies so clearly described and analyzed by Prof. Ringgren.[2])

The literary category of instructions for neophytes changed considerably when catechisms were expanded into veritable tracts of a fairly comprehensive size. I mention here above all the Hermetic gnostic writings with their dialogues between Hermes and Tat by means of which Tat is initiated into the divine mysteries.[3]) In this connection I should also like to refer to Philo, for he speaks of initiation into the sacred mysteries and it is certainly wrong to see here only metaphorical language.[4])

In further calls for notice in this context that the didactic element was prominent even in ancient American culture, as was so ably demonstrated by Dr. Lanczkowski in his paper, where he treated the esoteric language communicated from father to son and handed

---

[1]) Cf. DUPONT-SOMMER, *Les écrits esséniens*, 1959, p. 57 ff.; 61 f.; and for the instruction in secret writings WIDENGREN, *NUMEN* X, 1963, p. 54 f.

[2]) Cf. RINGGREN, *The initiation Ceremony of the Bektashi*.

[3]) Cf. FESTUGIÈRE, *La révélation d'Hermes Trismegiste*, 2, p. 34 ff.; Reitzenstein, *Poimandres*, 1904, p. 117 on this instruction and its possible Hellenistic-Greek sources.

[4]) As BRANDT does, cf. *ERE* VII, 324 f. GOODENOUGH, *By Light Light*, 1935, p. 263, has shown that there are "several striking hints of actual mystic organization", GOODENOUGH has drawn attention *inter alia* to the following fragment: "It is not permitted to speak out the sacred mysteries to the uninitiated until they shall have been purified with the perfect purification. For the uninitiated and the facile person . . ., since he is unable to hear or see immaterial and conceptual nature, is deceived by the thing which is made manifest to his sight and so casts reproach upon the irreproachable. To declare the Mysteries to the uninitiated would mean the destruction of the laws of the most sacred Mystery", *ib*. p. 260 (HARRIS, *Fragments of Philo Judaeus*, 1886, p. 69).

over to the officials before their entrance into their new stage of life.[1])

6. The process by which a rite of tribal initiation was changed into a rite of religious significance, i.e. an initiation into a community of essentially religious character as a new member of that community, may conveniently be illustrated by referring to the role played by circumcision in Judaism and Islam. While its real meaning in Jewish religion and social life is quite clear, its role in Islam constitutes a special problem. What does circumcision in Islam really signify? I mention this problem because Prof. Watt in his very accurate and substantial paper in which he surveyed the whole field of membership of the Islamic community did not treat circumcision as a rite of initiation within Islam.[2]) Accordingly we have to ask: is the imporance of this rite merely social or is it also possessed of some religious significance? In order to be able to answer this question we must consider whether this rite is a necessary requisite when a new member is accepted into the Muslim *'ummah* or whether it may be left out. Curiously enough the Qur'ān contains no commandment on circumcision, and it has therefore been assumed that the Apostle of God took it for granted that all Arabs were circumcised—which was, however, not the case. The ordinance of circumcision is also insufficiently based on tradition.[3]) For this reason the *maḏāhib* are divided on this point, the schools of Ibn Hanbal and Shāfiʿī affirming the obligatoriness of circumcision, whereas those of Malik and Abu Hanifah deny it. The Shiʿites too think the rite obligatory for a Muslim. The result of this uncertainty is a non-observance of this rite during certain periods and in certain parts of the Islamic world. There can be no doubt about the fact that van Gennep is right when looking on the circumcision as a *rite de passage*, this rite being primarily possessed of a social importance, indicating the passing over from one stage of life to another.[4]) On the other hand circumcision has acquired in popular Islam (alongside with the taboo on eating pork) the meaning of "the shibboleth of Islam".[5]) Here, therefore, the change of a tribal ceremony into a religious rite is definitely ascertained. For Muslims in general, circumcision is possessed of the same importance as it has for the Jewish people. The difference lies therein, that, contrary to

---

[1]) Cf. Lanczkowski, *Die Sprache von Zuiva als Initiationsmittel.*

[2]) Cf. Watt, *Conditions of membership of the Islamic community.*

[3]) Cf. *ERE* III, 677. From this article, written by Margoliouth, I draw my material when not otherwise indicated.

[4]) Cf. Wensinck, *Hdwb d Isl*, p. 317.

[5]) Cf. Wensinck, *op. cit.*, p. 315, quoting Snouck Hurgronje.

what is the case in Jewish religion, no theological sense is attached to this rite; it is *not* the symbol and sign of a covenant between God and His people. This fact presumably discloses the non-religious, originally exclusively social character of circumcision in Arabia.

7. In such a complex, and obviously in the, at least to some extent, syncretistic ritual of the Bektashi initiation ceremonies,[1] we must ask ourselves whether some special methods could be used in order to make further analysis possible, both functional and historical. It seems to me that at least two ways of research would be worth trying.

1. A philological investigation of the origin of various technical terms, in the first place their geographical and linguistic origins: Arabic, Persian, Turkish; in the second place according to the social and military context in which such terms have their proper place.

2. This leads us to the second possibility, viz. the ascertaining of the social background of the Bektashi order. Its military importance, as also in other Turkish darwish orders, and—in a general sense—the *futuwwah* confraternities, is very conspicuous.

Now as I have said, it is more often than not easier to formulate abstract principles of method than to follow a certain method in actual research work. For that reason I should like to single out some special terms possessed of a definite social-military background. In the *futuwwah* societies the place where the fraternity comes together is called *maidān*, an interesting term in this connection for it means "field, ground", and is in ancient Iran a designation of the battlefield as well as the polo-ground.[2] This term accordingly directs our thoughts to the field where the warrior organizations, the "Männerbünde", as well as the followings of kings and feudal lords were accustomed to assemble.[3] In his initiation the new member receives trousers—for the Iranian horseman the most typical article of dress—and has a girdle attached to him as his waist-belt. Sometimes also an apron and weapons are handed over to him. The trousers are called by their New Persian name *šalvār*, and this also outside Iran. Belt and

---

[1] This fact was well brought out in the instructive paper read by Prof. RING-GREN.

[2] Cf. WOLFF, *Glossar* zu Firdosis Schahname, 1935, p. 788 "1. Turnierplatz, Rennbahn, 2. Schlachtfeld".

[3] It is a matter for regret that I have found time to publish neither my monograph *Feudalismus im alten Iran* nor my lecture *Le symbolisme de la ceinture*. I hope their publication will be possible this year.

arms belong together, the arms being attached to the girdle which is
above all a symbol of the follower's obedience to his lord.[1]) The
apron is reminiscent of the smith Kāvah, a leader of the insurrection
against the tyrant and a model figure of the leader of the artisan's
fraternities.[2])

Thus several traits in the initiation of the *futuwwah* societies take us
back to special social-military organizations in pre-islamic Iran to
which cultural context the New Persian terminology also points.
From the *futuwwah* we might then proceed to the Bektashi and other
militant darwish orders in Ottoman Turkey. Here also the connection
with the artisan's guilds as a possible body of recruitment of the
orders should not be lost sight of. The initiation into a guild or
artisan's confraternity evidently preserved much of the initiation
ceremonies, as they were connected with a real religious initiation.[3])

The technical language associated with the initiation ceremonies
is above all New Persian, as a preliminary survey has clearly shown.
I give below a list of such words, of necessity quite imperfect because
the Turkish texts are inaccessible to me:

ābdast	= ablution
āyīnah	= mirror
butxānah	= House of Idols
čirāɣ	= candle, torch
dār	= wood, gallows
dargāh	= throne-seat
dastūr	= permission
ğām	= cup

---

[1]) This I tried to demonstrate above all in *Le symbolisme de la ceinture*.

[2]) Cf. CHRISTENSEN, *Smeden Kaväh og det persiske Rigsbanner*, 1919. It should be
noted that Kāvah has nothing to do with *kavi* (ELIADE, *Forgerons et alchimistes*,
1956, p. 88 has been misled by ALTHEIM, *Attila*, french transl. 1952, p. 128;
(cf. German ed. p. 97). Actually CHRISTENSEN, *Les gestes des rois*, 1936, p. 37, took
the trouble to point out that Kāvah and *kavi* have of course nothing to do with
each other. It is essential that phenomenological work should be based on solidly
established facts.

[3]) WACH, *Sociology of Religion*, Engl. ed. 1947, p. 187 f., 251 treats these phenomena, but in this case this fine scholar has not seen the real sociological implications and presents no more than a bare skeleton of positivistic facts. His treatment
is a disappointment to everyone who looks for an analysis of the Turkish darwish
orders from the sociological point of view. Some hints are given in my *Religionens
värld*, 2. ed. 1953, p. 438 f. (a German transl. *Die Welt der Religion* will be published
shortly by Töpelmann).

ǧān	= soul
gulbāng	= "shout" [1]
kamarbastah	= girded
maidān	= polo ground, battlefield
mai-gūn	= wine-coloured
maixānah	= drinking place
mast	= intoxicated
nāmard	= unmanly, unworthy
namāz	= worship
niyāz	= reverence
parvāz	= flying, ecstasy
pīr i moγān	= The Old of the Magians [2]
pōst	= skin
pōst-nišīn	= sitting on the skin
rāhbar	= guide
tāǧ	= cap, crown
tabar	= double axe
tarǧumān	= interpreter [3]
tēγband	= sword-belt
xumxānah	= wine shop

The term *mardān*, men, typically enough is the designation of the initiated mystics, so both in al-Huǧwīrī (transl. Nicholson, p. 327 f.); in Bābā Tāhir, (ed. and transl. HERON-ALLEN, p. 62 poem 62: 4, not understood by the editor who think that it denotes "mankind" in general); and in the life of 'Alā'uddīn (cf. NICHOLSON, *The Mystics of Islam*, 1914, p. 147). These references might easily be multiplied.

The Iranian background of the antinomistic tendency among the sufis, the socalled *malāmatīyah*, was demonstrated by me 10 years ago when I pointed to the New Persian term *ǧuvānmardī* and its

---

[1]) Originally this term denotes the note of the nightingale, then the song of the singers in a tavern, cf. JACOB, *Orientalische Studien Th. Nöldeke gewidmet*, II, 1906, p. 1071 f. It is, however, allegorically interpreted already in Persian poetry. This word is found in Ḥāfiẓ, ed. BROCKHAUS, 534. 4 as JACOB points out.

[2]) Curiously enough this term in Ḥāfiẓ denotes the tavern-keeper but it is quite evident that the word is allegorically interpreted already there, cf. JACOB, *op. cit.*, p. 1061 f., and not only among the Bektashis as BIRGE, *The Bektashi Order of Dervishes*, p. 268 would seem to believe.

[3]) This word denotes in Bektashi ceremonies a ritual prayer or recitation usually used by the (*rāhbar>*) *rehber* in contradistinction to the (*gulbāng>*) *gül-benk*, a congregational prayer, though on occasion recited by only one person, then the Baba, cf. BIRGE, *op. cit.*, p. 166 f.

importance both among the sufis and in the *futuwwah*. I content
myself with a reference to this demonstration[1].)

We may arrange the loan-words enumerated above in various
groups:

1. The localities and places of initiation and utensils found there.
2. The initiators, prayers said by them, and other ritual acts under-
   taken.
3. The equipment of the darwish handed over to the candidate.
4. Words connected with wine and wine drinking (some overlapping here).
5. Words connected with the warriors' societies (some overlapping
   here).

Owing to the preliminary character of my observations I refrain
from entering into details but the reader can easily verify what is said
about the various classes of loan-words.

An ancient gnostic heritage is found in the technical language of
the poems *en vogue* among the Bektashis. We note e.g. the following
passage:

Departing from the way of darkness I have set foot on the straight
   path.
I have awakened from the sleep of indifference, I have opened the
   eye of the soul.

BIRGE, op. cit., p. 193

Here we meet with such well-known themes as the way of darkness,
the straight path (for which one has need of the guide, *rāhbar*), the
sleep of indifference, *ġaflah* (a ḳur'ānic term, but used in Islamic
gnostic language in a different meaning), the eye of the soul.

This gnostic language as used here is strongly reminiscent of that
found in the writings of the "Pure Brethren" but this fact may be due
to the common Shī'itic background.

A very curious circumstance is the fact that even the three "signs"
of Manichaeism presumably have been taken over by the Bektashis,
where, however, pure Turkish words are used for them, *elbagi*, the
"binding" of the hand, *dil bagi*, the "binding" of the tongue, *bel bagi*,
the "binding" of the loins (cf. BIRGE, *op. cit.*, p. 192 n. 3). This

---

[1] Cf. WIDENGREN, Harlekintracht und Mönchskutte, *OrSuec* II/1953, p. 105.
More material has been found by me since I published this article, part of which
was used in a Swedish pocket-book of mine, *Kungar, profeter, harlekiner*, 1961.
I therefore intend to republish my monograph in a revised and enlarged form.

corresponds to the *signaculum manuum*, *signaculum oris*, and *signaculum sinus* (Augustine, *De moribus Manichaeorum*, X).

Hāǰǰi Bektaš Veli, the founder of the Bektashi order, had his origin from Xorasan, and this fact will explain the strong Iranian influence in his order; even Xorasan is mentioned there in the initiation ceremonies, for we have the "*Horasan postu*" (this time however constructed according to Turkish grammatical rules). In addition we know that already the Seldjuk sultanate in Asia Minor was impregnated with Persian language and culture—at least in the upper classes. These facts will account to some extent for the New Persian terminology.

The very strong Shī'itic tendencies within the order, on the other hand, appear to be associated above all with the Arabic language. Geographically Syria may have been the homeland of this language of Shī'itic type. We also know of some connections between the Nuṣayris and the Bektashis, a fact which also points to Syria as the country from which Arabic terms may have spread northwards to the Bektashis of Anatolia. However, all this needs careful examination. Shī'ah in its Persian form as well as the New Persian mystic-didactic poetry will of course have contributed to the strong influx of New Persian words and technical expressions. Here the field is open for extensive researches. I may mention the poetry of Nāṣir i Xosrau as a possible source of influence. It is quite remarkable that the idea of *rāhbari*, guidance, plays a prominent role in his *dīwān* (cf. e.g. ed. 1339 a.H. p. 12: 13). Dervishes should be guides, *rāhbarān*, to each other (cf. Huǧwīrī, transl. NICHOLSON, p. 344).

In concluding these quite provisional observations I should also like to draw attention to the possible existence of "loan-translations". So e.g. the Turkish word *erenler*, "those who have attained" (cf. BIRGE, *op. cit.*, p. 261), corresponds well to the New Persian term *rasīdagān*, found in Huǧwīrī and elsewhere, from the verb *rasīdan*, to attain, also a technical term in the mystical language, connected with the idea of the "way" to be followed in order to reach the ultimate goal. On the whole the notion of the "way" could be traced back to the technical language of the gnostics, with its Iranian background.

8. One point which calls for notice is the special religious, "technical" language used in connection with the initiation as far as the new, esoteric knowledge is concerned.

Here attention may be drawn to the very special expression "the eye of the soul" and its possible origin. I think its migration may be traced from the Upanishads to Pahlavi Zoroastrian texts, *perhaps* based on Avestic sources. We then come across the same expression further west, in the technical language of the early Christian monks as well as in the Ps. Clementine writings—a remarkable fact. The same expression must have passed rather early into Islam for Sufi writers at an early date use the term *'ayn al-qalb*, corresponding to the Hellenistic term ὄμμα τῆς ψυχῆς. And as we learned from Prof. Ringgren's lecture the expression "the eye of the soul" was used in the ritual of the Bektashi initiation. Now the history of such a technical expression hints at common psychological experiences of the neophyte on the occasion of his being initiated into a knowledge of quite another kind than ordinary knowledge. To see with the eye of the soul, in Pahlavi *gyān čašm*, is put in contradistinction to physical sight with the eye of the body, *tan čašm*. This *inner* vision is something characteristic of the initiated, the gnostic or the mystic also being initiated into an esoteric, divine knowledge.[1]

This *vision*, experienced at the occasion of one's initiation, in the mysteries of the Hellenistic-Roman period, generally called *epopteía*, was a vision of the Godhead, but it is—as far as my knowledge goes— not so clearly spoken of as meaning an insight into a higher, esoteric *knowledge*. Admittedly, however, our own knowledge of the, so to speak, interior side of the mystery initiation ceremonies is still very imperfect. It therefore seems to me very important that we find in the Hermetic writings not only the expression "the eye of the mind", but also "the eye of the heart." [2]

9. Prof. BLEEKER in his introductory lecture mentioned the well-known fact that initiation generally implies a new period in life. This fact is universally accepted as a characteristic trait of initiation.[3] If we think of the initiatory ceremonies in the Hellenistic mysteries we find that initiation means a complete transformation. The *epopteía* of the Godhead means that the neophyte not only *sees* the Godhead

---

[1]) Cf. WIDENGREN, *Die Welt der Religion*, Ch. XVII where a short history of this expression is given.

[2]) The expression "the eye of the mind" is found e.g. ed. NOCK-FESTUGIÈRE, I p. 51: 3; p. 114: 20 "the eye of the heart" I p. 53: 12 f.; p. 81: 6 (cf. the commentary given p. 82). It is interesting to observe that the Sufi language above all takes up the second expression. Because of the undeniable mystery background of the Hermetic writings both expressions may reveal something of the aspects of the *epopteía* (this word is however absent in these writings).

I may add that the New Persian expression, *čašm i dil*, is found e.g. in the work of Huǧwīrī.

[3]) Cf. ELIADE, *RGG*³ III, 753.

but actually is himself changed into a divine being. This is why the
mystery texts always speak of "the transformation", *metamorphoústhai*,
of the initiated. Prof. Kerényi in his paper also mentioned the fact
that the hero Herakles was changed into another being in the *netherworld*.[1]

There is also a Christian *mystérion*. Baptism meant that the neophyte
—to quote Prof. Brandon—was placed "beyond the temporal process
through ritual assimilation to the immortal transcendent Christ."
Baptism symbolized a dying with Christ, but also a returning with
him to new life, a participation in Christ's resurrection (Paul, *Romans*
6: 4, 8). The Christian will "walk in the newness of life". The initiation
by means of baptism meant a new life.[2] Now, this gift of a new life
could be thought of in various symbolical categories. To the Christian
it was quite natural to lay stress on the difference between the First
Adam and the Second Adam, Christ. Adam was denied eternal life;
Christ received it. So the newly baptized, too, received life with
Christ. To express this truth several ancient cultic symbols were
made use of. The Syrian Father Aphrem in his hymns addressed to
the newly baptized Christians will accordingly say to them:

> The fruit which Adam did not partake of in Paradise
> to-day is joyfully put in your mouth.
>
> *Hymns of Epiphany* XIII 17 [3]

Adam was refused the fruit from the Tree of Life. Christ, being the
Tree of Life, according to a widely-spread symbolical language, is
given to the Christian neophyte after his baptism in the shape of the
fruit from the Tree of Life—because receiving in holy communion
the elements of Christ, the Tree of Life, he receives the fruits of this
Tree, viz., the body and blood of Christ. In this case the idea of

---

[1] Cf. for the "transformation" in mystery religions above all REITZENSTEIN,
Die hellenistischen Mysterienreligionen, 3. ed. 1927, p. 40, 77, 357. In the last passage
he treats PAUL's conception in II Cor. III 18.

[2] I cannot agree with NOCK, *Conversion*, 1933, p. 58 where he argues: "Initiation
in fact corresponds not to baptism but to some additional act of special devotion,
such as joining the third order of St. Francis." This is a rather curious idea.
I hope that it will be sufficient to read our exposition here in order to see the
phenomenological agreement between baptism and initiation. I further refer to
Die Welt der Religion, Ch. VII where of course much more could be said in the
same direction. I was more interested in showing that some of the initiatory
rites in the ancient Near East were developed from the royal coronation rites, cf.
below p. 21 f.

[3] Cf. WIDENGREN, *Mesopotamian Elements in Manichaeism*, 1946, p. 128.

Christ as the Tree of Life can be traced back to Mesopotamian ideas about Tammuz, the Tree of Life.[1]) The fruit of Life is further interchangeable with the herb of Life, in Syriac *sam ḥayyē* of which Ignatius speaks in his letters, the φάρμαχον ἀθανασίας, the medicine of immortality. Actually the *sam ḥayyē* is the late Christian successor of the Mesopotamian *šam balāṭi*, the herb of Life, which Gilgamesh tried to gain.[2]) Essential to the understanding of these notions is that "Life" as acquired by means of communion is symbolized by some external subject, *some real food*.

Obviously it was not possible to imagine partaking of Life without imagining this Life as contained in some concrete object, the fruit of Life or the herb of Life. Life, in the sense of divine and therefore eternal Life, had to be assimilated, incorporated with the *baptizand* by his consuming its *outward*, concrete symbol. The internal factor, Life, was acquired in the shape of an *outward*, tangible object. It seems to have been impossible for people of those generations and of those civilizations to imagine such an idea as "Life" without associating it with a concrete thing. An internal experience had to be visualized in an external symbol. There was here a clear tendency to see the transcendent divine quality in the shape of an immanent earthly object.

The same holds true of baptism itself. The meaning of early Christian baptism was touched upon in Mr. BARCLAY's instructive paper on the internal significance of baptism as contrasted with its external ritual. Why should internal moral purification be symbolized by external ablution in water? Or rather: how came it that waterpurification rites were interpreted as signifying moral purification, leading into a new existence—as a member of a community practising a new, holy life? Why was initiation into this new life symbolized by a water-baptism? These questions can only be answered by a reference to the actual historical background. This background explains, to some extent at least, the deeper meaning attributed to water-purifications. Sin, i.e. moral perversion, being a transgression of the divine will, meant that the body too was impure, for soul and body belonged together. These ideas must be supposed to be behind the wide-spread use of water-ablutions as an initiatory rite in the Ancient World; they are to be found e.g. also in the mystery-religions

---

[1]) Cf. WIDENGREN, *op. cit.*, p. 125 ff.; for Tammuz cf. *The King and the Tree of Life*, 1951, p. 8-15; *Religionens värld*, p. 167, 250 ff., 277, German ed. *Die Welt der Religion*, Ch. IX.

[2]) Cf. WIDENGREN, *Mesopotamian Elements*, p. 129 f., 139 ff.

of the Hellenistic-Roman period as in the Isis mysteries and Mithras mysteries. Apuleius refers to the water purifications before initiation (*Metamorphos.* XI 23) and Tertullian (*De baptismo* 5) says: *sacris quibusdam per lavacrum initiantur*. As reason for this ceremony Tertullian gives *regeneratio* and *impunitas*.

The sinful man, according to prevailing ideas in the Ancient Near East, was a prey to the demons of sickness who took possession of him. To be free from one's sins meant that the sick person was cured —from his psychical as well from his physical infirmities and evils, as we should say. Baptism accordingly included not only liberation from moral sins, but also liberation from physical illness, from sickness, the demons being driven out of the sinner's body in and by means of baptism. The Syriac homily on Constantine's baptism relates how the Emperor, suffering from leprosy, was cured by being baptized.[1] Man is a psycho-physical entity. His moral evil cannot be seen isolated from his psychical perversity. The passing over into a new existence thus means to him freedom from all evil and the gain of a new, perfect Life, free from all moral as well as bodily evil.

That difficulties were felt concerning the *external* aspect of Christian baptism is shown by Tertullian's treatise on baptism. Here the author tries to demonstrate in every possible way that water is an element possessed of special importance, and that since the act of creation (cf. e.g. ch. 3-4). Other, but similar solutions were offered in the Ps. Clementine writings where it is argued on the one hand that God's creative power was present in the water, by which it effects the rebirth of man; and on the other hand that baptism is a substitute for sacrifice, effecting man's purification.[2]

10. In his accurate and interesting paper on initiation in Mazdaism Prof. DUCHESNE-GUILLEMIN left a few problems open, so that it may be possible to add something to his valuable observations.

In the first place I think it important to note that Parsi initiation takes place between the ages of seven and fifteen years. These numbers are important for that reason that we know how the boy, having reached the age of 7 years, was handed over to his masters to be instructed *inter alia* in the use of arms and in horsemanship. The age of 15 in Iran was considered the ideal age, the young man or girl being held to have reached maturity at that age. Nevertheless a young man

---

[1] Cf. WIDENGREN, *Religionens värld*, p. 187 f.; *Die Welt der Religion*, Ch. VII where more material is to be found.

[2] Cf. BRANDT, *Die jüdischen Baptismen*, 1920, p. 95-97.

of 15 was still looked upon as *apurnāyīk*; he was not yet a *full* member of society. From the historical novel called *"Kārnāmak i Artaxšēr i Pāpakān"* where the exploits of Artaxšēr, the founder of the Sassanian empire, are related with much legendary material, we know that Artaxšēr was sent to the court of Ardavān, the last of the Parthian kings, to have his education completed. This took place when Artaxšēr was 15 years old, KN I 24. At the age of 20 the young man—hitherto an *apurnāyīk*—was a full member of society and a trained horseman and warrior. We further know that the member of the warriors' confraternities received a girdle, indicating his attachment to the leader of the fraternity; later on, however, showing the follower's obedience to his feudal lord.[1])

The admission into the Parsi community accordingly corresponds to the age-old admission into the warrior's societies, in the same way as the Parsi *kustī* would seem to constitute a heritage from the Sassanian and Parthian periods with their *kustīk* or *kamar*, the belt given to the adult member of society, probably at the age of 15, because at that age he was considered capable of using his arms. As indicated above his sword and dagger were attached to his girdle, his belt being above all a sword-belt.[2]) The admission as a *bihdīn*, in Sassanian times a *vēhdēn*, a member of the Good (i.e. Zoroastrian) Religion, means that the young Zoroastrian is incorporated into the total sum of all *dēnīkān*: people belonging to *dēn*, Religion (i.e. Zoroastrian religion). Thus it seems that in Iran the admittedly late, and certainly syncretistic, religious ceremonies of initiation had been taken over from an earlier stage when they were used in a simple form for initiation into society as full members, above all as admitted to the warriors' societies as trained warriors. That this process started very early, probably in pre-Sassanian times, is perfectly conceivable. Once the social pattern was there it was but natural that religion should follow suit—here as elsewhere. Personally I am also inclined to think that the initiation into the *Mithras* mysteries may be seen against this background, for there, too, there were originally *two* different initiation ceremonies, the *leontica*, the fourth grade, being the higher grade, coming after the third grade, the *miles*, "soldier". The three lower grades ending with "soldier", did not allow the initiated to

---

[1]) Cf. above p. 9 f. and the text from the Fārsnāmah of Ibnu'l Balxi transl. in WIDENGREN, *Iranische Geisteswelt*, 1961, p. 303 f. My work *Feudalismus im alten Iran*, Ch. III will treat of education and various stages of age in pre-islamic Iran.

[2]) Cf. above p. 9 f.

participate in the mysteries. The members of these grades were only "servants", ὑπηρετοῦντες, whereas those who had received the *leontica* were "participants", μετέχοντες. More than 20 years ago it was demonstrated by an Uppsala scholar that this division, found also in the Eleusinian mysteries, corresponds to a universal phenomenon in the ceremonies of illiterate peoples.[1]) It is essentially a social division into two moieties, though this dual organization aims at mutual assistance not only to meet social needs (exogamy above all) but also when it comes to the fulfilment of cultic functions.

In Buddhism a parallel development may be traced, for there one was allowed to be a novice at the age of 15, but not to be a monk until one had reached the age of 20 years.[2]) Accordingly we meet here again with the same two dates in man's life, 15 and 20 years, as the two essential dates of religious initiation; and we may surmise that these two dates were chosen because of their importance for the young man's admission as a full member into society.

To sum up: in Iran the historical connection between religious and social initiation would seem to be fairly well established, probably so also in Buddhism. This fact agrees with what was found in two other world religions, Judaism and Islam, where circumcision, originally a purely social ceremony ultimately acquired religious significance, though much less in Islam than in Judaism.

11. An important part of the initiation ceremonies is the confession of faith on the part of the neophyte.[3]) We have already hinted at this phenomenon but postponed the treatment of it.

In Zoroastrian Iran such a confession of faith is found in the religious instructions which we may call catechisms—to use a term taken from Christian religion, where it is perhaps more to the point. Such a Zoroastrian text is the so-called "*Pandnāmak i Zartušt*". It has often been observed here that such an instruction was part of the preparation for initiation. The man to be initiated had to be instructed. The confession formulas, on the other hand, also contained a confession of faith. This fact would seem to correspond to what happened

---

[1]) Cf. Forsberg, *Une forme élémentaire d'organisation cérémoniale*, 1943; for the *Mithraic* mysteries p. 101 f., and for the social character of this dual organization p. 17 with its quotation from Malinowski, *Crime and custom in savage society*, 1932, p. 25.

[2]) Cf. Pischel, *Leben und Lehre des Buddha*, 4. ed. 1926, p. 107; Oldenberg, *Buddha*, 9. ed. 1921, p. 394 with reference to Mahāvagga I 75. (20 years counted from the conception).

[3]) For this whole section cf. Widengren, *Die Welt der Religion*, Ch. VIII.

in initiation: the putting away of the old and the taking up of something new. Originally then, we may assume that the confession of sins corresponded to the old status, whereas the declaration of faith was pronounced as a symbol of the new status upon which the man to be received into the Zoroastrian community entered by means of initiatory ceremonies. When used for people who were already members of the community, both confession of sins and confession of faith to some extent lost their character of marking a decisive step in life, a real initiation, but they presumably still preserved their quality of being a *rite de passage* from one stage to another.

The late and syncretistic composition of Parsi initiation ceremonies makes it impossible to present an historical analysis without carrying out very far-reaching and penetrating researches. I have no hesitation in saying that the lines indicated by prof. Duchesne-Guillemin will certainly prove useful in this respect.

12. As we have had more than one occasion to emphasize, the passing through the initiation leads the neophyte on into a new existence, and this highly characteristic trait—easily discernible in tribal initiations [1]—has often been noticed in research (up to now). The baptized Christian is a "new creature", καινὴ κτίσις. [2] Baptism also creates a feeling of being something entirely new, the Christian taking leave of his old sinful existence and entering upon a new life, free from sin, filled with righteousness. The case of Augustine may be taken as typical. *Et baptizati sumus et fugit a nobis sollicitudo vitae praeteritae. nec satiabar in illis diebus dulcitudine mirabili, considerare altitudinem consilii tui super salute generis humani. quantum flevi in hymnis et canticis tuis suave sonantis ecclesiae tuae vocibus commotus acriter. voces illae influebant auribus meis et eliquabatur veritas in cor meum et exaestuabat inde affectus pietatis, et currebant lacrimae, et bene mihi erat cum eis,* Confessiones IX 6.[3]

After his initiation Lucius too was filled with gratitude and happiness. Only with difficulty was he able to part with the goddess. *Paucis dehinc ibidem commoratus diebus inexplicabili voluptate simulacri*

---

[1] Cf. *ERE VII* 317 f. "simulation of death and resurrection", "granting of a new name".

[2] Cf. Paul, II Cor. 5: 17; Galatians 6: 15 with the commentaries of LIETZMANN, An die Korinther I-II, 3. ed. 1931, p. 126; WINDISCH, *Der zweite Korintherbrief*, 1924, p. 189 f.

[3] For this state of mind in Augustine after baptism I have not been able to find in literature any special psychological analysis. Interest has been focussed on other aspects.

divini perfruebar, inremunezabili quippe beneficio pigneratus, sed tandem ...
pro meo modulo supplicue gratiis persolutis, tardam satis domuitionem comparo,
vix equidem abruptis ardentissimi desiderii retinaculis, Metamorphos. XI 24.[1])

Concluding remarks. In his illuminating paper on "Initiation in
Ancient Egypt" Prof. BLEEKER put forward the question: who were
the initiated in Egypt? He offered three answers to that question:
by his divine nature the king was first of all initiated; secondly the
priests, who were his representatives in the cult; thirdly ordinary
religious people were apparently under certain conditions ultimately
allowed access to the sphere of cultic mystery.[2])

Accordingly we should expect initiation ceremonies to possess a
character of royal rites, and this is actually the case. Prof. E. O.
JAMES in his very important book "Christian Myth and Ritual" in a
most instructive way worked out the royal pattern underlying the
rites of baptism, and this point of view has been a leading principle
in much of my own work on the correspondence between enthronement ceremonies and baptismal rites, in which I have tried to follow
the development of a ritual complex in the centre of which we find
the king, from Mesopotamia to post-exilic Judaism, and then further
to gnostic movements as well as to Christian baptismal rites.[3])

It is especially illuminating to note that the ritual element of *hieros
gamos*, well motivated in the enthronement ceremonies, is not altogether missing from gnostic and Christian baptism and baptismal
texts. I should like to illustrate this by quoting from Aphrem's
Epiphany hymns some passages where he says:

The Bride-chamber that faileth not, my brethren, ye have received.
Your vesture is shining, and goodly your crowns.
Crowns that fade not away, are set on your heads.
Who should not rejoice, in your Bride-chamber, my brethren?

LAMY, *Ephraemi Syri Hymni et Sermones,* I, col. 109, XIII 3, 5, 11, 13 [4])

---

[1]) For this state of happiness in the mind of the *alter ego* of Apuleius, Lucius,
cf. NOCK, *Conversion,* p. 146 f. This chapter is one of the best in NOCK's book.

From here we should follow the development to mystical experiences as connected with initiation, a problem treated by Dr. VERENO in his interesting paper
on "Spirituelle Nachfolge und Initiation". Space and time do not allow me to
enter upon a discussion of this line of research which I consider highly important,
because rather neglected up to now.

[2]) This survey may serve as a historical background of the Isis mysteries in
the Hellenistic-Roman period.

[3]) I refer to the book *Die Welt der Religion,* the section in the chapter on rites
dealing with rites of initiation where some special monographs and articles of
mine are quoted and utilized.

[4]) Cf. WIDENGREN, *Mesopotamian Elements,* p. 111.

has also prevented me from venturing into the field of Indian religion,

For the reasons indicated I have therefore followed in my work a line of research leading from royal ceremonies directly to baptismal rites of an initiatory character—in gnosticism as well as in Christianity—whereas Prof. Bianchi in his paper "Initiation, mystère, gnose" would seem to establish under all circumstances a fourfold pattern which I should like to see elaborated in more detail. Already now, however, I should be inclined to stress the possible symbolic character of gnostic baptismal rites.[2]

How important initiation ceremonies are in the life of a people living on the level of tribal organization and tribal civilization is also clear from the very exact terminology concerning initiation as it is elaborated among such a people. This was demonstrated in a highly instructive way by Prof. ZAHAN in his paper *Terminologie Bambara concernant l'initiation.*

If this and other important aspects of tribal initiation ceremonies have been only slightly touched upon, or perhaps not mentioned at all in this paper of mine, this regrettable fact is due to the circumstance that my own special studies have been concentrated on the high cultures of the Near East, including Judaism, Christianity, and Islam. Tribal ceremonies there belong to the historical background— and I have tried not to neglect the historical dimension—and other aspects come to the fore in the treatment of initiatory ritual.

However, even so my general reflections are quite fragmentary.[3] I feel it to be quite especially regrettable that my lack of first-hand knowledge in Buddhism—except for a very small section of Hinayana —has prevented me from digesting and evaluating the fine contributions to Buddhist religion.[4] The same lack of first-hand knowledge

---

[2] I thus take exception to the qualification of *all* gnostic ritual as "magic". The neophyte who was initiated in the gnostic mysteries by means of baptism says that he is both "confirmed" and "redeemed", Irenaeus I 21, 3, cf. SAGNARD, *La gnose valentinienne*, 1947, p. 422. In this case, where the verbs ἐστήριγμαι and λελύτρωμαι are used, a comparison with other, both Christian and gnostic baptismal texts, surely does not reveal any difference *of principle* in their meaning. It goes without saying that this cannot be demonstrated in this context.

[3] Had I had more time at my disposal I would have said something about the father-son relations between the initiator and the candidate, a very important aspect, already treated by DIETRICH in his book on the so-called Mithras-liturgy, and conspicuous everywhere in the Pauline *corpus* of epistles.

[4] I was fortunately able to be present at the lectures given by Prof. HOFFMANN on *Initiation in Late Buddhism* and by Miss BLACKER on *Initiation Rites in Japanese Shugendo.*

where, moreover, I was not present at any other contributions than that of Dr. Presler.[1]) But I should like to end these fragmentary reflections by once more expressing our thanks to the scholars who contributed such illuminating papers on Indian and Far Eastern religion. Miss Blacker's lecture was also from the aesthetic point of view a delight to follow, thanks to her beautiful film—and I do not think that the aesthetic factor ought to be neglected in our researches, as it mostly has been.

From my personal point of view I have thus tried to present some general reflections, and I hope that my marginal notes have, in at least a few cases, indicated some possible lines of research on which I and my collaborators at Uppsala are concentrating. Other scholars would have presented other views. It is especially a matter for regret that prof. Eliade was prevented by illness from coming and presenting a survey of his positions.

---

[1]) Dr. PRESLER's lecture on *Hindu-Moslem Participation in the Same Rituals: Informal Initiation* was more instructive than many books, thanks to his highly realistic films. In such cases the picture is more telling than words.